About Island Press

Island Press is the only nonprofit organization in the United States whose principal purpose is the publication of books on environmental issues and natural resource management. We provide solutions-oriented information to professionals, public officials, business and community leaders, and concerned citizens who are shaping responses to environmental problems.

In 2006, Island Press celebrates its twenty-second anniversary as the leading provider of timely and practical books that take a multidisciplinary approach to critical environmental concerns. Our growing list of titles reflects our commitment to bringing the best of an expanding body of literature to the environmental community throughout North America and the world.

Support for Island Press is provided by the Agua Fund, The Geraldine R. Dodge Foundation, Doris Duke Charitable Foundation, The William and Flora Hewlett Foundation, Kendeda Sustainability Fund of the Tides Foundation, Forrest C. Lattner Foundation, The Henry Luce Foundation, The John D. and Catherine T. MacArthur Foundation, The Marisla Foundation, The Andrew W. Mellon Foundation, Gordon and Betty Moore Foundation, The Curtis and Edith Munson Foundation, Oak Foundation, The Overbrook Foundation, The David and Lucile Packard Foundation, The Winslow Foundation, and other generous donors.

Conservation of the Black-Tailed Prairie Dog

Frontispiece. Reprinted with permission of *Varmint Hunter* magazine.

Conservation of the Black-Tailed Prairie Dog

Saving North America's Western Grasslands

. . .

Edited by

John L. Hoogland

Washington • Covelo • London

Library of Congress Cataloging-in-Publication Data

Conservation of the black-tailed prairie dog : saving North America's western grasslands / edited by John L. Hoogland.— 1st ed.

p. cm.

Includes bibliographical references and index.

ISBN 1-55963-497-9 (cloth : alk. paper) — ISBN 1-55963-498-7 (pbk.)

1. Black-tailed prairie dog. 2. Black-tailed prairie dog—Conservation. 3. Grassland ecology—West (U.S.) I. Hoogland, John L.

QL737.R68C656 2005

333.74′16′0978—dc22

2005020628

British Cataloguing-in-Publication data available.

Printed on recycled, acid-free paper ♻

Design by Brighid Willson

Manufactured in the United States of America

10 9 8 7 6 5 4 3 2 1

At least fifty organizations are
working to conserve prairie dogs.

By volunteering their time, energy,
and professional expertise, members of these
groups repeatedly amaze me with their passionate
commitment to the long-term survival
of their, and my, favorite animal.

To these unsung heroes I dedicate
Conservation of the Black-Tailed Prairie Dog.

Contents

Preface

On 31 July 1998, the National Wildlife Federation (NWF) petitioned the United States Fish and Wildlife Service (USFWS) to add the black-tailed prairie dog to the Federal List of Endangered and Threatened Wildlife and Plants (FLETWP). In July 1999, I attended a two-day meeting in Denver, Colorado, regarding NWF's petition. The meeting included wildlife managers with expertise in different aspects of the biology of prairie dogs. I was there, for example, because I had studied the ecology and social behavior of prairie dogs for 15 years; Dean Biggins had evaluated methods for estimating current numbers of prairie dogs throughout their geographic range; Jack Cully was investigating the impact of plague on prairie dog populations; Pete Gober was the USFWS agent primarily responsible for handling NWF's petition; and so forth. During the meeting, I mused about the importance and utility of a book that would summarize all the available information regarding the conservation of prairie dogs.

On the return trip from Denver to my job at the University of Maryland's Appalachian Laboratory in Frostburg, Maryland, I decided to initiate such a book immediately. Within a week, however, I realized that the task was too Herculean for a single author. Recreational shooting, plague, keystone species, the Endangered Species Act (ESA), focal areas, translocations—these were only some of the pertinent topics about which I was mostly clueless. I therefore decided to edit a volume of chapters written by experts. The result is *Conservation of the Black-Tailed Prairie Dog.*

In this volume, other authors and I provide information for in-the-field biologists who are on the front lines of the battle to save the prairie dog. We also have written for local, state, and federal politicians who are trying to make responsible decisions about prairie dogs. In addition, we have aimed for the thousands of passionate, curious naturalists who are struggling to save colonies that are threatened by new supermarkets and housing developments in cities such as Boulder, Colorado, and Lubbock, Texas. Finally, we have tried to write for those ranchers and farmers who concede that prairie dogs deserve a chance.

Because so many members of our intended audience are not professional biologists, we have tried to avoid technical language and scientific jargon. But such avoidance is sometimes impossible. The glossary provides definitions for over 100 technical or semi-technical terms that we commonly use. Appendix B lists the full names for our many acronyms. We use only common names for plants and animals, but Appendix A shows the scientific names for all organisms mentioned. For those readers who want more details, we have included almost 700 references and the addresses of all authors.

For outstanding assistance with all aspects of the preparation of the manuscript, I thank Barbara Jenkins. Barb has been supremely competent with the conversions of files to the proper format, editing of tables and figures, tweaking photographs, meeting deadlines, and every other imaginable task.

For financial assistance during the editing of this volume, I thank the National Science Foundation, the National Fish and Wildlife Foundation, The United States Fish and Wildlife Service, The United States Bureau of Land Management, The United States Forest Service, and the Appalachian Laboratory of the University of Maryland's Center for Environmental Science.

Pete Gober encouraged me to pursue *Conservation of the Black-Tailed Prairie Dog* from the outset. He helped me to select authors, and he also helped me to obtain financial support for my role as editor. Because Pete is so familiar with, and knowledgeable about, all issues regarding prairie dogs, I invited him to be a co-editor. Unfortunately, the demands of his job would not allow him to collaborate with me.

For comments and suggestions for particular chapters, I thank Stanley Anderson, Steve Archer, Charles Brown, Mary Brown, Steve Buskirk, Len Carpenter, Archie Clark, Michael Coffeen, Sharon Collinge, Layne Coppock, Steve Dinsmore, Jo Ann Dullum, Kathleen Fagerstone, Ken Gage, Pete Gober, Richard Hart, Rodney Heitschmidt, Judy Hoogland, Scott Hygnstrom, Lynn Irby, Craig Knowles, Charles Lee, Susan Linner, Randy Matchett, Sterling Miller, L. Scott Mills, Wendy Orent, Paul Stapp, Dan Uresk, Bill Van Pelt, Dallas Virchow, David Wilcove, and Rosie Woodroffe. Hugh Britten, Laura Carrithers, Barbara Dean, Robert Hilderbrand, and Nicole Rosmarino read the entire manuscript and offered copious, detailed, and astute suggestions for improvement.

Several professional and semiprofessional photographers allowed me to use their (or their employees') images at no charge or at a greatly reduced rate. In particular, I thank John Anderson, Don Baccus, Kathy Boucher, Rick Boyle, Sven Cowan, James Faulkner, Ray Gehman, Debra Guenther, Judy Hoogland, Greg Lasley, Frederic Nichols, Jonathan Pauli, David Stern, Linda Stoll, Eric Stone, Cliff Wallis, and Melissa Woolf.

For minimizing my formal teaching responsibilities so that I could pursue my research with Utah prairie dogs and also have time to edit chapters while on campus, I thank the two directors of the University of Maryland's Appalachian Laboratory during the preparation of this volume: Robert Gardner and Louis Pitelka. I also thank Donald Boesch, president of the University of Maryland's Center for Environmental Science.

CHAPTER 1

Introduction: Why Care About Prairie Dogs?

John L. Hoogland

Black-tailed prairie dogs—hereafter, simply "prairie dogs"—are burrowing rodents that inhabit the grasslands of western North America. Coloniality is perhaps the most striking feature of these plump, brown, non-hibernating, herbivorous squirrels that stand about 30 centimeters (12 inches) tall, weigh about 700 grams (1.5 pounds), and forage aboveground from dawn until dusk.

Whether or not one likes prairie dogs, they are hard to ignore. Their colony-sites sometimes contain thousands of residents and extend for kilometers in all directions. The vegetation at colony-sites is unusually short, because prairie dogs systematically consume or clip grasses and other herbs that grow taller than about 30 centimeters (12 inches). Colony-sites contain hundreds of large mounds—as high as 0.75 meter (2.5 feet) and with a diameter as great as 2 meters (7 feet)—that surround most burrow-entrances.

After emerging from their burrows at dawn, prairie dogs forage, fight, chase, "kiss," vocalize, and play aboveground until they submerge for the night at dusk. Prairie dogs thus differ markedly from other burrowing mammals, such as pocket gophers and moles, which people rarely see. Further, colony-sites foster the growth of plants such as black nightshade, fetid marigold (also called prairie dog weed), pigweed, and scarlet globemallow—all of which are uncommon away from colony-sites. Finally, colony-sites attract fun-to-see animals such as American badgers, American bison, black-footed ferrets, bobcats, burrowing owls, coyotes, ferruginous hawks, golden eagles, mountain plovers, prairie falcons, pronghorn, and swift foxes.

About 200 years ago, prairie dogs inhabited eleven states, Canada, and Mexico, and their numbers probably exceeded five billion. As pioneers moved west, however, they often viewed prairie dogs as pests. Ranchers observed the reduced amount of grass at colony-sites and logically deduced that prairie dogs must compete with their livestock for food. Ranchers also concluded, again logically, that their livestock would incur leg fractures after stepping into prairie dog burrows. Farmers learned that the large mounds at burrow-entrances impede plowing and the growth of crops, and that prairie dogs sometimes eat crops.

Often with assistance from local, state, and federal agencies, ranchers and farmers have shot and poisoned billions of prairie dogs, or have converted prairie dog habitat to farmland. More recently, plague (a disease introduced into North America from Asia) has killed millions of prairie dogs, and urban development has eliminated some of the best prairie dog habitat. The current number of prairie dogs is less than 2% of the number that Meriwether Lewis described as "infinite" 200 years ago (Burroughs 1961).

Because of the drastic decline in numbers of prairie dogs over the last two centuries, the United States Fish and Wildlife Service (USFWS) concluded in 2000 that the prairie dog was a candidate species (i.e., was under consideration for the Federal List of Endangered and Threatened Wildlife and Plants (FLETWP) (Chapter 12). In 2004, USFWS reversed this decision by concluding that the prairie dog is no longer a candidate species (Chapter 12). Regardless of technical designation, the inescapable conclusion is that prairie dog populations have declined sharply over the last 200 years and are still victimized today by recreational shooting, poisoning, plague, and elimination of habitat.

"So what?" you might say. Should we care that the prairie dog, once so common, now occurs at less than 2% of its former numbers? The answer, I think, should be yes, as briefly outlined below and as further explored in the next 17 chapters.

Many people think about problems in terms of dollars and cents, so let's talk first about the finances regarding prairie dogs. Since poisoning began in the late 1800s, thousands of people per year have worked together to eliminate prairie dogs, with a cumulative cost of billions of dollars (Chapter 8). But the financial costs of eradication often exceed the benefits (Chapters 5, 8 and 9), because: poisons and the efforts necessary to dispense them are expensive; colonies often repopulate quickly after poisoning; competition between domestic livestock and prairie dogs is sometimes insignificant; and livestock only rarely step into prairie dog burrows. Perhaps money used for widespread poisoning could be reallocated for financial compensation to those ranchers and farmers who lose money because of prairie dogs (Chapters 14 and 17). This solution would cost less than trying to eradicate prairie dogs, would satisfy most ranchers and farmers, and would allow prairie dog populations to recover.

Most people think that all organisms have the right to exist, and that deliberate eradication of any native species is unacceptable. Indeed, this reasoning was a major factor in the passage of the Endangered Species Act (ESA) and applies specifically to prairie dogs (Chapters 7, 17, and 18).

Every species affects other species, and this axiom is especially relevant for prairie dogs (Johnsgard 2005; Chapters 4 and 5). Via foraging and clipping of vegetation and the mixing of topsoil and subsoil during excavations, prairie dogs alter floral species composition at colony-sites. Their burrows and colony-sites provide shelter and nesting habitat for myriad other animals such as tiger salamanders, mountain plovers, burrowing owls, black-footed ferrets, and hundreds of insect and arachnid species.

In addition, prairie dogs serve as prey for numerous mammalian and avian predators, such as American badgers, black-footed ferrets, bobcats, coyotes, ferruginous hawks, golden eagles, and prairie falcons. Consequently, conservation is important not only for the prairie dogs themselves, but also for the many plants and animals that associate with prairie dogs and depend on them for survival. Many conservation biologists—probably most—are more concerned about the grassland ecosystem than about prairie dogs (Chapters 4, 12, 17, and 18).

Prairie dogs provide several direct benefits to humans. Many people, for example, enjoy watching them and the many other animals attracted to their colony-sites (Chapter 15). Further, laboratory research with prairie dogs has led to a better understanding of the mammalian kidney and of diseases of the human gallbladder (Chapter 18). By removing woody plants such as honey mesquite, and by improving the nutritive value and digestibility of certain grasses, prairie dogs sometimes improve the habitat for livestock (Chapter 5). Finally, because they are uniquely social, prairie dogs have helped researchers to understand perplexing issues such as inbreeding and infanticide that affect humans and other social animals (Chapters 2 and 3).

So, yes, I think that we should care that prairie dog populations have plummeted over the last 200 years. I also think that we must try to reverse this trend. For the conservation of prairie dogs, at least four aspects are noteworthy:

- Regarding natural history, we know more about prairie dogs than we do about most other species that are on, or candidate species for, FLETWP. At Wind Cave National Park, South Dakota, for example, I studied eartagged, marked prairie dogs of known ages and genealogies for 15 consecutive years (Hoogland 1995). The prospects thus are higher than usual for using information about ecology, demography, and population dynamics to formulate realistic, promising plans for conservation.

- Many endangered animals affect only a small geographic area; consequently, their impact is often localized, and sometimes almost undetectable. The prairie dog, by contrast, originally inhabited eleven states and parts of Canada and Mexico and is highly conspicuous. Its perceived impact on ranching and farming is gargantuan.
- The rarity of most endangered species has resulted, incidentally rather than deliberately, from human activities such as conversion of habitat for agriculture, suppression of fire, and construction of factories and houses. These activities also have contributed to the decline of prairie dogs, but in addition there has been a calculated war with poison that has killed billions of prairie dogs over the last 100 years (Chapters 8 and 9).
- The outlook for many endangered species is dim—indeed, almost hopeless. For prairie dogs, however, the potential for conservation is enormous. Chapter 16, for example, lists 84 potential sites for large sanctuaries. Chapters 5 and 9 suggest ways to minimize competition between prairie dogs and livestock. Chapter 11 tells us which areas are least prone to outbreaks of plague, and Chapter 3 emphasizes how prairie dogs have a knack for overcoming seemingly impossible odds.

The purpose of *Conservation of the Black-Tailed Prairie Dog* is threefold. In Part I, other authors and I summarize the biology and natural history of prairie dogs. To formulate rigorous plans for conservation, we need good information on issues such as when they breed, how far they disperse, how they affect other organisms, and how much they compete with livestock. In Part II, we summarize how poisoning, plague, recreational shooting, and loss of habitat have caused a precipitous decline of prairie dog populations over the last 200 years—so that we can correct these problems and avoid similar mistakes in the future. In Part III, we propose practical solutions that we hope will ensure the long-term survival of the prairie dog and its grassland ecosystem, and that also will be fair to landowners. We cannot expect farmers and ranchers to incur all the costs for the conservation of prairie dogs while the rest of us enjoy all the benefits.

PART I

Natural History of Prairie Dogs

John L. Hoogland

We cannot save an animal without knowing its biology—where it lives, what it eats, its predators and parasites, and so forth. The next four chapters summarize the natural history of prairie dogs. With this information, politicians, environmentalists, and wildlife managers will be better able to make prudent decisions about conservation.

In Chapter 2, I explain that prairie dogs are colonial, burrowing rodents. Within colonies, they live in territorial family groups called coteries, which usually contain one adult male and several genetically related adult females (mothers, daughters, granddaughters, sisters, nieces, and so forth). Because young males disperse from the natal coterie and thereby preclude matings with mothers and sisters, and because older males do not remain in the same coterie for more than two consecutive years and thereby preclude matings with daughters, incest among prairie dogs is rare. But prairie dogs regularly mate with more distant kin such as first and second cousins. Information about the prairie dog's social organization and mating patterns leads to better conservation. When trying to establish new colonies via translocation, for example, knowledgeable wildlife managers can assemble new coteries whose ages and sex ratios resemble those of coteries under natural conditions.

Wildlife managers also benefit from knowing about the prairie dog's demography and population dynamics, which I summarize in Chapter 3. Such information helps managers to know when livetrapping is least likely to cause unwanted mortalities or, conversely, when recreational shooting is most likely to severely reduce colony size. Because both male and female prairie dogs are able to reproduce as long as they live, managers do not need to worry that translocated prairie dogs will be too old. And because prairie dogs commonly disperse 2–3 kilometers (1–2 miles), and sometimes as far as 6 kilometers (4 miles), managers can estimate how to optimize spacing of colonies when establishing a new sanctuary—an important consideration, because new, small colonies are unlikely to persist if they are too isolated. The more we can learn about prairie dogs, the better we can conserve them.

Following the identification of the prairie dog as a keystone species about ten years ago, efforts to conserve them have skyrocketed. Amateur naturalists, conservationists, environmentalists, and wildlife managers suddenly have begun to appreciate more fully that prairie dogs affect ecological phenomena such as cycling of nutrients and minerals, and that colony-sites provide prey, shelter, and suitable habitat for hundreds of diverse organisms. The prairie dog is thus a linchpin of the grassland ecosystem of western North America. But what exactly is a keystone species? When examined closely, does the prairie dog warrant designation as a keystone species? In Chapter 4, Natasha Kotliar, Brian Miller, Richard Reading, and Tim Clark try to answer these controversial questions.

As a keystone species, the prairie dog substantially affects myriad other organisms. Kotliar et al. list numerous species that depend on prairie dogs for survival and reproduction, and they examine three species that are especially dependent: black-footed ferrets, mountain plovers, and burrowing owls. More important, these authors argue that scores of other vertebrate and invertebrate species probably also depend on prairie dogs, but that documentation of such dependence is arduous. They also emphasize that dependence varies over space and time. Finally, Kotliar et al. point out that recognition of keystone status enhances efforts to conserve not only the prairie dog, but also its grassland ecosystem.

Most ranchers think that prairie dogs compete with their livestock for forage. Do they? This is perhaps the most important and provocative question addressed in all of *Conservation of the Black-Tailed Prairie Dog*. In Chapter 5, Jim Detling concludes that the simple answer is yes: prairie dogs eat many of the same plants that livestock otherwise would consume. Chapter 5 thus substantiates the ranchers' age-old disdain for prairie dogs. Especially within young colony-sites, however, vegetation often is more nutritious than vegetation on the outside. Consequently, livestock commonly prefer to feed at colony-sites, so that the net effect of competition is less than might be expected simply from the amount of forage consumed by prairie dogs. Further, prairie dogs sometimes improve the habitat for livestock by removing woody plants such as honey mesquite. Finally, prairie dogs often colonize areas that already have been overgrazed by livestock—and thus commonly are the effect, rather than the cause, of overgrazing. With prudent management of grazing by livestock, ranchers sometimes can deter colonization of new areas by prairie dogs.

CHAPTER 2

Social Behavior of Prairie Dogs

John L. Hoogland

Investigation of an animal's social behavior tackles issues such as spacing of individuals; timing of mating, parturition (i.e., giving birth), and weaning; and how individuals defend against predators. Information on these issues is essential for good conservation (Caro 1998; Durant 2000; Moller 2000; Sutherland and Gosling 2000; Holt et al. 2002; Dobson and Zinner 2003; Gosling 2003). A recovery plan for a species whose individuals live solitarily, for example, will differ from a plan for a species whose individuals live in colonies. And translocations are more likely to be successful if we can avoid them at certain points of the annual cycle (e.g., during the breeding season, or when juvenile nutrition still results solely from suckling).

In this chapter I summarize information on the social behavior of prairie dogs. In particular, I focus on issues germane to conservation. I start by addressing taxonomy (i.e., scientific classification), so that we all can agree on the animal that we are trying to save. I also discuss methods that make it possible for ecologists like me to identify social groupings such as coteries, colonies, and complexes. I then examine the prairie dog mating system, which inevitably leads to a consideration of genetic drift and inbreeding, both of which can hinder conservation.

Taxonomy of Prairie Dogs

The prairie dog's common name is misleading, because it is not really a "dog" at all. The first part of the common name refers to its grassland habitat (Hollister 1916; Clark 1977). The second part refers to the prairie dog's alarm call, which reminded early settlers of a domestic dog's bark (Smith et al. 1976, 1977; Clark 1979).

Prairie dogs are burrowing, colonial mammals that belong to the genus *Cynomys* of the squirrel family (Sciuridae; Table 2.1). Other members of the squirrel family include chipmunks, flying squirrels, ground squirrels, marmots, and tree squirrels (Hafner 1984; Harrison et al. 2003).

The genus *Cynomys* has five similar species. Adults of all species stand about 30 centimeters (12 inches) tall, weigh 500–1,500 grams (1–3 pounds), have brown fur, and live in colonies. Key physical characteristics for identifying the different species are length and color of tail, and presence or absence of a black or dark brown line above each eye. Vocalizations are also distinctive for each species (Waring 1970; Hoogland 1995; Frederikson 2005).

Mammalogists recognize two subgroupings within the genus *Cynomys* (Hollister 1916; Pizzimenti 1975; see Table 2.1). The black-tailed subgroup (subgenus *Cynomys*) contains black-tailed and Mexican prairie dogs. The white-tailed subgroup (subgenus *Leucocrossuromys*) contains Gunnison's,

Table 2.1. Taxonomy of prairie dogs and other North American squirrels. Reference: Hafner 1984.

- Order Rodentia
  - Suborder Protrogomorpha
    - Family Sciuridae
      - Subfamily Petauristinae
        - Genus *Glaucomys* (flying squirrels)
      - Subfamily Sciurinae
        - Tribe Tamiini
          - Genus *Tamias* and *Eutamias* (chipmunks)
        - Tribe Sciurini
          - Genus *Sciurus* and *Tamiasciurus* (tree squirrels)
        - Tribe Marmotini
          - Subtribe Marmotina
            - Genus *Marmota* (marmots)
          - Subtribe Spermophilina
            - Genus *Spermophilus* and *Ammospermophilus* (ground squirrels)
            - Genus *Cynomys* (prairie dogs)
              - Subgenus *Cynomys*
                - Species *ludovicianus* (black-tailed prairie dog)
                - Species *mexicanus* (Mexican prairie dog)
              - Subgenus *Leucocrossuromys*
                - Species *gunnisoni* (Gunnison's prairie dog)
                - Species *leucurus* (white-tailed prairie dog)
                - Species *parvidens* (Utah prairie dog)

Utah, and white-tailed prairie dogs. Salient differences between the two subgroups include the following:

- Mexican and black-tailed prairie dogs have long (7–10 centimeters, or 2–3 inches) black-tipped tails, but the other prairie dog species have shorter (3–7 centimeters, or 1–2 inches), white- or gray-tipped tails.
- Mexican and black-tailed prairie dogs do not hibernate, but Gunnison's Utah, and white-tailed prairie dogs remain underground for about four months during late fall and winter.
- Mexican and black-tailed prairie dogs live at elevations of 700–2,200 meters (2,300–7,200 feet) above sea level, but the other species live at higher elevations of 1,500–3,000 meters (4,900–9,800 feet).
- Vegetation within colonies of Mexican and black-tailed prairie dogs is rarely more than 30 centimeters (12 inches) tall, but shrubs within colonies of Gunnison's, Utah, and white-tailed prairie dogs are commonly more than 50 centimeters (20 inches) tall.

Overlap of the geographic ranges of the five species is trivial, so that locality alone is diagnostic for identification (Figure 2.1).

All five species of prairie dogs are rare (Zeveloff and Collett 1988; Biodiversity Legal Foundation 1994; Hoogland 2003a). As endangered and threatened species, respectively, the Mexican and Utah prairie dogs are on the Federal List of Endangered and Threatened Wildlife and Plants (FLETWP) (USFWS 1970, 1984). Petitions to add Gunnison's and white-tailed prairie dogs as threatened species to FLETWP are pending (Center for Native Ecosystems et al. 2002; Rosmarino 2004). The United States Fish and Wildlife Service (USFWS) concluded in 2000 that the black-tailed prairie dog is a candidate for FLETWP as a threatened species, but reversed that conclusion in 2004 (USFWS 2000a, 2004; Chapter 12). In this book, other authors and I focus on conservation of the black-tailed prairie dog, the species of *Cynomys* for which we have the most information (Figure 2.2). Many of our arguments apply to the other four species of prairie dogs as well.

The scientific name for the black-tailed prairie dog is *Cynomys ludovicianus*, for which Hollister (1916) recognized two subspecies: *Cynomys ludovicianus ludovicianus* and *Cynomys ludovicianus arizonensis*. Pizzimenti (1975: 64) argued, however, that ". . . there is no reason to support subspecific designation. . . ." This is an important distinction, because, if correct, it means that we need to conserve one subspecies rather than two.

Their geographic ranges are distinct (see Figure 2.1), but black-tailed and Mexican prairie dogs are remarkably similar. Black-tailed prairie dogs usually have shorter tails than Mexican prairie dogs, and only the distal one-third

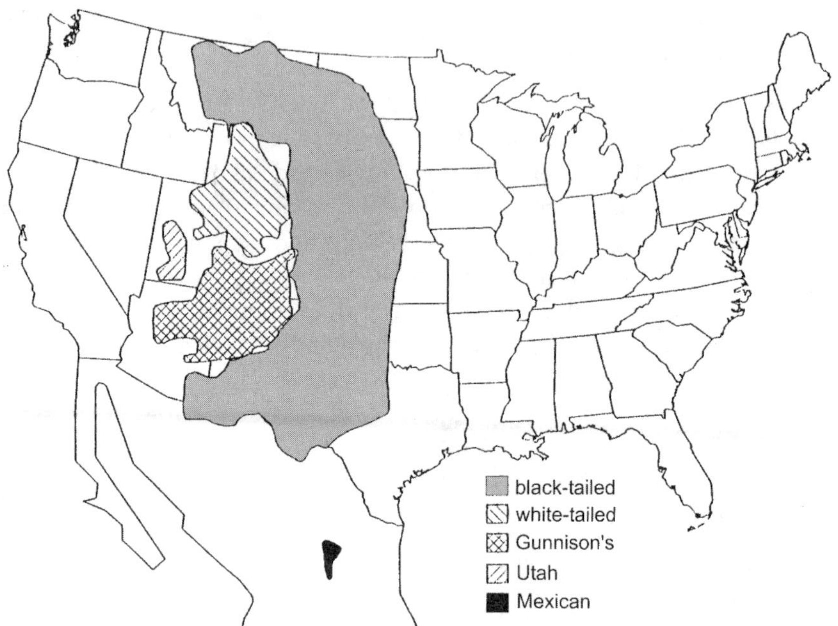

Figure 2.1. Geographic ranges of the five species of prairie dogs. This map shows the approximate distribution of prairie dogs about 200 years ago, before the massive decline of all species resulting from recreational shooting, poisoning, loss of habitat, and plague.

(versus the distal one-half) of the tail is usually black—but overlap for both of these measurements is substantial (Hollister 1916; Pizzimenti 1975; Hoogland 1996a). Classification of black-tailed and Mexican prairie dogs as separate species, rather than as isolated populations or subspecies of the same species, is somewhat arbitrary (Hollister 1916; Kelson 1949; Pizzimenti 1975; McCullough et al. 1987).

As noted above, black-tailed prairie dogs do not hibernate—even in colonies as far north as Saskatchewan, Montana, and North Dakota. In warm, sunny weather, individuals usually emerge from their burrows at about dawn and forage aboveground until about dusk. Individuals do, however, sometimes remain underground for several consecutive days during inclement weather in late autumn and winter (Koford 1958; Thomas and Riedesel 1975; Harlow and Menkens 1986; Bakko et al. 1988; Lehmer et al. 2001). Rarely, an individual or small group of individuals remains underground for a month or more during severe winter weather (Hoogland 1995). These temporary periods of underground inactivity mean that visual counts of individuals in winter will be underestimates of colony size (see also Chapter 6).

Figure 2.2. Black-tailed prairie dog. Note the long tail whose distal third is black. Photo by Greg W. Lasley.

Relative to the other four species of *Cynomys*, the black-tailed prairie dog is the most common, the most conspicuous, and the one most likely to be found in zoos. When scientists, nonscientists, farmers, ranchers, or city dwellers use the term "prairie dog," they usually mean the black-tailed prairie dog. Similarly, other authors and I are referring only to the black-tailed prairie dog when we use the term "prairie dog" in this book.

Colonies and Complexes

Prairie dogs live in aggregations called colonies, which are also called towns or villages (King 1955, 1959; Costello 1970). About 200 years ago, colonies sometimes contained millions of prairie dogs, and inhabited areas that extended for scores of kilometers in all directions. Today's colonies are much smaller (Chapter 16).

Colony density is the number of prairie dogs per hectare (2.471 acres). The only exact way to determine colony density is to mark all residents and to determine the area inhabited by the colony (Chapter 6). Such precise determinations of colony density, available from only five studies, range from 8 to 68 individuals per hectare (Tileston and Lechleitner 1966; Garrett et al. 1982; see summary in Hoogland 1995). With an understanding that densities vary over space and time with factors such as climate, forage, predation, and disease (King 1955; Hoogland 1995; Chapter 11), a rough estimate of colony density before the first emergences of juveniles from their natal burrows is 25 adults and yearlings per hectare (10 adults and yearlings per acre). Colony density approximately doubles when juveniles first appear aboveground from their natal burrows in May and June (Hoogland 1995). A rough estimate of colony density following first juvenile emergences is therefore 50 adults, yearlings, and juveniles per hectare (20 adults, yearlings, and juveniles per acre).

When unsuitable habitat such as a hill, tall vegetation, or a stream divides a colony, the resulting subcolonies are called wards (King 1955). Residents of one ward can see and hear residents of an adjacent ward, but movements between wards are uncommon.

A complex of prairie dogs is a group of two or more colonies in which each colony is less than 7 kilometers (4 miles) from another colony, so that individuals commonly can disperse between colonies (Forrest et al. 1985; Chapters 14 and 16). Complexes are important for conservation, because we want prairie dogs from nearby colonies to repopulate colonies that disappear (e.g., because of plague; see Chapter 11).

Costs of coloniality are substantial for prairie dogs (Hoogland 1979a, 1995). When compared to loners and individuals in smaller colonies, individuals in large colonies engage in more aggressive behavioral interactions and therefore incur more injuries that are sometimes fatal. They harbor more fleas, lice, and ticks, and therefore are more likely to contract diseases such as plague. And individuals in large colonies are also more likely to temporarily or permanently lose offspring in a crowd that includes others' juveniles, to accidentally care for others' offspring, and to lose offspring to infanticide.

Perhaps the single benefit of coloniality is lower predation (Hoogland 1981a, 1995): even though individual prairie dogs spend less time scanning for predators in large colonies, the collective time spent scanning by all colony members is greater. Consequently, individuals in large colonies detect enemies more quickly and more often than do isolates and individuals in smaller colonies. Because large colonies confer safety against predators, colony size is an important consideration for conservation (see also Chapter 16).

After detecting a predator, a prairie dog sometimes gives an alarm call, which is a series of high-pitched "chirk" sounds (King 1955; Waring 1970; Smith et al. 1977). About 50% of adults and yearlings of both sexes call during an attack, but juveniles only rarely call (Figure 2.3).

Prairie dogs have only one distinct alarm call, but variations in the rate of calling might indicate either differences in the level of danger posed by the same predator (e.g., running coyote versus trotting coyote), or different types

Figure 2.3. Alarm calling. During a predator's attack, about half of adult prairie dogs give an alarm call. Both males and females call, and callers usually have offspring or other kin within earshot. Photo courtesy of Wind Cave National Park.

of predators (e.g., aerial versus terrestrial) (King 1955; see also Slobodchikoff et al. 1991, and Placer and Slobodchikoff 2004, for fascinating research with Gunnison's prairie dogs). Alarm calls warn not only nearby offspring, but also other kin such as parents, siblings, nieces/nephews, and first cousins. After an aerial predator has flown out of sight or a terrestrial predator has trotted away from the colony, a prairie dog commonly jumps straight up and gives a jump-yip, or all-clear call, that sounds roughly like a human sneeze ("Atch-choo") (Figure 2.4). The jump-yip is contagious, and amusing, indeed, is the sight of 30–40 jump-yipping prairie dogs after a predator's departure.

Vegetation differentiates prairie dog colony-sites from surrounding areas in two ways. First, composition of the plant community is radically different within colony-sites (Koford 1958; Foster and Hygnstrom 1990). Certain plants such as scarlet globemallow, black nightshade, pigweed, and fetid marigold

Figure 2.4. Jump-yip. Male-08 gives jump-yip, or all-clear call, at burrow-entrance-A6. Prairie dogs jump-yip after a predator has disappeared from view, when a snake is in the home territory, and during territorial disputes with other prairie dogs. Photo by John L. Hoogland.

(also called prairie dog weed), for example, are most common within prairie dog colony-sites (King 1955; Chapters 4 and 5). Second, the height of vegetation is markedly shorter within colony-sites (King 1955; Tileston and Lechleitner 1966; Chapter 5) (Figure 2.5).

Short vegetation results not only from daily foraging, but also because prairie dogs use their teeth to clip plants more than 30 centimeters (12 inches) tall at the base without consuming them—presumably to enhance the detection of predators (King 1955; Hoogland 1995). Further, prairie dogs commonly colonize areas where the vegetation is already low (Koford 1958; Clark 1979; Snell 1985; Knowles 1986b; Chapter 5). Height of vegetation should be an important consideration when wildlife managers evaluate sites that might serve as sanctuaries for prairie dogs (Chapters 13 and 16).

As recently as 100 years ago, one colony in Texas contained approximately 400 million prairie dogs (Merriam 1902a; Clark 1979; Grossmann 1987). Because of recreational shooting, poisoning, loss of habitat, and plague, colonies of this magnitude no longer exist (Chapters 12 and 16).

Figure 2.5. Short vegetation. The low vegetation at prairie dog colony-sites results from normal foraging, from clipping of tall plants, and from the tendency to colonize habitats where the vegetation is already low. Shown here is a family of prairie dogs during the winter months. Notice how the short vegetation facilitates behavioral observations. Photo courtesy of Wind Cave National Park.

Methods for Studying Prairie Dogs

How do we know that prairie dogs live in family groups, that both males and females give alarm calls, that females sometimes live as long as eight years, and that infanticide is a major cause of mortality? All these discoveries result from watching marked prairie dogs living under natural conditions. Here I briefly describe the methods that I used to study prairie dogs from 1975 through 1989 at the Rankin Ridge Colony at Wind Cave National Park, South Dakota (Hoogland 1995).

I capture prairie dogs with 15-centimeter × 15-centimeter × 60-centimeter (6 inches × 6 inches × 24 inches) double-door livetraps (Tomahawk Livetrap Company, Tomahawk, Wisconsin) baited with whole oats. A conical, cloth bag facilitates handling, sexing, and determination of body mass. Numbered National fingerling eartags (National Band and Tag Company, Newport, Kentucky) work well for permanent identification (Hoogland 1995).

To observe prairie dogs from a distance, I paint numbers or symbols on their flanks with Nyanzol-D fur dye (Greenville Colorants, Clifton, New Jersey; Figure 2.6).

When a female mates with two or more males, I do not know which male sires the offspring. For analysis of paternity following mating with multiple males, I collect several capillary tubes of blood (from a clipped toenail) from the mother, all her offspring, and all possible sires, and then resort to biochemical techniques such as starch-gel electrophoresis, DNA-fingerprinting, or polymerase chain reaction (PCR) (Hoogland 1995; see also Haynie et al. 2003).

Juvenile prairie dogs—also called pups or young—are less than 9 months old and first emerged from the natal burrow (when about 6 weeks old) less than 8 months ago. Yearlings are at least 9 months old but less than 21 months old, and adults are at least 21 months old. For many studies, including several in this volume, the term "adult" includes both adult and yearling prairie dogs.

Good conservation requires information about survivorship and reproductive success of prairie dogs of known ages (Chapter 3). By prying open the mouth with ring-pliers and measuring the height of the cusps of molar teeth with a vernier caliper, wildlife managers can classify live, older-than-juvenile prairie dogs as either yearlings, two-year-olds, or older than three years (Hoogland and Hutter 1987; Cox and Franklin 1990). Body mass increases with age for the first three to four years, but extensive overlap precludes aging from body mass except for the simple distinction between adults and yearlings (Chapter 3). Aging live adult and yearling prairie dogs with complete reliability is possible only if they are first permanently marked (e.g., with numbered eartags) as juveniles.

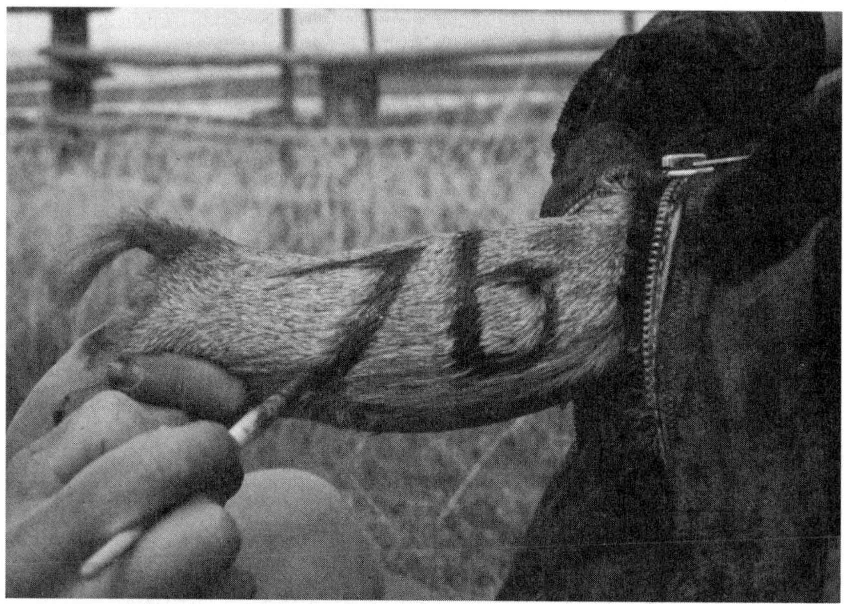

Figure 2.6. Marking with Nyanzol dye. While one person holds the front legs of a prairie dog restrained in a canvas bag, the other person holds the rear legs and applies a number with Nyanzol dye. Dye is light brown when first applied, but it turns to black in about five minutes. Photo by Judy G. Hoogland.

Curiously, most research with wild prairie dogs has occurred at Wind Cave National Park in South Dakota. John King (1955) did the benchmark study and thereby started a chain reaction of later research (e.g., Garrett et al. 1982; Garrett and Franklin 1983, 1988; Coppock et al. 1983a, 1983b; Wydeven and Dahlgren 1985; Cincotta et al. 1987a,b, 1989; Loughry 1987a, 1987b, 1988, 1992; Whicker and Detling 1993; Kildaw 1995; Detling, Chapter 5; J. F. Cully, research in progress; Chapter 15). As noted above, I also studied prairie dogs at Wind Cave National Park.

Family Groups Called Coteries

Within colonies, prairie dogs live in territorial family groups called coteries (King 1955). The number of adults and yearlings in a coterie ranges from 1 (the rare isolated individual) to 26, with an average of about 6 (Hoogland 1995) (Figure 2.5). The typical coterie contains one breeding male, two to three adult females, and one to two yearlings of each sex. Large coteries sometimes contain two breeding males who are commonly close kin, such as father and son or full brothers. Conversely, a single breeding male sometimes dominates two small, adjacent groups of females.

Behavioral interactions among prairie dogs are conspicuous and frequent. When two individuals from different coteries meet, they typically engage in a territorial dispute that involves staring, tooth-chattering, flaring of the tail, bluff charges, defense barks, and reciprocal sniffing of scent glands at the base of the tail (King 1955) (Figure 2.7). Territorial disputes commonly persist for more than 30 minutes, and sometimes include fights and chases. Within coteries, interactions are usually amicable and include play, grooming, and mouth-to-mouth contacts that resemble kisses (Figure 2.8).

Amicability within coteries turns to fighting and chasing in February through April, when pregnant and lactating females vigorously defend nursery burrows against all coterie-mates. Peace within the coterie returns in May, when juveniles first appear aboveground from their nursery burrows (King 1955).

Debra Shier's research indicates that translocations of prairie dogs are more successful when individuals are moved together as coteries (Box to Chapter 13). Curiously, however, research by Dustin Long et al. indicates that keeping coteries together does not enhance either survivorship or reproductive success of translocated prairie dogs (Chapter 13). The relevance of this conflict for conservation is enormous, but more research is necessary for a resolution.

Figure 2.7. Territorial dispute between male-24 and male-33. Territorial disputes commonly persist for more than 30 minutes and sometimes include fights and chases. Note the flared tails of both males. By recording where disputes occur, I can map the territories of all coteries within the study-colony. Photo by John L. Hoogland.

Figure 2.8. Kissing. Prairie dogs commonly kiss other prairie dogs of the home coterie, but usually fight and chase prairie dogs from other coteries. Sometimes I have seen as many as six prairie dogs kissing each other at the same time. Photo courtesy of Wind Cave National Park.

Coterie members have a well-defined territory that they defend from prairie dogs of other coteries (King 1955). Territories range in size from 0.05 hectares (0.12 acres) to 1.01 hectares (2.50 acres), with an average of about one-third of a hectare (0.8 acres) (Hoogland 1995). Boundaries between territories sometimes coincide with unsuitable habitat containing tall vegetation, rocks, or poor drainage. More commonly, though, territories are contiguous, and their boundaries are undetectable to human observers from physical features alone. The area and configuration of a territory usually remain constant across generations. Several territories at Wind Cave National Park, for example, remained the same size and shape for 14 consecutive years (Hoogland 1995).

Unlike males, which usually remain in the natal territory for only about one year after weaning, females usually remain in the natal territory for their entire lives (Chapter 3). Consequently, females are invariably surrounded by close kin such as mothers, grandmothers, daughters, granddaughters, sisters, aunts, nieces, and cousins. This kinship helps to explain why most interactions among females of the same coterie are amicable—except, as noted above, during the periods of pregnancy and lactation (King 1955; Hoogland 1995).

Within territories, prairie dogs depend on elaborate tunnels for rearing offspring and for protection from weather and predators. Burrows are typically 20–30 centimeters (8–12 inches) in diameter at the entrance, but the underground diameter is smaller (Merriam 1902a; King 1955, 1984; Sheets et al. 1971). Burrows are usually about 5–10 meters (16–33 feet) long and 2–3 meters (7–10 feet) deep, but some are as long as 33 meters (108 feet) and as deep as 5 meters (16 feet). A burrow typically has two entrances, each with a large mound called either a dome crater or a rim crater (King 1955; Cincotta 1989). Dome craters are unstructured mounds of dirt, have a basal diameter of 1–2 meters (3–7 feet), and are usually no higher than 0.2–0.5 meters (1–2 feet). Rim craters resemble miniature volcanoes, have a basal diameter of 0.5–1.5 meters (2–5 feet), and are sometimes as high as 0.75 meters (2.5 feet); rim craters result from the careful molding of moist soil by prairie dogs working alone or in small groups (Figure 2.9).

Dome and rim craters inhibit flooding after rainstorms, provide vantage points from which to scan for predators, and enhance underground ventilation (Vogel et al. 1973; Vogel 1989; Hoogland 1995).

Figure 2.9. Construction of rim crater. After scraping dirt from around the burrow-mound, male-08 uses his nose like a jackhammer to pound dirt into the rim of burrow-entrance-204. Rim craters deter flooding of nest-chambers, serve as vantage points to scan for predators, and enhance underground ventilation. Photo by John L. Hoogland.

The number of burrow-entrances per territory ranges from 5 (for an isolated prairie dog) to 214, with an average of 69 (Hoogland 1995). Burrow-entrances of the same territory commonly connect underground to one or two other entrances, but burrow-entrances of different territories do not connect.

Except when pregnant or lactating females are defending nursery burrows, all coterie members have access to all the numerous burrows within the home territory during the day and at night—that is, each prairie dog does not have its own private burrow or set of burrows. In large coteries, for example, as many as 14 prairie dogs sometimes spend the night in the same burrow in late fall and early winter.

Burrows affect conservation of prairie dogs in two specific ways. First, wildlife managers sometimes estimate the number of prairie dogs at a colony-site from the number of burrow-entrances there (Chapter 6). Second, ranchers worry that their horses and cattle will step into burrows and thereby will incur leg fractures. Over the years, I have chatted with more than 100 ranchers in Colorado, South Dakota, and Wyoming and have asked about broken legs. All the ranchers fretted about leg fractures, but only one could muster an example: a cow that sometimes foraged in a field with prairie dogs somehow sustained a broken leg (Hoogland 1995; see also Dold 1998). The implication is that the frequency of leg fractures from prairie dog burrows is trivial—probably because conspicuous dome and rim craters render burrow-entrances easy for domestic livestock to avoid.

Mating System and Reproductive Cycle

Knowing the prairie dog's mating system fosters good conservation. Such information might help wildlife managers determine when to treat females with a chemical that inhibits conception and implantation (Pfeiffer and Linder 1973; Garrett and Franklin 1983), for example, or when to minimize disturbance at a colony that is especially important for some reason (e.g., as habitat for black-footed ferrets).

A female prairie dog is sexually receptive for several hours on only one day of each year. Because 98% of matings occur underground, documenting them is a formidable task. A typical mating sequence involves most or all of the following:

- The first of about six co-submergences of a breeding male with a receptive female occurs at about noon, and the last co-submergence occurs at about 1530 hours (3:30 p.m.). By contrast, non-receptive females almost never co-submerge with a breeding male.

- Most co-submergences are short (less than 3 minutes), but at least one usually persists for at least 40 minutes.
- Aboveground fights and chases involving breeding males and a female number about 60 on the day when the female is receptive, versus fewer than 20 on previous and later days. The breeding male gives a unique mating call in response to the receptive female on about three separate occasions, and takes several mouthfuls of dry grass into a burrow before consorting with her there.
- The receptive female remains aboveground as much as 60–90 minutes after the other (non-receptive) females in her coterie have submerged for the night.
- Usually on the first day after mating, a female selects a nursery burrow, which she fills with nesting material and defends vigorously for the next eleven weeks of pregnancy and lactation (Figure 2.10).

Figure 2.10. Nest building. Female-4stripe, who is pregnant, takes mouthful of dry grass into burrow-entance-07. Usually on the day after mating, a female selects a nursery burrow and then begins to build a nest there and to defend it from other prairie dogs. Defense continues throughout pregnancy (usually 34 or 35 days) and lactation (about six weeks). Photo by John L. Hoogland.

By tracking co-submergences of breeding males and females and the associated aboveground behaviors, students and I can document more than 90% of matings each year. Most females mate with only one male during the short period of sexual receptivity, but some mate with two or three different males (Figure 2.11).

The earliest date of mating at my study-colony in South Dakota occurred on 16 February, the latest on 13 April, and the average was 7 March (Hoogland 1995).

The timing of matings each year largely determines the timing of other reproductive events as well. Because matings at my study-colony in South Dakota occurred in late February through early March each year, for example, females were pregnant in late February through mid-April, the period of nursing offspring began in late March and extended into May, and nearly weaned juveniles first emerged from their natal burrows in mid-May through early June (Hoogland 1995). Knowing this schedule of reproductive events is useful for many aspects of conservation (Chapter 3).

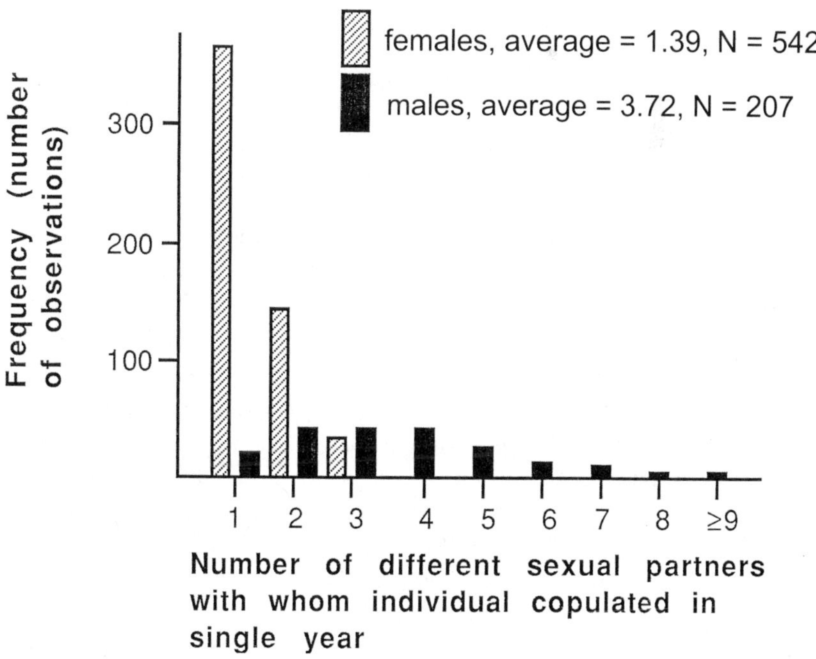

Figure 2.11. Number of sexual partners per year for male and female prairie dogs. This graph excludes data from individuals that did not mate at least once during the breeding season. For more details about annual reproductive success (ARS), see Hoogland 1995.

Multiple paternity occurs when two or more males each sire at least one offspring of a single female's litter (Hanken and Sherman 1981; Foltz and Schwagmeyer 1989). At least 5% of prairie dog litters show multiple paternity, and the actual frequency might be as high as 10% (Hoogland 1995). The main reason for these low frequencies is that 67% of estrous females preclude multiple paternity by mating with only one male (see Figure 2.11).

Most female prairie dogs (84%) mate exclusively with the resident breeding male(s) of the home coterie; 11% mate with the resident breeding male(s) and also with a male from a different coterie; and 4% mate exclusively with males from different coteries. When a male from a different coterie sires offspring, the result is cuckoldry of the resident breeding male. Cuckoldry occurs in about 8% of prairie dog litters.

Females that mate exclusively with males from outside the home territory are less likely to wean a litter than are females that mate with the resident adult male (13% versus 54%). For this and other reasons, disrupting prairie dogs during the mating season of February and March—via recreational shooting of breeding males, for example, so that the females of victimized coteries must solicit matings from outside males to reproduce—can drastically undermine the production of juveniles. Disruption during the periods of pregnancy and lactation can also seriously impede reproduction.

Genetic Drift and Inbreeding

A small, isolated population cannot contain all the genetic variation present throughout the prairie dog's extensive geographic range. Over time, variation will continue to diminish by chance. These factors are different aspects of a phenomenon known as genetic drift, which will hinder efforts to conserve prairie dogs (Roughgarden 1979; Freeman and Herron 2004; Trudeau et al. 2004). Reduced variation makes populations more vulnerable to extinction, because they are less able to respond to changing environmental conditions.

Within small, isolated populations, the only available mates sometimes are close kin. In combination with genetic drift, inbreeding reduces genetic diversity because inbred offspring are more susceptible to diseases, parasites, and environmental changes (Williams 1975; Falconer 1981; Stearns 1987; Seger and Hamilton 1988; Hedrick and Kalinowski 2000). Because it exposes rare deleterious alleles (i.e., variations of the same gene), inbreeding also increases the probability of genetic anomalies such as birth defects and albinism (Tate 1947). Outbreeding, on the other hand, sometimes disrupts valuable combinations of alleles that might be adaptations to local conditions (Dobzhansky 1951; Shields 1982; Waser 1993). Further, individuals sometimes must risk predation and exposure to harsh weather as they disperse long distances in search of unrelated mates (Dobson and Jones 1985; Garrett and Franklin 1988). Natural selection therefore should favor individuals that avoid both extreme inbreeding (incest) and extreme outbreeding, so that some level of "moderate" inbreeding results (Shields 1982; Bateson 1983; Keane 1990a, 1990b).

Prairie dogs have several mechanisms to avoid extreme inbreeding. Young males usually disperse from the natal territory before reaching sexual maturity, and consequently cannot mate with mothers, aunts, and sisters. Older males usually do not remain in the same breeding territory for more than two consecutive years, and therefore are gone when their daughters reach sexual maturity as two-year-olds (Chapter 3). Despite the regular dispersal of young and older males, sexually mature close kin of the opposite sex sometimes end up in the same coterie territory. When this happens, females assume the responsibility for avoiding incest. Some females do not become sexually receptive when the only resident breeding male is a father, brother, or son. Such females miss an entire breeding season, because they do not get another opportunity to mate until 12 months later. Other females with breeding male kin in the home coterie become sexually receptive, but only mate with unrelated (or distantly related) males from outside the home territory. To accomplish this task, the receptive female either solicits the unrelated male to temporarily invade her home territory, or she briefly visits his territory.

The four mechanisms just described work well, because only about 5% of prairie dog matings involve extreme inbreeding with parents, offspring, or siblings. Even though they avoid incest, however, prairie dogs routinely mate with more distant kin such as full and half first and second cousins. In 1988, for example, 68% of matings at my study-colony involved such moderate inbreeding (Hoogland 1995). The combination of rare incest with frequent moderate inbreeding probably results because prairie dogs easily can learn to recognize and avoid close kin such as parents, offspring, and siblings as members of the home coterie—but cannot easily recognize and avoid more distant kin such as first and second cousins from outside coteries.

Occasional incest and frequent moderate inbreeding evidently did not lead to deleterious consequences for prairie dogs at my study-colony (Hoogland 1992, 1995). Does this mean that wildlife managers can ignore inbreeding for the conservation of prairie dogs? The answer is no, for at least two related reasons. First, the disadvantage of extreme inbreeding in prairie dogs might be as low as 3%–4%. This disadvantage would be sufficient over time to lead to the demise of small, isolated colonies in which extreme inbreeding eventually might predominate but would require huge sample sizes for detection. Second, the existence of four mechanisms of avoidance indicates that incest often must yield inferior offspring. Otherwise, why would young and old males risk the perils of dispersal, and why would females sometimes forfeit an entire breeding season, to escape incest?

Summary

- The prairie dog is a burrowing rodent that lives in colonies. Within colonies, prairie dogs live in family groups called coteries. Coterie size ranges from 1 to 26, but the typical coterie contains 1 breeding male, 2–3 adult females, and 1–2 yearling offspring of each sex.
- Coterie members have a well-defined territory that they defend from prairie dogs of other coteries. The area and configuration of a territory usually remain constant across generations.
- To capture prairie dogs, researchers use double-door livetraps baited with whole oats. To mark them, researchers use eartags (for permanent identification) and Nyanzol fur dye (for identification from a distance).
- Most females (84%) mate exclusively with the resident breeding male of the home coterie; 11% mate with the resident breeding male and also with a male from a different coterie; and 4% mate exclusively with males from different coteries.
- At least 5% of prairie dog litters show multiple paternity, and the actual frequency might be as high as 10%.
- In South Dakota, matings among prairie dogs occur in late February and early March. Consequently, females are pregnant in late February through mid-April, the period of nursing offspring begins in late March and extends into May, and nearly weaned juveniles first emerge from their natal burrows in mid-May through early June. Knowing this schedule of reproductive events is useful for many aspects of conservation.
- Small isolated colonies are likely to lose genetic variation because of genetic drift and extreme inbreeding. Reduced variation renders populations more vulnerable to extinction, because they are less able to respond to changing environmental conditions.
- The more we know about the natural history and social behavior of prairie dogs, the better we can conserve them.

CHAPTER 3

Demography and Population Dynamics of Prairie Dogs

John L. Hoogland

The study of demography focuses on topics such as average and maximal lifespan, litter size, age of first reproduction, senescence, annual and lifetime reproductive success, and predation and other causes of mortality. Population dynamics includes issues such as dispersal, population crashes, repopulation after crashes, stable versus growing populations, and sex ratio at different times of the year. Conservation is easier when we have rigorous information on all these issues (Durant 2000; Young and Clarke 2000; Holt et al. 2002; Dobson and Zinner 2003; Hedrick 2004). Translocation of mostly juveniles to recipient-sites might work well for a species when we know that individuals first breed as yearlings, for example, but it is less likely to work for a species in which individuals defer first breeding until the second year. Because we know that American badgers are especially likely to prey on translocated prairie dogs, then wildlife managers probably will want to transfer prairie dogs into recipient-sites where badgers are rare, or to move badgers away from recipient-sites. If we know how far prairie dogs can safely disperse when they switch colonies, then we can more effectively design complexes of colonies within sanctuaries.

In this chapter I begin by summarizing demographic information that is pertinent to the conservation of prairie dogs. Specifically, I discuss gestation (pregnancy) and lactation, litter size, causes of mortality, age of first reproduction and age versus survivorship and reproduction, life tables, sexual dimorphism, and ways to estimate reproductive success. I then turn my attention to relevant issues of population dynamics: sex ratios, variation in colony size, and dispersal. Finally, I investigate why prairie dogs reproduce slowly in some colonies but quickly in others, and then point out that the prairie dog's resilience makes it difficult to eradicate. Most of the information in this chapter comes from my study of prairie dogs from 1975 through 1989 at the Rankin Ridge Colony of Wind Cave National Park, South Dakota (Hoogland 1995).

Parturition, Gestation, and Lactation

A prairie dog gives birth (i.e., parturition) underground in the nursery burrow that she has been defending for most of her pregnancy. The most obvious indication of parturition is that a mother's body mass suddenly drops precipitously, sometimes by more than 100 grams in less than 24 hours. Another diagnostic sign of parturition is a dramatic behavioral change. Pregnant females usually emerge early in the morning, spend the entire day foraging aboveground, and are among the last to submerge for the night. On the same day that a mother's body mass plummets, however, she is usually one of the last to appear aboveground in the morning—sometimes emerging as much as four to five hours after all other individuals. Further, the mother usually visits the home nursery burrow once or twice for a long time (one to two hours) on the day of, and for the first few days after, parturition. Parturition usually occurs early in the morning, but sometimes occurs late in the afternoon. The identification of parturition is essential for documenting the lengths of gestation and lactation.

The length of gestation is the number of days between mating and parturition, and the length of lactation is the number of days between parturition and weaning. The length of gestation for prairie dogs ranges from 33 to 38 days, but 88% of gestations are either 34 or 35 days (Hoogland 1995). This length is longer than previous estimates, all flawed because the researchers could not detect matings (Anthony and Foreman 1951; Tileston and Lechleitner 1966; Costello 1970; Burt and Grossenheider 1976; Chace 1976; Nowak and Paradiso 1983). At birth, juveniles are about 4 centimeters (1.5 inches) long, weigh about 15 grams (0.5 ounces), are blind, and have no fur. Fur appears about three weeks after birth, and the eyes open about two weeks later (Johnson 1927).

Female prairie dogs that mate do not invariably give birth. Failure to give birth can result either from failure to conceive or from abortion of all embryos after conception (Anthony and Foreman 1951; Knowles 1987). Of the females that I could unambiguously score as having mated, 82% gave birth. The probability of giving birth after mating is higher for adults than for yearlings (89% versus 54%) (Hoogland 1995).

I have found no easy way to discriminate between failure to conceive versus abortion of all embryos sometime after conception. Both probably occur. The second estrus of a few females in the same breeding season is almost certainly a response to failed conception, for example (Hoogland 1995). On the other hand, late abortion of all embryos probably explains the large teats of certain females that never give birth. Pregnant females sometimes abort certain implanted embryos and later give birth to the others (Anthony and Foreman 1951; Foreman 1962; Tileston and Lechleitner 1966; Knowles 1987).

After birth, juvenile prairie dogs remain underground for several weeks before appearing aboveground. Pre-emergent juveniles depend primarily on their mother's milk for nourishment, but they also eat plants brought underground by the mother. Conversely, emergent juveniles depend primarily on their own foraging for nourishment, but they also continue to nurse at night for a week or more after first appearing aboveground. These patterns make it difficult to specify the day of weaning and the length of lactation. One way to estimate the length of lactation is to determine the interval between parturition and first juvenile emergence from the natal burrow. This interval for prairie dogs ranges from 37 to 51 days, with an average of 41 days (Hoogland 1995).

Successful reproduction depends on many factors, which I discuss below, but the periods of mating, gestation, and lactation are especially critical. To secure prairie dogs for translocations, wildlife managers should avoid livetrapping during these periods. Otherwise, females ready to mate or to give birth might end up in livetraps, or lactating females might get separated from their dependant offspring. If reduction of a colony is important, on the other hand, then managers might want to encourage recreational shooting or other methods of elimination during the periods of mating, gestation, and lactation.

Litter Size

Because parturition occurs underground, information on litter size at birth is scarce for prairie dogs. Laboratory studies and dissections of pregnant and lactating females indicate that litter size at birth ranges from one to eight (Wade 1928; Anthony and Foreman 1951; Foreman 1962; Tileston and Lechleitner 1966; Knowles 1987). When juveniles first emerge from their burrows when they are about six weeks old, litter size ranges from 1 to 6, the most common litter size is 3, and the average is 3.08 (Figures 3.1 and 3.2).

Upon first emergence from the natal burrow in May or June, the average juvenile body mass is 147 grams (5 ounces) for males (range = 68–288 grams) and 141 grams (5 ounces) for females (range = 60–258 grams). Several months

Figure 3.1. Litter size when juveniles first emerge from the natal burrow. Litter size at first emergence ranges from one to six, and the most common litter size is three. Juveniles at first emergence are about six weeks old. Photo by John L. Hoogland.

later, in October, the average body mass has increased to 556 grams (20 ounces) for males (range = 243–964 grams) and 532 grams (19 ounces) for females (range = 270–819 grams) (Hoogland 1995).

The volume of maternal milk available for each juvenile is probably copious when a litter contains only one juvenile. However, a mother's milk might be limiting when litter size is five or six. Probably as a consequence, juvenile body mass at first emergence declines with litter size (Figure 3.3).

The percentage of juveniles in a litter that survives for at least one year varies directly with juvenile body mass at first emergence (Figure 3.4). Juveniles that survive for at least one year average about 15 grams (0.5 ounces) heavier at first emergence than shorter-lived juveniles (152 grams [5.4 ounces] versus 137 grams [4.8 ounces]).

Causes of Mortality for Prairie Dogs

The three main causes of mortality for prairie dogs are predation, infanticide, and inability to survive the winter.

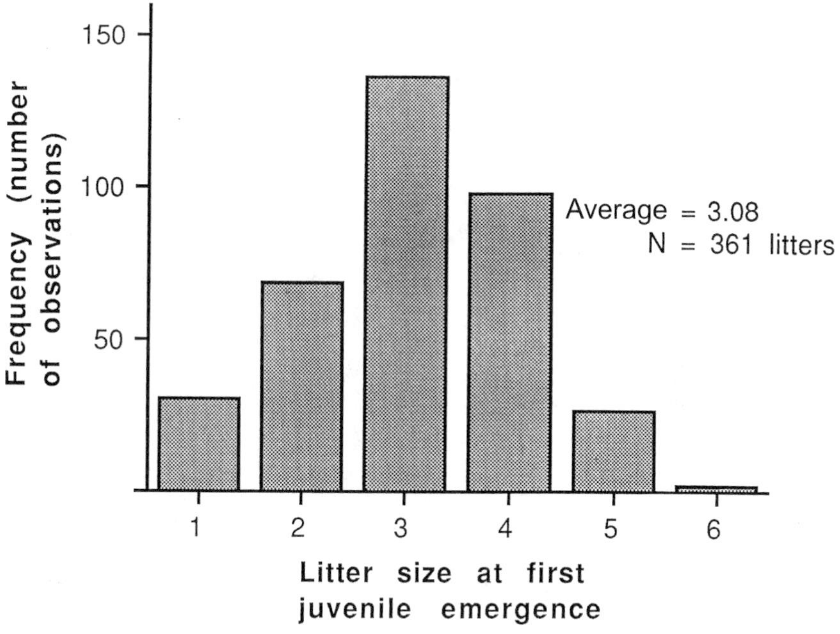

Figure 3.2. Litter size at first juvenile emergence.

Predation

Enemies that prey on prairie dogs are numerous (Sperry 1934; Scheffer 1945; King 1955; Halloran 1972; Olendorff 1976; Campbell et al. 1987; Hoogland 1995). Major mammalian predators include American badgers, bobcats, coyotes, long-tailed weasels, black-footed ferrets, and humans. Other mammals that occasionally prey on prairie dogs include swift foxes, red foxes, common gray foxes, grizzly bears, and mountain lions. Reptilian predators include bull snakes and rattlesnakes (Scheffer 1945; Owings and Owings 1979; Halpin 1983; Owings and Loughry 1985; Loughry 1987a, 1987b). Avian predators include golden eagles, northern goshawks, northern harriers, peregrine falcons, prairie falcons, Cooper's hawks, ferruginous hawks, red-tailed hawks, and several other species of buteo and accipiter hawks. All these terrestrial and aerial enemies commonly prey on other animals besides prairie dogs. The only exception is the black-footed ferret, which dines almost exclusively on prairie dogs (Hillman 1968; Sheets and Linder 1969; Clark 1989; Chapter 4). In an effort to detect predators before it is too late, prairie dogs spend about one-third of their time scanning for enemies (Figure 3.5).

Burrowing owls are small, diurnal raptors that commonly live in burrows abandoned by prairie dogs (Scheffer 1937, 1945). Contrary to popular opinion

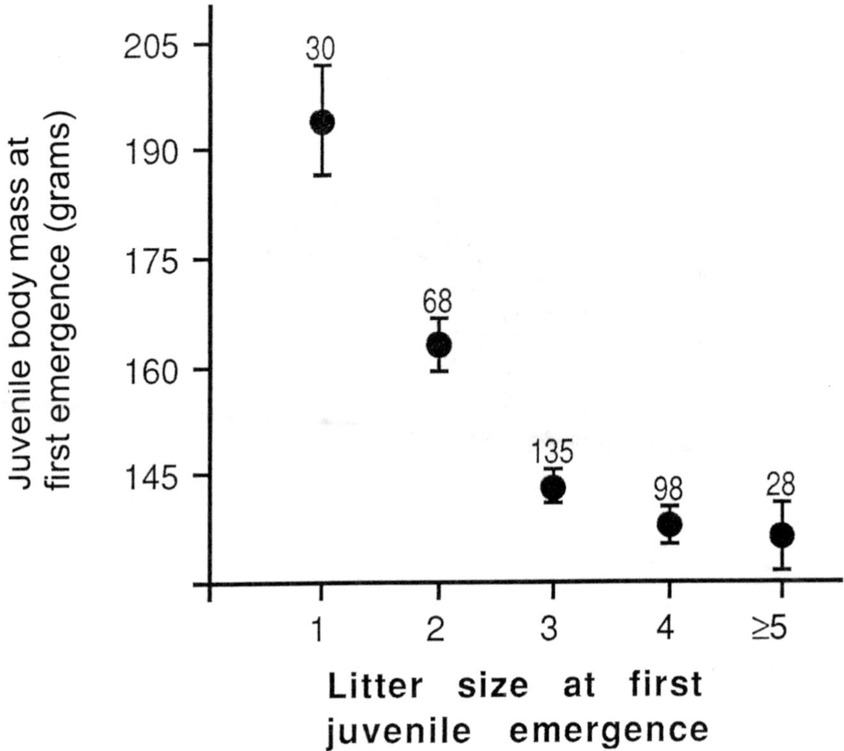

Figure 3.3. Juvenile body mass versus litter size at first juvenile emergence. Circles represent averages, and lines above and below the circles show standard errors (SE); the number above each SE line indicates the number of litters.

(e.g., Swenk 1915; Hollister 1916; Allen 1967; Costello 1970), burrowing owls usually do not attack adult or juvenile prairie dogs.

Infanticide

Nonparental infanticide, the killing of another prairie dog's juvenile offspring, accounts for the partial or total demise of 39% of all litters within colonies, and thus is a major cause of mortality (Hoogland 1995). Infanticide commonly occurs in three different contexts.

In Type-I infanticide, marauding lactating females kill the unweaned offspring of close kin living in the home-coterie territory. Victimized mothers are most commonly half-sisters, full sisters, mothers, or daughters of the killer. Marauders usually kill, and then cannibalize, all juveniles in a litter, but partial-

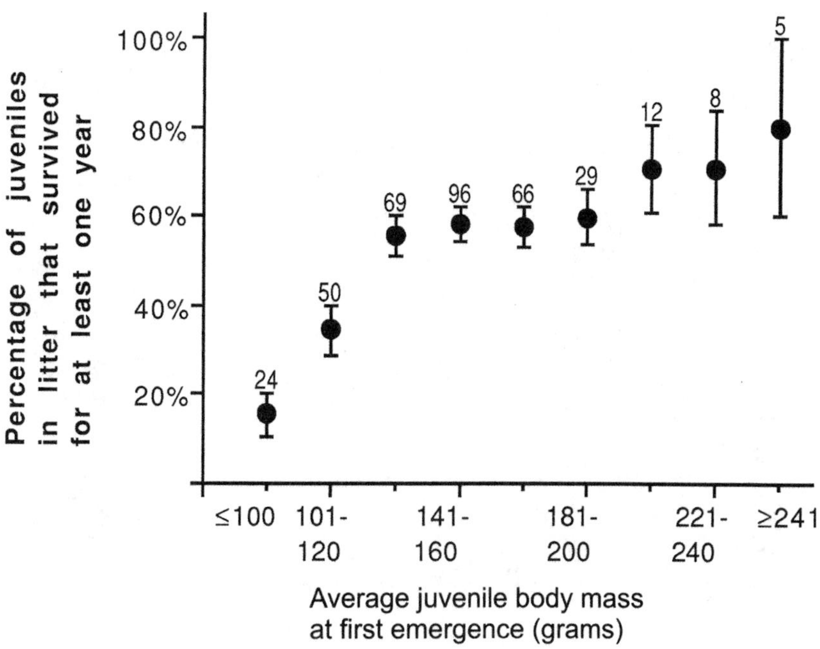

Figure 3.4. Survivorship in the first year versus juvenile body mass at first emergence. Circles represent averages, and lines above and below the circles show standard errors (SE); the number above each SE line indicates the number of litters.

litter infanticide also occurs. Of the three types of infanticide, Type-I is the most common. The frequency of litters partially eliminated by such marauding is 6%, and 16% are totally eliminated. Of several possible benefits (Hrdy 1979; Sherman 1981), the most likely is increased sustenance. Specifically, marauders gain additional nutrition from cannibalism (e.g., protein or rare minerals), and thus are better able to nurture themselves and their offspring through the six weeks of lactation.

Type-II infanticide involves killing of abandoned litters. On the day after mating, most female prairie dogs start to show conspicuous maternal behaviors such as building an underground nest, defense of the nursery burrow with that nest, spending the night alone in the nursery burrow, and so forth (Hoogland 1995). The females who mate and then show maternal behaviors give birth and then attempt to rear their litters to weaning. Those females who mate and do not show maternal behaviors usually give birth as well, but commonly abandon their offspring within a day or two after giving birth. With the mother at the time of parturition are other coterie members, who kill and cannibalize

Figure 3.5. Scanning for predators. Prairie dogs frequently look around for enemies such as coyotes, bobcats, golden eagles, and prairie falcons. Individuals in small colonies scan longer and more often than individuals in larger colonies. Photo by Judy G. Hoogland.

the abandoned neonates. Type-II infanticide accounts for the total elimination of 10% of litters.

Type-III infanticide involves invading males. Male prairie dogs frequently change territories within the home colony—either as yearlings from the natal territory to a breeding territory or as adults from one breeding territory to another. Most of these transfers occur in May or June, when territories contain young juveniles that have recently emerged from their natal burrows. Invading males are commonly both infanticidal and cannibalistic, as evidenced by maimed, partially consumed carcasses that commonly appear aboveground following takeovers. Type-III infanticide accounts for the total or partial demise of 7% of litters (Hoogland 1995).

Infanticide is sometimes a pathological response to overcrowding in captivity (Calhoun 1962; Diamond and Mast 1978; Packard et al. 1990) or in nature (Fox 1975; Curtin and Dolhinow 1978; Boggess 1984; Polis et al. 1984). Four lines of evidence indicate that infanticide within prairie dog colonies is adaptive rather than pathological:

- The density of prairie dogs at my study-colony was not unusually high: of five colony densities estimated from studies of marked individuals, the density at my study-colony was higher than two but lower than two others (Hoogland 1995).
- Garrett's observation of aboveground infanticide (described in Hoogland 1995) occurred at a young (less than ten years old), expanding colony with abundant forage (Garrett et al. 1982). The Pringle Colony, where I observed three instances of marauding, also was young and expanding.
- Poor female reproduction in other studies suggests the ubiquity of infanticide (King 1955; Tileston and Lechleitner 1966; Garrett et al. 1982; Knowles 1985, 1987; Halpin 1987; Garrett and Franklin 1988; Stockrahm and Seabloom 1988). Further, killing is not limited to a few idiosyncratic individuals. Rather, 84 prairie dogs at my study-colony were infanticidal: 38 females that killed the offspring of close kin, 2 immigrant female marauders, 24 females that killed abandoned juveniles, and 20 invading male marauders.
- Infanticide among prairie dogs involves one unique behavior (careful licking of the front claws) and one almost-unique behavior (rubbing of the face in the dirt). The coupling of complex behaviors such as these with a particular phenomenon suggests evolutionary design and adaptation rather than pathology (Williams 1966; Dawkins 1976).

The high frequency of infanticide means that prairie dogs are sometimes their own worst enemies. If we can better understand this bizarre phenomenon, then perhaps wildlife managers will be able to create conditions that promote infanticide at certain colonies where expansion would be problematic. If so, then we can bypass the expense, effort, and public resistance to measures such as poisoning and recreational shooting. Conversely, finding ways to discourage infanticide might help to establish colonies and promote their expansion in areas under consideration for reintroduction of black-footed ferrets.

Inability to Survive the Winter

As noted in Chapter 2, prairie dogs do not hibernate. Food is scarce during late fall, winter, and early spring, however, and surviving the winter depends in large part on fat accumulated during the months of summer and early fall. Middle-aged individuals are heavier than older and younger individuals and therefore are more likely to survive the winter. Most prairie dogs that do not survive the winter die underground, but occasionally I find carcasses of emaciated individuals aboveground (see Hoogland 1995).

Age of First Reproduction

Most prairie dogs first become sexually mature and mate in the second February or March following birth, approximately 21 months following first emergence from the natal burrow (King 1955; Stockrahm and Seabloom 1988; Hoogland 1995). However, some individuals first mate as yearlings (35% of females, 6% of males). The probability of a yearling's producing emergent juveniles is low for both sexes but is higher for females than for males (9% versus 2%). Conversely, some individuals delay sexual maturation until the third year. Again a sexual asymmetry prevails, with males being more likely than females to delay (24% versus 5%).

Age of first reproduction affects conservation of prairie dogs in many ways. Because prairie dogs commonly defer sexual maturation until age two, for example, translocations with a majority of adults and yearlings are more likely to be successful than juvenile-biased translocations (Chapter 13).

Age Versus Survivorship and Reproduction

In general, both annual survivorship and reproductive success should increase up to a certain age, after which they should steadily decline—as one or both do for numerous wild animals (Williams 1957; Hamilton 1966; Alexander 1987). Prairie dogs also show this trend. Middle-aged individuals of both sexes survive better than older and younger individuals (Figure 3.6), as noted above. Further, middle-aged individuals produce more weanlings and more yearlings (Hoogland 1995).

Menopause is the permanent cessation of ovulation among older females of mammalian species (Hrdy 1981). By channeling all their remaining investment into extant, older offspring, menopausal females might experience higher reproductive success than do other females that ignore older offspring and attempt to reproduce until death (Williams 1957; Dawkins 1976). Menopause is not evident among female prairie dogs. Ninety-five percent of six-year-old females come into estrus and mate, for example, as do 75% of seven-year-old females (Hoogland 1995). Older males also reproduce successfully. Wildlife managers therefore do not need to fret that translocated prairie dogs might be too old.

Life Tables and Lifespans for Male and Female Prairie Dogs

Life tables summarize data on survivorship and reproduction (Caughley 1977; Sherman and Morton 1984). A cohort-specific life table—also called a gener-

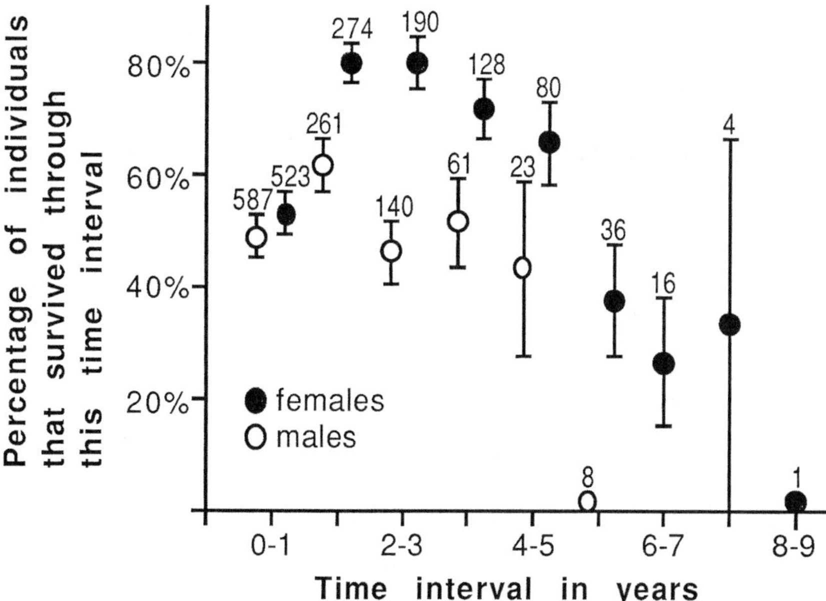

Figure 3.6. Age-specific survivorship of male and female prairie dogs. Circles represent averages, and lines above and below the circles show standard errors (SE); the number above each SE line indicates the number of individuals alive at the beginning of each interval. For both sexes, survivorship increases with age up to a certain point, and then decreases; females always survive better than males.

ation, composite, or horizontal life table—requires the tracking of an entire cohort (group of individuals born at approximately the same time) over time and involves numerous related symbols (Deevey 1947; Caughley 1977). The letter *x* indicates the age of the individuals at the beginning of a certain time interval; *nx* indicates the number of individuals alive at the beginning of the interval *x*; *lx* indicates the proportion of the original number of individuals that is still alive at the beginning of interval (or age) *x*; *mx* indicates the average number of offspring produced at age *x*; *lxmx* is the product of *lx* and *mx* and indicates the relative proportion of offspring contributed by each age class; *Ro* is the sum of the *lxmx* values for all ages and indicates whether the population is declining ($Ro < 1.0$), stable ($Ro = 1.0$), or increasing ($Ro > 1.0$). Tables 3.1 and 3.2 show cohort-specific life tables for male and female prairie dogs.

For both sexes, the biggest demographic hurdle is to survive the first year, during which mortality averages 53% for males and 46% for females; mortality is slightly lower in middle age for both sexes. Males that survive the first year commonly live two to three years, with a record of five years (Table 3.1).

Table 3.1. Cumulative cohort-specific life table for male prairie dogs that first emerged at the study-colony from 1975 through 1988. See text for definitions of *nx*, *lx*, *mx*, and *lxmx*. This life table includes both male and female offspring. Consequently, *mx* of 2.0 (rather than the usual 1.0 when one counts only daughters) indicates individual replacement in a single year, and *Ro* of 2.0 (rather than the usual 1.0) indicates stable population size. For more details, see Hoogland 1995.

Age (years)	*nx*	*lx*	*mx*	*lxmx*
0	587	1.000	0.000	0.000
1	261	0.468	0.084	0.039
2	140	0.287	2.926	0.840
3	61	0.135	4.206	0.568
4	23	0.058	4.920	0.285
5	8	0.020	5.750	0.115
≥6	0	0.000	—	—

Ro (offspring of both sexes) = sum of *lxmx* values = 1.847

Females that survive the first year commonly live four to five years, with a record of eight years (see Table 3.2).

Sexual Dimorphism

Sexual dimorphism in body mass of prairie dogs, with males being larger, is evident at all ages (Figure 3.7). During the first year, sexual dimorphism is slight but significant at first juvenile emergence and in October and November, trivial in February and March, and pronounced and significant in May and June. Among adults, males average about 10%–15% heavier than females throughout most of the year. Females in late pregnancy, however, sometimes outweigh adult males (Knowles 1987; Hoogland 2003b).

For both sexes, but especially for females, notice that body mass varies directly with age up to middle age, and then varies inversely with age for later ages (see Figure 3.7). This curvilinear (up and down) relationship between age and body mass is probably the reason for similar curvilinear relationships between age and survivorship (Figure 3.6) and between age and reproductive success (Hoogland 1995).

Statistics demonstrate a male-biased sexual dimorphism at most ages, but extensive intersexual overlap nonetheless occurs among small males and large females. Consequently, wildlife managers cannot use relative body mass to sex

Table 3.2. Cumulative cohort-specific life table for female prairie dogs that first emerged at the study-colony from 1975 through 1988. The notes for Table 3.1 also apply to this table.

Age (years)	*nx*	*lx*	*mx*	*lxmx*
0	523	1.000	0.000	0.000
1	274	0.543	0.230	0.125
2	190	0.422	1.657	0.699
3	128	0.324	1.939	0.628
4	80	0.225	1.966	0.442
5	36	0.132	1.478	0.195
6	16	0.059	1.000	0.059
7	4	0.015	0.000	0.000
8	1	0.004	0.000	0.000
≥9	0	0.000	—	—

Ro (offspring of both sexes) = sum of *lxmx* values = 2.148

unmarked prairie dogs from a distance. Unfortunately, no other obvious intersexual difference—in color, for example—exists that would allow sexing from a distance (King 1955; Chace 1976). That's too bad, because sexing from a distance would facilitate conservation. Regarding recreational shooting, for example, wildlife managers or landowners could deter population crashes by requiring that marksmen shoot only males if we could easily distinguish between males and females from a distance. And for a source of prairie dogs for translocations, colonies with an easily determined female-biased sex ratio would be more suitable than colonies with a higher proportion of males (Chapter 13).

Ways to Estimate Reproductive Success

One way to estimate reproductive success among prairie dogs is to count the number of offspring reared to first emergence from the natal burrow. Another, better, way is to count the number of offspring that survive for at least one year. Table 3.3 compares annual and lifetime reproductive success (ARS and LRS) for male and female prairie dogs.

Several factors promote ARS and LRS among prairie dogs (Hoogland 1995), including the following:

- As noted above, middle-aged individuals survive and reproduce better than older and younger individuals.

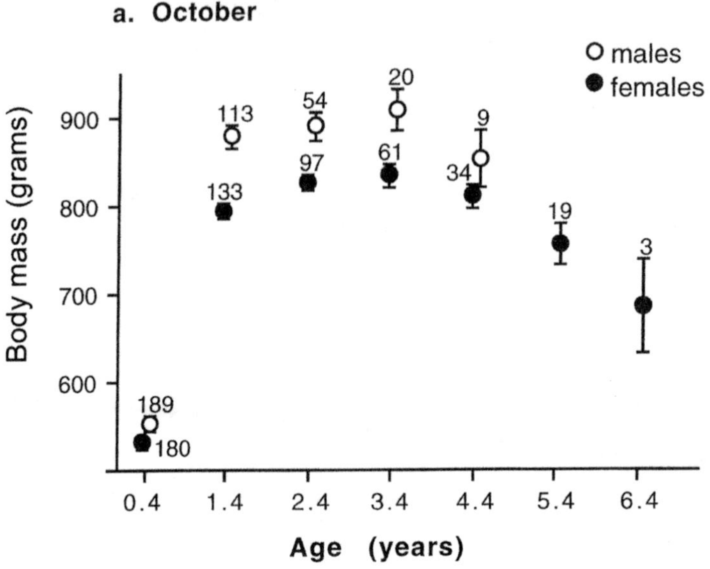

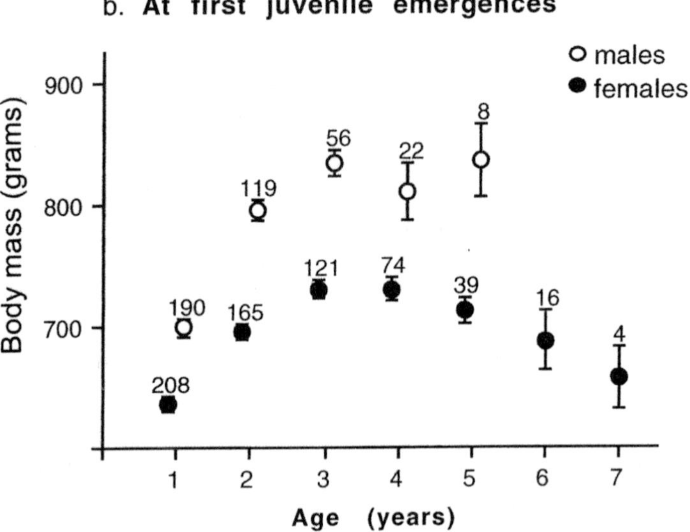

Figure 3.7. Sexual dimorphism in body mass at different ages: (a) in October, four months before the breeding season; (b) at first juvenile emergences in May and June. For both graphs, circles represent averages, and lines above and below the circles show standard errors (SE); the number above each SE line indicates the number of individuals weighed. For both October and May-June, body mass increases with age up to a certain age, and then decreases; males are always heavier than females.

Table 3.3. Annual and lifetime reproductive success (ARS and LRS) for male and female prairie dogs. Numbers shown here are averages; ranges and sample sizes are in parentheses. This table excludes data from individuals that did not mate at least once during the breeding season (for ARS) or at least once during their lifetimes (for LRS). See Hoogland 1995 for more details.

	Weaned juveniles produced in single year	*Yearlings produced in single year*	*Emergent juveniles produced over lifetime*	*Yearlings produced over lifetime*
Females	1.61 (0–6, N = 581)	0.77 (0–6, N = 551)	4.25 (0–18, N = 178)	2.14 (0–12, N = 173)
Males	4.17 (0–21, N = 219)	2.04 (0–12, N = 219)	7.06 (0–45, N = 124)	3.45 (0–24, N = 123)

- When a female mates with two or more males, the first male to mate sires more offspring than later-mating males.
- Large litters yield more yearlings in the following year than do smaller litters. Consequently, female ARS varies directly with litter size, which correlates positively with precipitation in the previous summer.
- Heavy individuals of both sexes are more likely than individuals of lower body mass to survive the winter, to mate, and rear numerous offspring (Figure 3.8).
- Females that mate early in the breeding season wean more juveniles than do later-mating females.
- For females, ARS is highest in multi-male coteries. For males, on the other hand, ARS is highest for those dominant individuals that can monopolize all the females of two adjacent coteries.
- More than any other factor, longevity enhances LRS for both males and females. Specifically, females that live six to seven years and males that live four to five years produce many more offspring over their lifetimes than do individuals that live only one to two years (Figure 3.9).

Sex Ratio Among Juveniles, Yearlings, and Adults

The sex ratio is the ratio of males to females in a population (Fisher 1958; Frank 1990). The first stage at which wildlife managers easily can measure the juvenile sex ratio among prairie dogs is first emergence from the natal burrow, approximately six weeks after birth. Because abortions and mortality of pre-emergent

Figure 3.8. Portly male prairie dog. When compared to prairie dogs of low body mass, heavy prairie dogs are more likely to survive the winter, to mate, and to rear numerous offspring. Among adults and yearlings, body mass ranges from 253 grams to 1,390 grams, with an average of 705 grams (Hoogland 1995, 2003b). Photo courtesy of Wind Cave National Park.

juveniles both occur, as noted above, the sex ratio within litters at first emergence is not equivalent to the sex ratio at either fertilization or birth. Of 1,100 juveniles that emerged from natal burrows at my study-colony from 1975 through 1988, 53% were males and 47% were females. These percentages, like those from other colonies (King 1955; Tileston and Lechleitner 1966; Halpin 1987; Garrett and Franklin 1988), do not differ significantly from the expected values if the numbers of males and females at first emergence are equal.

Among yearlings, the sex ratio in natural colonies is male-biased in some years and female-biased in other years. Among adults, the sex ratio is always female-biased (Table 3.4). To increase the probability of success, wildlife managers usually try to translocate groups of prairie dogs for which the ages and sex ratios approximate the ages and sex ratios within colonies under natural conditions (Chapter 13).

Population Dynamics

Colony size (i.e., the number of adults and yearlings) at my study-colony at Wind Cave National Park, South Dakota, varied substantially over my 14 years

a) female LRS versus final age

○ number of copulations over lifetime
● number of emergent juveniles over lifetime
Φ number of yearlings over lifetime

Estimate of female's lifetime reproductive success

Female's final age in years

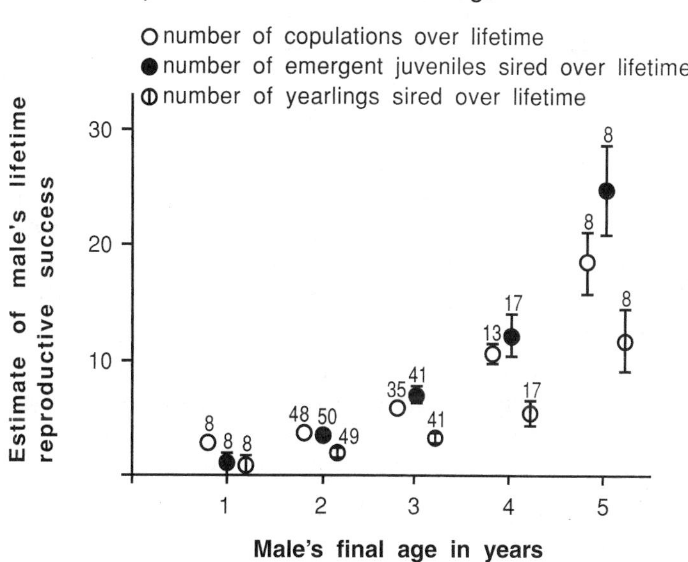

Figure 3.9. Lifetime reproductive success (LRS) versus longevity for (a) females and (b) males. Circles represent averages, and lines above and below the circles show standard errors (SE); the number above each SE line indicates the number of individuals for each final age. Longevity enhances LRS more than any other factor.

Table 3.4. Number of adults, yearlings, and juveniles in May of different years at the Rankin Ridge Colony at Wind Cave National Park, South Dakota. For more details about population dynamics of prairie dogs, see Hoogland 1995.

Time of Census	*Adult males*	*Adult females*	*Yearling males*	*Yearling females*	*Male emergent juveniles*	*Female emergent juveniles*
May 76	35	85	0	1	37	42
May 77	26	72	16	29	28	34
May 78	27	70	19	23	57	41
May 79	31	70	16	12	32	26
May 80	27	59	15	12	43	39
May 81	20	52	33	26	67	52
May 82	31	48	26	21	49	38
May 83	38	53	23	25	55	38
May 84	26	55	35	21	36	30
May 85	19	43	3	17	31	43
May 86	20	45	18	25	70	63
May 87	15	38	23	35	58	56
May 88	21	47	23	25	24	17
May 89	29	61	11	10	51	57

of research (1976 through 1989), from 92 to 143 (Table 3.4; Figure 3.10). The number of juveniles reared to first emergence from the natal burrow also fluctuated, from 41 to 133 (Figure 3.10). Curiously, the number of emergent juveniles did not vary systematically with colony size (Figure 3.10).

Salient annual variation at my study-colony occurred not only in colony size and in the number of emergent juveniles, but also in the date of mating, the date of first juvenile emergence, litter size at first juvenile emergence, the number and percentage of juveniles in a litter that survived for at least one year, and juvenile body mass at first emergence. Indeed, the only variable that did not show conspicuous annual variation is the sex ratio within litters at first emergence (Hoogland 1995). I have not probed the possible causes of annual variation in demographic measures, but meteorological factors such as average daily temperature, precipitation, and duration of snow-cover are obvious candidates (Knowles 1987).

Discriminating between animals that disappear because of long-distance dispersal and animals that disappear because of mortality is usually difficult (Caughley 1977; Pfeifer 1982; Sherman and Morton 1984). I had this problem with most of the 1,200 marked prairie dogs that disappeared from my study-

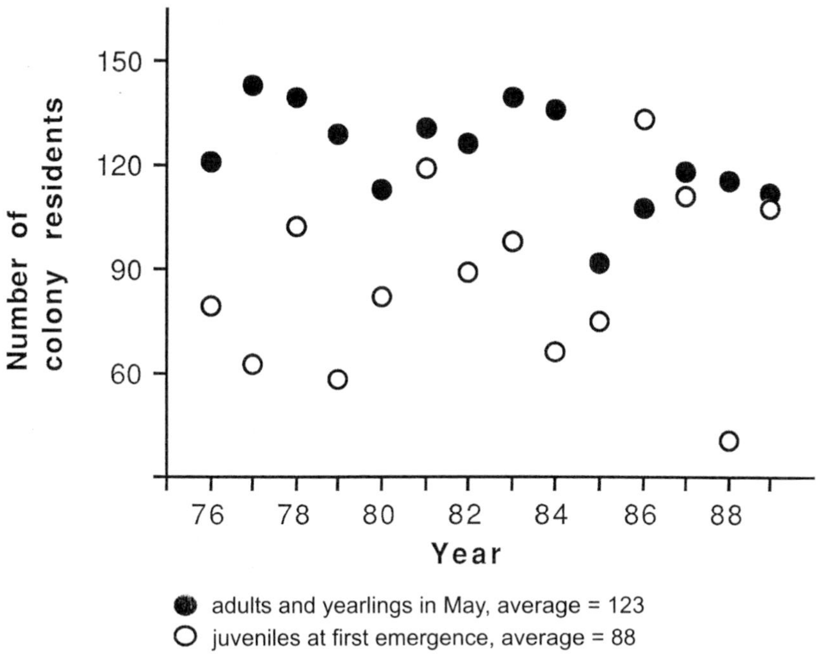

Figure 3.10. Annual variation in the number of adult, yearling, and juvenile residents at my study-colony. The number of emergent juveniles does not correlate with the number of adults and yearlings in May.

colony from February through June of 1975 through 1989. I documented death for only 52 individuals: 22 predations that I observed and 30 prairie dogs whose carcasses I found aboveground. I verified long-distance dispersal from my study-colony for only two individuals. In June 1980, I observed one marked yearling male living at the Pringle Colony, which is about 1 kilometer (0.6 miles) from the study-colony. In April 1988, James G. Daley livetrapped a male with eartags at the Sanctuary Colony, 2 kilometers (1.2 miles) away; this male was two years old at the time of capture, but he disappeared from the study-colony in June 1987 while still a yearling. I discuss dispersal in more detail in the next section.

Despite my ignorance of the reasons for disappearance of prairie dogs at my study-colony, I discovered a surprising pattern in the timing of disappearance (Hoogland 1995). Adult and yearling prairie dogs disappear more often during the short, warm interval of June through September than during the longer, colder interval of November through April. Juvenile prairie dogs disappear over five times more often during the warmer months. For the older individuals, long-distance dispersal might account for some of the higher rate of disappearance during the warmer months. Long-distance dispersal cannot account for the higher rate of disappearance of juveniles in warmer months, however, because prairie dogs do not disperse as juveniles. Some of the juvenile disappearances in June result when males invade new coterie territories and kill juveniles there (see above). Do infanticidal males continue to invade in July through September and thereby account for many of the juvenile disappearances during that interval? I was unable to investigate this intriguing possibility because I ended my field season each year in June.

Dispersal

Dispersal is the permanent movement of an individual from one area to another. Conservation is easier when good information on dispersal is available. Unfortunately, we know little about dispersal of prairie dogs. Before proceeding, let me define a few key terms. Natal dispersal is the emigration of a young individual from the area of birth, and breeding dispersal is the emigration of an older individual from the area where it mated (Greenwood 1980; Holekamp 1984). The natal territory is the area where a prairie dog is born, and the breeding territory is the area where an individual mates. An emigrant is a prairie dog who disperses away from one colony, and who might become an immigrant into another colony. A philopatric individual is one that remains in the natal territory. The avoidance of extreme inbreeding is clearly one impetus for individuals to move out of the home territory (Chapter 2 and Hoogland 1992, 1995), but certain prairie dogs probably disperse in search of territories with better options regarding food, burrows, or potential mates. In the discussion that follows, I first consider research at my study-colony, where I examined intracolonial natal dispersal, intracolonial breeding dispersal, and immigration. Later I consider studies by other researchers regarding intercolonial dispersal.

Intracolonial Natal Dispersal

To study natal dispersal of prairie dogs, I tracked movements of male and female juveniles that I had captured, eartagged, and marked within a few days after first emergence from the natal burrow. Of 190 females first marked as juveniles that survived for at least two years, only eleven (6%) moved from the natal territory to another territory within my study-colony (Figure 3.11). Ten of these dispersing females (91%) were victims of extraordinary circumstances such as abandonment by mother or eviction by invading females from another coterie (Hoogland 1995). Thus, most females spend their entire lives within the natal territory (i.e., are markedly philopatric).

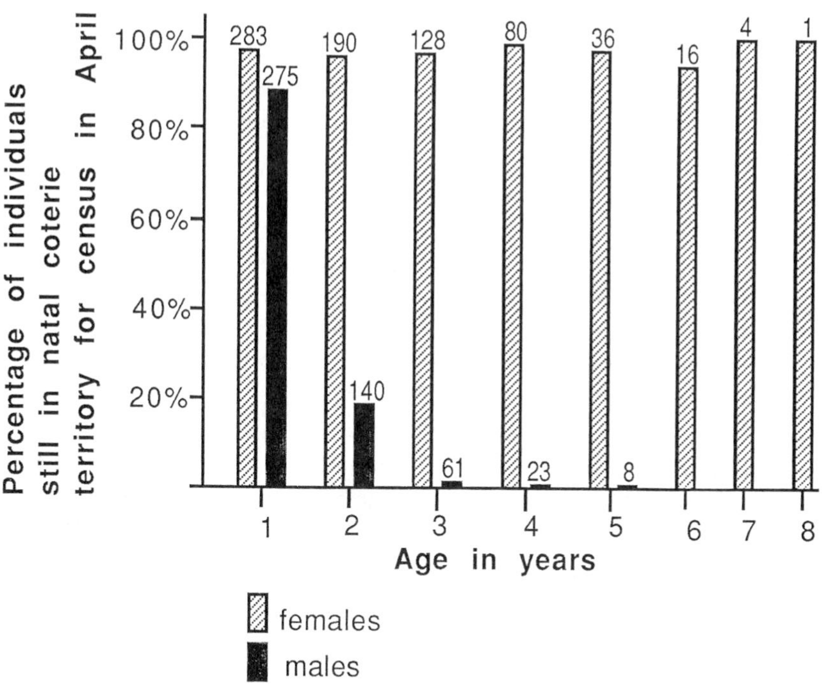

Figure 3.11. Percentage of males and females that still reside in the natal coterie territory at different ages. The number above each bar indicates the number of individuals alive and still residing at my study-colony. For all ages, the probability of still residing in the natal territory is higher for females.

By contrast, most male prairie dogs are philopatric for only the first year, after which they disperse before reaching sexual maturity in the second year. Of 140 males first marked as juveniles that survived for at least two years, 81% moved from the natal territory to another territory within my study-colony before mating for the first time (see Figure 3.11). Those rare males that remain in the natal territory for a second or third year have not yet attained sexual maturity (Hoogland 1995). Most intracolonial natal dispersal by yearling males occurs in May and June—just before, during, or just after the period when juveniles are first emerging from their natal burrows. Natal dispersal by males usually precludes incestuous matings with mothers, aunts, and sisters (Chapter 2).

Intracolonial Breeding Dispersal

After mating in one territory, no female prairie dog ever dispersed to another territory within my study-colony-site. Intracolonial breeding dispersal among male prairie dogs, by contrast, is common. Of 76 long-lived males (i.e., with lifespan of at least four years) at my study-colony, 97% remained in the same breeding territory for only one or two years before moving to a new territory (Hoogland 1995). Most breeding dispersals by adult males occur in late summer or fall. Breeding dispersal by males usually precludes father-daughter incest (Chapter 2).

Immigration

My discussions of intracolonial natal and breeding dispersal at my study-colony might indicate that males, and especially females, do not disperse often to different colonies. A consideration of immigration paints a different picture. From February through June of 1975 through 1989, 28 males and 21 females immigrated into my study-colony from some other colony and remained there long enough for me to mark them. Each immigrant arrived alone. A few other prairie dogs (N < 10) immigrated and then departed too quickly for capture during my five months of research each year (February through June). Other temporary immigrants might have visited during the seven months when I did not conduct research each year (July through January). I do not know the orginal colony-site for any of the 49 immigrants into my study-colony, but the two closest colonies were Pringle and Sanctuary (1 and 2 kilometers [0.6 and 1.2 miles] away, respectively).

Of 27 male immigrants, 59% mated at least once and 48% sired at least one emergent juvenile. The 28th male immigrant arrived in the last year of my research, so I do not have any information on his mating and siring success in later years. Of the 21 female immigrants, 24% reared at least one litter to first emergence. Most of the reproductively unsuccessful immigrants disappeared permanently from the study colony-site shortly after their arrival.

Intercolonial Dispersal

My findings on dispersal between colonies are all anecdotal, but the research of others (Knowles 1985; Cincotta et al. 1987a,b; Garrett and Franklin 1988; Roach et al. 2001; Milne 2004) has focused on this key issue and has led to several important discoveries, such as:

- Intercolonial dispersers sometimes travel as far as 6 kilometers (3.7 miles).
- Prairie dogs are more vulnerable to predation during the process of intercolonial dispersal than are individuals that remain in the safety of the home colony.
- Individuals that disperse from the home colony usually move into an established colony rather than attempting to initiate a new colony.

- Contrary to predictions that result from an analysis of intracolonial dispersal, females are almost as likely as males to show intercolonial dispersal.
- Most male intercolonial dispersers and about half of female intercolonial dispersers are yearlings. Because intercolonial dispersal by juveniles does not occur, the other dispersers are necessarily at least two years old.
- Intercolonial dispersal by yearlings and adults is most common in the month or so after the first emergences of juveniles from their natal burrows.
- Contrary to popular opinion and a few anecdotal reports (summarized in Costello 1970), prairie dogs disperse singly, not in groups.
- Of the females that disperse to other colonies as adults, some have not given birth in the year of dispersal (no visible teats); others have given birth but have lost their offspring before weaning (long, dry, flat teats); and still others evidently have reared juveniles to first emergence (long, turgid teats).

From my discussion of immigration and intra- and intercolonial dispersal, notice that male prairie dogs resort to either long-distance dispersal to different colonies (mostly as yearlings, rarely as adults) or short-distance dispersal within the home colony-site (either as yearlings or as adults). Most dispersing females, however, move long distances to other colonies (as either yearlings or adults)—that is, short-distance dispersal of females within the home colony-site is uncommon.

We know that prairie dogs sometimes disperse as far as 6 kilometers (3.7 miles), but is this distance a maximum that only a few dispersers ever achieve? To investigate this issue in a new way, Sara Milne (2004) recently has perused old and recent maps of colony-sites at Theodore Roosevelt National Park, North Dakota; Badlands National Park, South Dakota; Scott's Bluff National Monument, Nebraska; and Little Missouri National Grasslands, North Dakota. When a new colony appeared, Milne assumed that the founders of that colony originated from the nearest other colony. For 120 new colonies, the minimal distance dispersed by the founders ranged from 0.18 kilometers (0.11 miles) to 9.6 kilometers (6 miles), with an average of 1.8 kilometers (1.1 miles). For recolonization of 13 colony-sites in north-central Colorado where all residents had disappeared, Roach et al. (2001, Table 1) found that the minimal distance dispersed by recolonizing individuals ranged from 1.4 kilometers (0.9 miles) to 5.7 kilometers (3.5 miles), with an average of 2.7 kilometers (1.7 miles). These studies show that prairie dogs sometimes disperse long distances.

Why do some dispersers move to a distant section of the home colony-site when others leave the home colony and search for an established colony? Why do certain dispersers attempt to initiate a new colony? And how many dispersers die from predation or exposure to weather for every successful disperser? Our poor understanding of dispersal does not provide answers to these key questions. For conservation, perhaps the most important question of dispersal concerns the optimal distance between colonies. Regarding plague, for example, we want colonies to be far enough apart so that intercolonial transmission of plague via infected prairie dogs or some other mechanism will be low, but close enough so that the probability of eventual recolonization of a ravaged colony-site by dispersing prairie dogs will be high. Research by Roach et al. (2001) and Milne (2004) suggests that the optimal distance between colonies might be about 2–3 kilometers (1.2–1.9 miles).

In theory (e.g., Koenig et al. 1996; Peacock and Smith 1997), genetic markers via electrophoresis, DNA-fingerprinting, or polymerase chain reaction (PCR) might help to address certain questions about the dispersal of prairie dogs. In practice, however, information from genetic markers regarding dispersal is difficult to interpret (Chesser 1983; Daley 1992; Jones et al. 2005). Consider the nifty PCR research by Roach et al. (2001), for example, which indicates that about 39% of colony residents are either immigrants or offspring of immigrants. But these colonies were in an area where extinctions are common (because of either poisoning or plague) and colonies are young; 11 of their 13 study-colonies, for example, were only four years old or younger. The relevance of Roach et al.'s (2001) results is thus unclear regarding either prairie dogs living under more natural conditions or efforts to establish and maintain colonies in plague-free areas (Chapters 16 and 17).

Intercolonial Variation in Survivorship and Reproduction

My study-colony was at least 20 years old, had a stable population size, and had little room for expansion (Hoogland 1995). In this and other stable colonies showing little or no expansion, prairie dogs reproduce slowly. Five factors (all discussed in more detail either earlier in this chapter or in Chapter 2) are responsible for this slowness: survivorship in the first year is less than 55%, and is only slightly higher in middle age; females can wean a maximum of only one litter per year; the percentage of individuals that mate as yearlings is only 6% for males, and only 35% for females; the probability of weaning a litter for adult and yearling females is only 43% per year; for those females that wean offspring, the average litter size at first juvenile emergence is only 3.08.

Probably because of increased availability of food and reduced competition for resources, trends in demography and population dynamics are different in young, expanding colonies. When compared directly with prairie dogs at my study-colony, for example, prairie dogs at a younger, expanding colony survived better, showed faster juvenile growth rates, were more likely to mate as yearlings, and reared larger litters (Garrett et al. 1982). Survivorship and reproduction also increase dramatically in years following a population crash caused by poisoning, plague, or recreational shooting (Knowles 1986a, 1987; Chapters 8, 9, and 10). Even under ideal conditions, however, the reproduction of prairie dogs has certain unavoidable limits. Females never can rear more than one litter per year, for example, and the maximum litter size at birth is only eight. In efforts to predict population dynamics, wildlife managers must evaluate whether the colonies under consideration are old and stable or young and expanding.

Prairie Dogs Resist Eradication

Prairie dogs are easy to shoot and poison (Chapters 8, 9, and 10), but elimination of every resident within a colony is nonetheless difficult. With continued shooting and poisoning, prairie dogs become more wary and thus harder to locate and kill (Chapters 8 and 10). Further, colony-sites with good burrows and few or no prairie dogs are especially attractive to dispersers—and thus often do not remain deserted for long. Finally, as discussed above, colonies rebound quickly after natural or unnatural population crashes—because remaining individuals grow faster, survive better, are more likely to breed as yearlings, and have larger litters than do individuals in stable colonies.

By surviving 200 years of poisoning, plague, loss of habitat, and recreational shooting, prairie dogs have demonstrated that they can overcome formidable obstacles. With prudent conservation, the preservation of prairie dogs for future generations is eminently feasible (see also Chapters 11, 12, 17, and 18).

Summary

- The length of gestation for prairie dogs ranges from 33 to 38 days, but 88% of gestations are either 34 or 35 days. The interval between a juvenile's birth and its first emergence from the natal burrow ranges from 37 to 51 days, with an average of 41 days.
- Laboratory studies indicate that litter size at birth ranges from 1 to 8. When juveniles first emerge from their burrows when they are about six weeks old in May or June, litter size ranges from 1 to 6, the most common litter size is 3, and the average is 3.08.
- The three main causes of mortality for prairie dogs are predation, infanticide, and inability to survive the winter. Enemies that capture prairie dogs include mammalian, reptilian, and avian predators. Nonparental infanticide accounts for the partial or total demise of 39% of all litters. Both males and

females are infanticidal, and the most likely payoff is increased sustenance via the cannibalism that follows infanticide.

- For both sexes, the biggest demographic hurdle is to survive the first year. Males that survive the first year commonly live two to three years, with a record of five years. Females that survive the first year commonly live four to five years, with a record of eight years. Probably because they are heavier, middle-aged individuals of both sexes survive better and produce more offspring than do older and younger individuals.
- Sexual dimorphism in body mass, with males being larger, is evident at all ages, with only one exception: females in late pregnancy sometimes outweigh adult males.
- Most prairie dogs first become sexually mature and mate in the second February or March following birth, approximately 21 months following first emergence from the natal burrow.
- At first juvenile emergence, the numbers of male and female juveniles are approximately equal. Among yearlings, the sex ratio is male-biased in some years and female-biased in other years. Among adults, the sex ratio is always female-biased.
- Most females spend their entire lives within the natal territory. Most males remain in the natal territory for only the first year, after which they disperse.
- Prairie dogs sometimes disperse to another territory within the home colony-site, and other times they disperse to another colony. Rarely, dispersing individuals initiate a new colony.
- Five factors account for the slow reproduction of prairie dogs in stable colonies: survivorship in the first year is less than 55%, and is only slightly higher in middle age; females can wean a maximum of only one litter per year; the percentage of individuals that mate as yearlings is only 6% for males, and only 35% for females; the probability of weaning a litter for adult and yearling females is only 43% per year; for those females that wean offspring, the average litter size at first juvenile emergence is only 3.08.
- When compared with prairie dogs at old, stable colonies, prairie dogs at younger, expanding colonies survive better, grow faster as juveniles, are more likely to mate as yearlings, and rear larger litters.
- Prairie dogs are easy to shoot and poison, but elimination of every resident within a colony is nonetheless difficult.
- By surviving 200 years of poisoning, plague, loss of habitat, and recreational shooting, prairie dogs have demonstrated that they can overcome formidable obstacles. With prudent conservation, the preservation of prairie dogs for future generations is eminently feasible.

CHAPTER 4

The Prairie Dog as a Keystone Species

Natasha B. Kotliar, Brian J. Miller, Richard P. Reading, and Timothy W. Clark

The prairie dog has a pronounced impact on its grassland ecosystem (King 1955; Uresk and Bjugstad 1983; Miller et al. 1994; Society for Conservation Biology 1994; Wuerthner 1997; Johnsgard 2005). They maintain short vegetation by their grazing and by selective removal of tall plants and shrubs; provide shelter, foraging grounds, and nesting habitat for a diverse array of animals; serve as prey for many predators; and alter soil chemistry.

Do these impacts mean that the prairie dog is a keystone species? To investigate, we first scrutinize the definition for a keystone species. We then document both vertebrates and invertebrates that associate with prairie dogs and their colony-sites. We examine ecosystem processes at colony-sites, and then assess whether the prairie dog is a legitimate keystone species. Finally, we explore the implications of keystone status for the conservation of prairie dogs.

What is a Keystone Species?

Paine (1969) coined the term "keystone species" to describe the ecological role of the ochre sea star, whose selective predation of common mussels increases species richness (i.e., the number of species) in the rocky intertidal zone. The concept of keystone species subsequently expanded beyond predation to include modification of the habitat, mutualism, and other ecological phenomena (Mills et al. 1993; Jones et al. 1994). Power et al. (1996) later suggested two criteria for keystone status: the species must have significant effects on its ecosystem, and these effects must be disproportionately large relative to its abundance. Kotliar (2000) recently has added a third criterion: the effects must be unique.

Significant, unique effects on an ecosystem sometimes result from mere abundance of a species, in the absence of disproportionately large impacts. When this happens, Soulé et al. (2003) have suggested the term "foundation species," and have further suggested that keystone and foundation species be called "highly interactive species." Interactions with other species can vary across spatial and temporal scales, and can occur under diverse conditions. Identifying the factors that contribute to, or limit, the functions of keystone and foundation species is usually difficult (Mills et al. 1993; Power et al. 1996; Kotliar 2000; Davic 2003).

Because keystone and foundation species are so important, their disappearance drastically affects ecosystems and evolutionary processes (Estes et al. 1998; Crooks and Soulé 1999; Terborgh et al. 1999). Wildlife managers sometimes rely on conserving a single keystone or foundation species as a strategy for conserving an entire ecosystem—largely because the former is so much easier than the latter (Lambeck 1997; Simberloff 1998; Miller et al. 1999; Chapters 12, 17, and 18; Box to Chapter 12).

Prairie dogs directly and indirectly influence the grassland ecosystem via three primary pathways: grazing, burrowing, and as prey. In the sections that follow, we highlight these effects for organisms that associate with prairie dogs and for ecosystem processes. We then review the controversy regarding the prairie dog's keystone role.

Vertebrates That Associate with Prairie Dogs and Their Colony-Sites

Many vertebrate species use prairie dog colony-sites for food and shelter (Table 4.1). Prairie dogs serve as prey for predators such as American badgers, black-footed ferrets, coyotes, ferruginous hawks, golden eagles, and prairie falcons (Hoogland 1995; Kotliar et al. 1999; Kretzer and Cully 2001a; Chapter 2). Their burrows provide nest sites and refuge for American badgers, black-footed ferrets, burrowing owls, prairie rattlesnakes, and tiger salamanders (Clark et al. 1982; Ceballos et al. 2000; Kretzer and Cully 2001a). Clipping (i.e., cutting down of vegetation without consumption; see Chapter 2) and grazing by prairie dogs create open habitats preferred by avian grassland species such as mountain plovers and horned larks, and promote growth of grasses and forbs (i.e., herbaceous plants other than grasses and grass-like plants; see Chapter 5) preferred by large herbivores (Knowles et al. 1982; Reading et al. 1989; Detling 1998; Chapter 5).

Table 4.1. Vertebrate species that satisfy at least one of Kotliar et al.'s (1999) following four criteria for dependence of a species on prairie dogs: abundance is higher at prairie dog colony-sites than elsewhere; individuals use features that are specific to colony-sites (e.g., the prairie dogs themselves or their burrows); populations increase (or decrease) when populations of prairie dogs increase (or decrease); and survivorship or reproductive success is higher at colony-sites than elsewhere. Because of spatial and temporal variation, dependence sometimes occurs in some areas but not others, or in some seasons but not others. References: Kotliar et al. 1999; Kretzer and Cully 2001a; Lomolino and Smith 2004; Smith and Lomolino 2004.

Amphibians
Great Plains toad, plains spadefoot toad, tiger salamander, Woodhouse's toad
Reptiles
Texas horned lizard, ornate box turtle, prairie rattlesnake, western plains garter snake
Birds
American kestrel, burrowing owl, chestnut-collared longspur, eastern meadowlark, ferruginous hawk, golden eagle, horned lark, killdeer, mountain plover, western meadowlark
Mammals
American badger, American bison, black-footed ferret, black-tailed jackrabbit, coyote, deer mouse, eastern cottontail, northern grasshopper mouse, pronghorn, striped skunk, swift fox, thirteen-lined ground squirrel, white-tailed deer

Some species sporadically and opportunistically capitalize on the benefits provided by prairie dog colony-sites, whereas others have stronger associations (Kotliar et al. 1999). Several species that associate closely with colony-sites are endangered or declining, so that a continued decline in prairie dog numbers might further imperil these associates (Kotliar et al. 1999).

In the following sections, we briefly summarize the relationships between prairie dogs and three well-known species that are highly dependent on them: black-footed ferrets, mountain plovers, and burrowing owls.

Black-Footed Ferrets

With alarm calling, a high density of burrows, and the ability to detect predators quickly, coloniality of prairie dogs probably has evolved as a defense against large diurnal predators that cannot easily enter burrows (King 1955; Hoogland 1981a). Defenses that have evolved against certain predators might render prey especially susceptible to other predators, however (Hamilton

1971). Specifically, their dense coloniality works well against bobcats, coyotes, and golden eagles, but prairie dogs are vulnerable to predation by black-footed ferrets. Hunting within burrows at night when their quarry is inactive, ferrets feed almost exclusively on prairie dogs (Hillman 1968; Sheets and Linder 1969; Fortenberry 1972; Clark 1989; Seal et al. 1989; Miller et al. 1996). Ferrets also use prairie dog burrows for shelter and nesting. Kotliar et al. (1999) therefore designated ferrets as obligately dependent on prairie dogs.

The drastic decline of prairie dogs over the last 200 years (Chapters 8, 12, and 16) has contributed to the near extinction of the black-footed ferret (Clark 1989; Miller et al. 1996) (Figure 4.1). No known natural populations of ferrets exist, and survival of the species in the wild will depend on the success of reintroducing laboratory-reared ferrets—or free-living descendants of

Figure 4.1. The black-footed ferret, one of the rarest mammals in North America. Ferrets prey almost exclusively on prairie dogs, and use prairie dog burrows for shelter and nesting. Their survival hinges on the success of reintroducing laboratory-reared ferrets into the wild. Photo by Dean E. Biggins.

laboratory-reared ferrets—into natural prairie dog colony-sites (Chadwick 1993; Miller et al. 1996; Vargas et al. 1998; Dobson and Lyles 2000).

To date, the success of reintroducing ferrets has been marginal (Mike Lockhart, USFWS Black-footed Ferret Recovery Coordinator, personal communication, 9 September 2004). Reintroduced ferrets are declining or have disappeared at most sites, sometimes because plague has ravaged the recipient colonies of prairie dogs. The only population of ferrets that has consistently increased since its reintroduction in 1996 is at Conata Basin, Buffalo Gap National Grasslands, South Dakota, where plague among prairie dogs has never been detected. In nearby Custer County, South Dakota, however, plague recently has appeared (J. Kafka, *Casper Star-Tribune*, 27 September 2004). Further, the ferrets at Conata Basin are threatened by recent poisoning there following the removal of the prairie dog from the candidate list for the Federal List of Endangered and Threatened Wildlife and Plants (FLETWP) (USFWS 2004; Chapters 12 and 18). The long-term persistence of black-footed ferrets at Conata Basin and within other populations of prairie dogs is thus uncertain. Curiously, despite regular outbreaks of plague at both recipient-sites, populations of reintroduced ferrets are currently increasing among white-tailed prairie dogs at Shirley Basin, Wyoming, and among Gunnison's prairie dogs at Aubrey Valley, Arizona (Mike Lockhart, personal communication, 2004).

Mountain Plovers

Because they prefer open, level ground with short vegetation, mountain plovers frequently nest at prairie dog colony-sites (Knowles et al. 1982; Olson 1985; Knopf and Rupert 1996) (Figure 4.2). In response to declines in prairie dog numbers, populations of mountain plovers have decreased sharply in recent decades (Knopf 1996; Dinsmore et al. 2001). In Montana, the number of mountain plovers recently correlated with the decline and subsequent recovery of prairie dog populations from plague (Dinsmore et al. 2001). Because mountain plovers can nest in open, shortgrass prairie away from colony-sites, they are facultatively (versus obligately) dependent on prairie dogs for survival (Kotliar et al. 1999).

Burrowing Owls

Burrowing owls do not prey on prairie dogs (Chapter 2), but they benefit from foraging and nesting at prairie dog colony-sites for three reasons (Butts and Lewis 1982; Agnew et al. 1986; Haug et al. 1993; Hughes 1993; Desmond et al. 2000) (Figure 4.3). First, to find prey and facilitate the detection of predators,

Figure 4.2. The mountain plover. Mountain plovers prefer open terrain with short vegetation, and commonly nest at prairie dog colony-sites. Photo by Cliff Wallis.

burrowing owls prefer level ground and short vegetation that are trademarks of colony-sites. Second, they sometimes usurp prairie dog burrows for nesting. Third, the alarm calls of prairie dogs alert burrowing owls to enemies (such as coyotes and American badgers) that prey on both species. Probably because of these advantages, burrowing owls in Oklahoma feed and nest more frequently at prairie dog colony-sites than in other habitats (Smith and Lomolino 2004). Further, declines of burrowing owl populations in Nebraska correlate with crashes of prairie dog populations following poisoning (Desmond et al. 2000).

Burrowing owls prefer large prairie dog colonies over smaller colonies (Knowles and Knowles 1984; Griebel 2000; Knowles 2003), and reproductive success is higher at the former (Desmond et al. 2000). Burrowing owls also prefer colony-sites with high densities of burrow-entrances (Desmond 1991; Hughes 1993; Plumpton and Lutz 1993; Toombs 1997). Because they can survive and nest away from colony-sites, burrowing owls resemble mountain plovers by being only facultatively dependent on prairie dogs for survival (Kotliar et al. 1999).

Figure 4.3. Burrowing owl. Burrowing owls prefer to forage amidst the short vegetation at prairie dog colony-sites, and sometimes usurp prairie dog burrows for nesting. Photo by Don Baccus.

Other Kinds of Organisms That Associate with Prairie Dogs and Their Colony-Sites

To this point we have considered only vertebrates that associate with prairie dogs. But other kinds of organisms also associate. Numerous species of protozoans, arachnids, insects, and other invertebrate animals commonly live at prairie dog colony-sites, for example (King 1955; Koford 1958; Smith 1967; Agnew et al. 1986; Kretzer and Cully 2001b). And consider the parasites that infest prairie dogs. Most of the internal parasites (e.g., roundworms, spiny-headed worms, and tapeworms) are probably species-specific to, and therefore obligately dependent on, prairie dogs. Many of the fleas, lice, ticks, mites, and other external parasites that live on prairie dogs or in their nests probably are species-specific and obligately dependent as well (Pizzimenti 1975; Pfaffenberger et al. 1984; Kietzmann 1987; Hoogland 1995; Cully and Williams 2001).

Prairie dogs expose subsoil with their excavations, which affects the cycling of water and nutrients (Chapter 5). Further, prairie dogs commonly urinate and defecate aboveground (Hoogland 1995), and thereby fertilize the topsoil (Chapter 5). Finally, prairie dogs consume certain plants, and clip others (King 1955; Chapter 2). Consequently, at least four plant species usually are more common at colony-sites than elsewhere: black nightshade, fetid marigold (also called prairie dog weed), pigweed, and scarlet globemallow (King 1955; Farrar 2002; Chapter 5). Contrarily, honey mesquite and many species of grasses are less common at colony-sites (King 1955; Weltzin et al. 1997b; Stolzenburg 2004; Chapter 5).

Ecosystem Processes at Prairie Dog Colony-Sites

Burrowing by prairie dogs mixes subsoil and topsoil, redistributes nutrients and minerals, and promotes penetration and retention of moisture (Munn 1993; Whicker and Detling 1993; Outwater 1996) (Figure 4.4). The combination of burrowing, foraging, and clipping alters floral species composition, and affects the concentration of nitrogen in the soil and the rate of nitrogen uptake by plants (Koford 1958; Hansen and Gold 1977; Uresk and Bjugstad 1983; Uresk 1984; Weltzin et al. 1997b; Chapter 5). Prairie dogs reduce vegetational

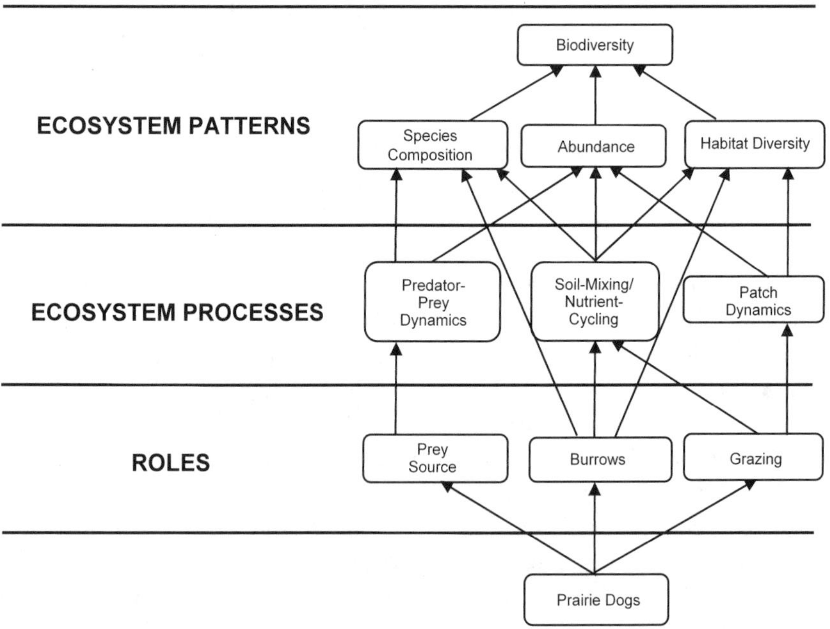

Figure 4.4. Primary pathways by which prairie dogs affect the grassland ecosystem. Reference: Kotliar et al. 1999.

biomass, but, especially at young colony-sites, they often enhance digestibility, protein content, and productivity of grasses and forbs (Coppock et al. 1983a; Chapter 5). Perhaps for this latter reason, American bison, pronghorn, and domestic livestock often prefer to forage at colony-sites (Coppock et al. 1983b; Whicker and Detling 1988a, 1988b; Guenther and Detling 2003; Lomolino and Smith 2004; Chapter 5).

At least four effects of prairie dogs on the grassland ecosystem are unique:

- Other species are important, but only prairie dogs provide such a broad spectrum of impacts (see Figure 4.4).
- Other mammalian species serve as prey and excavate burrows, but the prairie dog's combination of diurnality (daytime activity), large body mass, and high density of long, deep burrows is nonpareil (King 1955; Sheets et al. 1971; Hoogland 1995, 2003b).
- Far-ranging grazing by herbivores such as pronghorn and American bison affects the grassland ecosystem, but the concentrated herbivory and clipping by prairie dogs are exceptional because of the prairie dog's dense coloniality and reluctance to emigrate (King 1955; Hoogland 1995; Chapter 3).
- By serving as firebreaks, prairie dog colony-sites affect the role of fire in the ecosystems of western North America (Kotliar et al. 1999).

Does the Prairie Dog Qualify as a Keystone Species?

As noted above, a keystone species has a unique, significant, disproportionately large impact on its ecosystem. Arguing that more than 150 species associate with prairie dogs and their colony-sites, Miller et al. (1994) first proposed the notion that the prairie dog is a keystone species. Stapp (1998) and Kotliar et al. (1999) countered, however, that too few data are available to determine the level of dependence/association for most species commonly observed at colony-sites. Kotliar et al. (1999) argued that black-footed ferrets, mountain plovers, burrowing owls, and 6 other species clearly depend on prairie dogs for survival and reproduction; that 20 species opportunistically benefit at colony-sites; and that another 117 species have a natural history that suggests a benefit from associating with prairie dogs. Recent research indicates that additional species should be added to these latter three categories (e.g., see Manzano-Fischer et al. 1999; Ceballos et al. 2000; Desmond et al. 2000; Kretzer and Cully 2001a, 2001b; Lomolino and Smith 2003, 2004; Smith and Lomolino 2004). With further research, more additions are inevitable.

For species that associate with prairie dogs, the strength of the association varies with geography (space) and season (time) (Kotliar et al. 1999; Kretzer and Cully 2001a; Smith and Lomolino 2004). Consider Woodhouse's toads, for example, which positively associate with prairie dog colony-sites in Oklahoma (Lomolino and Smith 2003). At the Cimarron National Grasslands in Kansas, however, Woodhouse's toads were absent at colony-sites and present in nearby sites in 1977—but the reverse pattern occurred in 1996 (Kretzer and Cully 2001a). Seasonal variation in the use of colony-sites also occurs for many species (Kotliar et al. 1999; Lomolino and Smith 2003; Smith and Lomolino 2004). Ferruginous hawks, for example, frequently prey on prairie dogs in late autumn and winter, but less frequently in spring and summer (Berry et al. 1998; Seery and Matiatos 2000; Bak et al. 2001).

For amphibians, reptiles, and birds, the number of species observed at prairie dog colony-sites is similar to the number observed in nearby grasslands; for small mammals and certain insects, however, colony-sites usually have fewer species than nearby grasslands (Agnew et al. 1986; Stapp 1998; Kotliar et al. 1999; Kretzer and Cully 2001a, 2001b; Johnson and Collinge 2004). A comparison between species richness at and away from colony-sites is not necessarily the best way to assess keystone status, however (Kotliar et al. 1999; Kotliar 2000). Regardless of patterns of species richness, clear differences in species composition occur at colony-sites: some species prefer colony-sites, while other species avoid them (Agnew et al. 1986; Kotliar et al. 1999; Ceballos et al. 2000; Kretzer and Cully 2001a, 2001b; Winter et al. 2002; Chapter 5).

In summary, some characteristics of the prairie dog's influence on grassland ecosystems have been misinterpreted or overrated. Nevertheless, the prairie dog's impact on plant and animal communities is substantial and unique, is disproportionately large relative to its abundance, and is critical to the integrity of grassland ecosystems. We therefore conclude that the prairie dog is a legitimate keystone species (see also Miller et al., 1994, 2000; Kotliar et al. 1999; Kotliar 2000). Because some of its ecological functions are directly proportional to its abundance (e.g., nutrient cycling), the prairie dog is also a foundation species.

Implications of Keystone Status for the Conservation of Prairie Dogs

In the past decade, the keystone concept has been instrumental in focusing attention on the importance of protecting prairie dogs (Miller et al. 1994; Kotliar et al. 1999). Wildlife managers should try to understand the range of conditions that affect keystone functions. They should look at the larger landscape and should consider how the ecosystem varies over space and time to guide decisions at a local scale (Kotliar 2000). The shorter height of vegetation at prairie dog colony-sites might have more impact in mid-grass prairies than in short-grass prairies, for example (Detling 1998; Chapter 5). The frequency of fires, variation in weather, and the presence of other organisms also might affect the local influence of prairie dogs on the grassland ecosystem.

Because the prairie dog is a foundation species, its influence on grassland ecosystems varies with its abundance. But certain keystone functions also vary with abundance. Even though small, isolated colonies of prairie dogs are better than no colonies at all, for example, they cannot support the full complement of species that naturally associate with prairie dogs (Kotliar 2000; Lomolino et al. 2003; Johnson and Collinge 2004). More information on the loss of keystone functions with declining population size will foster better conservation of prairie dogs. About 200 years ago, both large and small colonies occurred throughout the prairie dog's geographic range (Chapter 16). A similar combination of small and large colonies is probably a good mechanism for maintaining today's prairie dogs and their keystone functions (Lomolino et al. 2003; Trudeau et al. 2004).

Agricultural interests have dictated artificially small limits on population sizes of prairie dogs for more than 100 years (Schenbeck 1981, 1985; Miller et al. 1990; Chapters 7, 16, and 17). Indeed, few prairie dog populations today are sufficiently large to support viable populations of black-footed ferrets (Chapters 16, 17, and 18). The keystone concept can promote conservation not only for the prairie dog, but also for its grassland ecosystem (Kotliar 2000; Miller et al. 2000; Soulé et al. 2003; Chapters 17 and 18; Box to Chapter 12).

A healthy grassland ecosystem includes areas with and without prairie dogs, allows for dispersal among colonies, and promotes colonization of new areas and recolonization of sites where prairie dogs lived in the recent or distant past. Because they currently inhabit only a tiny fraction of their original geographic range, more prairie dogs are pivotal for a healthy grassland ecosystem (Chapters 16, 17, and 18).

Regarding herbivory, redundancy (i.e., consumption of plants by several species rather than by a single species) is important for the persistence of ecosystems (Walker 1991; Ehrlich and Walker 1998). As redundancy decreases (e.g., following the drastic declines of American bison and prairie dogs from the grasslands of western North America), the vulnerability of an ecosystem increases. To preserve redundancy and other ecological phenomena in the grassland ecosystem, wildlife managers should try to identify species in addition to the prairie dog that merit protection.

Because it is a keystone and foundation species, conserving the prairie dog will help to save its grassland ecosystem. The concepts of keystone and foundation species thus are helpful for conservation.

Summary

- A keystone species satisfies three criteria: its effects on its ecosystem are unique, significant, and disproportionately large relative to its abundance. A foundation species has significant, unique effects that result from mere abundance.
- Prairie dogs influence the grassland ecosystem via three primary pathways: grazing, burrowing, and as prey. Numerous species use colony-sites for food and shelter. Black-footed ferrets, mountain plovers, burrowing owls, and at least 6 other species clearly depend on prairie dogs for survival and reproduction; at least 20 species opportunistically benefit at colony-sites; and at least 117 additional species have a natural history that suggests a benefit from associating with prairie dogs. With additional research, numbers in all three of these categories are certain to increase.
- Besides vertebrates, other types of organisms that associate with prairie dogs include numerous species of protozoans, arachnids, and insects, and at least four plant species.
- Burrowing by prairie dogs mixes subsoil and topsoil, redistributes nutrients and minerals, and promotes penetration and retention of moisture. The combination of burrowing, foraging, and clipping alters floral species composition and affects the concentration of nitrogen in the soil and the rate of nitrogen uptake by plants. Prairie dogs reduce vegetational biomass, but, especially at young colony-sites, they often enhance digestibility, protein content, and productivity of grasses and forbs.
- The prairie dog's influence on plant and animal communities is substantial and unique, disproportionately large relative to its abundance, and critical to the integrity of grassland ecosystems. The prairie dog is therefore a legitimate keystone species. Because some of its ecological functions are directly proportional to its abundance (e.g., nutrient cycling), the prairie dog is also a foundation species.
- Because it is a keystone and foundation species, conserving the prairie dog will help to save its grassland ecosystem. The concepts of keystone and foundation species thus are helpful for conservation.

Acknowledgments

Bruce Baker, Sharon Collinge, and Paul Stapp provided astute comments on earlier versions of the manuscript.

CHAPTER 5

Do Prairie Dogs Compete with Livestock?

James K. Detling

Because prairie dogs consume and clip vegetation, they have long been regarded as competitors with domestic livestock (cattle, horses, and sheep) and, consequently, as threats to the livelihoods of ranchers. The result has been a war against prairie dogs, involving recreational shooting (Chapter 10), poisoning (Chapter 8), and loss of habitat (Chapters 12 and 16). With the recent designation of the prairie dog as a keystone species of the grassland ecosystem worthy of conservation (Chapters 4, 12, and 17), the issue of competition between prairie dogs and livestock is more important than ever.

The level of competition between prairie dogs and livestock is scale-dependent. At a broad geographical scale, current overall competition must be relatively trivial—for the simple reason that today's prairie dogs inhabit less than 2% of the terrain that they occupied about 200 years ago (Chapter 16). At the local scale of a single paddock or ranch, however, where prairie dogs might inhabit a high percentage of the area, ranchers are legitimately concerned about possible competition between prairie dogs and livestock.

In this chapter I describe the vegetation in areas inhabited by prairie dogs, and then document the types and amount of vegetation consumed by prairie dogs. I examine the impact of prairie dogs on vegetation within colony-sites and investigate interactions among prairie dogs, livestock, and other large herbivores. I explore whether prairie dogs prefer to colonize areas heavily grazed by livestock and then tackle the most important and controversial question: what is the effect of prairie dogs on livestock?

Characteristics of Vegetation in Areas Inhabited by Prairie Dogs

Most prairie dogs live within the region of North America whose natural vegetation is classified as mixed-prairie and shortgrass steppe, but they also occupy areas of desert grasslands and shrublands in southern New Mexico and northern Mexico (Figure 5.1). These grasslands experience variable precipitation, and extended droughts are common. Average annual precipitation in the

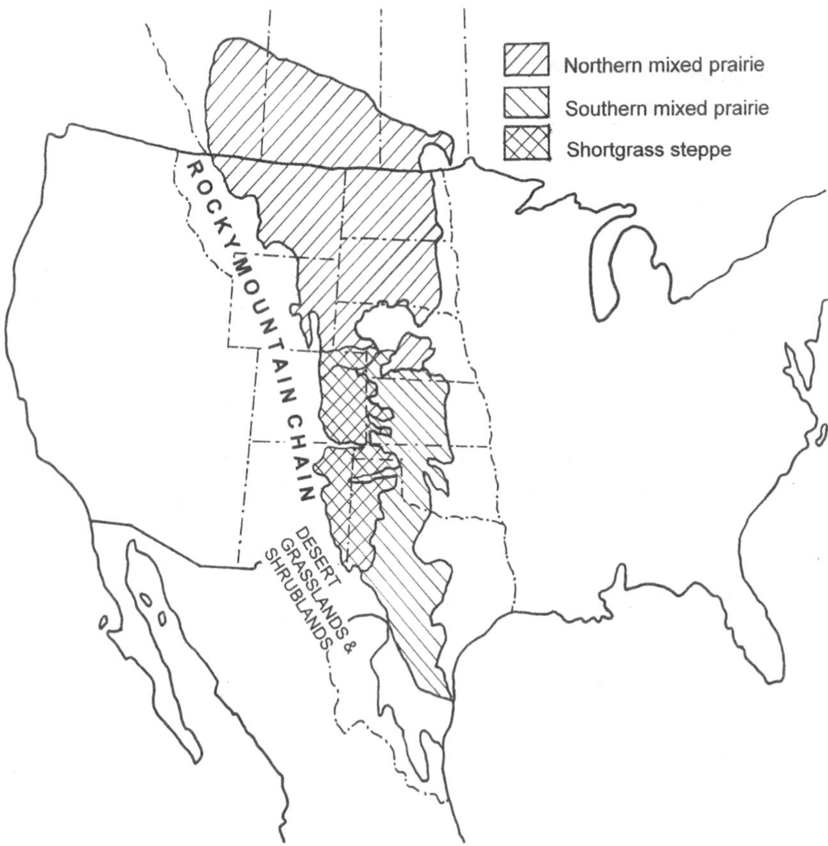

Figure 5.1. Distribution of northern mixed-prairie, southern mixed-prairie, and shortgrass steppe in western North America (Lauenroth and Milchunas 1992). Note how closely the distribution of these grasslands coincides with the distribution of prairie dogs (see Figure 2.1).

shortgrass steppe ranges from less than 30 centimeters (12 inches) in the west to more than 55 centimeters (22 inches) in the east, while in the mixed-prairie it ranges from 30 to 45 centimeters (12 to 18 inches) in the northern subregion to more than 60 centimeters (24 inches) in the southern subregion (Coupland 1992; Lauenroth and Milchunas 1992; Lauenroth et al. 1999). Winter is usually the driest season (less than 20% of the total annual precipitation), and summer is the wettest (Detling 1979; Coupland 1992; Lauenroth et al. 1999).

Perennial grasses are the dominant plants of the mixed-prairie and shortgrass steppe, but these grasslands also contain dwarf shrubs (i.e., predominately herbaceous plants with woody basal branches) (Stubbendieck et al. 1992) and perennial forbs (i.e., herbaceous plants other than grasses and grass-like plants) (Sims et al. 1978). The mixed-prairie is co-dominated by mid-height and short grasses, with mid-height grasses being more abundant during years of high precipitation and short grasses being more abundant in drier years (Clements 1920). As its name implies, the semi-arid, shortgrass steppe is dominated by short grasses. Table 5.1 shows the most abundant plant species that occur at or near prairie dog colony-sites. Many of these species are important food items for both prairie dogs and livestock.

In the cooler northern mixed-prairie, the most common graminoids (grasses and grass-like plants such as sedges) are mid-height, cool-season (C_3 photosynthetic pathway) species, although two warm-season (C_4) species are also important (see Table 5.1). All these native graminoids are perennials, and provide high-quality forage to livestock, prairie dogs, and other herbivores (Johnson and Nichols 1982; Stubbendieck et al. 1992). Farther south, warm-season graminoids predominate (Table 5.1; Teeri and Stowe 1976; Coupland 1992; Epstein et al. 1997; Lauenroth et al. 1999). Some warm-season grasses provide high-quality forage, but most are medium to low quality (Stubbendieck et al. 1992). The shortgrass steppe shares many species with the mixed-prairie (see Table 5.1), but is dominated by blue grama and buffalo grass (Sims et al. 1978; Lauenroth and Milchunas 1992). Both the mixed-prairie and the shortgrass steppe have diverse assortments of forbs and dwarf shrubs (Sims et al. 1978), which only rarely achieve dominance.

Annual aboveground net primary production (ANPP) of grasslands varies directly with annual precipitation (Lauenroth 1979; Sala et al. 1988; Epstein et al. 1997; Lauenroth et al. 1999). Estimates of ANPP in the mixed-prairie region range from 250 g/m^2 (grams per square meter) to 600 g/m^2 (Coupland 1992); estimates for the shortgrass steppe range from 50 g/m^2 to 325 g/m^2 (Lauenroth and Milchunas 1992). At many grassland sites, root biomass is several times greater than aboveground biomass (Sims and Singh 1978; Ingham and Detling 1984).

Table 5.1. Some major graminoid species, together with their life-forms and quality of forage, in grasslands of the central Great Plains of western North America. Abbreviations for life-form characteristics: CS = cool season (C_3) species, WS = warm season (C_4) species, SG = shortgrass, MG = mid-height grass. Abbreviations for forage quality: E = excellent, G = good, F = fair, P = poor. For more details, see Sims and Singh 1978; Sims et al. 1978; Coupland 1992; Lauenroth and Milchunas 1992; Schmutz et al. 1992, and Stubbendieck et al. 1992.

Major species	*Life-form*	*Forage quality*
Northern mixed-prairie		
western wheatgrass	CS, MG	G
thickspike wheatgrass	CS, MG	G
needle-and-thread grass	CS, MG	F-G
porcupine grass	CS, MG	G
prairie junegrass	CS, MG	E
sun sedge	CS, SG	G
needleleaf sedge	CS, SG	G
blue grama	WS, SG	G
buffalo grass	WS, SG	E
Southern mixed-prairie		
western wheatgrass	CS, MG	G
prairie junegrass	CS, MG	E
silver bluestem	WS, MG	F
sideoats grama	WS, MG	G
blue grama	WS, SG	G
hairy grama	WS, MG	F
buffalo grass	WS, SG	E
little bluestem	WS, MG	F–G
curly mesquite	WS, SG	F
Shortgrass steppe		
blue grama	WS, SG	G
buffalo grass	WS, SG	E
red threeawn	WS, MG	P
western wheatgrass	CS, MG	G
needle-and-thread grass	CS, MG	F-G

What, and How Much, Do Prairie Dogs Eat?

A principal concern of ranchers is that prairie dogs consume many of the same plant species as cattle and other livestock. Available data support this concern, but rigorous research with cattle and prairie dogs in the same grasslands is lacking. In addition, prairie dogs sometimes clip, but do not consume, certain vegetation that livestock might otherwise have eaten (King 1955; Koford 1958; Hoogland 1995), thereby further reducing the availability of forage. Table 5.2 shows dietary information for prairie dogs and cattle on the shortgrass steppe of Colorado. Nine plant species accounted for 95% of the diet of prairie dogs in the first study (Hansen and Gold 1977): seven graminoids, a forb (scarlet globemallow), and a dwarf shrub (fringed sagewort). These same species accounted for about 85% of the diet of cattle. Dietary overlap between prairie dogs and cattle on the shortgrass steppe is thus substantial (see also Van Dyne et al. 1983; Mellado et al. 2005). Dietary overlap between prairie dogs and horses is also significant (Hansen et al. 1977; Hanley and Hanley 1982; Krysl et al. 1984).

Competition does not necessarily occur simply because two species use the same resource. Rather, competition occurs when sharing of resources adversely affects one or both species (Ricklefs and Miller 2000). Unfortunately, competition is difficult to document under natural conditions. In the absence of such documentation, it nonetheless seems logical to conclude that dietary overlap adversely affects livestock, or both livestock and prairie dogs, at least under some circumstances.

Table 5.2. Plant composition in the diets of prairie dogs, cattle, domestic sheep, American bison, and pronghorn sampled on the shortgrass steppe of northeastern Colorado. References: Hansen and Gold 1977 (for prairie dogs and cattle) and Van Dyne et al. 1983 (for cattle, sheep, bison, and pronghorn). Species with an asterisk (*) were not listed by Van Dyne et al. 1983.

	Percentage (%) in diet					
Plant species	*Prairie dogs*	*Cattle (Hansen and Gold 1977)*	*Cattle (Van Dyne et al. 1983)*	*Sheep*	*Bison*	*Pronghorn*
sedges (several species)	36	23	9	15	14	<1
blue grama	20	10	33	20	55	9
sand dropseed	13	10	*	*	*	*
fringed sagewort	8	<1	18	23	3	6
scarlet globemallow	7	6	8	12	4	22
buffalo grass	4	2	*	*	*	*
western wheatgrass	3	26	18	9	13	3
needle-and-thread grass	2	6	*	*	*	*
Indian ricegrass	2	<1	*	*	*	*

In the northern mixed-prairie, the diet of prairie dogs consists primarily (at least 80%) of perennial graminoids (Table 5.3), especially during spring and summer (Summers and Linder 1978; Fagerstone and Williams 1982; Uresk 1984). Forbs, dwarf shrubs, and cacti are more important food items during winter (Fagerstone et al. 1981; Fagerstone 1982). Many of the species consumed by prairie dogs in South Dakota's mixed-prairie are the same species eaten by calves and lambs in the same state (Volesky et al. 1990), by prairie dogs and cattle in southeastern Wyoming's mixed-prairie (Samuel and Howard 1982), and by prairie dogs, cattle, and domestic sheep in Colorado's shortgrass steppe (see Table 5.2). Prairie dogs avoid certain grass species (e.g., tumblegrass and red threeawn), and livestock often avoid the same species as well (see Table 5.2; Stubbendieck et al. 1992).

Diets of prairie dogs and livestock overlap, but how much do prairie dogs consume? C. Hart Merriam was one of the first to address this question more than 100 years ago. Regarding a prairie dog colony in Texas that inhabited approximately 64,000 square kilometers (25,000 square miles) and contained

Table 5.3. Relative plant cover (percentage) and percentage in diet of prairie dogs for plants in northern mixed-prairie of the Conata Basin in South Dakota's Buffalo Gap National Grasslands. Data are averages for May, July, August, and September. Reference: Uresk 1984.

Plant category	*Relative plant cover (percentage)*	*Percentage in diet of prairie dog*
Graminoids		
buffalo grass	35	3
blue grama	24	22
needleleaf	9	17
tumble grass	10	2
red threeawn	9	<1
sand dropseed	1	20
wheatgrass	<1	11
Japanese brome	<1	<1
sixweeks fescue	<1	*
other graminoids	<1	9
Forbs		
scarlet globemallow	6	11
fetid marigold	3	*
plains pricklypear	1	<1
milkvetch	<1	1
other forbs	2	2

approximately 400 million prairie dogs, Merriam (1902a) wrote: "According to the formula for determining the relative quantities of food consumed by animals of different sizes (kindly given to me by Prof. W. W. Cooke), 32 prairie dogs consume as much grass as 1 sheep, and 256 prairie dogs as much as 1 cow. On this basis the grass annually eaten by these pests in the great Texas colony would support 1,562,500 head of cattle. Hence, it is no wonder that the annual loss from prairie dogs is said to range from 50 to 75 percent of the producing capacity of the land. . . ." Using data from Kelso (1939), Koford (1958) later calculated that 335 prairie dogs eat as much as 1 cow—that is, that competition is not as severe as hypothesized by Merriam (1902a). Koford (1958) also calculated that a single prairie dog would eat an average of 70 grams (2.5 ounces) of forage per day (26 kilograms [57 pounds] per year). With Koford's (1958) estimate and the assumption that the density is about 25 adult and yearling prairie dogs per hectare (10 per acre; Chapter 2), the consumption by prairie dogs is about 625 kilograms per hectare per year (63 g/m^2/year); this calculation does not include consumption by juveniles, for which the density is roughly 25 per hectare (10 per acre) in late spring (Chapter 2). Given the range of ANPP cited above, such consumption rates might remove as much as 100% of ANPP at the least productive shortgrass steppe sites or as little as about 10% of ANPP at the most productive mixed-prairie sites. Prairie dog densities, and hence consumption rates, vary from one area to another, however (Hoogland 1995; Chapter 6). Further, as density of vegetation increases, clipping of vegetation probably also increases. The proportion of vegetation consumed or clipped by prairie dogs thus varies with local conditions.

Another way to estimate consumption and clipping of forage by prairie dogs involves using exclosure cages. Cages are placed on the ground and, after a certain period, biomass of vegetation is determined by weighing plant material collected inside and outside the cages. Biomass inside cages is assumed to be ANPP during the period of exclosure, and biomass outside cages is vegetation that remains after consumption by prairie dogs and other herbivores. From two colony-sites at Wind Cave National Park, South Dakota, April Whicker and I obtained ten samples per month (May through September) from each of the following four regions: at the edge where expansion was under way; in slightly older but still young, grass-dominated sections; in older sections dominated by forbs and dwarf shrubs; and in nearby uncolonized grasslands. American bison foraged frequently in all four regions. Consumption ranged from 20% to 40% of ANPP in grass-dominated areas off the colony-sites to 60% to 75% of ANPP in grass-dominated areas within colony-sites (Figures 5.2 and 5.3). Consumption in parts of the colony-sites dominated by forbs and dwarf shrubs varied substantially, possibly in response to

Figure 5.2. American bison and prairie dogs. Probably because the vegetation is more nutritious at prairie dog colony-sites, bison commonly prefer to feed there. Bison also rest at colony-sites, and use wallows (depressions with little or no vegetation) and burrow-mounds there for "dust-baths." Photo by Dean E. Biggins.

variation among coteries in density of prairie dogs (Hoogland 1995). Unfortunately, however, we could not discriminate at colony-sites between forage consumed by bison versus forage consumed by prairie dogs.

In another study at Wind Cave National Park, Cid et al. (1991) set up a series of plots (50 meters × 50 meters, or 55 yards × 55 yards) and exclosures on a large, 27-year-old prairie dog colony-site to establish four conditions from May through September. These conditions were: both prairie dogs and bison present; prairie dogs present but bison excluded; bison present but prairie dogs excluded; both prairie dogs and bison excluded. In the first year of the study, ANPP at the colony-site was low because of a drought that lasted through July, and no differences in productivity among plots were evident. Rainfall was more abundant in the second year, however, and it came early in the growing season, so that ANPP was high (more than 200 g/m^2). In Year 2, plots with only prairie dogs excluded had a 36% greater aboveground plant biomass than plots with both prairie dogs and bison present, while plots with only bison excluded had a 37% greater biomass than plots with both prairie dogs and bison. Bison and prairie dogs thus removed almost identical amounts of plant biomass.

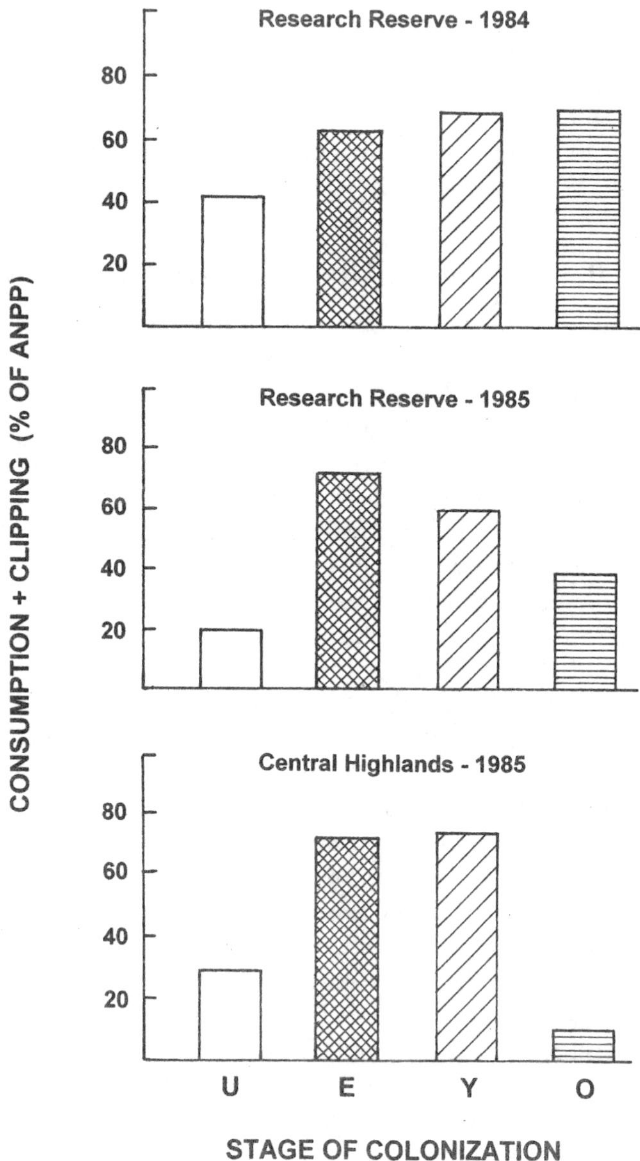

Figure 5.3. Estimates of clipping (i.e., vegetation felled but not consumed) and consumption of forage (percent of aboveground net primary production, or ANPP) versus stage of colonization at three prairie dog colony-sites at Wind Cave National Park. Symbols are: U = uncolonized grassland grazed by American bison; E = edge of prairie dog colony-site; Y = young part of colony-site dominated by graminoids; O = older part of colony-site dominated by forbs and dwarf shrubs.

To summarize: prairie dogs mainly consume native, perennial graminoids and a few common perennial forbs. Dietary overlap among prairie dogs, native ungulates, and livestock is substantial. Depending on factors such as climate, precipitation, and density at colony-sites, prairie dogs might consume as little as about 10% of ANPP of graminoids at colony-sites, or as much as almost 100%.

Impact of Prairie Dogs on Vegetation Within Colony-Sites

One of the most striking visual features of prairie dog colony-sites is the presence of large, sparsely vegetated soil mounds—called dome craters and rim craters—around burrow-entrances (King 1955; Archer et al. 1987; Whicker and Detling 1988a; Cid et al. 1991; Hoogland 1995; Chapter 2). Burrow-mounds can be as high as 0.75 meters (2.5 feet) and can have a diameter of 2 meters (7 feet), and they number from 50 to 300 per hectare (20–120 per acre). Despite this high density, burrow-mounds typically occupy less than 4% of the total area of colony-sites in Montana, Colorado, and Texas (Farrar 2002). Some rim craters have additional denuded areas surrounding them from which prairie dogs have scraped soil, which they use to fortify the mounds (see Figure 2.9 of Chapter 2). These denuded areas increase the cumulative percentage of disturbance resulting from burrowing to about 6% of a colony-site's overall surface area. Despite their conspicuousness, burrow-mounds thus represent a small loss of available forage to livestock. On the positive side, plant species such as western wheatgrass, buffalo grass, and scarlet globemallow sometimes grow well on, or at the periphery of, burrow-mounds, and both prairie dogs and livestock consume these species (Farrar 2002).

When prairie dogs move into uncolonized grassland, they immediately begin to consume or clip the vegetation. Consequently, the height of vegetation is usually dramatically lower at colony-sites than at nearby uncolonized grassland (Chapter 2). In separate studies on the northern mixed-prairie at Wind Cave and Badlands national parks in South Dakota, for example, the average height of vegetation adjacent to prairie dog colony-sites was about 25 centimeters (10 inches), but the average height within colony-sites was less than 10 centimeters (4 inches) (Archer et al. 1987; Whicker and Detling 1988a; Russell and Detling 2003; Chapter 6). Because of intensive grazing by prairie dogs and other herbivores, plant biomass is concentrated much closer to the soil surface at colony-sites than at uncolonized areas. In uncolonized mixed-prairie at Wind Cave National Park, for example, the height of 75% of the aboveground plant biomass ranged from 1 to 22 centimeters (0.5 to 9 inches), but the height of 75% of the biomass at a prairie dog colony-site was less than 8 centimeters (3 inches) (Day and Detling 1994). The difference in height of vegetation on and off prairie dog colony-sites is less dramatic in the more arid shortgrass steppe. In eastern Colorado, for example, vegetation on shortgrass pastures with cattle only averaged 12 centimeters (5 inches) tall, but vegetation on sites with both cattle and prairie dogs averaged only 6.4 centimeters (2.5 inches) tall (Guenther and Detling 2003). One consequence of the shorter vegetation at colony-sites is that ungulates probably cannot obtain as much biomass per bite.

As prairie dogs clip and consume vegetation over time, grasses become weak and lose their ability to compete with other plants. Within two years of colonization at a mixed-prairie site at Wind Cave National Park, for example, cover of grasses decreased by 50% (Archer et al. 1987; Figure 5.4). Most of the initial reduction resulted from a decrease in the abundance of mid-height

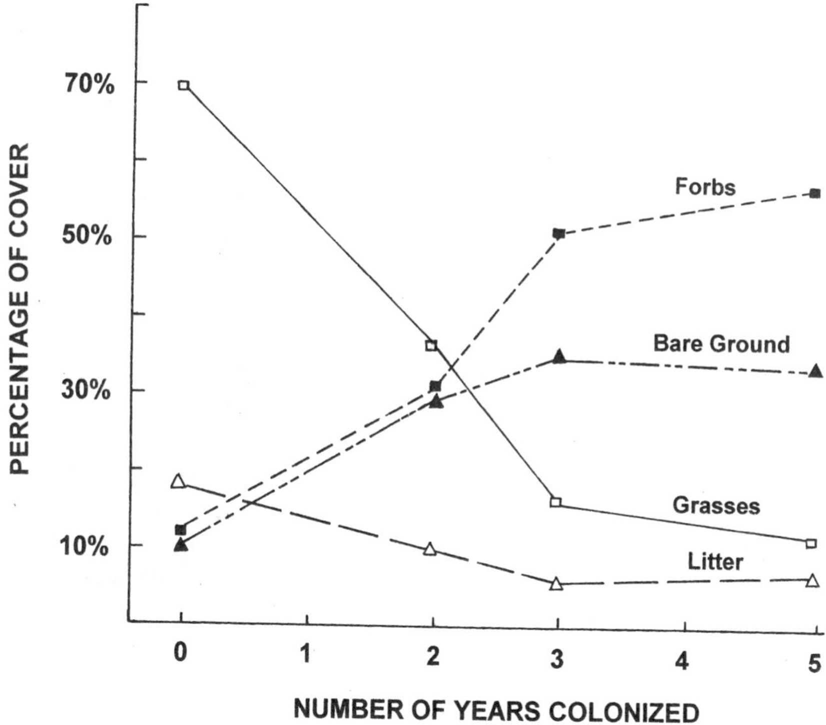

Figure 5.4. Cover of grasses, forbs, bare ground, and litter versus time since colonization of Wind Cave Canyon colony-site at Wind Cave National Park. Data for zero years inhabited are from an uncolonized area adjacent to the prairie dog colony-site. Litter includes dead, partially decomposed plant material lying aboveground. Reference: Archer et al. 1987.

grasses—because they were less tolerant of grazing and because prairie dogs preferred them. As cover of grasses declined, cover of forbs increased and was almost equal to cover of grasses within two years after colonization. Within three years, annual forbs such as fetid marigold and perennial forbs such as bracted spiderwort and scarlet globemallow had attained dominance. The time varies for transition from grasses to forbs (and dwarf shrubs), but studies of other colony-sites in the northern mixed-prairie show similar patterns (Coppock et al. 1983a; Fahnestock and Detling 2002; Fahnestock et al. 2003).

Changes in vegetation following colonization in the southern mixed-prairie are similar to those described above for the northern mixed-prairie. At two prairie dog colony-sites in Texas that were at least 50 years old, for example, total aboveground herbaceous biomass was three to four times greater away from the colony-sites than at them (Weltzin et al. 1997a, 1997b). This difference resulted mainly from lower standing crops of mid-height grasses at the colony-sites. In contrast to studies in other grasslands, however, forbs in southern mixed-prairies were more abundant away from colony-sites than at colony-sites. By preventing establishment of woody plants such as honey mesquite via destruction of seeds or girdling, prairie dogs help to maintain southern grasslands and savannas, and thereby improve the habitat for livestock (Weltzin et al. 1997a, 1997b).

The effects of prairie dogs on vegetation within the shortgrass steppe appear to be less dramatic than their effects at northern and southern mixed-prairies. Although aboveground biomass of dominant grass species in the shortgrass steppe is lower at colony-sites than at adjacent uncolonized sites (Farrar 2002), elimination or near-elimination of these species at colony-sites evidently does not occur. In shortgrass steppe of northeastern Colorado, for example, the cover of blue grama ranged from 9% to 16% at colony-sites and from 16% to 24% at nearby off-colony sites (Bonham and Lerwick 1976). Similar trends occurred at other shortgrass steppe sites in northeastern Colorado, southwestern Kansas, and southeastern Colorado (Winter et al. 2002; Guenther and Detling 2003).

Just as aboveground plant biomass declines over time following colonization by prairie dogs, belowground biomass declines as well, often substantially. Root biomass declined steadily from the youngest, lightly grazed (by native ungulates), uncolonized grassland sites to the oldest parts of colony-sites within Wind Cave National Park (Figure 5.5), for example. The decline is probably largely attributable to reduced photosynthetic production in heavily grazed plants with lower leaf area, and to a diversion of carbohydrates from roots to growth of new shoots (Detling et al. 1979; Briske and Richards 1995). As grazing continues, the reduced availability of carbohydrates to roots and the

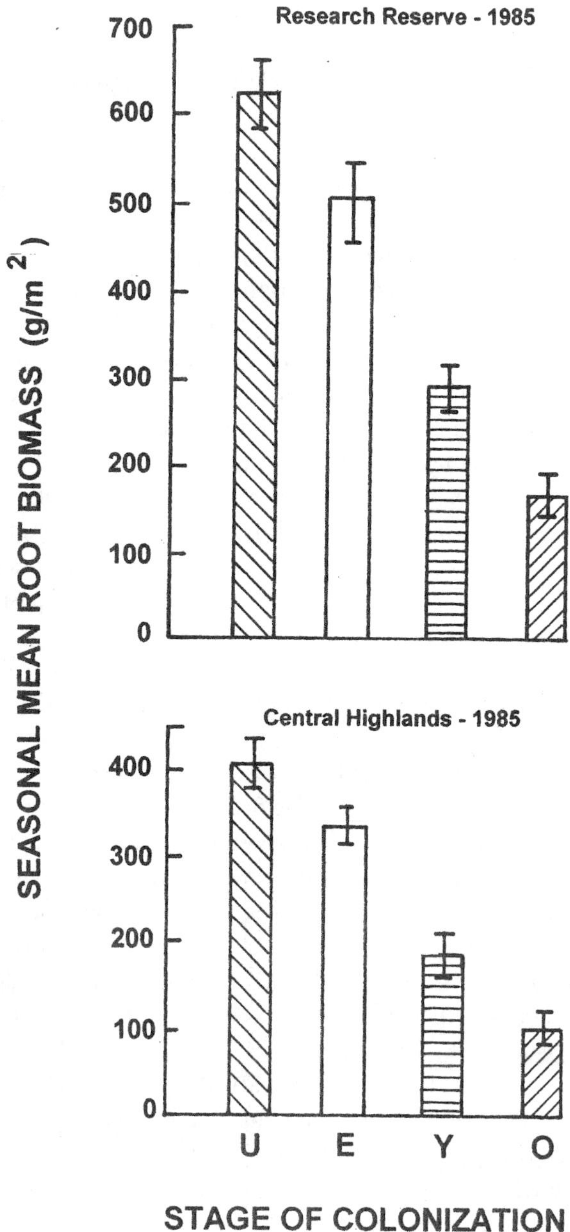

Figure 5.5. Root biomass averaged over the growing season from two prairie dog colony-sites at Wind Cave National Park. Symbols for state of colonization as in Figure 5.3. Bars indicate averages, and lines at the top of the bars show standard errors. Reference: Detling 1998.

resulting deterioration of the root system impairs the plant's ability to acquire water and nutrients, further reducing its ability to compete with other plants.

The proportion of dead plant material relative to living plant material is lower at prairie dog colony-sites (Coppock et al. 1983a; Whicker and Detling 1988b; Detling 1998). Consequently, the percentage of dead leaves in the diet of American bison grazing at colony-sites during the summer at Wind Cave National Park is only 1%–5%, but is 5%–18% for bison grazing off colony-sites (Vanderhye 1985). Further, leaves of plants at colony-sites are more easily digested, and often contain higher concentrations of protein, than leaves of the same species away from colony-sites (Coppock et al. 1983a; Krueger 1986; Whicker and Detling 1988b). Herbivores that feed at colony-sites thus might obtain better nutrition than herbivores that feed on the same plant species away from colony-sites. Reductions in plant biomass at colony-sites will, of course, partially offset the enhanced quality of forage. Prairie dogs thus create a tradeoff between enhanced quality versus reduced quantity of forage at colony-sites. Assessing the consequences of this quality-quantity tradeoff for cattle and other livestock is complicated because it depends on factors such as type of grassland, length of occupancy by prairie dogs, current and past strategies for managing livestock, and recent precipitation.

Calculations from a mixed-prairie at Wind Cave National Park illustrate the tradeoff between quality versus quantity of vegetation at prairie dog colony-sites (Coppock et al. 1983a). Pringle Valley in 1979 encompassed 120 hectares (297 acres), of which prairie dogs inhabited 36 hectares (89 acres, or 30%; Table 5.4). On the basis of time occupied by prairie dogs, three zones at the colony-site were evident: old (occupied more than 26 years), young (3–8 years), and edge (less than 3 years). Because graminoids comprise the majority of the forage used by most livestock, I have limited my calculations to graminoids, and have examined three attributes: average biomass during the growing season, protein, and digestible dry matter. For all three, the effect of prairie dogs depended on the length of occupancy (Table 5.4). At the edge of the colony-site, for example, average biomass of graminoids per unit area was only 28% lower than on uncolonized grassland. In the oldest part of the colony-site, however, average biomass was 98% lower than on uncolonized grassland. And now for some tradeoffs: even though average biomass per unit area at the colony-site's edge was 28% lower than average biomass on uncolonized grassland, the total mass of protein per unit area was only 12% lower at the edge of the colony-site than at off-colony sites. Reductions of protein in other zones of the colony-site also were not proportionately as great as reductions in biomass. Similar but less pronounced trends occurred for digestible dry matter (Table 5.4).

When it occurs at high concentrations within leaves, silica sometimes deters consumption by herbivores (McNaughton and Tarrants 1983;

Table 5.4. Area (in hectares) of mixed-prairie inhabited by prairie dogs at various stages of colonization, and average mass per unit area (kilograms per hectare) of live graminoids, protein, and digestible dry matter in each of these areas averaged over the entire growing season. Numbers in parentheses represent percent change in each feature relative to the value of that feature in uncolonized grassland. Data are from Pringle Valley, Wind Cave National Park. Reference: Coppock et al. 1983a.

	Off colony	*Edge of colony*	*Young colony*	*Old colony*	*Total*
Area occupied in Pringle Valley (hectares)	84	12	15	9	120
Mass per unit area in Pringle Valley (kilograms per hectare)					
Live graminoids	990	710 (–28%)	410 (–59%)	20 (–98%)	—
Crude protein	80	71 (–12%)	41 (–49%)	2 (–90%)	—
Digestible dry matter	449	383 (–23%)	221 (–56%)	11 (–98%)	—

McNaughton et al. 1985) and therefore might affect the suitability of plants for livestock. Concentrations of silica within leaves are higher for grasses at prairie dog colony-sites than for grasses at nearby off-colony areas (Brizuela et al. 1986; Cid et al. 1989, 1990). Despite these higher concentrations of silica, however, bison and pronghorn graze preferentially at colony-sites (Coppock et al. 1983b; Krueger 1986; Green 1998).

In summary: burrow-mounds have a small effect on aboveground biomass of vegetation at prairie dog colony-sites. Most of the reduction in graminoid biomass is a result of grazing and clipping of vegetation by prairie dogs. Over time, grasses are weakened by continued defoliation and are replaced by forbs and dwarf shrubs. Although graminoid biomass is lower at prairie dog colony-sites, the quality of the forage, as estimated from protein content and digestibility, is sometimes higher at colony-sites—especially at young colony-sites, or at the edges of older colony-sites. This higher quality of forage usually is not sufficient to completely offset the reduction in biomass, however.

How Do Prairie Dogs, Livestock, and Other Large Herbivores Interact?

As noted above, American bison prefer prairie dog colony-sites. They frequently graze on the younger parts of colony-sites that are still dominated by graminoids and use the older areas dominated by forbs and dwarf shrubs for resting and wallowing (Coppock et al. 1983b). Like bison, pronghorn prefer to forage at prairie dog colony-sites (Figure 5.6) (Krueger 1986). Unlike bison, however, pronghorn prefer to forage in the older areas of colony-sites rather than the younger areas.

Many factors can reduce or enhance the association between large herbivores and prairie dogs. In one valley at Wind Cave National Park, for example, bison increased their use of off-colony sites in the year following a prescribed burn in part of the uncolonized portion of the valley—and consequently decreased their use of colony-sites (Coppock and Detling 1986). The effect of burning was short-lived, however, because usage of the burned area decreased—and usage of colony-sites increased—to pre-burn levels by the second year following the fire (Bock and Bock 1989). Weather, especially precipitation during the growing season, also might influence the association between

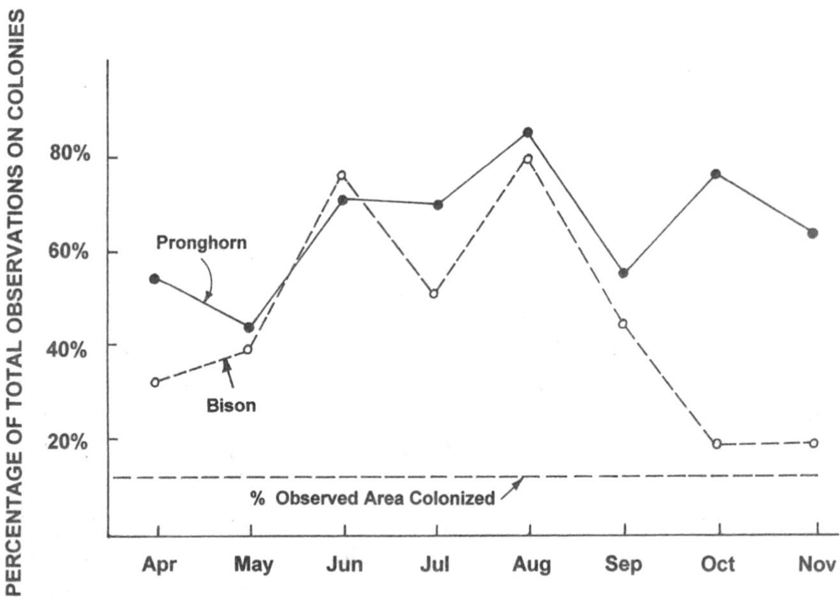

Figure 5.6. Seasonal use of prairie dog colony-sites by American bison and pronghorn at Wind Cave National Park. Censuses were conducted two to five times per week in 1983 from mid-April through November by traveling a route that went through all major habitats in the park, and included 12% prairie dog colony-sites, 73% uncolonized grassland, 13% coniferous forest, and 2% other habitats (see Coppock et al. 1983b for details). Each data point is the average of all census values collected in a month. The horizontal dashed line represents random use of prairie dog colony-sites (12%); points above the line indicate attraction to colony-sites; and points below the line would indicate avoidance of colony-sites. References: Krueger 1986; Whicker and Detling 1988b.

bison and prairie dogs. Bison cow-calf herds preferentially foraged, rested, and wallowed at colony-sites at Wind Cave National Park in a year of high precipitation, for example, but used colony-sites randomly (i.e., in proportion to their availability) in a year of low precipitation (Green 1998).

In a recent study on the shortgrass steppe of northeastern Colorado, cattle used prairie dog colony-sites in proportion to their availability (Figure 5.7); that is, they neither preferred nor avoided colony-sites (Guenther and Detling 2003). Further, cattle grazed as intensively at colony-sites as they did in other habitats not occupied by prairie dogs. Specifically, they foraged about the same proportion of the time regardless of whether they were at colony-sites, and their foraging efficiencies (bites per step) and foraging rates (bites per minute) were similar at and away from colony-sites. These data from interactions between livestock and prairie dogs come from shortgrass steppe, but data from interactions between American bison and prairie dogs come from northern mixed-prairie (Coppock et al. 1983b; Krueger 1986; Green 1998). At this point we do not know whether the lack of preference for colony-sites by cattle results from differences in grazing behavior between cattle and bison, or from differences in type of grassland.

Figure 5.7. Cattle and prairie dogs on the shortgrass steppe of Colorado. Cattle commonly forage at colony-sites. More research is necessary for a better understanding of competition for forage between prairie dogs and cattle. Photo by Debra A. Guenther.

Do Prairie Dogs Prefer to Colonize Areas Heavily Grazed by Livestock?

Tall, dense vegetation in mixed-prairies hinders establishment and expansion of prairie dog colony-sites (Allan 1954; Koford 1958; Smith 1967; Licht and Sanchez 1993). By contrast, prairie dogs in northeastern Montana are more likely to colonize areas that have been intensively grazed by cattle or that have man-made roads and trails, for the following four reasons (Knowles 1986b):

- Habitats preferred by cattle are often the best habitats for prairie dogs as well.
- Areas heavily grazed by cattle have lower vegetation than ungrazed areas, and therefore require less removal of tall vegetation by prairie dogs during the initiation or expansion of colonies.
- Trails and roads facilitate dispersal of prairie dogs, and migrating individuals therefore have a higher probability of locating other suitable habitat (e.g., other areas with livestock) via roads.
- Because of improved visibility for the prairie dogs due to shorter vegetation, predation at grazed colony-sites is probably lower than predation at ungrazed colony-sites.

The implication from these considerations is that the presence of prairie dogs is often an effect of prior heavy grazing by domestic livestock, rather than the initial cause of possible damage to the rangeland (Koford 1958; Knowles 1985, 1986b; Vermeire et al. 2004; Chapter 9).

What Is the Effect of Prairie Dogs on Livestock?

Most of the past and current rationale for systematic eradication of prairie dogs derives from the assumption that prairie dogs have substantial detrimental effects on the raising of livestock (Merriam 1902a; Collins et al. 1984; Chapters 7, 8 and 9). Rigorous testing of this assumption will require large-scale, long-term field experiments that involve numerous pastures, with and without prairie dogs, in different types of grassland. In the absence of such large-scale experiments, we must rely on results from small-scale field studies and computer simulations.

As discussed above, American bison and other ungulates often use prairie dog colony-sites to a greater extent than would be expected from the proportion of the landscape occupied by the colony-sites—perhaps because digestibility and the concentration of protein are higher for plants at colony-sites. To investigate whether bison benefit, in terms of body mass, from grazing at colony-sites, Vanderhye (1985) modified Swift's (1983) model for nutrition of ungulates. She used Krueger's (1986) estimate of food consumption by bison and Coppock et al.'s (1983a) estimate of seasonal differences in quality of forage, as well as her own estimates of live-versus-dead forage in the diet of bison, at and away from colony-sites, at Wind Cave National Park. The model simulated gain in body mass of mature female bison and immature yearlings from mid-June through late August as a function of the proportion of feeding at prairie dog colony-sites.

Vanderhye's (1985) model suggests that American bison can receive significant nutritional advantage by feeding at colony-sites. For both adult females and yearlings, seasonal gain in body mass increases directly with percentage of time spent grazing at colony-sites (Figure 5.8). Over six years, bison used colony-sites 39% of the time during the growing season, even though colony-sites comprised only 12% of the area studied. At this usage, the model estimates that adult bison gain 18% more body mass than by feeding exclusively off colony-sites, and 10% more than by feeding randomly regarding colony-sites. For mature females, most of the increased body mass involves fat,

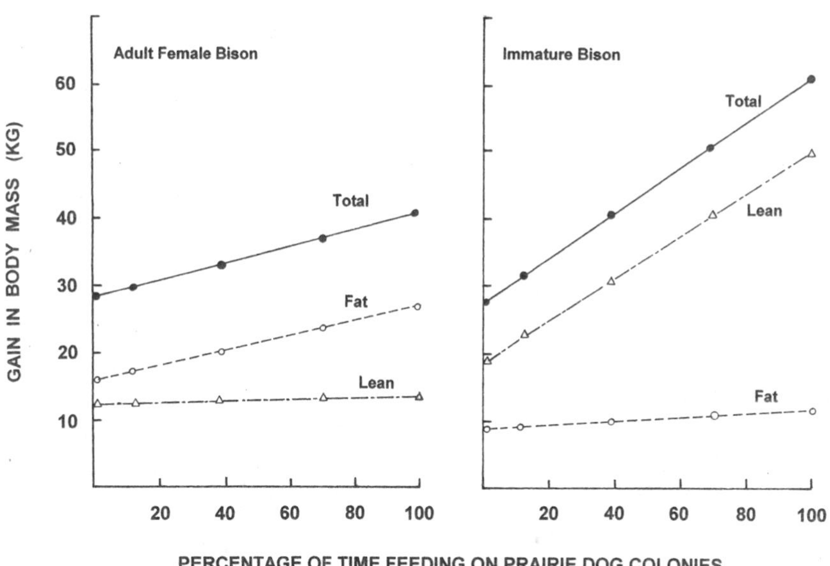

Figure 5.8. Simulated gain in body mass (kilograms) of adult female American bison and immature yearling bison feeding for various proportions of time at prairie dog colony-sites from mid-June through late August at Wind Cave National Park. One kilogram is equivalent to 2.20 pounds. Reference: Vanderhye 1985.

but for yearlings most of the increase involves lean body mass (Figure 5.8) (Vanderhye 1985).

Vanderhye's (1985) computer simulations indicate that bison can benefit from grazing at prairie dog colony-sites. The same is probably true for cattle and other ungulates, but, as noted above, preferences of bison and cattle for colony-sites are not available from the same types of grassland. In any event, caution is needed in interpreting and extrapolating from Vanderhye's (1985) results. A key assumption of her model is that sufficient forage is available to feed the bison—that is, shortages of forage are not simulated. Further, the model examines only the potential benefits of improved quality of forage—that is, the model does not consider tradeoffs between increases in quality versus decreases in quantity of forage at colony-sites.

In a study on the northern mixed-prairie near Wall, South Dakota, Uresk and Paulson (1988) used a linear programming approach (Bottoms and Bartlett 1975) to estimate how the size of prairie dog colony-sites affects carrying capacities of cattle on a pasture of 2,100 hectares (5,189 acres). In their model, consumption of preferred plant species varies from 20% to 80%, and size of colony-sites varies from 0 to 40 hectares (0 to 99 acres), the approximate range of areas for colony-sites at Uresk and Paulson's (1988) research site. Their model assumes that adequate forage is always available; that foraging by cattle does not affect foraging by prairie dogs, and vice-versa; that the density of prairie dogs is 44 individuals per hectare (18 individuals per acre), which is similar to John Hoogland's estimate of 50 adults, yearlings, and juveniles per hectare (Chapter 2), but which is almost two times the density of 25 individuals per hectare (adults and yearlings only) that I used earlier in this chapter; and that consumption by an individual prairie dog is 11 kilograms (24 pounds) per year (i.e., 30 grams per day; see Hansen and Cavender 1973), which is less than 50% of the estimate of 26 kilograms per year that I used earlier in this chapter. With these assumptions, Uresk and Paulson's (1988) estimate of consumption by prairie dogs is 482 kilograms per hectare per year, which is close to my estimate of 625 kilograms per hectare per year.

Uresk and Paulson's (1988) simulations suggest that a mixed-prairie pasture of 2,100 hectares (5,189 acres) can support from 40 cow-calf units (at 20% consumption of ANPP with no prairie dogs) to 161 cow-calf units (at 80% consumption and no prairie dogs; Table 5.5). Most cattle operations plan about 40% to 60% consumption of ANPP (Lacey and Van Poolen 1981); within this range, a pasture should support 81–121 cow-calf units in the absence of prairie dogs. At all rates of consumption by cattle, the addition of 20 hectares (49 acres) of prairie dogs causes a decline in carrying capacity of about two cow-calf units. At a rate of consumption by cattle of 60%, for example, the model predicts a 3.3% decline in cow-calf carrying capacity (from

Table 5.5. Estimates of six-month carrying capacities for cow-calf units on a 2,100-hectare (5,189-acre) mixed-grass pasture in South Dakota versus area of prairie dog colonies (0–40 hectares [0–99 acres]) and total consumption of forage by cattle-plus-prairie dogs in the entire pasture (20%–80%). Reference: Uresk and Paulson 1988.

	Area inhabited by prairie dogs (hectares)		
	0	*20*	*40*
Percentage of forage consumed	*Number of cow-calf units*		
20	40	39	37
40	81	79	77
60	121	119	117
80	161	159	157

121 to 117 cow-calf units) when prairie dogs inhabit 40 hectares (99 acres, or 2% of the pasture's area). Unfortunately, the model only works for pastures for which prairie dogs inhabit 2% or less of the total area, and Uresk and Paulson (1988) caution against extrapolation beyond the limits of their simulations. From their model we therefore cannot predict the effect on carrying capacity for cattle when prairie dog colony-sites inhabit more than 2% of a pasture, as they commonly do.

At the Conata Basin of South Dakota, Collins et al. (1984) examined increases in vegetation following partial elimination of prairie dogs with zinc phosphide, and then calculated the economic benefits of poisoning. Treatment of more than 7 hectares (17 acres) of a prairie dog colony-site was necessary to gain one animal unit month (AUM, the amount of forage required by a mature cow, with or without calf, for one month of grazing) (Heady and Child 1994) per year. Poisoning with zinc phosphide was cost-effective only if the area that needed to be poisoned in later years was less than 10% of the area initially poisoned. Thus, even though poisoning prairie dogs leads to additional forage for cattle, the resulting increase in body mass of cattle is rarely sufficient to offset the substantial cost (see also Chapters 8 and 9).

In a controlled field study in Oklahoma, O'Meilia et al. (1982) introduced prairie dogs into certain "experimental" pastures but did not introduce prairie dogs into other "control" pastures. They then tracked body mass of steers for two years in pastures with and without prairie dogs. Pastures with prairie dogs (21–30 per hectare, or 8–12 per acre) contained only about 60% as much grass as pastures without prairie dogs, but availability of forbs did not differ significantly between pastures with and without prairie dogs (Table 5.6). Steers on pastures with no prairie dogs consumed about 37% more total forage (average over two years) than steers on pastures with prairie dogs (1,105 versus 805 kilograms per hectare per year), but gains in body mass did not differ significantly in either year for steers in control pastures versus steers in experimental pastures (Table 5.7).

Possible explanations for these provocative, unexpected results include the following (O'Meilia et al. 1982; see also above):

- Steers on pastures with prairie dogs consumed a higher proportion of forbs than steers in control pastures, and protein content is typically higher for forbs than for grasses.
- Plants on pastures with prairie dogs matured slowly because of repeated defoliation, and therefore had higher concentrations of protein, and were more digestible, than more mature plants of the same species in control pastures.
- Feces and urine of prairie dogs fertilized the plants at colony-sites.

Table 5.6. Average availability and consumption of forage (kilograms per hectare) on pastures with and without prairie dogs near Woodward, Oklahoma. Reference: O'Meilia et al. 1982.

Year	*Treatment*	*Grass*	*Forbs*	*Total*
1977				
	Steers only			
	Availability	1469	131	1600
	Consumption	1184	98	1282
	Percent consumption	81%	75%	80%
	Prairie dogs and steers together			
	Availability	875	141	1016
	Consumption	830	134	964
	Percent consumption	95%	95%	95%
1978				
	Steers only			
	Availability	924	80	1004
	Consumption	853	75	928
	Percent consumption	92%	94%	92%
	Prairie dogs and steers together			
	Availability	534	136	670
	Consumption	513	132	645
	Percent consumption	96%	97%	96%

Table 5.7. Annual gain in body mass (kilograms per individual) of cattle in pastures with and without prairie dogs near Woodward, Oklahoma. Numbers shown are averages ±1 standard deviation; 1 kilogram is equivalent to 2.2 pounds. Sample size was six steers per treatment each year; differences between groups were not statistically significant either year. Reference: O'Meilia et al. 1982.

	Annual gain in body mass (kilograms)	
Years	*Prairie dogs absent*	*Prairie dogs present*
1976–77	162.3 ± 13.4	148.8 ± 22.8
1977–78	138.5 ± 11.8	130.7 ± 21.3

One problem with O'Meilia et al.'s (1982) experimental design is that small sample sizes (six steers per treatment) coupled with large variation in gains in body mass might have precluded statistically significant results. Another problem is that cattle in the experimental pastures were confined to grazing amongst prairie dogs—a highly artificial condition. Finally, O'Meilia et al.'s colony-sites were only three years old when grazing trials were initiated. Time since colonization was therefore too short for large shifts in plant species composition that typically have occurred at older colony-sites. More field studies are necessary for a better understanding of the effects of prairie dogs on livestock.

In summary: one model indicates that ungulates might benefit by foraging at prairie dog colony-sites because of higher-quality forage there (Vanderhye 1985). Another model indicates, however, that for every 20 hectares (49 acres) inhabited by prairie dogs in a 2,100-hectare (5,189 acre) pasture, the carrying capacity diminishes by about two cow-calf units (Uresk and Paulson 1988). In a field study, body mass of cattle that fed exclusively at colony-sites did not differ from body mass of cattle that fed exclusively away from colony-sites (O'Meilia et al. 1982). Large-scale field studies are necessary to clarify the effect of prairie dogs on livestock. With so much controversy and so many economic implications, the paucity of such studies is disappointing.

Summary

- Despite over a century of controversy, we still cannot accurately determine the effect of prairie dogs on the raising of domestic livestock.

- Prairie dogs and livestock consume many of the same native species of graminoids and forbs. Competition does not necessarily occur simply because two species use the same resource, however. Unfortunately, competition is difficult to document under natural conditions. In the absence of such documentation, it nonetheless seems logical to conclude that dietary overlap adversely affects livestock, or both livestock and prairie dogs, at least under some circumstances.
- Via consumption and clipping, prairie dogs reduce the quantity of several plant species that livestock otherwise could consume, and plant species less palatable to livestock usually increase over time at colony-sites. Older colony-sites, with little available biomass of graminoids, sometimes become unsuitable for grazing by livestock. On the other hand, prairie dogs in some areas prevent the establishment of woody plants such as honey mesquite and thereby improve the habitat for livestock.
- Partially offsetting the decrease in quantity of forage for livestock at prairie dog colony-sites is an increase in quality of forage, especially at younger, grass-dominated colony-sites (or in young sections of old colony-sites). Specifically, plants at young colony-sites have more protein, and are more digestible, than the same plants away from colony-sites. The negative effect on raising livestock thus might not be as large as would be predicted solely from either the amount of forage that prairie dogs consume and clip, or the area of rangeland inhabited by colonies.
- Large-scale field studies—involving numerous pastures, with and without prairie dogs, in different types of grassland—are necessary to clarify the effects of prairie dogs on domestic livestock. With so much controversy and so many economic implications, the paucity of such studies is disappointing.

Acknowledgments

NSF Grant DEB-0217631 to the Shortgrass Steppe Long Term Ecological Research Project at Colorado State University supported preparation of this chapter.

PART II

Why Have So Many Prairie Dogs Disappeared?

John L. Hoogland

We will be better able to conserve prairie dogs if we can understand those factors that have led to their drastic decline in population size over the last 200 years. The next seven chapters summarize how poisoning, recreational shooting, conversion of colony-sites to cropland, and plague have ravaged colonies. This information will help politicians, conservation biologists, and wildlife managers to make shrewd decisions regarding the conservation of prairie dogs—and to avoid mistakes of the past.

Because prairie dogs are so conspicuous, tracking their numbers should be easy. Unfortunately, however, not all residents of a colony are aboveground and visible at the same time. Further, determining the area inhabited by a colony of prairie dogs is elusive. Even if we can somehow obtain a good estimate, the area does not accurately predict how many individuals live there because the density of prairie dogs varies enormously. Finally, the geographic range of prairie dogs is vast, extending from southern Canada to northern Mexico. In Chapter 6, Dean Biggins, John Sidle, David Seery, and Andrea Ernst summarize the numerous methods for counting prairie dogs and for determining the area inhabited by prairie dogs at local and larger scales. Biggins et al.'s synopsis should help wildlife managers to decide which strategies are best for different objectives.

Is it really true that all ranchers and farmers of the western United States disdain prairie dogs, and that people everywhere else cherish them? In Chapter

7, Berton Lamb, Rich Reading, and Bill Andelt summarize current opinions about prairie dogs. Unless we understand how people think about prairie dogs, we cannot hope to change myths and misconceptions that have persisted for generations.

Staggering, indeed, are the numbers of prairie dogs—and the numbers of other species that live at prairie dog colony-sites—that have been killed by poisoning over the last 150 years. In 1923 alone, for example, poisoning devastated 1.5 million hectares (3.7 million acres) inhabited by prairie dogs. From 1903 through 1912, poisoning killed 91% of Colorado's prairie dogs; over the next eleven years, poisoning killed another 31 million prairie dogs in Colorado. In many regions in the early 1900s, the objective of poisoning was complete extermination. In Chapter 8, Steve Forrest and Jim Luchsinger explain these and other disturbing aspects of poisoning. In many respects, Chapter 8 is depressing. In one respect, however, Chapter 8 offers encouragement: if prairie dogs are so resilient that they can withstand more than 100 years of intense poisoning, then finding a solution to ensure their long-term survival should be easy.

In theory, because the prairie dog is a keystone species of the grassland ecosystem whose current numbers are less than 2% of former numbers, poisoning of prairie dogs should never again be necessary. In practice, however, poisoning continues (Figures Part II.1 and Part II.2). Because the purchase and

Figure Part II.1. All-terrain vehicle (ATV) modified for the distribution of oats poisoned with zinc phosphide. The large boxes on each side distribute toxic oats via a mechanism operated from the handlebar. Photo by David Stern.

Figure Part II.2. Victim of toxic oats. Most victims die underground, but this prairie dog expired aboveground one day after distribution of oats poisoned with zinc phosphide at its colony-site. Photo by David Stern.

dispensing of poisons are expensive and because prairie dog numbers usually increase so rapidly after control, Bill Andelt notes in Chapter 9 that the costs of poisoning often exceed the benefits. Andelt also points out that the limitation or postponement of grazing by domestic livestock might deter colonization of new areas by prairie dogs, and also might inhibit expansion of extant colonies—so that poisoning will be unnecessary.

Besides prairie dogs, toxicants kill other animals that consume poisoned bait at colony-sites. Further, fumigation kills not only prairie dogs, but also all other organisms within targeted burrows. Finally, by removing prairie dogs, poisons adversely affect the many plants and animals that depend on prairie dogs for survival. For these reasons, Steve Forrest and Jim Luchsinger (Chapter 8) persuasively argue that poisoning should be the last resort for controlling today's prairie dogs.

Recreational shooting of prairie dogs has been common for more than 100 years. Historically, recreational shooting usually has not seriously depressed populations. In the last decade or so, however, interest in recreational shooting has soared, and marksmen have begun to use high-technology, long-range rifles. Today's losses from recreational shooting therefore can be substantial. In South Dakota in 2000, for example, recreational shooters killed 1.2 million prairie dogs. In Chapter 10, Archie Reeve and Tim Vosburgh discuss the immediate and long-term impacts of recreational shooting on prairie dog populations.

Farmers and ranchers sometimes profit by charging a fee to persons who come from afar to shoot prairie dogs. Consequently, rather than delete colonies via poisoning, landowners sometimes want their colonies to persist and try to protect them from over-shooting. Paradoxically, colonies where marksmen pay to shoot might persist longer than colonies with no shooting—because income from shooting gives farmers and ranchers a reason to conserve, rather than eradicate, colonies. I hesitate to mention this rationale, because shooting prairie dogs is so repugnant to me and many other people. But the reality is that income from allowing others to shoot prairie dogs often might induce farmers and ranchers to maintain colonies on their lands. Allowing landowners to manage their colonies for income via recreational shooting is the sort of compromise that conservation biologists and wildlife managers perhaps should be willing to make to improve the probability of long-term survivorship of prairie dogs—especially because so many of today's prairie dogs live on private lands.

An introduced disease, plague commonly eliminates entire colonies of prairie dogs. *Yersinia pestis*, the bacterium that causes plague, is the same enemy (the "Black Death") that killed about 40% of the human population in Europe between 1347 and 1352. I know all about the devastation of plague, because in 1995 it obliterated not only my study-colony of marked Gunnison's prairie dogs at Petrified Forest National Park in Arizona, but also my study-colony of marked Utah prairie dogs at Bryce Canyon National Park in Utah.

Questions abound regarding plague among prairie dogs. What happens to plague between outbreaks, for example? Does the disease persist quietly among small, nocturnal rodents that live at or near colony-sites, and then suddenly reappear among prairie dogs and annihilate colonies when the conditions are right? Is plague among prairie dogs a threat to humans? Why is plague absent in the eastern one-third of the prairie dog's geographic range? Can we do anything to reduce the impact of plague on prairie dogs? In Chapter 11, Jack Cully, Dean Biggins, and David Seery address these questions and investigate how plague is complicating conservation.

Whether for or against prairie dogs, many persons were troubled or confused by the United States Fish and Wildlife Service (USFWS) designation in 2000 of the prairie dog as a candidate species for the Federal List of Endangered and Threatened Wildlife and Plants (FLETWP). What does this designation really mean, and what are the definitions for key terms such as *endangered*, *threatened*, *warranted-but-precluded*, and *listing priority number*? And what induced USFWS to reverse itself in 2004 by concluding that the prairie dog is no longer a candidate species? For answers and clarification, I have sought help from Rob Manes (Chapter 12) and Nicole Rosmarino (Box to Chapter 12).

CHAPTER 6

Estimating the Abundance of Prairie Dogs

Dean E. Biggins, John G. Sidle, David B. Seery, and Andrea E. Ernst

Prairie dog populations have declined by about 98% over the last 200 years because of recreational shooting, poisoning, loss of habitat, and plague (Chapters 10, 11, 12, and 16). These numbers imply that we know how many prairie dogs existed 200 years ago, and how many remain today. In reality, however, accurate estimates of former and current numbers of prairie dogs are elusive.

One way to estimate numbers of prairie dogs is to count them. Counting prairie dogs is feasible only for small areas, however. For larger areas, an easier way to estimate the number of prairie dogs is to determine the area inhabited by them. When considering trends in the population size of prairie dogs within a particular state or across the former geographic range, biologists always focus on the cumulative area inhabited, from which they can (roughly) estimate the number of prairie dogs.

Early estimates of the abundance of prairie dogs are understandably nonrigorous and incomplete (e.g., the 1804 journals of Lewis and Clark, as reviewed by Burroughs 1961 and Marsh 1984; see also Chapter 16). But recent estimates also reveal the difficulty of estimating abundance. An estimate in 2000 of 38,000 hectares (94,000 acres) inhabited by prairie dogs in Colorado, for example, ballooned to 255,000 hectares (630,000 acres) in 2004 after completion of new, more accurate surveys (Chapter 12). Similarly, an estimate in 2000 of 4,000 hectares (9,884 acres) inhabited by prairie dogs in Oklahoma swelled to 26,000 hectares (64,000 acres) in 2004 (Chapter 12). For its designation of the prairie dog as a candidate species for the Federal List of Endangered and Threatened Wildlife and Plants (FLETWP) in 2000, the United

States Fish and Wildlife Service (USFWS) calculated that prairie dogs inhabited 311,000 hectares (768,000 acres) throughout the entire geographic range (USFWS 2000a; Chapter 12). We now know, however, that prairie dogs inhabit somewhere between 0.5 and 0.8 million hectares (1.2–2.0 million acres) (USFWS 2004; Chapter 16). The larger estimates from 2004 for Colorado, Oklahoma, and the entire geographic range did not result because prairie dog populations proliferated from 2000 through 2004, but rather because the values from 2000 were serious underestimates.

Behavioral ecologists might need to count only the prairie dogs within a single colony to obtain information about demography and population dynamics (e.g., King 1955; Hoogland 1995). Similarly, wildlife managers might need to count only the prairie dogs within one or a few colonies on a national wildlife refuge to determine if grazing by domestic livestock is having a positive or negative impact. Governors, on the other hand, might want to know how many prairie dogs occur throughout their states, so that they can fairly evaluate the disparate claims and petitions of ranchers versus environmentalists. And USFWS officials wanted numbers throughout the entire former geographic range when they deliberated addition of the prairie dog to, and its later removal from, the list of candidate species for FLETWP (USFWS 2002a, 2004; Chapters 12 and 16). Objectives and scale for estimating the abundance of prairie dogs thus vary, and accuracy is always a priority. In this chapter we start by reviewing methods for determining the area inhabited by a colony of prairie dogs and then discuss ways to find and map colonies. We then explain different methods for estimating colony size and colony density.

Determining the Area Occupied by a Colony of Prairie Dogs

One common method to estimate the area occupied by a colony of prairie dogs involves forming a polygon by connecting the outermost burrow-entrances on a map of a colony-site (e.g., King 1955; Tileston and Lechleitner 1966; Hoogland 1995). Unfortunately, however, outermost entrances are difficult for wildlife managers to find, for two reasons. First, outermost entrances usually have small burrow-mounds, or no mounds at all; central entrances, by contrast, usually have large burrow-mounds called dome craters or rim craters (King 1955; Chapter 2). Second, outermost entrances typically are surrounded by tall vegetation (more than 30 centimeters [12 inches] high), whereas central entrances usually are in areas with low vegetation. Further, prairie dogs sometimes forage beyond outermost entrances (King 1955), so what do we really mean by area occupied? Despite these problems, outermost burrow-entrances yield a good estimate of area inhabited by prairie dogs.

The clip-zone is the central area of a colony-site where vegetation is low because of normal foraging, and also because prairie dogs sometimes clip vegetation without consumption—presumably to enhance detection of predators and conspecifics (King 1955; Hoogland 1995; Chapter 2). A second common method to determine the area inhabited by a colony is to map the clip-zone. Such mapping is easier said than done, however. The clip-zone is hard to detect in years of drought, for example, or when grazing by ungulates is especially heavy. Conversely, the clip-zone is also equivocal in years of copious precipitation, when the growth of vegetation outpaces foraging and clipping by prairie dogs. Further, the clip-zone varies with changing seasons and with the density of prairie dogs. Finally, prairie dogs commonly forage far outside the clip-zone (King 1955; Hoogland 1995).

Mainly because prairie dogs forage farther from the clip-zone than from outermost burrow-entrances, clip-zones are less accurate than outermost entrances for estimating a colony's area of occupancy. On the other hand, estimates of area from clip-zones are usually faster, less expensive, and more feasible from afar (e.g., from aircraft or satellites).

Finding and Mapping Prairie Dog Colony-Sites

To monitor the abundance of prairie dogs, biologists map the spatial location (i.e., latitude and longitude) and size of colony-sites. We then import these maps into a Geographic Information System (GIS), so that we can simultaneously view variables such as slope, predominant vegetation, altitude, and annual precipitation in relation to colony boundaries. Biologists commonly use three methods to find and map colony-sites: direct observations, aerial photography, and satellite imagery.

Direct Observations

One way to find prairie dog colonies is to look while walking or driving. Observers on foot or on all-terrain vehicles delineate boundaries of colony-sites by carrying Global Positioning System (GPS) receivers while searching for outermost burrow-entrances (Plumb et al. 2001). Though accurate, the combination of direct observations with GPS is slow, and therefore is only suitable for monitoring colonies within relatively small areas, such as Native American reservations, national parks, and national wildlife refuges.

For larger areas (e.g., entire states), biologists sometimes use direct aerial observations to map prairie dog colony-sites. Observers in airplanes fly line-intercepts and record the flight path and length of lines flown above colonies

(Sidle 1999; Sidle et al. 2001), and then estimate the cumulative area of colonies from the percentage of the flight path intercepted by colony-sites.

Aerial Photography

Remote sensing provides information about the earth's surface from an overhead perspective (Campbell 1996). Methods of remote sensing include cameras mounted on airplanes (Table 6.1) and sensors attached to satellites. Dome craters and rim craters usually are visible in aerial photographs, and clip-zones are sometimes visible as well (Figure 6.1). Burrow-entrances in tall vegetation outside the clip-zone, or burrow-entrances without mounds, usually are not visible from aerial photographs.

Aerial photography is available at multiple scales, with resolution ranging from coarse (e.g., 1:250,000) to fine (e.g., 1:12,000). By varying the type of film and using different kinds of filters (e.g., haze-reducing), wildlife managers can obtain different types of information about prairie dog colony-sites.

Table 6.1. Use of conventional aerial photography to monitor prairie dog colonies.

Source	*Location*	*Type*	*Scale*
Cheatheam 1973	Texas	Black-and-white	1:7,920
Bishop and Culbertson 1976	North Dakota	Black-and-white	Various
Dalstead et al. 1981	South Dakota	Color, Color infrared, Black-and-white	1:15,840
Ernst 2001	Texas panhandle	Color, 35 mm	Ground resolution: 2 meters
Luse and Wilds 1992	Montana	SPOT	1:24,000
Nichols and Daley 1995	Colorado	Color, 35 mm (remote-controlled airplane)	1:4,200
Powell and Robel 1994	Kansas	Color, 35 mm	1:8,000 (enlarged)
Schenbeck and Myhre 1986	South Dakota	Black-and-white, Color infrared	1:16,000
Teitjen et al. 1978	South Dakota	Black-and-white	1:15,840
Uresk and Schenbeck 1987	South Dakota	Black-and-white, Color infrared	1:16,000
Vanderhoof and Robel 1994	Kansas	Color, 35 mm	1:8,000 (enlarged)

Figure 6.1. Aerial photograph of prairie dog colony-site near Lubbock, Texas. The light circles indicate burrow-mounds. Photo by Lubbock County Farm Service Agency.

Aerial photography is fast, inexpensive (sometimes less than $10 per photograph), and suitable for large areas such as entire states. Digital aerial photos provide high resolution and require neither film nor its processing. Computer hardware and software can enhance the utility of aerial photographs for mapping colony-sites. Further, archives of aerial photographs sometimes can provide a mechanism to track the inception, expansion, or demise of certain colonies. Aerial photography has several drawbacks, however. Bare soil and short vegetation away from colony-sites erroneously might indicate the presence of prairie dogs, for example, especially with images of low resolution. Further, delineation of small colony-sites (less than 5 hectares [12 acres]) is sometimes difficult from aerial photographs of low resolution. Perhaps the most important shortcoming is that aerial photographs usually cannot verify the presence of live prairie dogs, and therefore do not allow discrimination between active colony-sites versus colony-sites that recently have lost all prairie dogs (because of plague or poisoning, for example). Such verification requires direct observations from the ground (i.e., "ground-truthing") or from low-flying aircraft.

Satellite Imagery

For investigations across the prairie dog's cumulative geographic range of 160 million hectares (395 million acres) from Canada to Mexico, satellite imagery is more practical and consistent than aerial photography (Table 6.2). The low spatial resolution of traditional satellite systems such as Landsat (28.5-m resolution), Satellite pour l'Observation de la Terre (SPOT, 10-m), and Indian Remote Sensing (IRS, 5-m), however, has been only marginally successful for defining boundaries of colony-sites (Johnson et al. 2004). With one-meter resolution that clearly shows burrow-mounds within the clip-zone, Ikonos satellite imagery potentially solves the problem of defining boundaries (Sidle et al. 2002; Figure 6.2). At present, however, the cost of Ikonos is prohibitive for use throughout the geographic range of prairie dogs. Costs for similar results might decline if private companies launch satellites with one-meter resolution sensors that are independent of, and less expensive than, Ikonos. Like aerial photographs, satellite images cannot discriminate between active colony-sites versus recently deserted colony-sites.

Figure 6.2. Ikonos satellite image of prairie dog colony-site. The light circles indicate burrow-mounds. Image by Space Imaging Incorporated.

Table 6.2. Advantages and disadvantages of several methods for estimating area inhabited by prairie dogs. Accuracy indicates how close our estimate is to the true value. Precision indicates variation among repeated estimates that use the same method.

Technique	*Precision*	*Accuracy*	*Cost*	*Processing time*	*Spatial resolution*	*Required equipment*	*Availability*	*Necessary training*	*Advantages*	*Disadvantages*
Global Positioning System (GPS)	High	High	High	Fast	High	GPS receiver	Not available, but easy to do	Little	High accuracy with good GPS receiver	Time-consuming; land accessibility might be difficult
Aerial transects	Low	Medium	High	Fast	Medium	Airplane, laptop computer, GPS receiver	Not available, but easy to do	Extensive	Coverage of large area	Time-consuming; high variation in data from different researchers
Aerial photography	Medium	Medium	Medium; low for archived imagery	Slow	High	Airplane, specialized software and tools	Available for parts of range only	Extensive	Low cost; high spatial resolution	Time-consuming; photographic quality and coverage both limited
Digital aerial photography	High	Medium	Low	Medium	High	Airplane	Available for entire range	Little	Low cost; high spatial resolution	Easy to lose digital data

Low-resolution satellite imagery	Medium	Low	Low	Slow	Low	Specialized Software	Available for entire range	Extensive	Low cost; extensive archives available	Low spatial resolution; detection of small colonies difficult
High-resolution satellite imagery	High	High	Currently high per image; might decrease over time	Slow	High	Specialized Software	Available for entire range	Little	Clearly defines colony-site boundaries; good for monitoring plots	High cost is prohibitive for entire range

Estimating Colony Size and Colony Density

Colony size is the number of prairie dogs that live in a colony. Biologists sometimes use the term for the number of adults and yearlings within a colony (Hoogland 1995; Chapter 2), but colony size for this chapter includes juveniles as well. Colony density is the number of adults, yearlings, and juveniles per hectare. The exact way to determine colony size and colony density is to mark all colony residents (King 1955; Hoogland 1995). Because catching and marking prairie dogs is so difficult and impractical, however, this method is reasonable for only a small number (less than about five) of small colonies (each with fewer than about 200 residents).

If colony density were constant, then accurate mapping of colony boundaries instantly would tell us colony size. But densities of prairie dogs vary over space and time with natural factors such as precipitation, vegetation, age of colony, and predation (King 1955; Hoogland 1995; Chapters 2 and 3), and with unnatural factors such as plague, recreational shooting, and poisoning (Chapters 8, 10, and 11). Methods for estimating colony size and colony density include visual counts, capture-mark-recapture (CMR), and inferences from number and density of burrow-entrances.

Visual Counts

Counting unmarked individuals is probably the most popular technique for estimating numbers of prairie dogs. With the aid of binoculars or a telescope, wildlife managers usually count prairie dogs from an elevated vantage point (with or without a blind) or from a parked vehicle (Figure 6.3). Jack Cully et al. used visual counts, for example, to document how plague ravaged prairie dog colonies at the Rocky Mountain Arsenal National Wildlife Refuge in the 1980s and 1990s (Chapter 11). The primary problem with visual counts is bias. Specifically, counts are invariably lower than true colony size for two reasons. First, even though prairie dogs are diurnal and spend many daylight hours aboveground, they frequently submerge for various reasons. Mothers commonly submerge into the home nursery burrow to nurse offspring, for example, or into another mother's nursery burrow for infanticide; males also submerge to kill juveniles; both sexes submerge for mating; and both sexes also submerge to escape predators, human observers, excessive heat or cold, and precipitation (Hoogland 1995; Lehmer et al. 2001). Prairie dogs submerged for these reasons will be invisible during a visual count. Second, vegetation and burrow-mounds sometimes conceal prairie dogs that are aboveground, and poor lighting and certain background colors also impede the detection of prairie dogs by wildlife managers (Fagerstone and Biggins 1986; see also Menkens et al. 1990). Count-

Figure 6.3. Visual count. One way to estimate colony size is to count the number of visible prairie dogs. A visual count is always an underestimate because some prairie dogs are underground during the count, and because vegetation and burrow-mounds impede the detection of individuals. This visual count shows four individuals, but is that a fifth prairie dog—or a rock—on the burrow-mound in the distance? Photo by Kathy Boucher of Prairie Dog Specialists.

ing unmarked prairie dogs is easier than catching and marking, but nonetheless is suitable only for small- to medium-scale operations (less than about 100 colonies).

Estimates of the percentage of resident prairie dogs visible to human observers on a typical day range from 55% (Severson and Plumb 1998) to 57% (Biggins et al. 1993) to 86% (Knowles 1986b). Observers thus detect about two-thirds of the residents with each visual count.

Capture-Mark-Recapture (CMR)

Another way to estimate colony size involves capture-mark-recapture (CMR), for which precision varies directly with the number of prairie dogs that are livetrapped. Prairie dogs violate the assumption of equal probability of capture, however, because certain individuals repeatedly enter livetraps, whereas others rarely enter (Hoogland 1995). Consequently, unless they can capture most or all residents within a colony, researchers must incorporate statistical techniques that accommodate unequal probability of capture (Otis et al. 1978; Fagerstone and Biggins 1986; Severson and Plumb 1998; see also Menkens and Anderson 1993). Methods for evaluating data from CMR are available in a program called MARK for personal computers (White and Burnham 1999).

Burrow-Entrances as Indicators of Prairie Dog Abundance

Wildlife biologists disagree about whether the number and density of burrow-entrances correlate with the number and density of prairie dogs. The conclusion of "no reliable index" (King 1955, p. 23) overstates the case, because presence of entrances demonstrates presence (past or current) of prairie dogs, and absence means absence of prairie dogs (Biggins et al. 1993). The following phenomena imply, however, that the correlation between colony size and the number of burrow-entrances must be highly variable (King 1955; Hoogland 1981a, 1995; Chapter 2):

- Individuals within a coterie enter and exit numerous burrow-entrances in a typical day. Further, several individuals of the same coterie commonly spend the night in the same entrance, or enter the same entrance during the day to escape from predators. Thus, each prairie dog does not have its own private burrow-entrance or set of entrances.
- A single burrow commonly has two or more entrances.
- The number of prairie dogs within a colony fluctuates seasonally and annually, but the number of burrow-entrances for that colony remains remarkably stable. At John Hoogland's (1995) study-colony at Wind Cave National Park, for example, the number of adults, yearlings, and juveniles ranged from 92 to 250 over 15 years, but the number of burrow-entrances over the same 15 years was always almost exactly 1,600.

Regarding the inference of colony size from the number of burrow-entrances, critics (Powell et al. 1994; Severson and Plumb 1998) and supporters (Biggins et al.1993; Johnson and Collinge 2004) understandably interpret the utility of the inference relative to their own data and objectives. An inference that Jack King (1955) considered unreliable for his research might satisfy requirements for other research. Similarly, John Hoogland concluded (1995, page 36) that ". . . neither the number nor density of burrow-entrances accurately predicts prairie dog colony size . . . or colony density." But might an "inaccurate" prediction be suitable for other purposes? The debate regarding burrow-entrances versus colony size probably should refocus on whether the correlation is high enough for the specific problem under investigation.

For small-scale research, mapping burrow-entrances within all or part of a single colony-site might be possible (e.g., King 1955; Hoogland 1995). For larger-scale research, one way to estimate the number of entrances at a colony-site is to use strip transects (Biggins et al. 1993). Counting only "active" burrow-entrances might increase the accuracy of estimating colony size from the number of burrow-entrances; Biggins et al. (1993) defined an "active" entrance as one with fresh scat (i.e., fecal pellet that is greenish, black, or dark brown rather than bleached) on the burrow-mound or less than one meter away. Counts of active entrances correlated with the decline of white-tailed prairie dogs at Meeteetse, Wyoming, over ten years (Figure 6.4; see also Biggins and Kosoy 2001a). From colonies with good estimates of colony size from visual counts of residents (adults, yearlings, and juveniles), the average number of active burrow-entrances per black-tailed prairie dog is 3.9 (N = 39

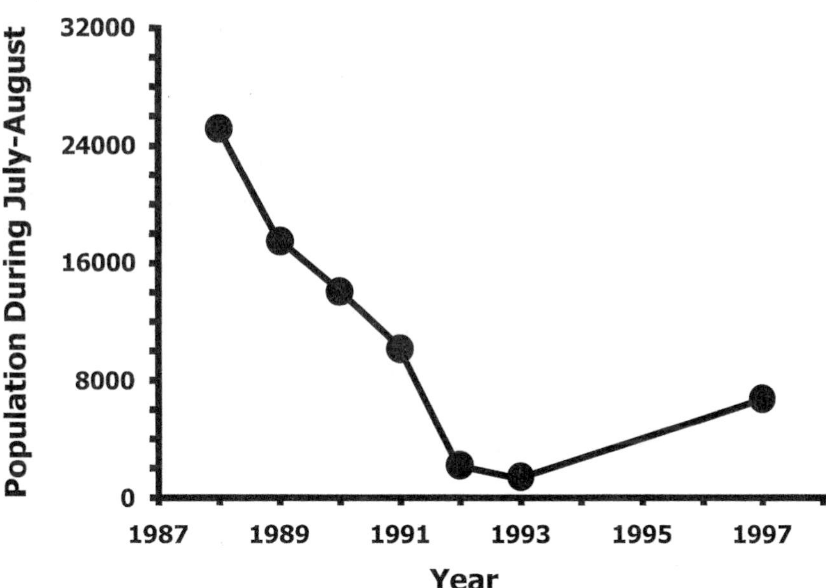

Figure 6.4. The number of adult and juvenile white-tailed prairie dogs in the vicinity of Meeteetse, Wyoming, estimated from strip transect surveys of active burrow-entrances in July and August (from Biggins and Kosoy 2001a). The population, which originally contained several colonies, crashed because of plague. The average number of active burrow-entrances per white-tailed prairie dog is 11.5.

colonies); the average number of active burrow-entrances per white-tailed prairie dog is 11.5 (N = 30 colonies) (Biggins et al. 1993).

Scale evidently affects the ability to detect relationships between densities of prairie dogs and densities of burrow-entrances. We use the term "scale" here to indicate the number of sampled colony-sites and their geographic range, and the ranges of densities for prairie dogs and burrow-entrances. In a large-scale study of 22 colonies in Colorado, density of prairie dogs (estimated from visual counts of adults, yearlings, and juveniles) correlated positively with densities of active burrow-entrances (range of prairie dogs per hectare = 32–120 [13–49 per acre] and range of active entrances per hectare = 100–674 [40–273 per acre]) (Johnson and Collinge 2004). A similar positive correlation was evident in another large-scale study of 39 colonies sampled over a three-state region (range of prairie dogs per hectare = 0.8–54.2 [0.3–21.9 per acre] and range of active entrances per hectare = 0.4–156.4 [0.2–63.3 per acre]) (Biggins et al. 1993). On smaller scales, densities of prairie dogs and burrow-entrances did not significantly correlate in either South Dakota (12 colonies; range of prairie dogs per hectare = 8–41 [3–17 per acre]; Severson and Plumb 1998) or Kansas (5 colonies; range of prairie dogs per hectare = 29–79 [12–32 per acre]; densities of active entrances rated as low, medium, or high; Powell et al. 1994).

The stability of the number of burrow-entrances over time, a disadvantage for tracking short-term changes in colony size (King 1955; Powell et al. 1994; Severson and Plumb 1998), can be an advantage for attempts to evaluate the suitability of habitat. The number of prairie dogs that inhabited (or might inhabit) a colony-site ravaged by plague, for example, sometimes can be estimated from the total number of burrow-entrances—because entrances are sometimes recognizable for as long as five years after prairie dogs have disappeared.

Which method should a conservation biologist, wildlife manager, or environmentalist use to estimate the abundance of prairie dogs? The answer will depend on the size of area under investigation, objectives, budgetary constraints, available equipment, and the necessary level of accuracy.

Summary

- One common method to estimate the area occupied by a colony of prairie dogs involves forming a polygon by connecting the outermost burrow-entrances on a map of a colony-site. A second common method is to map the clip-zone (the central area of a colony-site where vegetation is low because of foraging and clipping).
- To find and map prairie dog colonies, biologists rely on direct observations, aerial photography, and satellite imagery. Direct observations are adequate

for finding and mapping colonies within small areas such as national parks and national wildlife refuges. For larger areas such as entire states or groups of states, observations and photographs from airplanes are appropriate.

- For estimating the area inhabited by prairie dogs throughout their entire geographic range, satellite imagery is more practical than aerial photography. With one-meter resolution that clearly shows burrow-mounds, Ikonos satellite images of colony-sites are excellent. The current cost of Ikonos, however, is exorbitant. Cheaper, similar results might soon be available if private companies launch satellites with one-meter resolution sensors.
- If density of prairie dogs were constant, then mapping boundaries of a colony-site would accurately indicate the number of prairie dogs living there. But densities of prairie dogs vary over space and time with natural factors such as precipitation, vegetation, age of colony, and predation, and with unnatural factors such as plague, recreational shooting, and poisoning.
- The most accurate method for estimating colony size and colony density is to capture all the prairie dogs and mark them. Because this method is so difficult, however, catching and marking is reasonable for only a small number (less than about five) of small colonies (each with fewer than about 200 residents). When wildlife managers can capture some but not all colony residents, we can use various statistical techniques to estimate colony size.
- The second most accurate method for estimating colony size and colony density is to count unmarked prairie dogs. These counts usually indicate only about two-thirds of the resident prairie dogs, however, because some individuals are usually underground for various reasons and because all aboveground individuals are not visible. Counting unmarked prairie dogs is easier than catching and marking, but nonetheless is suitable only for small- to medium-scale operations (less than about 100 colonies).
- Numbers and densities of prairie dogs roughly correlate with numbers and densities of active burrow-entrances, and these correlations are better for large-scale operations (i.e., numerous large colonies spread over several counties, with hefty variation in densities of both prairie dogs and burrow-entrances) than for smaller-scale operations.
- The most appropriate method for estimating numbers of prairie dogs will depend on size of area under investigation, objectives, budgetary constraints, available equipment, and the necessary level of accuracy.

CHAPTER 7

Attitudes and Perceptions About Prairie Dogs

Berton Lee Lamb, Richard P. Reading, and William F. Andelt

We sometimes get the impression that all ranchers and farmers of the western United States hate prairie dogs, and that people everywhere else love them. This generality contains elements of truth, but better documentation of attitudes and perceptions is paramount for good conservation. In this chapter we examine attitudes and perceptions about prairie dogs, and how state and federal actions affect these viewpoints. We also investigate how wildlife managers might respond to attitudes and perceptions about prairie dogs.

Attitudes and Perceptions

People in western states who are directly affected by prairie dogs (i.e., human stakeholders) include ranchers, farmers, environmentalists, public land and wildlife managers, outdoor recreationists, Native Americans, political activists, and residents of some rural and urban areas. Except for those who identify themselves as "environmentalists" or urban residents, most people from other stakeholder groups dislike, or are apathetic about, prairie dogs (Randall 1976a; Dolan 1999; Reading et al. 1999; Lamb and Cline 2003). Because so many people live in urban areas, however, the majority of people express support for prairie dogs—but this support is generally weak. In a survey of residents in eleven states with prairie dogs, for example, 69% said that deciding the fate of prairie dogs was less important than other environmental issues or not an issue at all, whereas 31% said prairie dogs have the same or more importance than other issues (Sexton et al. 2001). The most common perception of prairie dogs among rural people is that they are pests. In 1989, for example, 78% of the general public in western Kansas regarded prairie dogs as pests, and only 18% viewed them as ecologically important (Lee and Henderson 1989; see also Fox-Parrish 2002).

The most important factor that instills a negative attitude toward prairie dogs is direct experience with them (Zinn and Andelt 1999; Lamb et al. 2001). Farmers and ranchers usually express antagonism, for example, but urban dwellers usually like prairie dogs. Some people do not believe that the prairie dog is an important environmental issue, but nonetheless favor a balanced approach. The most important issues identified by citizens regarding prairie dogs are prevention of disease (42%), ranching and farming (25%), and protection of habitat (11%) (Sexton et al. 2001).

The attentive public consists of people who are knowledgeable and politically active about a subject that they view as important (Miller et al. 1996). Almost every issue concerning prairie dogs has an attentive public. Political participation (e.g., signing petitions, writing representatives, belonging to interest groups) is linked to knowledge about prairie dogs, and those who are politically active are more likely to appreciate the importance of conservation (Lamb and Cline 2003). In the sections that follow, we summarize the attitudes and perceptions of several groups regarding prairie dogs, with the understanding that great variation exists within each group.

Ranchers and Farmers

Most ranchers believe that prairie dogs compete with their domestic livestock for food, and that horses and cows break their legs if they step into prairie dog burrows. Consequently, ranchers generally dislike prairie dogs (Chace 1973; O'Meilia et al. 1982; Fox-Parrish 2002; McCain et al. 2002; Chapters 5, 17, and 18). Ninety-seven percent of ranchers in Montana favor reducing prairie dog populations, for example, and 91% believe that financial losses caused by prairie dogs on public lands are unacceptable (Reading and Kellert 1993; see also Kayser 1998). Ranchers in other states have similar perspectives (Lee and Henderson 1989; Wyoming Agricultural Statistics Service 2001; Fox-Parrish 2002).

A minority of ranchers favors the retention of small to medium-sized prairie dog colonies on public grazing-lands (Table 7.1) (Carr 1973; Reading 1993). Further, 23% of Wyoming ranchers, and especially those with ranches of more than 6,000 hectares (14,800 acres), would accept financial compensation for maintaining prairie dog colonies on their domains (Wyoming Agricultural Statistics Service 2001; see also Chapter 14). Many ranchers in Colorado would participate in a similar program administered by the Colorado Division of Wildlife; three counties, however, have threatened to pass

Table 7.1. Percentage of Montana residents who want different percentages of public land to be inhabited by prairie dogs. Reference: Reading et al. 1999.

	Percentage (%) of public lands that should be inhabited by prairie dogs			
Respondents	*0*	*<2*	*2–5*	*>5*
Ranchers	56	30	13	2
Rural residents	36	36	17	11
Urban residents	18	27	25	30
Conservation group members	7	21	27	46

regulations designed to discourage participation in this program (Reading et al. 2002, 2005).

In addition to the obvious financial concerns, ranchers dislike prairie dogs for the following four reasons, some of which have more subtle financial implications:

- Prairie dogs are symbols of poor land stewardship.
- Management of prairie dogs might lead to a loss of control over public and private grazing lands.
- Conservation of wildlife, especially for species protected by the Endangered Species Act, might lead to restrictions on ranching operations.
- Conservation of prairie dogs poses a threat to rural western lifestyles (Carr 1973; Reading and Kellert 1993; Reading et al. 1999, 2002).

Many western farmers also disdain prairie dogs. They worry that prairie dogs consume crops, that burrows drain fields of precious water, and that burrow-mounds damage farm equipment (USFS 1978; Fox-Parrish 2002).

Rural and Urban Residents

As for many other animals (Woodroffe et al. 2005), protecting prairie dogs is more important to suburban and urban residents than to rural residents (Table 7.2). Of the residents of Fort Collins, Colorado, who live adjacent to prairie dogs, 70% report problems with them; 84% of respondents living near prairie dogs, and 68% of the general population, favor management that includes poisoning, but also preservation (Zinn and Andelt 1999). Among the urban, suburban, and rural residents of Boulder County, Colorado, 73% agree, and only 19% disagree, that prairie dogs should be controlled if they damage land; only one-third consider prairie dogs a nuisance and health hazard, whereas 41% consider them important members of the grassland ecosystem (The Public Information Corporation 1998). Wildlife managers are less likely to encounter opposition if they relocate, rather than poison, prairie dogs (Zinn and Andelt 1999; Chapter 13).

Men and Women

Perhaps because women usually have less direct experience with prairie dogs, four studies have shown that women are more likely than men to favor the conservation of prairie dogs (Reading 1993; The Public Information Corporation 1998; Lamb et al. 2001; Fox-Parrish 2002).

Hunters

Hunters are more favorable than nonhunters to the conservation of prairie dogs, for two reasons (Randall 1976b; Reading 1993). First, hunters are more aware that the prairie dog is a keystone species of the grassland ecosystem. Second, many hunters like to shoot prairie dogs. Most hunters, however, oppose the notion of reintroducing prairie dogs into areas where they are currently absent.

Environmentalists

More than two-thirds of the citizens of the United States call themselves environmentalists (Ungar 1994). However, environmentalism is a complicated

Table 7.2. Percentage of respondents living in or near shortgrass prairies who indicated high to low benefits for conserving prairie dogs on public and private lands. Reference: Sexton et al. 2001.

	Benefit from conservation of prairie dogs				
Respondents (%)	*High*		*Neutral*		*Low*
Urban	13	16	28	15	28
Suburban	6	11	22	16	44
Rural	5	9	22	14	51
All	8	12	23	15	42

indicator of attitudes and preferences, and individuals are commonly pro-environment on some issues and anti-environment on others (Guber 2003). Part of this variability reflects the ambiguity of the term "environmentalist," with some people focused on issues such as pollution while others are concerned about loss of biodiversity. Many environmentalists appreciate the keystone role of prairie dogs to the grassland ecosystem, and commonly favor the moral and ethical arguments for conserving prairie dogs as well (Reading and Kellert 1993; Graber et al. 1998; Reading et al. 1999). Most environmentalists expect benefits from careful management, and therefore regard conservation of prairie dogs as a serious issue (Lamb et al. 2001).

Native Americans

Some reservations allow recreational shooting of prairie dogs (Chapter 10), but most Native American tribes nonetheless appreciate the importance of conservation. The Sioux on the Rosebud Reservation in South Dakota, for example, limit the number of licenses for recreational shooting (Graber et al. 1998; Dolan 1999), and the Cheyenne River Sioux have developed a conservation plan that emphasizes the keystone role of prairie dogs (Roemer and Forrest 1996). This emphasis probably results, at least in part, because several Native American tribes harvest prairie dogs for food—and therefore do not want them to disappear (Hoogland 1995; Bourland and Dupris 1998; Graber et al. 1998).

Effect of State and Federal Actions on Attitudes and Perceptions About Prairie Dogs

In response to the disdain of most ranchers and farmers for prairie dogs, many state and federal agencies have actively tried to eliminate prairie dogs—mainly via poisoning (Long 1998; Chapter 8), but also by encouraging recreational shooting (Chapter 10). The United States Fish and Wildlife Service (USFWS) has designated reintroduced populations of black-footed ferrets as "experimental and nonessential"; this designation frees landowners from legal responsibility if ferrets are harmed in the shooting or poisoning of prairie dogs, and consequently makes the landowners more likely to respond favorably to reintroductions. Until 2000, every state with prairie dogs designated them as pests and encouraged eradication. Many state and federal agencies (including the National Park Service) regularly have poisoned prairie dogs as part of "good-neighbor" policies (Chapters 15 and 17). Other states have required control of prairie dogs if a neighboring landowner demands it.

The view of prairie dogs by state and federal agencies is changing. In 2000, for example, USFWS designated the prairie dog as a candidate species for the Federal List of Endangered and Threatened Wildlife and Plants (FLETWP) (USFWS 2000a; Chapter 12). Most states with prairie dogs are now participating in a multi-state conservation plan (Chapter 14). Further, state and federal agencies are considering incentive programs by which landowners will receive financial compensation if they maintain prairie dog colonies on their domains (Wyoming Agricultural Statistics Service 2001; Colorado Division of Wildlife 2002b, but see above; Chapter 14). Such changes in state and federal policies might lead to improved public perceptions of, and attitudes toward, prairie dogs, especially if agency personnel (from agricultural agencies, in particular) embrace these changes (Miller et al. 1990, 1996).

The petition to list the prairie dog as a threatened species (Graber et al. 1998; Chapter 12), and the subsequent designation of it as a candidate species for FLETWP (USFWS 2000a; Chapter 12), probably promoted positive attitudes among some human stakeholders. For other human stakeholders, however, the petition and designation as a candidate species perhaps promoted further disdain, which might have led to increased efforts to eradicate prairie dogs before they were eligible for rigorous protection following listing. We are unaware of quantitative data that support or refute these speculations.

In 2004, USFWS concluded that the prairie dog is no longer a candidate species for FLETWP (USFWS 2004). We suspect that some human stakeholders favor this reversal, and that others oppose it—but once again we have no rigorous information to support our speculation (but see Chapters 17 and 18).

How Should Wildlife Managers Respond to Public Attitudes and Perceptions About Prairie Dogs?

The conservation of prairie dog colonies and associated species such as black-footed ferrets, burrowing owls, and mountain plovers will require developing more positive attitudes and perceptions among key human stakeholders (Reading et al. 1999; Chapter 17). Because personal experience and peer pressure exert the greatest influence on attitudes and perceptions, the best results are likely to come from education programs that are comprehensive and practical, rather than simply informative (Reading and Kellert 1993). Such programs should work to correct misperceptions, and to cultivate positive attitudes (Reading et al. 1999).

Financial incentives for conserving prairie dogs perhaps provide the best hope for changing attitudes and perceptions (Chapters 10 and 14). But simply paying people to allow prairie dogs to persist supports the idea that they are pests (Reading et al. 2005; Chapter 17). We need programs that reward landowners for adopting practices that maintain colonies and promote positive values about prairie dogs. The changing of attitudes that have evolved over many generations will be an onerous task. Thus, even well-designed programs probably will require years before significant changes in attitudes occur. Wildlife managers should work with agricultural and ranching agencies to develop innovative programs that recognize the value of prairie dogs to the grassland ecosystem, but minimize interference with farming and ranching.

Summary of Review of Literature

- Many ranchers believe that prairie dogs compete with their livestock for forage, and that a horse or cow will break a leg after stepping into a prairie dog burrow. Many farmers worry that prairie dogs consume crops, that burrows drain fields of precious water, and that burrow-mounds damage farm equipment.
- Many state and federal agencies actively have tried to eliminate prairie dogs. These actions support the notion that the prairie dog is a pest.
- The petition to list the prairie dog as an endangered species (in 1998), and the subsequent designation as a candidate species for FLETWP (in 2000), probably promoted positive attitudes among some human stakeholders and negative attitudes among others. The later removal of the prairie dog from the candidate list (in 2004) probably has had similar mixed results on attitudes among human stakeholders.
- The conservation of prairie dog colonies and associated species such as black-footed ferrets, burrowing owls, and mountain plovers will require developing more positive attitudes and perceptions among key human stakeholders. Financial incentives for conserving prairie dogs perhaps provide the best hope for changing attitudes and perceptions.
- Wildlife managers should work with agricultural and ranching agencies to develop innovative programs that recognize the value of prairie dogs to the grassland ecosystem but minimize interference with farming and ranching.

CHAPTER 8

Past and Current Chemical Control of Prairie Dogs

Steve C. Forrest and James C. Luchsinger

Prairie dogs were once abundant throughout the Great Plains of North America. They numbered perhaps five billion individuals, and occupied about 30 million hectares (74 million acres) (Bailey 1905; Miller et al. 1994; Johnsgard 2005; Chapter 16). Some colony-sites had diameters of more than 100 kilometers (62 miles) (Messiter 1890; Knowles et al. 2002). Today's cumulative population size for prairie dogs is between 12.5 and 20 million adults and yearlings, less than 5% of their population size of 200 years ago (Chapter 16). Poisoning is a major reason for this steep decline of prairie dog populations. Other factors that have contributed to the decline include loss of habitat, recreational shooting, and plague (Chapters 10, 11, and 16).

In this chapter, we examine chemical control (i.e., poisoning) of prairie dogs, but we do not consider ethical and humane issues regarding control of wildlife in general, and poisoning of prairie dogs in particular. We start by examining how settlement of the western United States affected prairie dogs. We then document past and current levels of poisoning. We investigate the effect of environmental awareness of poisoning, and conclude by speculating on the future role of chemical control.

How Did Settlement of the Western United States Affect Prairie Dogs?

Because they often lack suitable rainfall and access to irrigation, the short- and mixed-grass prairies of the western United States were some of the last areas to be settled. Early pioneers, seeing prairie dogs while traveling to more productive homesteads, often viewed them benignly:

> This interesting little animal . . . never fails to attract the attention of every traveler on the western prairies . . . an approach to one of their settlements is always hailed with delight. (Kennerly 1855, quoted in Oakes 2000)

Sympathy was rare, however, among later pioneers who settled amongst the prairie dogs, and who viewed the rodents as enemies of farming and ranching. Attempts to eliminate prairie dogs began as soon as settlement occurred (Clark et al. 1986b; Oakes 2000). Early methods of control were labor-intensive, and sometimes crude. Plowing was effective, for example, and led to significant loss of prairie dog habitat in states such as Kansas, where about two-thirds of the 13.4 million hectares (33.1 million acres) of suitable habitat changed to cropland after settlement (Choate et al. 1982). Other methods of killing included drowning, shooting, trapping, and poisoning with chemicals such as arsenic, strychnine, potassium cyanide, carbon bisulfide, and concoctions such as "Lee's Peerless Gopher Killer" (Lantz 1903; Edgar and Turnell 1978; Hubbard and Schmidt 1984).

America's farm population grew by 2.2 million from 1900 to 1910. In Montana, for example, cultivated land rose from 100,000 hectares (250,000 acres) in 1909 to 1.4 million hectares (3.5 million acres) in 1919 (Manning 1995). Concurrently, ranchers were fencing large areas of open range into pastures for grazing (Palmer 1901; Oakes 2000). Farmers and ranchers pressured state and federal agencies to eradicate prairie dogs (Lantz 1903; Burnett 1915). The resulting cooperation set the course for managing prairie dogs for the next 50 years.

Organized Chemical Control of Prairie Dogs

Starting in 1900, Texas was the first state to promote organized efforts to eliminate prairie dogs. As Palmer (1899, p. 65) described it:

> In Texas certain stock raisers in the Panhandle proposed to exterminate prairie dogs by means of a bill requiring landowners to destroy all the dogs on their property on or before August 1, 1900, under a penalty not exceeding $100 for each section of land on which the animals were allowed to remain.

The language of this bill and the severity of the penalty indicate that the intent was far-ranging extermination. The bill failed, however, partly due to opposition from owners of large ranches, who would have incurred substantial costs because they had so many prairie dogs to poison (Palmer 1899).

After Texas, other states also initiated programs to poison prairie dogs. The purpose of legislation in Kansas in 1901 was that ". . . nothing short of the entire extermination of the animals should satisfy a community or township" (Lantz 1903, p. 156). Colorado enacted and funded efforts to control prairie dogs with the Pest Inspection Acts of 1911 and 1915 (Gillette 1912; Burnett 1915). As in Texas and Kansas, the goal once again was far-ranging eradication (e.g., Silver 1919).

State programs had varied success. By 1911, prairie dogs were gone from 809,000 hectares (2 million acres) in Kansas (Lantz 1903; Nelson 1920; Choate et al. 1982). From 1903 through 1912, strychnine-treated grain deleted 91% of Colorado's prairie dogs; from 1912 through 1923, more poisoning killed an additional 31 million prairie dogs (Burnett 1919; Bell 1926; Clark 1989; Wuerthner 1997) (Figure 8.1).

Figure 8.1. Prairie dogs killed by poisoning. This collection, from about 1917, resulted even though most poisoned individuals perish underground. Photo courtesy of United States National Archives.

What about federal involvement? In 1896, C. Hart Merriam, first chief of the Bureau of Biological Survey (BBS), bemoaned ". . . the pernicious effects of laws providing bounties for the destruction of mammals and birds" (Merriam 1896). By 1901, however, BBS was receiving hundreds of complaints from western farmers and ranchers, and Merriam recognized that reducing prairie dog populations could provide a mission, and therefore financial support, for BBS (Palmer 1901). Vernon Bailey, a BBS biologist who viewed prairie dogs as an impediment to economic development of the west, became the chief spokesman for the eradication of prairie dogs (Oakes 2000). By 1902, BBS reports described the prairie dog not merely as a species of economic impact, but as a "scourge" to be destroyed (Merriam 1902b). "The Prairie Dog of the Great Plains" (Merriam 1902a) was a "masterful piece of propaganda designed to expand the role of BBS in prairie dog eradication" (Oakes 2000).

The first years of the federal effort to control prairie dogs (1905–1915) involved demonstrating, and marshalling financial support for, different methods of poisoning (Oakes 2000). Starting in 1915, however, BBS's budget included funds specifically for the administration and implementation of eradication (Dunlap 1988; Miller et al. 1996). By 1918, BBS was cooperating with several states to conduct widespread poisoning of prairie dogs, ground squirrels, pocket gophers, and a host of other "economically injurious" species (Burnett 1919; Bell 1921). Thousands of people joined the war against prairie dogs (Merriam 1902b; Swenk 1915; Randall 1976a; Clark 1979) (Figure 8.2). New Mexico BBS agents felt that an aggressive campaign could finish the job of exterminating prairie dogs in the state by 1921 (Oakes 2000).

In 1931, Congress passed the Animal Damage Control Act, which sanctioned partnerships between Predatory Animal and Rodent Control (PARC, the division within BBS responsible for controlling prairie dogs) and states, individuals, and public and private agencies. Additional funding to poison prairie dogs became available through other federal programs during the 1930s (Oakes 2000).

The BBS kept detailed records of chemical control. South Dakota, for example, poisoned approximately 1.2 million hectares (3 million acres) of prairie dogs from 1915 to 1965. During the same period, Montana and Texas poisoned 3.4 and 3.8 million hectares (8.4 and 9.4 million acres), respectively. Arizona poisoned about 0.5 million hectares (1.2 million acres) from 1918 to 1922, and extirpated the prairie dog from the state by 1932 (Alexander 1932; Oakes 2000). Records for some states combined poisoning statistics for all species of prairie dogs, and occasionally with statistics for ground squirrels as well, so that data specifically for black-tailed prairie dogs are elusive. Wyoming, for

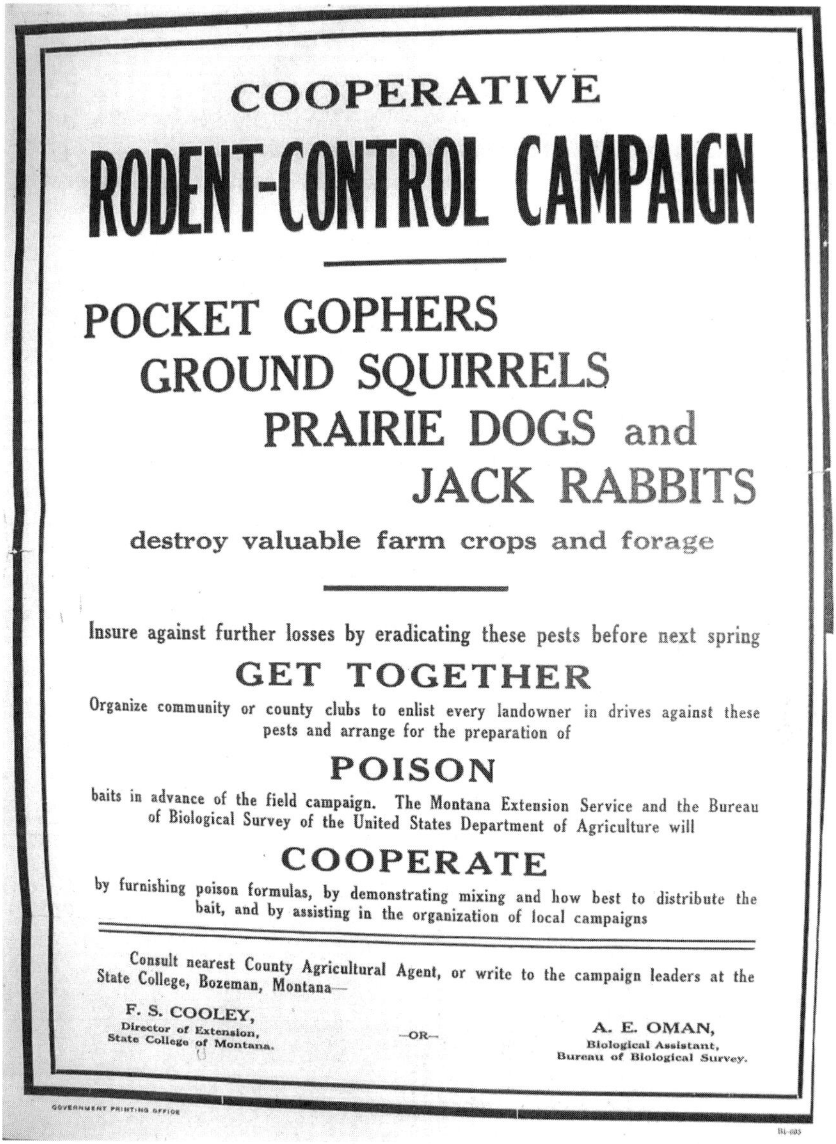

COOPERATIVE

RODENT-CONTROL CAMPAIGN

POCKET GOPHERS
GROUND SQUIRRELS
PRAIRIE DOGS and
JACK RABBITS

destroy valuable farm crops and forage

Insure against further losses by eradicating these pests before next spring

GET TOGETHER

Organize community or county clubs to enlist every landowner in drives against these pests and arrange for the preparation of

POISON

baits in advance of the field campaign. The Montana Extension Service and the Bureau of Biological Survey of the United States Department of Agriculture will

COOPERATE

by furnishing poison formulas, by demonstrating mixing and how best to distribute the bait, and by assisting in the organization of local campaigns

Consult nearest County Agricultural Agent, or write to the campaign leaders at the State College, Bozeman, Montana—

F. S. COOLEY,
Director of Extension,
State College of Montana.

—OR—

A. E. OMAN,
Biological Assistant,
Bureau of Biological Survey.

GOVERNMENT PRINTING OFFICE

Figure 8.2. Montana poster from 1923 that urges participation in poisoning of prairie dogs. Photo courtesy of United States National Archives.

example, reported only combined statistics for white-tailed and black-tailed prairie dogs through 1965.

The total area across all states poisoned from 1915 to 1965 attributable exclusively to black-tailed prairie dogs was more than 12.1 million hectares (30 million acres) (Figure 8.3), and probably was more than 15 million hectares (37 million acres). The peak year was 1923, when poisoning affected 1.5 million hectares (3.7 million acres). Precise estimates for the cost of the war against prairie dogs are unavailable, but the cumulative cost over the years has been billions of dollars.

By 1960, prairie dogs probably inhabited less than 5% of their geographic range of the early 1800s (Berryman and Johnson 1973; Miller et al. 1994). Survivors persevered on lands with low productivity, in areas with poor access, and on scattered public lands (Anderson et al. 1986; Oakes 2000). Most colonies inhabited less than 10 hectares (25 acres), and only a few complexes (i.e., groups of nearby colonies) inhabited more than 2,500 hectares (6,200 acres) (Linder et al. 1972; Chapter 12). Victims of their own success, poisoning

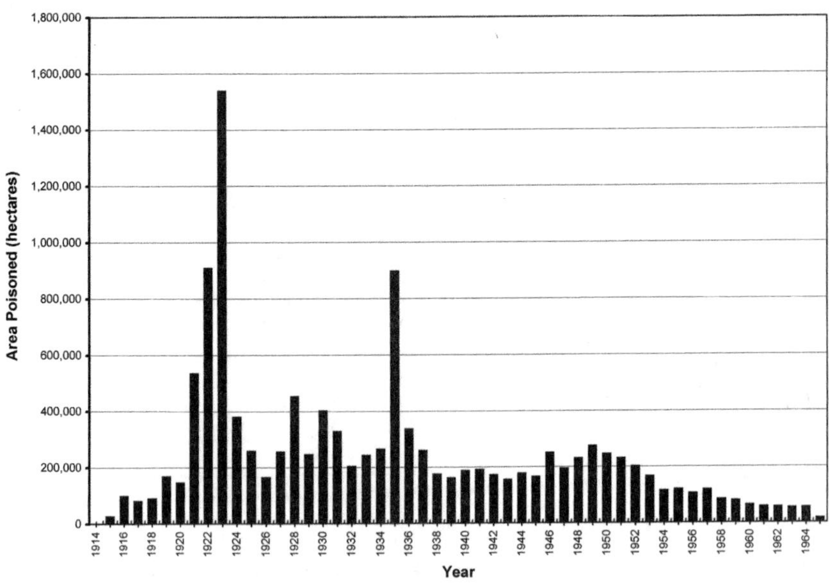

Figure 8.3. Area poisoned annually (by all methods) for elimination of black-tailed prairie dogs from 1915 to 1965 for all states except Wyoming, and including only the years 1918–1935 for New Mexico and 1921–1923 for Colorado. References: Progress reports and summary tables from USFWS and BBS for 1916–1939; state summaries from PARC for 1941–1967; statistical reports 1916–64, Record Group 22, United States National Archives.

programs started to wane. For the first time, federal agencies began to talk about "stabilizing" efforts to control prairie dogs (Berryman and Johnson 1973).

The Effect of Environmental Awareness on the Poisoning of Prairie Dogs

Despite widespread support, some resistance to federal poisoning of prairie dogs was evident from the outset (Jackson 1917; Silver 1919). Opposition usually did not result from concern for prairie dogs in particular or the environment in general, however. Rather, most opponents simply objected to the cost of poisoning, or wanted to avoid entanglements with government-sponsored programs (Oakes 2000). Some Native Americans resisted poisoning prairie dogs on religious grounds (Oakes 2000).

As programs for controlling rodents and predators expanded in the 1920s, some biologists began to question the notion of complete eradication. The American Society of Mammalogists testified before Congress in 1931 against fervid poisoning by BBS—but nothing changed regarding federal regulation of poisoning (Dunlap 1988).

Following World War II, renewed interest in the environment led to greater concern for conservation. The United States Fish and Wildlife Service (USFWS) was becoming increasingly sensitive to shifting public opinion. As one state director put it (Everett Mercer 1961, quoted in Oakes 2000):

> My efforts presently are directed toward seeing that extermination of prairie dogs in this state [New Mexico] will not finally be held by the public to have been brought about by the Bureau of Sport Fisheries and Wildlife [BSFW, a division of USFWS].

Rachel Carson's *Silent Spring* (1962) ". . . awakened the [general] public to the idea of the interdependence of man and other organisms with which he shares the earth" (Matthiessen 1987). Soon thereafter came the Leopold Report (1964), an influential critique of PARC. While conceding the occasional utility of toxicants to control prairie dogs, Leopold (1964) cautioned against excessive poisoning.

Discovery of black-footed ferrets in South Dakota occurred in 1964, just as USFWS was about to declare the species extinct (Miller et al. 1996). *Must They Die?* (McNulty 1971) publicized the ongoing poisoning of prairie dogs, and the disastrous consequences of such poisoning for ferrets. Many farmers and ranchers still wanted to eradicate prairie dogs (e.g., Carr 1973), but public sentiment was shifting toward responsible conservation.

Before and during World War II, the preferred toxicants for prairie dogs were carbon bisulphide and strychnine (Hansen 1993)(Table 8.1). After the war came Compound-1080, which is tasteless, extremely lethal, and highly effective (Atzert 1971). Both Compound-1080 and strychnine have undesirable consequences, however: nontarget animals die after consuming baits treated with either poison, and strychnine also kills scavengers that consume poisoned prairie dogs (Cain et al. 1972; Berryman and Johnson 1973). In 1972, President

Table 8.1. Toxicants formerly and currently used to eliminate prairie dogs. References: Lantz 1903; Matschke and Hegdal 1985; Uresk et al. 1986; Hyngstrom and Virchow 1994; USEPA 1996, 1998; unpublished records of BBS.

Poison	*Method of use*	*Period of use*	*Typical mortality (%)*	*Annual amount used (kilograms/ year)*	*Comments*
Strychnine	with grain	1880s–1988	83–90	495,000 (grain + strychnine, 1935)	Use limited by court injunction
Potassium cyanide/ calcium cyanide	with grain	1880s–1950s	Variable	Unknown	Replaced by more effective poisons
Carbon bisulphide	fumigant	1880s–1950s	Unknown	Unknown	Replaced by more effective fumigants
Compound-1080 (sodium fluoroacetate)	with grain	1940s–1990	98	47,000 (grain + 1080, 1963)	Prohibited for use as rodenticide by USEPA in 1990
Red squill	with grain	1950s–1960s	Unknown	5,000 (1959)	Replaced by more effective poisons
Aluminum phosphide/ magnesium phosphide	fumigant	1950s–present	85–95	2,700–4,000 (1987–1996)	Currently in use
Gas cartridges	fumigant	1950s–present	95	Unknown	Currently in use
Zinc phosphide	with grain	1976–present	95	25,000 (1990) 6,400 (2001)	Currently in use

Richard Nixon issued Executive Order 11643, which banned the use of toxicants on public lands or via federal programs (Nixon 1972; Berryman and Johnson 1973; Wagner 1988). Unfortunately for prairie dogs, Nixon's order applied only to federal lands and federal use of toxicants. Compound-1080 usage by states, cities, and individuals increased by a factor of 20 from 1972 through 1988. Usage of strychnine by non-federal agencies also increased from 1972 through 1988.

Other factors in the 1970s also affected the poisoning of prairie dogs. The Endangered Species Act of 1973 provided legal protection for the black-footed ferret and thereby kindled interest and concern for prairie dogs. Protection for ferrets included restrictions from the United States Environmental Protection Agency (USEPA) regarding use of certain toxicants for prairie dogs; some poisons, for example, were available only to certified applicators. Surveys for ferrets prior to poisoning prairie dogs became prerequisite when federal money or federal lands were involved. Surveys added "considerable costs to control operations" (Hansen 1993), and therefore discouraged poisoning. Efforts to save ferrets thus promoted, albeit indirectly, the conservation of prairie dogs.

Current Level of Chemical Control

Today, poisoning most often occurs when people perceive that prairie dogs are competing with domestic livestock for forage; interfering with agriculture; threatening human health via transmission of diseases such as plague and monkeypox; or interfering with the commercial development of land. Poisoning is most commonly cyclic, but occasionally continues for many consecutive years at the same colony-sites (Figure 8.4).

The effects of one-time or infrequent poisoning of prairie dogs are usually short-lived, because colonies frequently recover almost completely within only two to three years after a single poisoning (Chapter 9). These recoveries result because it is difficult to obtain 100% mortality in a single treatment. People dispensing poison inadvertently might miss certain sections of the target colony-site, for example, and certain prairie dogs avoid toxic bait for inexplicable reasons. Further, prairie dogs survive and reproduce well under the conditions of low population density and reduced competition that follow poisoning of some, but not all, colony residents (Knowles 1986a; Radcliffe 1992; Chapter 3). Systematic poisoning at the same colony-sites over time can effectively eliminate prairie dogs regionally, however, as it did in Arizona and southwest New Mexico (Alexander 1932; Oakes 2000).

Repeated poisoning also can lead to the decline of prairie dogs in another, more subtle way. In Kansas, for example, the total area inhabited by prairie dog

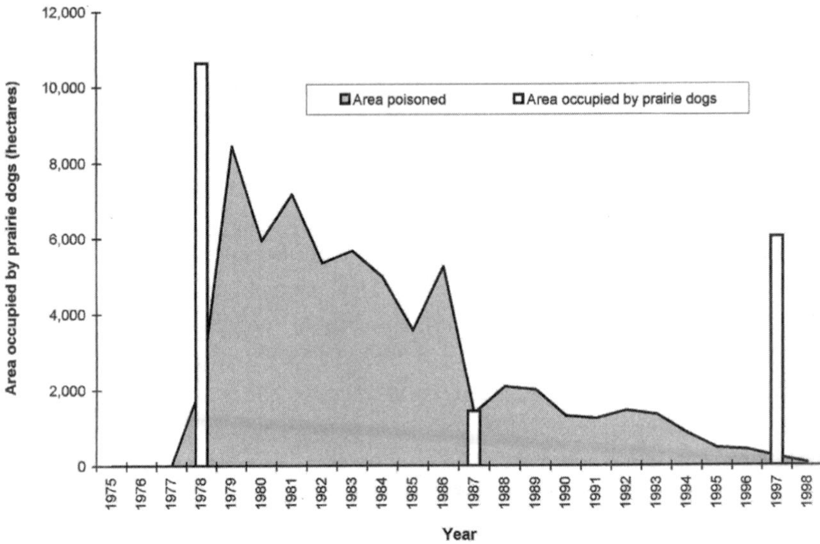

Figure 8.4. Area inhabited by prairie dogs versus area poisoned on the Buffalo Gap National Grassland, 1977–1997. References: M. Peterson, Supervisor, Nebraska National Forest, personal communication, 2005; USFS Annual Prairie Dog Control Reports, Fall River and Wall Ranger Districts, 1995–1998; G. Schenbeck, Nebraska National Forest, personal communication, 2005.

colonies declined by 19% between 1977 and 1991, but the number of colonies increased by 28% (Vanderhoof and Robel 1992). Plague was absent throughout most of Kansas in the 1980s and continues to be absent today (Chapter 11), so the decline in area inhabited by prairie dogs probably resulted mostly from poisoning. The pattern observed in Kansas is classic fragmentation: large colonies are broken up into more numerous, more isolated, smaller colonies. Fragmentation of this type increases the probability of local extinctions, because small, isolated colonies are vulnerable to random environmental variation, genetic drift, and inbreeding (Wilcox and Murphy 1985; Miller et al. 1996; Lomolino and Smith 2003; Chapter 2). As colonies disappear, the probability of extinction for remaining colonies increases because immigration—and hence the arrival of both new genetic variation and potential mates who are not close kin—becomes more unlikely as intercolonial distance increases (Garrett and Franklin 1988; Chapter 3).

Since 1973, the two most commonly used USEPA-approved toxicants are zinc phosphide (administered via oats or some other grain) and fumigants (administered via insertion into burrows); both toxicants can negatively impact nontarget species (Johnson and Fagerstone 1994; Chapter 9). Fumigants are of two types: tablets that release hydrogen phosphide (also called phosphine) as they dissolve in underground moisture, and gas cartridges that release carbon monoxide following ignition (Chapter 9). Wildlife Services (WS), a division of the Animal and Plant Health Inspection Service (APHIS) and called Animal Damage Control (ADC) before 1997, poisoned about 2.3 million burrow-entrances per year (i.e., 15,000–46,000 hectares [37,000–114,000 acres] per year) from 1990 through 2000 (Figures 8.5–8.7).

What Is the Future of Chemical Control?

For more than 100 years, poisoning has been the primary method for eradicating prairie dogs. The magnitude of today's poisoning is low relative to poisoning over the last century, however, due to simple numerics: because today's cumulative population size is less than 5% of the former population size, comparatively few prairie dogs are left to poison. Levels of poisoning should remain relatively low for the following reasons:

- Economic incentives might increase tolerance of prairie dogs on private lands and therefore discourage poisoning (Chapters 10, 14, 17, and 18).

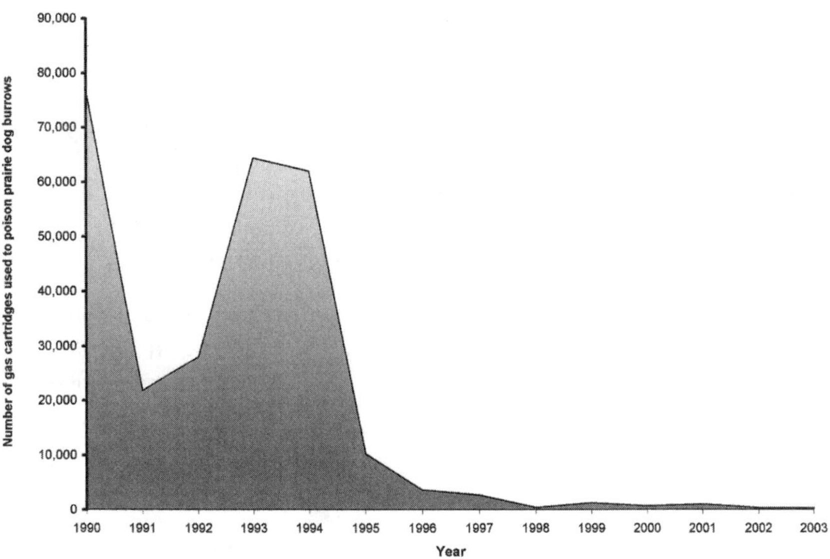

Figure 8.5. Number of gas cartridges (ignitable fumigants) used or distributed by WS to control black-tailed prairie dogs, 1990–2003. References: USDA 2003 and unpublished WS reports, 1990–1995.

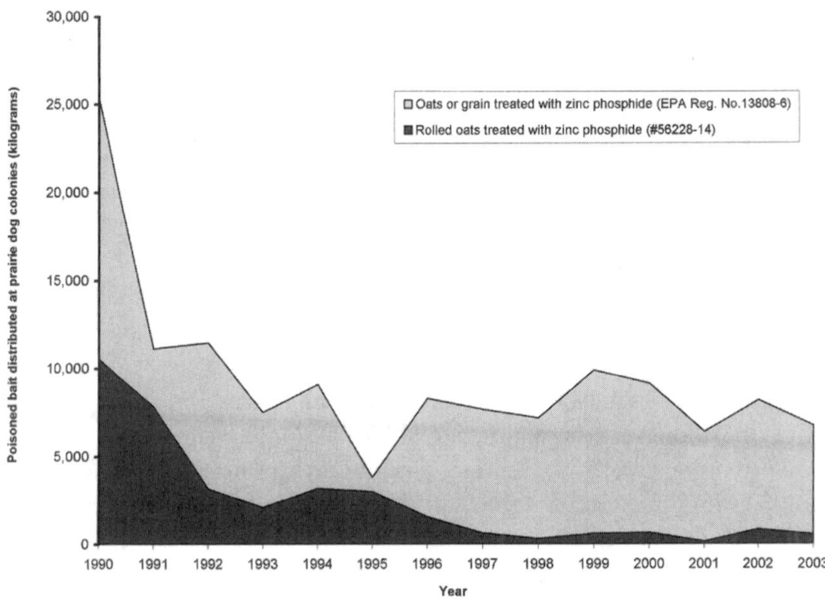

Figure 8.6. Amount of bait poisoned with zinc phosphide used or distributed by WS to control prairie dogs, 1990–2003. References: USDA 2003 and unpublished WS reports, 1990–1995.

- Federal and state lands probably will play a new, greater role in the conservation of prairie dogs and species that associate with them (Chapters 15 and 16), so that poisoning on these lands will be less likely.
- Better conservation of prairie dogs on federal and state lands should lead to fewer conflicts with agricultural and ranching operations on private lands, and consequently fewer requests for poisoning (Chapter 16).

Despite these trends regarding the magnitude of today's level of poisoning relative to levels of poisoning over the last century, poisoning on federal, state, and private lands has increased since August 2004 following the removal of the prairie dog from the candidate list for the Federal List of Endangered and Threatened Wildlife and Plants (FLETWP) (Chapters 12 and 18). The future of chemical control for the management of prairie dogs is thus hard to predict.

Besides prairie dogs, toxicants kill other animals that consume poisoned bait at colony-sites. Nontarget victims include granivorous (i.e., seed- and grain-eating) birds and insects, and also granivorous mammals such as various species of ground squirrels, chipmunks, and rabbits. In addition, scavengers sometimes die after consuming poisoned prairie dogs (Deisch et al. 1989;

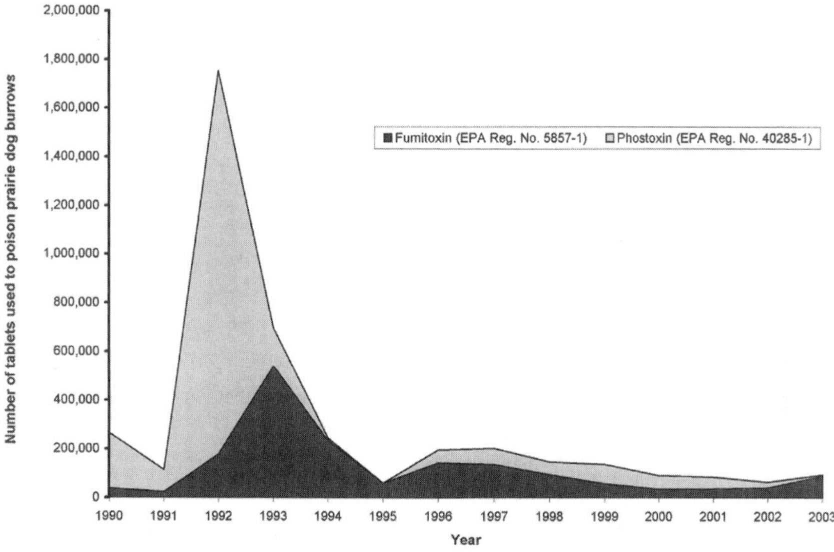

Figure 8.7. Number of aluminum phosphide tablets (fumigants) used or distributed by WS to control black-tailed prairie dogs, 1990–2003. Fumitoxin and Phostoxin are trade names for aluminum phosphide tablets. References: USDA 2003 and unpublished WS reports, 1990–1995.

Sharps and Uresk 1990; Johnson and Fagerstone 1994; Chapter 9). Further, fumigation kills not only prairie dogs, but also all other organisms within targeted burrows (Chapter 9). Finally, by removing prairie dogs, toxicants and fumigants adversely affect the many plants and animals that depend on prairie dogs for survival (Chapter 4). As for other animals sometimes regarded as pests (Woodroffe et al. 2005), poisoning should be the last resort for controlling today's prairie dogs.

Summary

- Early settlers of western North America considered prairie dogs as enemies of farming and ranching. Early methods for elimination included drowning, shooting, trapping, and poisoning with chemicals such as arsenic, strychnine, potassium cyanide, and carbon bisulfide.
- In 1900, Texas was the first state to organize efforts to eliminate prairie dogs. By the 1920s, federal programs to poison were operational in every state with prairie dogs.

- *Silent Spring* (1962), the Leopold Report (1964), and *Must They Die?* (1971) stirred opposition to the poisoning of prairie dogs. President Richard Nixon's Executive Order 11643 in 1972 slowed poisoning of prairie dogs on federal lands, as did protection of black-footed ferrets in 1973 via the Endangered Species Act.
- The effects of one-time or infrequent poisoning of prairie dogs are usually short-lived. Colonies commonly recover almost completely within only two to three years after a single poisoning—because it is difficult to obtain 100% mortality in a single treatment, and because prairie dogs survive and reproduce so well under the conditions of low population density and reduced competition that follow poisoning of some, but not all, colony residents.
- Since 1973, the two most commonly used USEPA-approved toxicants have been zinc phosphide (administered via oats or some other grain) and fumigants (administered via insertion into burrows).
- The magnitude of today's poisoning is low relative to poisoning over the last century due to simple numerics: because today's cumulative population size is less than 2% of the former population size, comparatively few prairie dogs are left for poisoning.
- Despite the trends regarding the magnitude of today's level of poisoning relative to levels over the last century, poisoning has increased over the last year following the removal of the prairie dog from the candidate list for FLETWP. The future of chemical control for the management of prairie dogs is thus hard to predict.
- Besides prairie dogs, toxicants kill other animals that consume poisoned bait at colony-sites. Further, fumigation kills not only prairie dogs, but also all other organisms within targeted burrows. Finally, by removing prairie dogs, toxicants and fumigants adversely affect the many plants and animals that depend on prairie dogs for survival. For these reasons, poisoning should be the last resort for controlling today's prairie dogs.

Acknowledgments

We thank Sherm Blom, Guy Connolly, Kathy Fagerstone, Jonathan Proctor, David Roemer, Al Steuter, and two anonymous reviewers for help with our manuscript. SF thanks Jonathan Proctor and Dave Roemer for sharing data from a previously unpublished manuscript. For financial assistance, SF thanks the World Wildlife Fund (J. M. Kaplan Fund) and USFWS; JL thanks The Nature Conservancy and USDA-APHIS-WS.

CHAPTER 9

Methods and Economics of Managing Prairie Dogs

William F. Andelt

People have been managing prairie dogs for more than 100 years (Chapter 8). In this chapter I focus on the methods and economics of managing prairie dogs, but do not consider ethical and humane issues regarding various methods of elimination. First I summarize methods that do and do not work well. I then discuss how prairie dog colonies quickly repopulate after control. Finally, I investigate whether poisoning prairie dogs is worth the cost for farmers and ranchers, and then offer some recommendations.

Methods That Do Not Work Well for Managing Prairie Dogs or Are Too Expensive

Alteration of Habitat

Treatment with 2,4-D (a herbicide) reduces the number of forbs and shrubs at colony-sites, but evidently does not reduce body mass or numbers of prairie dogs (Fagerstone et al. 1977). Similarly, the following items do not significantly reduce numbers of prairie dogs (Knowles 1987): piles of logs or rocks; freshly cut ponderosa pines; telephone poles (to facilitate perching by predatory birds such as ferruginous hawks); and hay bales.

Predator Odors

Cage litter from black-footed ferrets placed in burrow-entrances evidently does not affect either the survivorship or reproduction of prairie dogs (Andelt and Beck 1998).

Translocation

Wildlife managers sometimes reduce the population size of prairie dogs in one area by moving individuals to another area (i.e., translocation; Chapter 13). A paucity of nearby suitable recipient-sites for translocated prairie dogs often limits the utility of this form of management, however, as does the high cost. Though translocations are usually impractical for reducing numbers of prairie dogs in one area, they are crucial for initiating colonies in other areas (Chapter 13).

Contraceptive Agents

With growing opposition to the use of lethal methods for controlling prairie dogs (Miller et al. 1990, 1994; Roemer and Forrest 1996; Chapter 8), contraceptive agents might provide an alternative. Immunocontraceptives (i.e., chemicals that involve the immune system to deter conception) might limit prairie dog reproduction, for example. Immunocontraceptives administered via treated bait, however, are quickly denatured and inactived by digestion before they can be absorbed into the circulatory system (Miller et al. 1998). For immunocontraceptives to be useful for conservation, researchers must find an easy, inexpensive, effective method for administering them to wild prairie dogs.

Administered via oats, diethylstilbestrol (DES) is a synthetic estrogen that dramatically reduces reproduction among prairie dogs by deterring the implantation of, and increasing the resorption of, embryos (Pfeiffer and Linder 1973; Garrett and Franklin 1981, 1983). Because DES accumulates in tissues, however, one detrimental consequence is that it might inhibit the reproduction of predators and scavengers that consume DES-treated prairie dogs (Fagerstone and Ramey 1996). Contraceptive agents such as DES are currently unavailable for public use.

In theory, sterilization of 100% of male prairie dogs within a colony should preclude all reproduction. In practice, however, sterilization of all males is difficult and expensive. Surgical sterilization of as many as 50% of males within a colony does not significantly reduce reproduction (Schwartz 2002), because females in coteries with sterilized males mate with fertile males from other coteries (Hoogland 1995).

Gas Exploding Devices

The Rodentorch (Mertens' Repair Shop, Orovada, Nevada) and the Rodex-4000 (Rodex Industries, Midvale, Idaho) are explosive devices for controlling prairie dogs. Both mechanisms inject a gaseous mixture of propane and oxygen through tubes inserted into the burrow-entrance, and then ignite the mixture to create an explosion within the tunnel. Gas exploding devices can reduce numbers of prairie dogs by more than 50% (Sullins and Sullivan 1992; Randy Buehler, Logan County Pest Control District, Sterling, Colorado, personal communication, 2002). The Rodentorch and Rodex-4000 are expensive and hazardous, however, and are illegal in some states.

Visual Barriers

Prairie dogs depend on low vegetation that allows visual contact with coterie members, identification of trespassers from other coteries, and detection of predators (Hoogland 1995). Barriers that diminish visibility sometimes reduce use of an area by prairie dogs (Franklin and Garrett 1989), but other times they do not (Hygnstrom 1995). Most barriers are expensive and require regular maintenance (e.g., because of wind or rubbing by ungulates), and thus are usually impractical for use in pastures with domestic livestock.

Methods That Do Work Well for Managing Prairie Dogs

Limitation or Postponement of Grazing by Livestock

Prairie dogs commonly prefer areas with intensive grazing by livestock and avoid areas with taller vegetation (Allan 1954; Koford 1958; Smith 1967; Licht and Sanchez 1993). One implication of this finding is that prairie dog colonies can be an effect, as well as a cause, of reduced availability of forage (Chapter 5). Another implication is that limitation or postponement of grazing by livestock will deter colonization of new areas by prairie dogs—especially in mixed-prairies with tall and mid-height grasses, versus the shortgrass steppe with lower vegetation (Chapter 5)—and also will inhibit expansion of extant colonies (Uresk et al. 1981; Knowles 1986b; Cincotta et al. 1987a,b; Truett and Savage 1998). Numerous lines of circumstantial evidence support both these implications (e.g., Koford 1958; Snell and Hlavachick 1980; Snell 1985; Cable and Timm 1988; Knowles and Knowles 1994; Chapter 5).

If limitation of grazing deters the initiation of new prairie dog colonies and the expansion of current colonies, then why don't more ranchers practice such limitation? At least three reasons are important. First, as noted above, the benefits of limiting grazing are most pronounced in tall- and mid-grass prairies—but the benefits are probably meager for many ranches on the short-grass prairie. Second, many ranchers do not believe the notion that heavy grazing by livestock can improve the habitat for prairie dogs (Chapters 5 and 7). The third reason concerns short-term versus long-term perspectives. In a particular year, a rancher might realize a higher profit if he or she allows livestock to heavily forage throughout the ranch—so that the number and size of prairie dog colonies probably will increase while vegetation for livestock decreases. Over many years, however, the same rancher might earn more money by limiting or postponing grazing in many areas—so that the number and size of colonies will remain the same or decrease while vegetation for livestock increases.

We need more research to investigate the feasibility of reducing prairie dog numbers by limiting grazing by livestock. With so many economic implications, and because limiting grazing has few negative side effects for other organisms, the dearth of rigorous information about this method for controlling prairie dogs is perplexing.

Recreational Shooting

Recreational shooting reduces size and density of prairie dog colonies. Recreational shooting is the subject of a separate chapter (Chapter 10), so I will not discuss this issue further.

Zinc Phosphide

The only toxicant registered for use on bait for prairie dogs is 2% zinc phosphide. Baits with zinc phosphide are classified as Restricted Use Pesticides, and landowners must obtain certification from the United States Environmental Protection Agency (USEPA) before using them. Precipitation deactivates zinc phosphide, which is most effective during clear weather with moderate temperatures (Tietjen 1976a), probably because prairie dogs are most active under the same conditions (Hoogland 1995). Zinc phosphide also is more effective when vegetation at colony-sites has become dry and dormant—that is, when natural food is scarce, so that prairie dogs are more likely to consume poisoned bait (Tietjen 1976a). Extermination with zinc phosphide usually is legal only from 1 July through 31 December or 31 January, and therefore does not occur during the periods of mating, gestation, and lactation (Chapter 2).

Prebaiting with untreated oats two to three days prior to baiting with zinc phosphide is a legal prerequisite and is important for maximal elimination of prairie dogs (Tietjen and Matschke 1982). Efficiency of zinc phosphide, measured as percentage of prairie dogs killed, ranges from 66% to 97% after prebaiting (Hygnstrom et al. 1998), but the range is only 30% to 73% without prebaiting (Holbrook and Timm 1985). Highest efficiency involves spreading approximately 4 grams (about 1 heaping teaspoon) of toxic bait at the base of every burrow-mound and near every burrow-entrance (Tietjen 1976b) (Figure 9.1). A typical prairie dog colony-site requires about 400 grams of toxic oats per hectare (6 ounces per acre).

Figure 9.1. Oats treated with zinc phosphide at burrow-entrance. Toxic oats kill not only prairie dogs but also grain-eating insects, birds, and mammals. Photo by David Stern.

Zinc phosphide reacts with acids in the stomach and produces hydrogen phosphide (also called phosphine), a colorless gas that smells like garlic and kills prairie dogs, usually underground. For humans, hydrogen phosphide can cause fatigue, ringing in the ears, vomiting, diarrhea, disorientation, convulsions, paralysis, coma, and sometimes death (Hood 1972; Degesch America 1999).

Zinc phosphide evidently does not accumulate in fat or muscle tissue, and therefore, in theory, should not harm scavengers that consume carcasses of poisoned prairie dogs (Bell and Dimmick 1975; Schitoskey 1975; Hill and Carpenter 1982; Matschke et al. 1992). Zinc phosphide also does not seem to harm certain species of birds and mammals that frequent prairie dog colony-sites (Tietjen 1976b; Uresk et al. 1987; Deisch et al. 1990; Apa et al. 1991). Zinc phosphide does, however, kill animals other than prairie dogs that consume poisoned bait at colony-sites. Nontarget victims include granivorous (i.e., seed- and grain-eating) birds and insects, and also granivorous mammals such as various species of ground squirrels, chipmunks, and rabbits (Deisch et al. 1989; Sharps and Uresk 1990; Johnson and Fagerstone 1994; Chapter 8). Further, by eliminating prairie dogs, zinc phosphide adversely affects the nontarget plants and animals that depend on prairie dogs for survival (Chapter 4).

Fumigants

Landowners sometimes eliminate prairie dogs by using fumigants, which are of two types: aluminum phosphide tablets and gas cartridges. Fumigants are most lethal to prairie dogs when used in moist soils (to reduce dissipation of gases) in early spring (Ramey and Schafer 1996). Because they are so expensive, fumigants are most cost-effective as a follow-up to toxic baits.

Fumigation with aluminum phosphide—which, like zinc phosphide, is a Restricted Use Pesticide—involves insertion of two tablets into a burrow-entrance, followed by plugging the entrance with newspaper and moist soil. Prairie dogs die in response to hydrogen phosphide, which is produced when the tablets react with moisture from the air or soil. Aluminum phosphide tablets typically kill at least 90% of targeted individuals, and are most lethal when soil temperatures are above 16°C (60°F) (Moline and Demarais 1987; Hygnstrom and VerCauteren 2000).

With a diameter of 4 centimeters (1.5 inches) and a length of 9 centimeters (3.5 inches), gas cartridges are incendiary devices, which are General Use Pesticides (i.e., USEPA certification is not required). Use involves punching a small hole in the end of the cartridge, inserting and lighting a fuse, gently rolling the cartridge into a burrow, and plugging the burrow-entrance with moist soil. Gas cartridges usually do not work well if the soil is dry. Combustion of cartridges produces carbon monoxide, a colorless, odorless gas that kills prairie dogs. For humans, carbon monoxide can cause headache, throbbing at the temples, disorientation, nausea, vomiting, unconsciousness, and sometimes death (Timm 1994).

Fumigation via aluminum phosphide or gas cartridges kills not only prairie dogs, but also all other organisms within targeted burrows. Applicators therefore must use caution to avoid fumigating burrows occupied by American badgers, black-footed ferrets, burrowing owls, prairie rattlesnakes, tiger salamanders, and other nontarget species. By eliminating prairie dogs, fumigants negatively impact the many nontarget organisms that associate with prairie dogs (Chapter 4).

Wildlife Services (WS, called Animal Damage Control [ADC] before 1997), a division of Animal and Plant Health Inspection Service (APHIS) of the United States Department of Agriculture (USDA), is the primary federal agency that helps landowners who want to eliminate prairie dogs. Some state agencies assist with poisoning, but others do not. In Wyoming, assistance is available from county agencies. Some landowners distribute the poisons themselves, and others hire commercial firms. Poisons are available from WS, some state departments of agriculture, and commercial vendors.

How Quickly Do Prairie Dog Colonies Repopulate After Treatment with Zinc Phosphide?

Colony size routinely increases by about 30% per year for several consecutive years following control with toxicants such as zinc phosphide (Collins et al. 1984; Apa et al. 1990). Following intense, but not total, elimination, colony size can increase by as much as 71% per year for one to two years before the rate of increase begins to diminish (Knowles and Knowles 1994; see also Uresk and Schenbeck 1987). Colonies usually require three to five years to attain pretreatment numbers following treatment of burrow-entrances with zinc phosphide throughout entire colony-sites, but need only one to two years to attain pretreatment numbers following treatment of peripheral entrances only (Schenbeck 1981; Knowles 1986a). Because prairie dog colonies repopulate so quickly, long-term management usually will require more than one treatment with zinc phosphide. Complete eradication might solve this problem of repopulation, especially for isolated colonies for which immigration from other colonies is unlikely, but 100% mortality via any method is formidably elusive.

Is Controlling Prairie Dogs Worth the Cost?

Wildlife managers all agree that controlling prairie dogs is expensive (Table 9.1), but they disagree about whether the benefits of control justify the costs (Stapp 1998). Bell (1921) concluded that the benefits to ranchers from controlling prairie dogs outweigh the costs. More recently, however, Schenbeck (1981) and Collins et al. (1984; see also above and Chapters 2 and 5) have argued that controlling prairie dogs with zinc phosphide usually is not worth the cost, for five reasons:

- Zinc phosphide and the bait necessary for poisoning are expensive.
- The effort necessary for dispensing poisoned bait is time-consuming, and therefore expensive.
- Colonies usually repopulate quickly after poisoning unless eradication is complete.
- Competition between livestock and prairie dogs is sometimes insignificant.
- Livestock only rarely step into prairie dog burrows.

Hygnstrom and VerCauteren (2000) have countered that controlling prairie dogs is profitable for ranchers when the protocol includes oats laced with zinc phosphide followed by fumigation of burrows with aluminum phosphide. One reason for the discrepancy among wildlife biologists regarding poisoning is that financial gains or losses are not constant, but instead vary with factors such as rainfall, type and abundance of vegetation, age and size of colonies, densities of prairie dogs and burrow-entrances, proximity of other colonies, method of control, and human effort (Schenbeck 1985; Knowles 1986a). Another reason is that biologists make different assumptions about costs and benefits when calculating the economics of controlling prairie dogs.

Table 9.1. Costs of various methods for controlling prairie dogs. Each cost is an estimate at the time of research. One hectare = 2.471 acres.

Method	*Cost per hectare ($)*	*References*
Zinc phosphide (applied with grain)	11.05–19.16	Schenbeck 1981; Collins et al. 1984; Roemer and Forrest 1996; Hygnstrom et al. 1998
Aluminum phosphide (fumigant)	75.00	Hygnstrom and VerCauteren 2000
Gas cartridge (fumigant)	96.88	Hygnstrom and VerCauteren 2000

Even when elimination of prairie dogs is 100%—and thus most likely to be worth the cost of control—such extermination does not necessarily guarantee the immediate recovery of terrain for grazing by livestock. Additional steps such as leveling of burrow-mounds, reseeding, and temporary exclusion of livestock, for example, might be necessary to rehabilitate deserted colony-sites.

Recommendations

For many reasons (Chapters 4, 8, 17, and 18), the elimination of prairie dogs can be imprudent. Further, the financial costs of many types of control sometimes exceed the benefits (see Table 9.1; Chapter 8). Before using any method to eliminate prairie dogs, farmers, ranchers, politicians, and wildlife managers should appraise both the costs and benefits. They also should carefully evaluate the negative effects for black-footed ferrets, burrowing owls, mountain plovers, and other species that depend on prairie dogs for survival.

Summary

- Methods that do not work well, or are impractical or too expensive, for the elimination or reduction of prairie dog colonies include alteration of habitat by killing certain plants or by adding perches for predatory birds; addition of cage litter from black-footed ferrets; translocation; contraceptive agents such as DES; sterilization of males; gas exploding devices; and visual barriers.
- Methods that do work well for eliminating prairie dogs include limitation or postponement of grazing by domestic livestock; recreational shooting; zinc phosphide; and fumigants.
- We need more research to investigate the feasibility of reducing prairie dog numbers by limiting grazing by livestock. With so many economic implications, and because limiting grazing has few negative side effects for other organisms, the dearth of rigorous information about this method for controlling prairie dogs is perplexing.
- Colony size routinely increases by about 30% per year for several consecutive years following control with toxicants such as zinc phosphide. Complete eradication might solve this problem of repopulation, especially for isolated colonies for which immigration from other colonies is unlikely, but 100% mortality via any method is formidably elusive.
- Efforts to eliminate prairie dogs are expensive. Regarding livestock, wildlife managers disagree about whether the benefits of controlling prairie dogs outweigh the costs. One reason for the discrepancy is that financial gains (or

losses) vary with factors such as rainfall, type and abundance of vegetation, age and size of colonies, densities of prairie dogs and burrow-entrances, proximity of other colonies, method of control, and human effort.

- Even when elimination of prairie dogs is 100%—and thus most likely to be worth the cost of control—such extermination does not necessarily guarantee the immediate recovery of terrain for grazing by livestock.
- Before using any method to eliminate prairie dogs, farmers, ranchers, politicians, and wildlife managers should appraise both the costs and benefits. They also should carefully evaluate the negative effects for black-footed ferrets, burrowing owls, mountain plovers, and other species that depend on prairie dogs for survival.

CHAPTER 10

Recreational Shooting of Prairie Dogs

Archie F. Reeve and Timothy C. Vosburgh

Recreational shooting of prairie dogs is controversial—entertaining to some, abhorrent to others. Because recreational shooting recently has killed more than two million prairie dogs per year, the implications for conservation are significant.

In this chapter we examine recreational shooting, but we do not consider ethical and humane issues regarding harvesting (shooting) of wildlife in general or recreational shooting of prairie dogs in particular. We begin with a brief history of recreational shooting, examine the impacts, and then investigate levels at which shooting might be sustainable. We document that juveniles and adult (at least one year old) females are most vulnerable, and discuss the management of colonies for recreational shooting. Finally, we examine the risks to humans from recreational shooting, and then explore the ironic possibility that recreational shooting sometimes might enhance the conservation of prairie dogs on private land.

History of Recreational Shooting

Many residents of western states remember their teenage "plinking" of prairie dogs with a slingshot, BB-gun, or 22-caliber rifle. For more than 100 years in Kansas, for example, shooting of prairie dogs has been common after school and on Sunday afternoons (Smith 1967). Reasons to shoot prairie dogs are numerous. Most people shoot them for fun (36%) or target practice (29%), while others view the opportunity as time with family and friends (13%) or time outdoors (11%); only 3% shoot for damage control (Keffer et al. 2001).

Occasionally people shoot prairie dogs for food (Hoogland 1995; Graber et al. 1998; http://www.freedomnet.cnchost.com/pdf/recipes.htm lists recipes for cooking prairie dogs).

Marksmen regularly search for new locations to shoot, and sometimes are willing to pay landowners for access to their prairie dog colonies. Farmers and ranchers who want to reduce or eliminate prairie dogs sometimes regard shooting as an alternative to poisoning, which is expensive (Chapters 8 and 9). Intense shooting for two consecutive years at small colony-sites of less than 6 hectares (15 acres), for example, can significantly reduce numbers of prairie dogs (Knowles 1988). Farmers and ranchers sometimes advertise access to prairie dog colonies in popular magazines such as *Varmint Hunter* or on Internet Web sites. Other landowners participate in "shooter placement" programs, which coordinate assignment of shooters to willing landowners (Wyoming Black-tailed Prairie Dog Working Group 2001).

Ninety-five percent of landowners in Wyoming try to reduce colonies of prairie dogs, and the majority (54%) strives to eliminate them (Wyoming Agricultural Statistics Service 2001). Over 85% of the farmers and ranchers that allow recreational shooting do not charge fees (Wyoming Agricultural Statistics Service 2001), evidently because they are unaware that shooting might generate income, are concerned about liability, or believe that reducing the number of prairie dogs is sufficient compensation.

Federal agencies such as the United States Forest Service (USFS) and the United States Bureau of Land Management (BLM) once encouraged recreational shooting on USFS and BLM lands to reduce prairie dog numbers, and often provided maps with directions to large, densely populated colonies (BLM 2001; Chapter 15). After the designation of the prairie dog as a candidate species for the Federal List of Endangered and Threatened Wildlife and Plants (FLETWP) in 2000 (USFWS 2000a), these agencies curtailed or eliminated shooting where prairie dogs have been decimated by plague and where reintroductions of black-footed ferrets have occurred or are under consideration (e.g., Thunder Basin National Grasslands, Wyoming; Phillips County, Montana) (Chapter 15). Following the removal of the prairie dog from the candidate list in 2004 (USFWS 2004), however, recreational shooting has resumed at many BLM and USFS colony-sites, including some with ferrets (e.g., Conata Basin, Buffalo Gap National Grasslands, South Dakota; see Chapters 15 and 18).

Several states recently have estimated numbers of shooters, recreation-days spent shooting, and, ultimately, numbers of prairie dogs killed by recreational shooting (Table 10.1). One recreation-day (equivalent to one shooter-day) is one recreational shooter spending one day in the field shooting prairie dogs;

four shooters on the same day = four recreation-days. Numbers of prairie dogs killed per recreation-day range from 6.5 (Colorado) to 12.6 (Nebraska).

The Lower Brule Sioux Reservation in central South Dakota monitored shooting of prairie dogs from 1993 through 2001 (Table 10.2). Over this nine-year period, a yearly average of 121 licensed recreational shooters killed an average of 14,200 prairie dogs per year while spending an average of 372

Table 10.1. Estimated intensity of recreational shooting of prairie dogs in three western states. For South Dakota, data are from non-Native American lands only. One recreation-day is one recreational shooter spending one day in the field shooting prairie dogs. References: Nebraska Game and Parks Commission 2001; South Dakota Prairie Dog Work Group 2001; Colorado Division of Wildlife 2002a.

Location	*Year*	*Total prairie dogs killed*	*Total shooters*	*Total recreation-days*	*Average killed per recreation-day*
Colorado	1998–1999	418,412	6,070	64,674	6.47
Nebraska	1998	301,000	7,100	33,400	9.01
Nebraska	1999	356,000	5,970	28,300	12.58
South Dakota	2000	1,186,272	Not reported	94,741	12.52

Table 10.2. Data from nine years of shooting prairie dogs on the Lower Brule Sioux Reservation, South Dakota. One recreation-day is one recreational shooter spending one day in the field shooting prairie dogs. Reference: Lower Brule Sioux Tribe 2002.

	Year								
Statistic	*1993*	*1994*	*1995*	*1996*	*1997*	*1998*	*1999*	*2000*	*2001*
Number of licenses sold	115	146	139	127	157	97	114	130	64
Total killed	17,700	28,000	4,600	10,700	15,300	16,700	12,100	14,800	8,069
Total recreation-days	367	503	334	486	372	392	363	319	211
Number killed per shooter per day	48	56	14	22	41	43	33	46	38
Average days per shooter	3.2	3.6	2.4	3.8	2.8	2.9	3.2	2.5	3.3

recreation-days on the reservation. Each shooter killed an average of 118 prairie dogs per year (about 38 per day, three times the highest rate in Table 10.1). The cumulative number of victims can be substantial. In South Dakota in 2000, for example, recreational shooters killed 1.2 million prairie dogs (see Table 10.1).

Especially in the last ten years or so, marksmen sometimes come from out of state to shoot prairie dogs (Vosburgh 2000; South Dakota Prairie Dog Work Group 2001). In North Dakota, for example, the number of licensed out-of-state shooters increased from 163 in 1989 to 1,326 in 2001 (S. Hagen, North Dakota Game and Fish Department, Bismarck, North Dakota, personal communication, 2003).

Extensive recreational shooting of prairie dogs, or extensive poisoning (Chapter 8), reduces the local food supply for large predators such as coyotes. As a result, coyotes might be more likely to attack domestic livestock. If this happens, we have no information about whether a landowner's gains from shooting or poisoning prairie dogs will outweigh losses from increased predation by coyotes on livestock.

Effects of Recreational Shooting on Prairie Dog Colonies

In response to recreational shooting, prairie dogs change their behavior: they spend less time aboveground and, when aboveground, devote less time to feeding and more time to scanning. Further, prairie dogs exposed to shooting submerge into burrows sooner and stay underground longer in response to humans (Vosburgh and Irby 1998; Keffer et al. 2001). Increased alertness and faster, longer, submergences are problematic for recreational shooters. In response, recreational shooters have improved the technology of their firearms. Today's shooters typically bring a variety of rifles, telescopes, rangefinders, shooting benches, and reloading equipment (Figure 10.1). Shooting prairie dogs at long distances entitles membership in the 500-Yard Club, sponsored by *Varmint Hunter* magazine. Some marksmen have been successful from 1,350 meters (1,500 yards).

Colony size for this chapter means the number of adult (at least one year old) and juvenile prairie dogs that inhabit a colony-site (see also Chapter 2). Colony size increases via births and immigration, and decreases via deaths and emigration. Information about the rate of population increase—sometimes called the "finite rate of increase" and symbolized by R in this chapter—is important for understanding potential effects of recreational shooting on colony size. The population size (N) one year is the product of the population size the previous year and the finite rate of increase, or $N(t + 1) = N(t) \cdot R$. If $R = 1$,

Figure 10.1. Recreational shooting of prairie dogs. Here one person shoots prairie dogs in Montana with a high-technology, long-range rifle, while an assistant helps to locate targets with a telescope. Because they can earn money by charging fees for recreational shooting, ranchers sometimes want to retain and manage prairie dog colonies that they otherwise would not tolerate. In recent years, recreational shooting has eliminated millions of prairie dogs. Photo by Jonathan N. Pauli.

then the population in the next year (N at time t + 1) is the same as the population in the current year, N(t). But, if a population of 200 increases 10% each year, R = 1.1 and N(t) = 200, N(t + 1) = 220, N(t + 2) = 242, N(t + 3) = 266, and so on, as the population grows exponentially. In this example, the population would remain constant at 200 if 20 individuals are shot each year, with the assumption that each prairie dog contributes equally to the next year's population.

The equation $N(t) = N(0) \cdot R^t$ is used to compute future population size if the initial population size, N(0), and R are known; see Appendix C for other expressions of population growth. In 20 years the population N(20) = 1,345 prairie dogs, for example, from an initial population of 200 when R = 1.1.

Finite rates of increase at colonies with no shooting vary from year to year. At the Rankin Ridge Colony in Wind Cave National Park, South Dakota, for example, colony size increased in some years but declined in others; finite rates of increase averaged 1.032 (range = 0.698–1.452; Table 16.1 of Hoogland 1995; Chapter 3). Because the Rankin Ridge Colony is surrounded by unsuitable habitat, its area remained constant for 15 consecutive years—so that R of about 1.0 might have been expected. Stable populations usually increase in response to factors such as additional food, reduced predation, and increased availability of suitable habitat (Caughley and Sinclair 1994). Mainly because of reduced competition, populations also increase following the removal of individuals (Caughley and Sinclair 1994). Table 10.3 shows how prairie dog colonies have increased under natural conditions or after artificial reduction.

Scars on a female's placenta indicate the number of embryos at the start of pregnancy (Foreman 1962; Tileston and Lechleitner 1966; Knowles 1987). At colony-sites in North Dakota subjected to 20+ years of recreational shooting, analysis of placental scars yielded an unexpected result: only 32% of yearling females attempted to reproduce—versus 90% of yearling females at colony-

Table 10.3. Population growth under natural conditions and following artificial reduction. References: (1) Knowles 1988, Table 2, for Charles M. Russell National Wildlife Refuge (CMRNWR); (2) B. Perry, USFS, Wall, South Dakota, personal communication, 2000, for Agate colonies in Conata Basin, Buffalo Gap National Grasslands; (3) and (4) Knowles 1986a, Table 2, for CMRNWR; (5) Radcliffe 1992, for Wind Cave National Park (WCNP); (6) Garrett et al. 1982, for WCNP; (7) Koford 1958, for area near Nunn, Colorado.

Location	*Method of reduction*	*Parameter measured*	*Duration of monitoring (years)*	*Estimate of average R*
(1) Montana	shooting	population	1	1.65
(2) South Dakota	shooting	number of active burrow-entrances	4	R undetermined
(3) Montana	toxicant	population	2	2.71
(4) Montana	toxicant	population	2	2.49
(5) South Dakota	removal and translocation	population	2	2.92
(6) South Dakota	no reduction; expanding colony	population	3	1.38
(7) Colorado	no reduction; expanding colony	population	1	2.93

sites with no shooting (Stockrahm and Seabloom 1988). Undisturbed colonies had more suitable habitat available for foraging and expansion, however. The differences in reproduction by yearling females probably resulted more from differences in availability of suitable habitat than from differences in levels of recreational shooting (Garrett et al. 1982; Chapter 3).

At What Level is Recreational Shooting Sustainable?

Populations do not grow indefinitely, of course. Diminishing resources available per individual eventually will lead to increased mortality, decreased reproduction, and possibly increased emigration as well. When population growth depends on current population size, the growth is called density-dependent (Akçakaya et al. 1999). One of the assumptions of density-dependent growth is that when a population approaches some level, called the carrying capacity (K), the growth rate will decline and eventually will reach R = 1.0 when N = K. The value of R at some time t, R(t), depends on the population size N(t) relative to K according to the equation, $R(t) = R_{max}^{(1 - N(t)/K)}$. When the population N(t) is small, the exponent (1–N(t)/K) is close to 1 and its growth rate R(t) will be close to the maximum possible, or R_{max}. But as the population grows and approaches its carrying capacity, R will be less than R_{max}. When the population reaches carrying capacity, R = 1.0. Density-dependent population growth (Figure 10.2), expressed as $N(t + 1) = N(t) \cdot R_{max}^{(1-N(t)/K)}$ (see also Appendix C), reveals that R_{max} is key to how quickly a population will reach K.

If farmers and ranchers regard prairie dogs as an economic resource via recreational shooting, their best strategy is to manage colonies so that the number of individuals shot is always replaced by either births or immigration—that is, they should manage for a sustainable yield. Population growth from 20 to 1,000 prairie dogs with $R_{max} = 2.0$ is simulated in Figure 10.3 along with the annual production (yield). The largest annual sustainable yield—also known as the maximal sustainable yield (MSY; see Appendix C)—occurs when the population is approximately 50% of carrying capacity, but managing for MSY is difficult (Caughley and Sinclair 1994). The formidable task is to determine the population size after shooting that will produce the best yield for the next year. If harvest exceeds the sustainable yield and if this trend continues over time, the population eventually will decline to zero.

Figure 10.4 shows that an initial population of 1,000 with $R_{max} = 2.0$ will stabilize at 585 prairie dogs with an annual harvest of 195. When 210 prairie dogs are harvested annually, the population declines toward zero. MSY in this example is 209, and any annual harvest less than 209 stabilizes the population at some level less than the carrying capacity. Constant harvesting at levels more

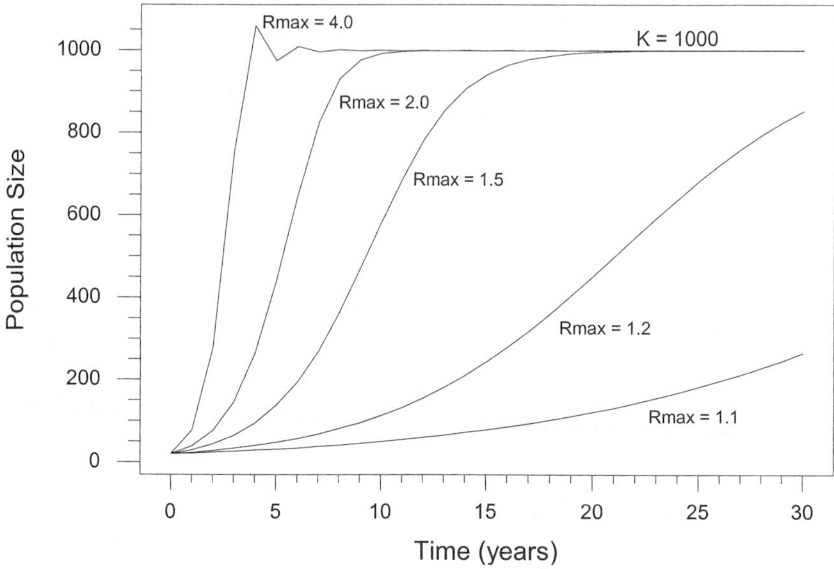

Figure 10.2. Density-dependent population growth from an initial population N(0) = 20 and carrying capacity K = 1,000 with different values for R_{max}. Population size = number of adult and juvenile prairie dogs. For this and all other figures in this chapter, the term "adult" includes yearlings, and population size = number of adults and juveniles.

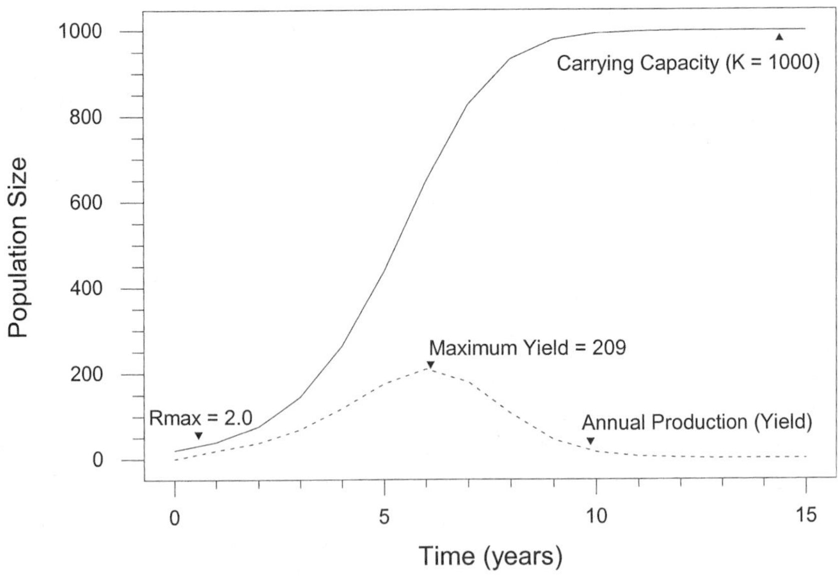

Figure 10.3. Example of density-dependent population growth (R_{max} = 2.0) and annual production (yield) over time as a population of prairie dogs reaches carrying capacity.

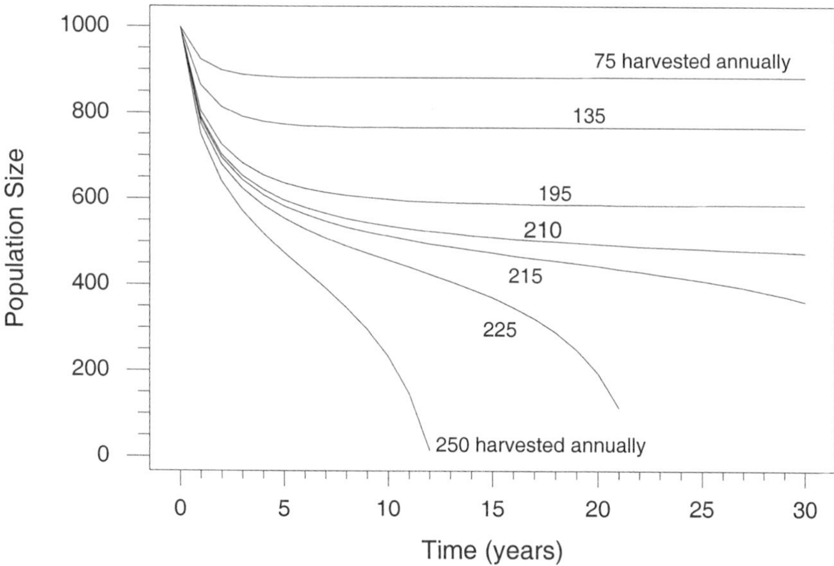

Figure 10.4. Effects of different levels of constant harvest annually on a population with density-dependent growth ($R_{max} = 2.0$) but no variation in survival and fecundity rates. Annual harvests of more than 209 prairie dogs cannot be sustained, and the population eventually will decline to zero.

than 209 reduces population size and growth rate, with eventual extinction (Caughley and Sinclair 1994; Akçakaya et al. 1999).

To this point, we have assumed population growth to be deterministic, with no variation in birth rate or death rate. Environmental variation from year to year, and from one locale to another, however, causes fluctuations in birth and death rates (Hoogland 1995). In addition, prairie dogs within the same population have different probabilities for survival and reproduction. Stochastic population models accommodate random annual fluctuations in mortality, individual differences in longevity and reproduction, and so forth.

In the simulation examples provided so far, the finite rate of increase at time t, R(t), is equal to $R_{max}^{(1-N(t)/K)}$. Annual variation in rates of birth, immigration, death, and emigration all contribute to variability of R(t). Annual variation in carrying capacity also will cause variation in R(t). We introduce variation by increasing or decreasing the computed value of R(t) by a random amount but within defined limits—for example, ± 20% of the computed value for R(t); this 20% includes demographic variation as well as random variation in carrying capacity. We used these values for 100 simulations to project population growth from an initial population of 20 prairie dogs with $R_{max} = 2.0$

and K = 1,000. The simulations show that the average population size stabilizes at approximately 1,000 (Figure 10.5); because of random variability of R(t), however, population size at t = 15 ranges from 797 to 1,230.

Juveniles and Adult Females are Most Vulnerable to Recreational Shooting

The timing of recreational shooting affects both reproduction and mortality among prairie dogs. Shooting from March through May is likely to kill pregnant and lactating females (Chapter 3), so that neither the females nor their offspring will reproduce in the following year (Knowles 1988). Unfortunately, shooters cannot distinguish between male and female prairie dogs (Chapter 3) and, except during late spring and early summer, cannot distinguish between adults and juveniles, either. In population projections used so far, we have assumed harvest of different age groups in populations to be proportional to their frequency in the population. Juvenile prairie dogs are more susceptible than adults to recreational shooting, however. Even though only 35% of a population in May and June were juveniles, for example, juveniles comprised

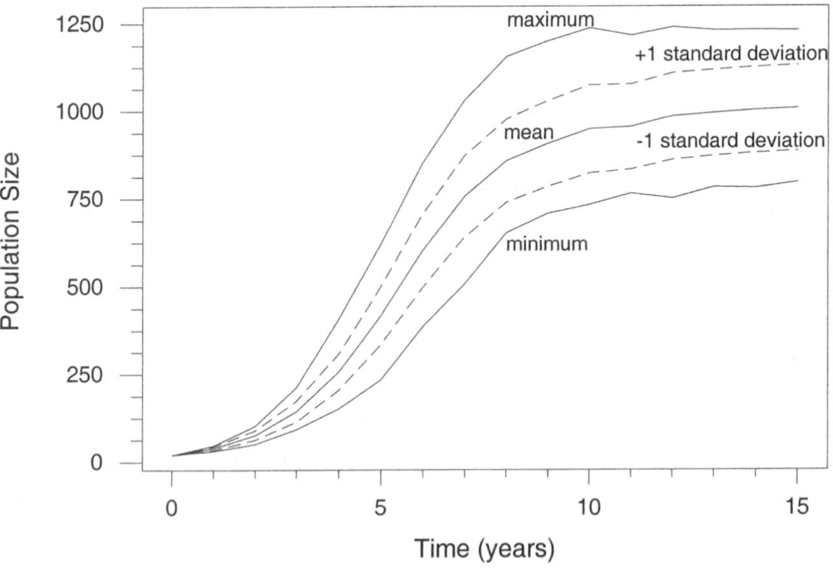

Figure 10.5. Results of 100 simulations of density-dependent population growth (R_{max} = 2.0, K = 1,000) but with random variation in the population growth rate each year (± 20% of R(t) after computation as $R(t) = R_{max}^{(1-N(t)/K)}$).

53% of the victims when 10% of the colony was shot during early to midsummer (Keffer et al. 2001). Higher levels of shooting (more than 20% mortality) on another colony also disproportionately targeted juveniles. Because adults are more likely than juveniles to reproduce in the following year (Chapter 2), the juvenile-biased susceptibility to recreational shooting probably means that colonies will decline more slowly than they would if susceptibility were either adult-biased or without bias.

Among adults, females are more vulnerable than males to recreational shooting (Vosburgh and Irby 1998; Keffer et al. 2001). During early summer in Montana, for example, the ratio of adult females to adult males within a colony before shooting was 100/96 (Vosburgh and Irby 1998). But in late summer after shooting, the ratio of adult females to adult males at the same colony was 100/167—that is, the survivorship of adult females during the period of shooting was only 57% of the survivorship of adult males. At a control colony with no shooting, by contrast, survivorship of adult females was 122% of the survivorship of adult males between early and late summer of the same year (Vosburgh and Irby 1998; see also Hoogland 1995). Because a single male can mate with several females (Chapter 2), the female-biased susceptibility to recreational shooting probably means that colonies will decline faster than they would if vulnerability were either male-biased or without sexual bias.

Intense recreational shooting sometimes might induce prairie dogs to disperse. With the assumption that disappearance = dispersal, 69% of surviving marked prairie dogs dispersed from a colony-site for which recent mortality from shooting was more than 20%. Similar dispersal of marked individuals did not occur at a nearby colony-site with less than 10% mortality from shooting (Keffer et al. 2001).

Management of Prairie Dog Colonies for Recreational Shooting

One common way to regulate recreational shooting of prairie dogs is to impose a quota on numbers shot (Caughley and Sinclair 1994). Regulating harvest by quotas is conceptually attractive: once the quota is reached, harvesting stops. Determining when quotas are reached is elusive, however, because such determination requires accurate records of prairie dogs killed versus number of bullets fired. At the Rosebud Sioux Reservation in South Dakota in 2000, 936 shooters reported a total of 156,307 rounds fired, with a death toll of 57,848 prairie dogs (Rosebud Sioux Department of Game, Fish, and Parks, unpublished data). This rate of one prairie dog killed for every 2.7 shots is similar to an observed rate of one prairie dog killed per 3 shots at the Fort Belknap

Reservation in Montana in 1999 (Vosburgh 2000). Under these conditions, a quota of 1,000 prairie dogs would mean permitting the discharge of approximately 3,000 bullets.

Figure 10.4 shows a major problem with fixed annual harvest quotas: constant numbers harvested each year, if too high, will lead to extinction. But Figure 10.4 assumes no variability in population growth rate. When random variation (±15% of the computed value for R(t)) is used to predict how an initial population of 1,000 (N(0) = K) with R_{max} = 2.0 will respond to an annual quota of 195, the results (Figure 10.6) are different from those generated by the deterministic model (Figure 10.4). The stochastic model predicts an average population of 406 (range = 0–819) after 30 years with average annual harvest of 183. The model also predicts a 23% chance that the population will become extinct by t = 30. Risk of extinction increases directly with level of random variation in R(t). With random variation ±10% of R(t), for example, extinction within 30 years occurs at a frequency of only 1%; with random variation ±20% of R(t), however, extinction within 30 years occurs at a frequency of 46%. To preclude extinction, the harvest quota must be low enough to accom-

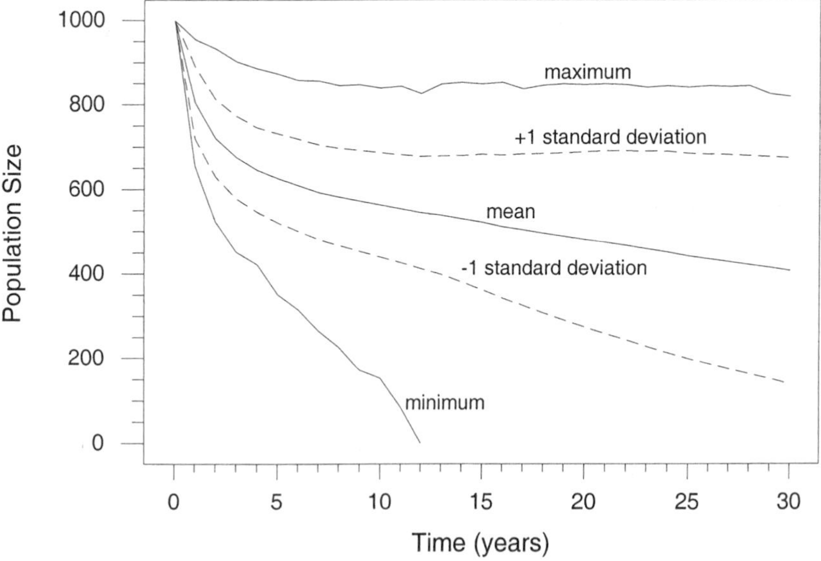

Figure 10.6. Results of 1,000 simulations of effects from an annual harvest quota of 195 prairie dogs to an initial population of 1,000 individuals with density-dependent population growth (R_{max}= 2.0) and random variation in the population growth rate each year (± 15% of R(t) after computation as $R(t) = R_{max}^{(1-N(t)/K)}$).

modate the lowest estimate of population size for the next year (Caughley and Sinclair 1994).

Another common way to regulate recreational shooting of prairie dogs is to regulate harvesting effort (Caughley and Sinclair 1994). Such regulation theoretically removes a certain proportion of the population rather than a fixed number. One way to control harvesting effort is to limit the duration of the harvest. Another way is to limit the number of shooters (Caughley and Sinclair 1994). For prairie dogs, Figure 10.7 shows the effects of various levels of annual harvest as percentages of the current population. When the rate of annual harvest = 25%, the long-term average harvest (from t = 0 to t = 30) is approximately 199 prairie dogs, and the population remains stable at 585. This is similar to the outcome in Figure 10.4 with a fixed quota of 195.

The same level of random variation in R(t) as in Figure 10.6 (±15% of the computed value for R(t)) was used to predict how an initial population of 1,000 (N(0) = K) with R_{max} = 2.0 will respond when the rate of annual harvest = 25%. The outcome of 1,000 simulations produces an average population of 580 prairie dogs (ranging from 439 to 744) after 30 years with average annual harvest of 197, but poses no risk of extinction (Figure 10.8)—unlike the

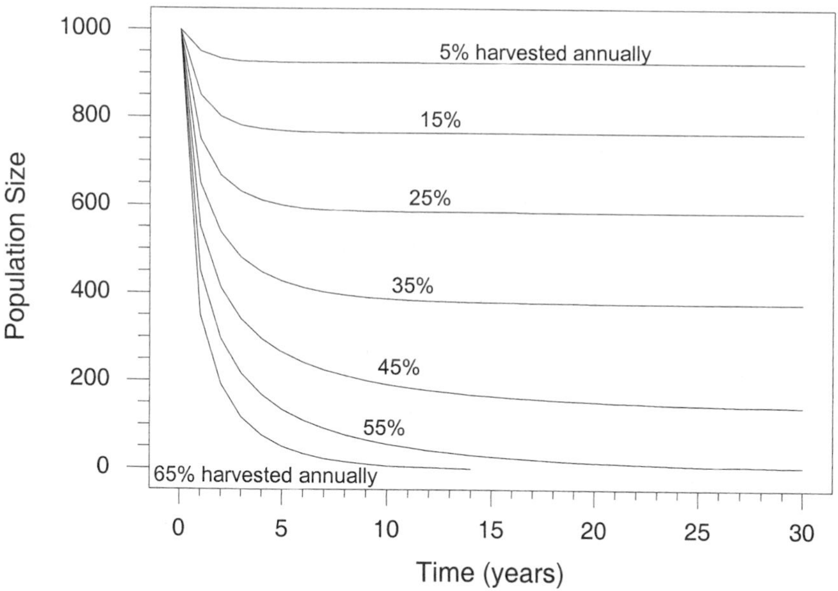

Figure 10.7. Deterministic predictions of different levels of constant proportional harvest annually on a population of prairie dogs with density-dependent growth (R_{max} = 2.0).

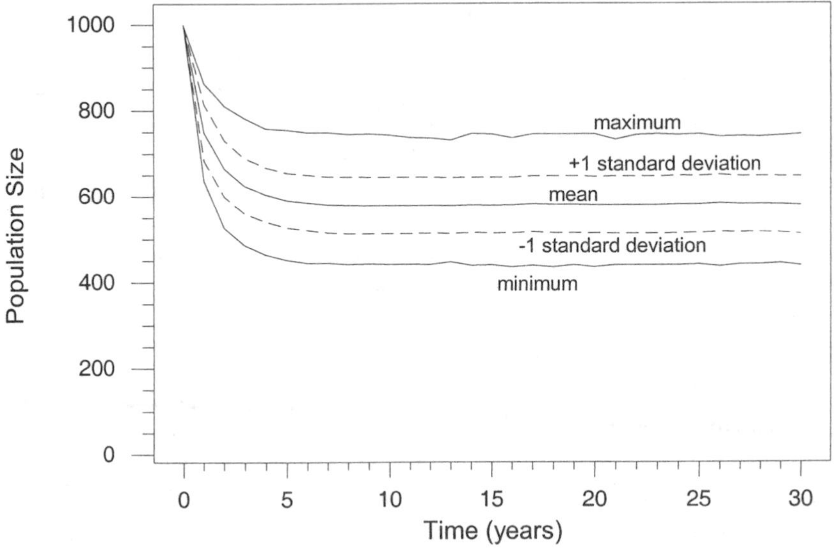

Figure 10.8. Results of 1,000 simulations when the annual rate of harvest = 25% of the population, initial population size = 1,000 prairie dogs, density-dependent population growth with R_{max} = 2.00, and random variation in the population growth rate each year (± 15% of R(t) after computation as $R(t) = R_{max}^{(1-N(t)/K)}$).

scenario with a fixed quota harvest (see Figure 10.6). With demographic and environmental uncertainty, populations are more likely to persist if harvested proportionally rather than by fixed quota.

Prudent regulation via either fixed quota or harvesting effort requires knowledge of the target population's carrying capacity and R_{max}. Unfortunately, however, good estimates of these parameters are seldom available. A population at approximately K/2, for example, is expected to produce the maximal number of prairie dogs each year (see Figure 10.3), which, in theory, could be harvested each year as MSY. But, random environmental events and individual variation in longevity and reproduction can lead to substantial fluctuations in population size—so harvest always should be well below the estimated MSY (Caughley and Sinclair 1994).

A third way to regulate recreational shooting of prairie dogs involves harvesting only when a population exceeds some threshold level. Threshold harvesting requires specific knowledge about population levels, and produces high annual variation in harvest because populations below threshold must be protected (Lande et al. 1997). Threshold harvesting might be feasible if a landowner has monitored population growth rates under various environmental conditions with no shooting or poisoning (Livieri 1999). Such information is never available, however, so threshold harvesting probably is not a practical option for recreational shooting of prairie dogs.

Farmers and ranchers hoping to profit from recreational shooting should learn about the population size of their colonies prior to the onset of shooting; estimate numbers harvested; and then determine if the population remains stable, increases, or declines. One easy way to evaluate trends in population size is to estimate the area inhabited by prairie dogs each year (Chapter 6). With good records, farmers and ranchers should be able to maximize long-term profits and minimize the probability that their colonies will go extinct. As noted above, one easy tactic is to regulate either the number of recreational shooters or the time spent shooting. Another tactic is to direct shooters to areas where density of prairie dogs is high, and away from areas where density is low.

Risks to Humans Associated with Recreational Shooting

Farmers and ranchers hoping to attract recreational shooters are concerned about liability for injuries that occur on their lands, particularly if they charge a fee. Many states have adopted "recreational use statutes," designed to encourage people to open their land for recreational uses without the fear of liability. Protection only applies, however, when no fee is charged (Table 10.4). When state or federal governments collect fees from recreational shooters and then transfer the money to landowners, the legal protection from recreational use statutes usually prevails (Kays 1997).

The definition of "charging a fee" regarding recreational use statutes is sometimes ambiguous. Further, a statute is often unclear regarding liability if

Table 10.4. Recreational use statutes and terms of liability protection in states where some landowners allow recreational shooting of prairie dogs.

State	*Recreational use statute*	*Protection if fee is charged?*
Colorado	State statutes: 33-41-103	No; see 33-41-103(2)(e)(I)
Montana	2001 State code: 70-16-302 and 87-1-267 (temporary)	No; see 87-1-265(4) and 87-1-267(8)
Nebraska	Legislative statute: 37-732	No; see 37-734
New Mexico	State statutes: 17-4-17	No; see 17-4-17(B)
North Dakota	2001 Century code: 53-09-02	No; see 53-08-05(2)
South Dakota	2002 Codified laws: 20-9-14	No; see 20-9-16(2)
Wyoming	2003 State statutes: 34-19-103	No; see 34-19-105

a landowner collects a fee for repair and maintenance of property rather than for the privilege of recreational shooting (Kays 1997). Farmers and ranchers hoping to charge fees for recreational shooting of prairie dogs probably should seek legal counsel regarding liability.

Shooting prairie dogs with high-powered rifles inevitably leads to accidents, but relevant information specifically related to recreational shooting of prairie dogs is unavailable. Information from other types of hunting, however, indicates that shooting of other humans and self-inflicted wounds are likely to occur with recreational shooting of prairie dogs (International Hunter Education Association 1998).

Recreational shooting of prairie dogs is hazardous not only to humans, but also to nontarget species. Burrowing owls, for example, are vulnerable because they nest at prairie dog colony-sites; are diurnal; and, when they stand on burrow-mounds, resemble prairie dogs (Johnsgard 1988; Haug et al. 1993). Most shootings of burrowing owls are probably accidental, but some are perhaps intentional (Marks and Ball 1983; James and Espie 1997; Restani et al. 2001). Wildlife managers and ranchers should evaluate the threat to nontarget species when trying to determine whether recreational shooting is acceptable.

Another concern for wildlife managers is lead poisoning among scavengers that consume prairie dogs killed by recreational shooting. Current information on lead poisoning is meager and inconclusive (Plumb et al. 2001; Stephens et al. 2003), but common sense tells us that such poisoning might be frequent when recreational shooting is rampant.

Might Recreational Shooting Enhance the Conservation of Prairie Dogs?

Most of the land currently inhabited by prairie dogs is privately owned (Chapters 15 and 16). In Nebraska, for example, prairie dogs currently inhabit 26,300–32,400 hectares (65,000–80,000 acres), 99% of which is on private lands (Nebraska Game and Parks Commission 2001). With so much private land containing habitat formerly or currently inhabited by colonies, landowners are pivotal to the future of prairie dogs (Chapters 15 and 16).

Of 660 farmers and ranchers surveyed in eastern Wyoming (Wyoming Agricultural Statistics Service 2001), 23% expressed interest in a program that provides financial compensation for allowing prairie dogs to inhabit their domains; young respondents (less than 50 years old) showed more interest than older ones. The survey proposed four overlapping types of state administration: management of recreational shooting; coordinated placement of recreational shooters; development of markets for prairie dogs as pets or for nature photography; and a "banking program," by which other states would compensate landowners in Wyoming who conserve prairie dogs. Of these, the "banking program" was most popular (59% interested), placement of shooters was second (57%), and management of recreational shooting was third (51%). Respondents who expressed interest in programs with financial compensation considered a reasonable level of compensation to be $74–$86 per hectare ($30–$35 per acre). Interest in maintaining or increasing the area occupied by prairie dogs varied directly with the level of financial compensation. To attain $74–$86 per hectare from recreational shooting, a landowner with 405 hectares (1,000 acres) of prairie dogs would need to charge four shooters $79–$92 per person per day to shoot during the period between Memorial Day and Labor Day (approximately 95 days). Whether a prairie dog population can sustain that level of recreational shooting, and whether a farmer or rancher can generate that level of business, will depend on factors discussed in this chapter.

If landowners in states other than Wyoming are similarly interested in programs that promote recreational shooting, then colonies managed for shooting might account for a significant percentage of the cumulative area inhabited by prairie dogs in the future. In addition, private organizations might play a role. *Denver Post* columnist Ed Quillen (1999) has raised an interesting concept tentatively entitled "Prairie Dogs Unlimited" (PDU), which would function much like Ducks Unlimited, Trout Unlimited, and Pheasants Forever. Like the latter groups, PDU could support the conservation of prairie dogs through land purchase, restoration and enhancement of habitat, public education, and political lobbying. And like Ducks Unlimited and Pheasants Forever, regarding their focal animals, PDU could advocate the recreational shooting of prairie dogs.

Many families of western North America have tried for generations to eradicate prairie dogs. New financial incentives from recreational shooting, however, might make it worthwhile for ranchers and farmers to preserve and manage prairie dog colonies that they otherwise would not tolerate. Consequently, and ironically, today's ranchers and farmers might willingly share responsibility for the long-term survival of prairie dogs.

Summary

- Recreational shooting of prairie dogs has been occurring for more than 100 years, and the cumulative number of victims can be substantial. In South Dakota in 2000, for example, recreational shooters killed 1.2 million prairie dogs.

- Juvenile prairie dogs are more susceptible to recreational shooting than adults. Among adults, females are more vulnerable than males.
- If landowners regard prairie dogs as an economic resource via recreational shooting, their best strategy is to manage colonies so that the number of individuals shot is always replaced by either births or immigration.
- One common approach to control harvesting of prairie dogs via recreational shooting is to impose a quota on numbers shot. Another approach is to regulate harvesting effort (e.g., by limiting the number of shooters).
- Recreational shooting involves several risks: self-inflicted wounds; accidental shooting of other humans or nontarget species such as burrowing owls; and lead poisoning among scavengers that consume prairie dogs killed by bullets.
- New financial incentives from recreational shooting might make it worthwhile for ranchers and farmers to preserve and manage prairie dog colonies that they otherwise would not tolerate. Consequently, and ironically, today's ranchers and farmers might willingly share responsibility for the long-term survival of prairie dogs.

Acknowledgments

We thank S. Dinsmore, L. Irby, C. Knowles, M. Lockhart, and R. Rothwell for helpful comments.

CHAPTER 11

Conservation of Prairie Dogs in Areas with Plague

Jack F. Cully, Dean E. Biggins, and David B. Seery

For most of the last 200 years, poisoning and loss of habitat have been primarily responsible for the sharp decline of prairie dog populations (Chapters 8 and 16). More recently, plague has been a key culprit as well, and has claimed millions of victims in the western portion of the prairie dog's geographic range.

Because it completely eliminates so many colonies, and partially eliminates so many others, the relevance of plague to the conservation of prairie dogs is clear. We begin this chapter with a description of plague and its transmission. We then examine whether plague is natural or introduced into North America, and how this might affect the vulnerability of prairie dogs. We investigate possible outcomes regarding the evolutionary battle of prairie dogs versus plague, and the transfer of plague from prairie dogs to humans. We then tackle one of the most vexing questions: what happens to plague between epizootics? We describe the puzzling rarity of this disease in eastern populations, and then explore ways to reduce plague's impact. We conclude by speculating on the long-term prognosis of prairie dogs versus plague.

Plague and Its Transmission

Plague, called sylvatic plague when it affects wild rodents, is a disease caused by a bacterium (*Yersinia pestis*). Because plague commonly infects large numbers of prairie dogs within groups of nearby colonies over a short period of time, biologists and wildlife managers commonly talk about epizootics (or epidemics) of plague. The usual vectors (i.e., organisms that transfer disease-causing microorganisms from one host to another) are fleas, which acquire plague bacteria when they ingest blood of infected mammals (Barnes 1993). Direct transmission of plague among fleas does not occur.

Plague bacteria sometimes cause a blockage at the front of a flea's stomach (Poland and Barnes 1979; Hinnebusch et al. 2002). When a flea with blockage attempts to feed, blood rushes into the gut and hits the block where it picks up plague bacteria; infected blood is then regurgitated back into the host. Because the flea cannot get blood into its stomach, it remains unsatisfied and often bites repeatedly. Blockage and regurgitation promote transmission of plague from fleas to prairie dogs (Gage 1998), but transmission also might occur via contaminated flea mouthparts without blockage (Ken Gage, quoted in Orent 2004).

Yersinia pestis is the same bacterium that killed about 40% of the human population of Europe between 1347 and 1352 (Gage 1998; Orent 2004). For humans and probably for other susceptible mammals as well, plague has three overlapping stages (Orent 2004). When transmitted by fleas it first attacks the lymphatic system, and infected lymph nodes swell into the lumps known as buboes (bubonic plague). Soon thereafter, plague bacteria enter the bloodstream and proliferate there (septicemic plague). Septicemic transmission occurs after contact with infected blood. During the final stages of plague, the infection sometimes enters the victim's lungs and causes pneumonia (pneumonic plague). Pneumonic transmission occurs when the host coughs out bacteria as respiratory droplets that are inhaled by others. Inhaled bacteria rapidly reproduce in the lungs and usually cause a serious infection, which is often fatal.

Prairie dogs sometimes cannibalize carcasses (Hoogland 1995), so direct (septicemic) transmission might occur if individuals cannibalize victims of plague. In the laboratory, pneumonic transmission of plague also can occur (T. E. Rocke, National Wildlife Health Center, Madison, Wisconsin, personal communication, 2002). For prairie dogs living under natural conditions, however, transmission of plague almost always involves fleas (Barnes 1993; Cully and Williams 2001; Hoogland et al. 2004).

Is Plague Natural or Introduced to Western North America?

The origin of plague in North America is uncertain. Perhaps plague arrived via the Bering Land Bridge during the Pleistocene (Biggins and Kosoy 2001b). From historical, biochemical, and genetic data, however, most researchers now believe that plague first arrived in the United States in 1899 or 1900 via commercial ships from China (Link 1955; Achtman et al. 1999; Biggins and Kosoy 2001a, 2001b; Orent 2004). In the vicinity of San Francisco, California, introduced plague flourished among house (black) rats. The first native rodent to be identified with plague was the California ground squirrel in 1908 (McCoy 1908; Wherry 1908). By the early 1920s, plague occurred in southern California to the south and in southern Oregon to the north (Link 1955). By the mid-1930s, plague occurred as far east as Wyoming, Utah, and Arizona, and by 1950 it had spread to its current distribution (Figure 11.1). Among the different species of prairie dogs, the first suggestion of plague was a die-off among Gunnison's prairie dogs in Arizona in 1932, but proof of plague in this species did not come until 1937 (Eskey and Haas 1940). Plague was documented among Utah prairie dogs in 1936 (Eskey and Haas 1940). The first demonstration of plague among black-tailed prairie dogs occurred in Kansas in 1945, in Texas in 1947, and possibly in Colorado in 1945 (Ecke and Johnson 1952; Miles et al.

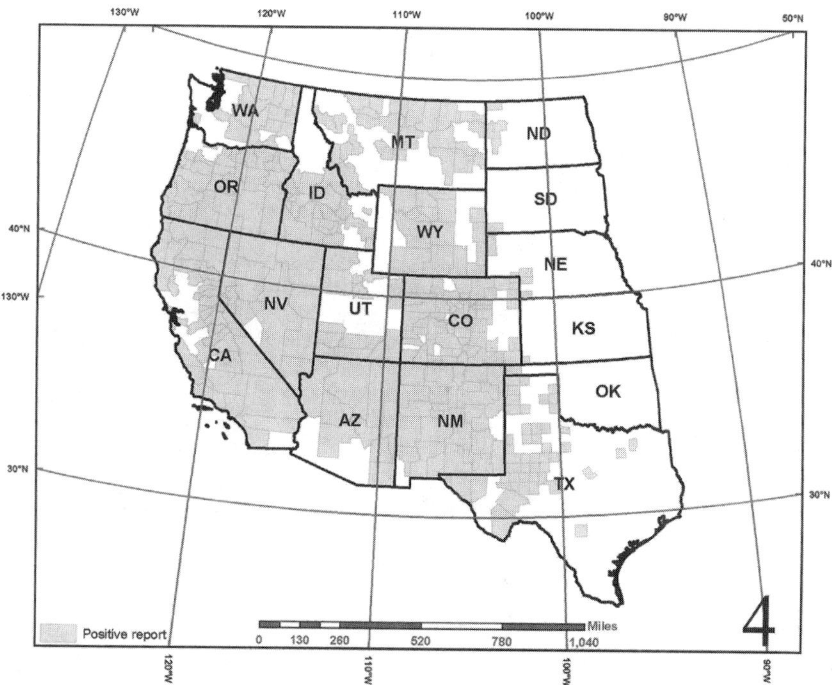

Figure 11.1. Counties with plague among humans, wild mammals, or fleas from 1970 through 2002. Undetected plague also might have occurred in other counties. The 102nd meridian is the approximate eastern boundary of plague. Map courtesy of Center for Disease Control.

1952; Cully et al. 2000). Varela and Vásquez (1954) recorded plague among Mexican prairie dogs in Coahuila, Mexico, but this report is questionable because none of the "infected" individuals died (see also Trevino-Villarreal et al. 1998).

Vulnerability of Prairie Dogs to Plague

When plague infects a prairie dog colony, mortality usually approaches 100% (Miles et al. 1952; Barnes 1993; Cully and Williams 2001). Indeed, we usually first suspect plague among prairie dogs by the sudden disappearance of most or all residents within a colony. Mortality results because plague bacteria release fatal toxins (Barnes 1993; Achtman et al. 1999). Most victims show no aboveground symptoms and perish underground. Occasionally an ailing, disoriented victim dies aboveground (Barnes 1993; see also Rayor 1985; Hoogland et al. 2004) (Figure 11.2). The time between initial exposure to plague and mortality varies for prairie dogs, but usually it is less than 14 days (Marinari and Williams 1998; Chapter 13).

Figure 11.2. Disoriented, wobbly juvenile prairie dog that is probably infected with plague. Plague-infected individuals usually die underground, but sometimes they wander aimlessly and then perish aboveground. Photo by Frederic Nichols.

Two factors, not necessarily mutually exclusive, might help to explain the extreme vulnerability of prairie dogs to plague. The first factor is that plague is an introduced disease to which prairie dogs have been exposed for only about 60 years. In this short time, prairie dogs probably have been unable to evolve a good defense—and consequently remain highly susceptible. The second factor involves the virulence of toxins produced by plague bacteria. After a prairie dog dies from the toxins, infected fleas from the carcass are probably more likely than infected fleas on live hosts to seek new hosts and thereby transmit plague. If so, then natural selection for increased virulence of plague (and consequently increased dispersal of infected fleas away from dead prairie dogs) might be stronger than natural selection for resistance among prairie dogs—so that prairie dogs remain highly susceptible. If plague is so virulent that it kills all the prairie dogs within the home and nearby colonies, however, then finding suitable hosts will be difficult for dispersing fleas.

Plague devastates populations of numerous species of marmots, ground squirrels, and chipmunks, but prairie dogs seem to be especially susceptible when compared to other species of ground-dwelling squirrels (Pollitzer and Meyer 1961; Olsen 1981; Barnes 1982, 1993; Biggins and Kosoy 2001b; Orent 2004). One likely explanation for this difference is that prairie dogs are more densely colonial than other squirrels (Hoogland 1981a; Michener 1983), and thus are more susceptible to costs of coloniality such as increased transmission of diseases (Alexander 1974; Hoogland 1979a, Cully and Williams 2001). On the other hand, their extreme vulnerability to plague relative to other taxonomic relatives might be an artifact that results because highly interactive prairie dogs in large colonies amidst low vegetation are easier to census and track than other, less interactive ground-dwelling squirrels that live in smaller colonies amidst taller vegetation (Miles et al. 1952; Lechleitner et al. 1968).

Plague Threatens the Conservation of Prairie Dogs

In combination with unpredictability regarding the place and timing of epizootics, the catastrophic mortality from plague inhibits efforts to conserve prairie dogs (Wuerthner 1997; Cully and Williams 2001; USFWS 2000a). Consider the recent history of prairie dogs at the Rocky Mountain Arsenal National Wildlife Refuge (RMA) in Colorado, for example. In 1988, prairie dogs at RMA inhabited 1,850 hectares (4,570 acres). Three epizootics ravaged colonies over the next 13 years, and at one point reduced RMA's cumulative area of occupancy to a mere 9 hectares (22 acres) (Figure 11.3). If devastation of this magnitude is typical and widespread, then conservation of prairie dogs will be exceedingly difficult.

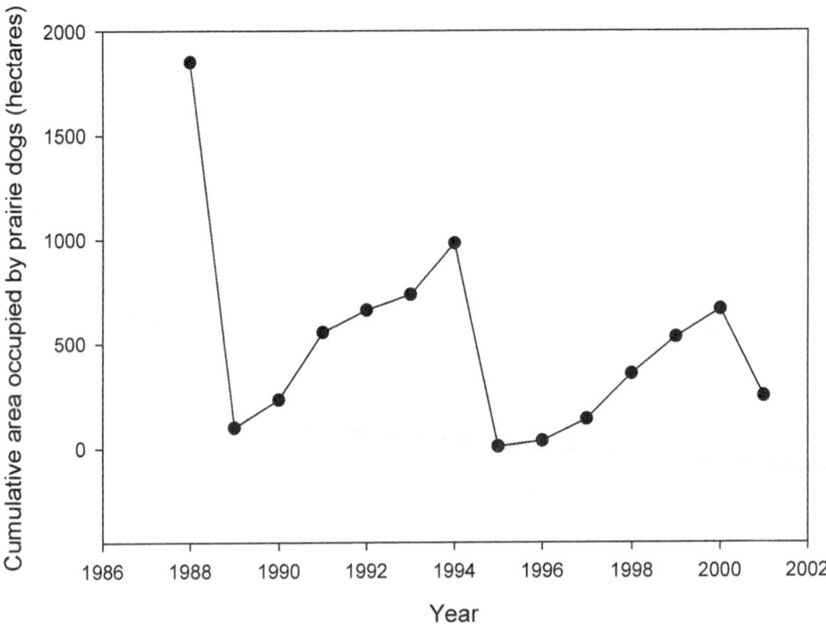

Figure 11.3. Annual variation in cumulative area inhabited by prairie dogs at Rocky Mountain Arsenal National Wildlife Refuge from 1988 through 2001. Epizootics of plague occurred in 1988–1989, 1994–1995, and 2000–2001.

Possible Outcomes Regarding the Evolutionary Battle of Prairie Dogs Versus Plague

In the future, at least three outcomes regarding the evolutionary battle of prairie dogs versus plague are possible, as described below.

- Prairie dogs might continue to go locally extinct wherever plague occurs. Some populations of prairie dogs have permanently disappeared after first exposure to plague, and others have been devastated by exposure to plague every four to five years or so (Barnes 1993; see also Figure 11.3). Consequently, the cumulative population of prairie dogs, as measured by cumulative area of colony-sites, has declined steadily since the introduction in the 1940s of plague into areas with prairie dogs. Other factors such as poisoning, loss of habitat, and recreational shooting also have decimated populations over the last 60 years, however (Chapters 8, 10, and 16), so that quantifying the historic effect of plague alone is impossible.
- Prairie dogs might become more resistant to plague. Some rodents in North America (Quan et al. 1985; Thomas et al. 1988), Asia (Kucheruk 1965; Rall

1965), and Africa (Isaäcson et al. 1983) have developed partial immunity to plague. In theory, prairie dogs also might evolve immunity. In practice, however, evidence for immunity is scarce. Small numbers of surviving Gunnison's, white-tailed, and Utah prairie dogs have developed serum antibodies after exposure to plague (Cully et al. 1997; Biggins 2001a, 2001b), but the colonies with survivors nonetheless have remained highly susceptible to later epizootics. Survival sometimes might result when exposure contains insufficient bacteria to ignite a lethal infection. Perhaps survivors are individuals that, for some unknown reason, require an unusually high number of initial bacteria for serious infection.

- Prairie dogs might develop a mechanism that reduces the impacts of plague. Today's colonies are smaller, rarer, and more isolated than they were before the arrival of plague in the 1940s (Chapters 12 and 16). These characteristics probably render today's prairie dogs less susceptible to plague (Cully and Williams 2001; Chapter 12). Today's population structure is almost certainly not an evolved response to combat plague, however—but rather is the inevitable consequence of poisoning, loss of habitat, and plague itself.

Transfer of Plague from Prairie Dogs to Humans

Human cases of plague resulting from prairie dogs and their fleas are few because humans rarely handle infected prairie dogs, and because prairie dog fleas tend to be highly host-specific and therefore avoid humans (Weber 1978; Polland and Barnes 1979; Barnes 1982; Levy and Gage 1999). Prairie dogs sometimes harbor fleas of the genus *Pulex*, which commonly bite people, but these fleas are poor vectors of plague (Burroughs 1947). Most cases of human plague in the United States result from association with rodents other than prairie dogs, especially ground squirrels. Ground squirrel fleas are less host-specific than prairie dog fleas, and therefore are more likely to bite humans and transmit plague (Weber 1978; Barnes 1982; Cully and Williams 2001).

People worried about plague should never handle prairie dogs. They also should avoid colony-sites where prairie dogs recently have vanished, because, as noted below, plague-positive fleas might persist at such deserted sites for more than one year.

What Happens to Plague between Epizootics?

After an epizootic of plague among prairie dogs, the disease typically vanishes, often for many years. Where does it go? At least four hypotheses might explain the maintenance of plague between epizootics:

- Plague-positive fleas can survive and maintain live bacteria for at least one year, and therefore might serve as an important reservoir for plague bacteria between epizootics (Lechleitner et al. 1968). Infected fleas remain inside burrows after an epizootic or come to burrow-entrances, and thus can infect other rodent species that visit burrows. Fleas also might jump onto large animals such as coyotes and pronghorn that routinely visit prairie dog colony-sites.
- Perhaps plague bacteria persist in the soil at colony-sites between epizootics (WHO 1970; Poland and Barnes 1979; Orent 2004). This mechanism seems unlikely, for two related reasons (Cully 1989). First, plague bacteria do not produce spores or other obvious devices that might aid long-term survival when the bacteria are outside hosts and vectors. Second, the interval between epizootics at the same colony-site is usually more than three years—probably too long for the bacteria to survive outside hosts and vectors.
- Perhaps prairie dogs themselves sometimes maintain the plague bacteria between epizootics (Cully and Williams 2001). White-tailed prairie dogs in the vicinity of Meeteetse, Wyoming, for example, have maintained plague continuously since 1985 (Anderson and Williams 1997), even though individuals are still extremely susceptible (E. S. Williams, personal communication, 2002). Because white-tailed prairie dogs are less social than black-tailed prairie dogs and usually occur in smaller colonies of lower density (Hoogland 1979b, 1995), opportunities for transmission of diseases probably are reduced (Cully and Williams 2001). Consequently, plague might not move within and between colonies of white-tailed prairie dogs so quickly as it usually does within and between colonies of black-tailed prairie dogs—so that 100% mortality of white-tailed prairie dogs within a complex of nearby colonies is less likely. Similar maintenance of plague might occur among black-tailed prairie dogs in areas where colony sizes and colony densities are unusually low for some reason (e.g., poor habitat, frequent poisoning, heavy predation, or plague itself) (see Chapters 3 and 6).
- In our opinion, the most likely hypothesis to explain the maintenance of plague between epizootics involves other rodent species. More than 70 species of mammals in North America contract plague, harbor plague-infected fleas, or have serum antibodies to plague bacteria (Barnes 1993). Some of these 70 species are rodents that commonly live at or near prairie dog colony-sites, such as deer mice, northern grasshopper mice, meadow voles, and certain species of ground squirrels (Kotliar et al. 1999; Chapter 4). These latter associates sometimes might have rates of recruitment that are higher than rates of mortality from plague—and thus might be able to maintain plague for many years at or near colony-sites (Cully and Williams

2001). When the conditions are right, plague infects prairie dogs once again and devastates colonies. Maintenance of plague between epizootics does not necessarily involve just a single rodent species that associates with prairie dogs, but rather might involve—either simultaneously or sequentially—several associated species.

Rarity of Plague in Eastern Populations of Prairie Dogs

Plague is rare among prairie dogs in the eastern part of the geographic range. Specifically, even though plague has been annihilating prairie dogs in the western two-thirds of the geographic range since the 1940s, plague is rare—indeed, almost totally absent—among prairie dogs east of a line that approximates the 102nd meridian (see Figure 11.1). Consequently, plague among prairie dogs is rare throughout most of Kansas, Nebraska, Oklahoma, North Dakota, and South Dakota. Reasons for the absence of plague in the eastern one-third of the range are elusive. Perhaps something about the climate is not conducive to the maintenance or transmission of plague in the mixed-grass prairies east of the 102nd meridian. Or perhaps the community of mammals—or the community of fleas—changes east of the 102nd meridian to a mix of species that cannot maintain plague. On the other hand, perhaps the rarity of plague farther east is merely accidental. If so, then migration to the east—after a stall at the 102nd meridian that has persisted for more than 60 years—might eventually occur.

Studies of mammals and fleas on both sides of the "plague line" are beginning to address the absence of plague among prairie dogs east of the 102nd meridian. At this point we only know that certain mammals that contract plague west of the line are present east of the line as well, as are several species of fleas that transmit plague. Examples of the former include prairie dogs themselves, deer mice, northern grasshopper mice, and thirteen-lined ground squirrels; examples of the latter include *Oropsylla hirsutus*, *Oropsylla tuberculatus cynomuris*, and *Pulex* spp. (Cully and Williams 2001).

Ways to Reduce the Impact of Plague on Prairie Dogs

Efforts to protect prairie dogs from plague have focused on killing fleas by infusing burrows with insecticide-dusts such as Pyraperm and Deltadust (Bayer Environmental Science, Montvale, New Jersey) (Figure 11.4). Pyraperm contains permethrin and reduces flea infestation within colonies of black-tailed prairie dogs for at least three months (Beard et al. 1992). At a 5-hectare (12-acre) colony-site of Utah prairie dogs, Pyraperm killed fleas and immediately halted an outbreak of plague in both 1998 and 2001 (Hoogland et al. 2004).

Figure 11.4. Infusion of burrows with insecticide-dust such as Deltadust, which kills fleas for as long as six months and thereby helps to protect prairie dogs from plague. Photo by Eric Stone.

Deltadust is an insecticide-dust that contains deltamethrin, a chemical similar to permethrin, but the formulation is more resistant to moisture and therefore kills fleas over a longer period of time after infusion of prairie dog burrows (Seery et al. 2003). Deltadust also suppresses fleas among other rodent species that associate with prairie dogs (Biggins 2001a).

Besides permethrin and deltamethrin, other insecticides also control fleas on small mammals (Hinkle et al. 1997). Possible choices for use on prairie dogs include insect growth regulators such as methoprene (Lang and Chamberlain 1986), lufenuron (Davis 1999), pyriproxyfen (Karhu and Anderson 2000), and fluazuron (Slowik et al. 2001). After application to the skin or fur, fipronil deters fleas on pets such as domestic dogs and domestic cats, and it might work for prairie dogs as well if simple, inexpensive methods of application can be developed (Metzger and Rust 2002).

We recognize that insecticide-dusts, in addition to killing fleas that transmit plague, also kill other arthropods within prairie dog burrows (e.g., other insects; arachnids such as mites, ticks, and spiders). Because of these negative side effects, we only recommend the use of insecticide-dusts where the conservation of prairie dogs is especially important (e.g., study-colony of marked individuals, or colony with black-footed ferrets).

In theory, vaccines also might help to protect prairie dogs against plague. In practice, however, the development of vaccines is still in its infancy (Creekmore et al. 2002).

Long-Term Prognosis of Prairie Dogs Versus Plague

Plague has found a home among prairie dogs of the western United States. Evidence that prairie dogs have begun to evolve resistance is minimal, so we should assume that plague will continue to ravage colonies. Because of so many unanswered questions, the best conservation strategy versus plague for now is to maintain numerous colonies of prairie dogs distributed throughout their geographic range, with special emphasis on the plague-free eastern one-third of the range (see also Chapters 12, 16, and 17).

Summary

- Plague, called sylvatic plague when it affects wild rodents, is a disease caused by a bacterium (*Yersinia pestis*). The usual vectors are fleas. Plague probably first arrived in the United States in about 1900 via commercial ships from China.
- Because they have been exposed to plague for only about 60 years, prairie dogs probably have been unable to evolve a good defense—and consequently remain highly susceptible. Mortality within infected colonies usually approaches 100%.
- In combination with unpredictability regarding the place and timing of epizootics, the catastrophic mortality from plague inhibits efforts to conserve prairie dogs.
- Human cases of plague resulting from prairie dogs and their fleas are few because humans rarely handle infected prairie dogs, and because prairie dog fleas tend to be highly host-specific and therefore avoid humans.
- After an epizootic of plague among prairie dogs, the disease typically vanishes, often for many years. Maintenance of plague between epizootics probably involves other rodent species such as deer mice, northern grasshopper mice, and meadow voles that frequently live at or near prairie dog colony-sites.
- For unknown reasons, plague is currently rare among prairie dogs in the eastern one-third of the geographic range.

- Efforts to protect prairie dogs from plague have focused on killing fleas by infusing burrows with insecticide-dusts such as Deltadust.
- Because of so many unanswered questions, the best conservation strategy versus plague for now is to maintain numerous colonies of prairie dogs distributed throughout their geographic range, with special emphasis on the plague-free eastern one-third of the range.

CHAPTER 12

Does the Prairie Dog Merit Protection Via the Endangered Species Act?

Rob Manes

The prairie dog and the Endangered Species Act (ESA) polarize people. Some argue that the prairie dog is an important species threatened with extinction, that it reflects the health of the fragile grassland ecosystem, and that it deserves ESA protection. Others protest that the prairie dog is a pest for farmers and ranchers of western states, and that ESA protection would hinder eradication.

In this chapter I summarize the history and purpose of ESA, and define some of the many associated terms. I then explain how a species comes under consideration for ESA's Federal List of Endangered and Threatened Wildlife and Plants (FLETWP), and clarify the distinction between endangered and threatened species. I examine the United States Fish and Wildlife Service (USFWS) reasons for classifying the prairie dog as a candidate species for addition to FLETWP in 2000, and why USFWS reversed this controversial classification in 2004. Finally, I discuss how politics might affect the addition of species to FLETWP.

History and Purpose of ESA

In 1966, Congress passed the Endangered Species Preservation Act, which authorized acquisition of land to protect imperiled native species. The Endangered Species Conservation Act of 1969 prohibited importation of endangered species from other countries. Next, in 1973, came ESA, which combined and strengthened earlier legislation by defining key terms; authorizing protection for plants as well as animals; establishing tougher standards for federal conservation programs; prohibiting killing and harassment of threatened and endangered species; and prescribing matching funds to state agencies for conservation. The purpose of ESA, which is under the jurisdiction of USFWS and the National Marine Fisheries Service (NMFS), is to prevent the disappearance of plants and animals that are, or might soon be, in danger of extinction. The full text of ESA is accessible at the following Internet address: http://endangered.fws.gov/esa.html.

Amendments to ESA in 1982 require that listing (i.e., addition of a species to FLETWP) be based on either scientific research or information from commercial operations; in theory, economic concerns are irrelevant. The 1982 amendments also impose certain deadlines regarding the listing process. The most recent amendments to ESA, in 1988, mandate monitoring of candidate and recovered species; propose improvements in species recovery; require financial accounting for all ESA actions; and strengthen protection of plants on federal lands. Usually with funds for implementation, ESA actions to protect listed species include land acquisition; cooperation with state agencies; restoration and conservation of suitable habitat; removal or reduction of causes of mortality; and prohibition of certain activities (e.g., shooting and poisoning), with associated enforcement and penalties that range from monetary fines to imprisonment.

The total number of plant and animal species in the United States on FLETWP was 1,264 on 31 December 2004. Thirty-four additional species have been removed from FLETWP because of either extinction or adequate recovery.

In this chapter I focus on issues that fall primarily under ESA's Section 4, which addresses the listing process. For prairie dogs, these issues include the following (see also Chapters 8, 9, 10, 11, 16, and 17): cumulative area currently inhabited; previous and continuing loss of habitat (mainly via conversion of grassland to cropland); recreational shooting; prairie dogs as pets; diseases such as plague; and poisoning.

Definitions of Key ESA Terms

Terms—such as *12-month finding, candidate species, listing process, threat, warranted,* and *warranted-but-precluded*—are in the glossary at the back of this book. These terms apply only to FLETWP. Even if a species is not on FLETWP or a candidate for listing, it might be on a state's list of endangered and threatened species.

When is a Species Added to FLETWP?

On its own initiative, USFWS (or NMFS) sometimes determines that a species should be considered for listing. More commonly, USFWS responds to a petition for listing from an outside person or organization. The listing process requires USFWS to make a *90-day finding* that indicates whether substantial information exists for possible listing. If the 90-day finding is affirmative, then USFWS solicits additional input and completes a *12-month finding* that determines whether listing is *warranted*, *not warranted*, or *warranted-but-precluded* (for more details, see http://endangered.fws.gov).

A finding of warranted-but-precluded means that a species should be added to FLETWP, but that addition is prevented or delayed by attention to species that are in greater danger of extinction. A species designated by USFWS as warranted-but-precluded is called a *candidate species*, and requires an annual *candidate assessment*, which is published in the *Federal Register* for public review. USFWS assigns each candidate species a *listing priority number* (LPN) from 1–12, with the following guidelines:

- LPN results from the magnitude and immediacy of threats. LPN of 1 indicates maximal danger of extinction, whereas LPN of 12 indicates minimal danger.
- LPN also reflects taxonomic uniqueness (i.e., the number of similar species). LPN will be lower (i.e., indicative of higher priority) for a species that is the only member of its genus than for a species with several congeners, for example. LPN also will be lower for a species with no subspecies than for a species that has several.
- Even for candidate species with low LPNs, eventual listing often depends largely on availability of funds.

After a designation of warranted-but-precluded, USFWS does not necessarily add the candidate species to FLETWP at a later date. Via an annual candidate assessment, for example, USFWS might remove a species from the candidate list. Such removal has occurred for the prairie dog—that is, USFWS determined that the prairie dog was a candidate species in 2000, but changed its status to "not warranted" in 2004. In theory, designation as a candidate species provides no formal protection via ESA. In practice, however, organizations and individuals often afford special consideration to candidate species regarding conservation—usually to avoid the regulations and restrictions that would accompany listing.

What Does It Mean to be an Endangered or Threatened Species?

If a candidate species eventually is added to FLETWP, it can be classified as either endangered or threatened. An *endangered species* is in jeopardy of extinction throughout all or a significant portion of its geographic range. A *threatened species* is likely to become endangered within the foreseeable future.

Two issues, in particular, are important to USFWS (or NMFS) regarding listing. First, evidence must indicate a plausible and predictive path by which a species is likely to become endangered or extinct within the foreseeable future. Specifically, a demonstrable decrease in overall population size, or a reasonable projection of such decrease, must be unambiguous. Further, the decrease in overall population size must be of such a magnitude that, if nothing changes, extinction probably will occur. The term "foreseeable future" has no formal definition and can vary for different species—or for the same species under different circumstances.

Second, for listing a species must exhibit a decline in population size "throughout all or a significant portion of its range." One common and reasonable way to address this issue is to compare the current geographic range with the best estimate of the former range. This approach, however, sometimes might lead to erroneous conclusions regarding possible extinction. Some fragile species, for example, might be able to withstand declining populations in only a small portion of the range before approaching extinction. More resilient species, on the other hand, might be able to withstand declines over much of the range. The existence of numerous separate populations does not necessarily guarantee persistence, because all the populations might be small and isolated, and therefore individually vulnerable (Chapter 2).

Populations of all species fluctuate in response to many factors, and many species are declining and less abundant than they were 200 years ago. These trends alone, however, are inadequate for ESA listing. To justify listing, evidence must demonstrate that current population declines probably will soon lead to endangerment or extinction.

Why Did USFWS Classify the Prairie Dog as a Candidate Species in 2000?

In summer 1998, the National Wildlife Federation (NWF) and the Biodiversity Legal Foundation (BLF) independently petitioned USFWS to add the prairie dog as a threatened species to FLETWP (Graber et al. 1998; BLF et al. 1998). NWF's petition requested an *emergency listing*. USFWS did not concur about the need for an emergency listing, and therefore initiated the normal listing process while BLF prepared to sue. The 90-day finding was affirmative—that is, USFWS concluded that NWF and BLF had compiled sufficient information for possible listing as a threatened species (USFWS 1999). Seeking additional input from state agencies, public organizations, and private citizens, USFWS then began to prepare its 12-month finding.

The best way to estimate numbers of prairie dogs is to count them. Counting is feasible only for small areas, however. For larger areas, a more practical way to estimate the number of prairie dogs is to determine the area they inhabit (Chapter 6). If prairie dog densities were constant over time and space, then an accurate estimate of the cumulative area they inhabit would yield an accurate estimate of the total number of prairie dogs. But densities vary with natural factors such as climate, availability of forage, age of colony, predation, and time of year, and with unnatural factors such as poisoning, plague, and recreational shooting (King 1955; Hoogland 1995; Severson and Plumb 1998; Chapters 6, 8, 10, and 11). When examining trends in prairie dog population size within a particular state or across the former geographic range, biologists consider these factors and focus on the cumulative area inhabited, from which they can (roughly) estimate the number of prairie dogs (Chapter 6).

About 200 years ago, prairie dogs inhabited parts of Canada, Mexico, and eleven states (Chapter 16). For its 12-month finding, perhaps the most difficult task USFWS faced was to determine and evaluate population trends over the last two centuries—a formidable challenge, because biologists are not unanimous regarding former or current numbers of prairie dogs (Chapters 6 and 16). Most biologists concur that prairie dog populations have declined seriously since the early 1800s (Seton 1929; Anderson et al. 1986; Miller et al. 1996; Chapter 16), but reliable estimates necessary for USFWS to reach a rigorous conclusion about listing were lacking in 2000. For those states that had information about current area inhabited by prairie dogs, the estimates sometimes varied tremendously (USFWS 2000a). In Nebraska, for example, estimates of area inhabited by prairie dogs in 2000 ranged from 6,070 to 32,375 hectares (15,000 to 80,000 acres); in Colorado, estimates ranged from 17,800 to 405,000 hectares (44,000 to 1 million acres).

Without reliable estimates, how could USFWS compare areas formerly and currently inhabited by prairie dogs? And how could USFWS determine if any identified declines would continue? In order to proceed, USFWS calculated its own estimate of cumulative area inhabited by prairie dogs in 2000. This estimate was 311,000 hectares (768,000 acres), of which 274,000 hectares (677,000 acres) were within the United States. Comparing this estimate with rough estimates of area formerly occupied by prairie dogs (Merriam 1902a; Burnett 1918; Oakes 2000; Knowles et al. 2002; Chapter 16), USFWS (2000a) concluded that today's prairie dogs inhabit less than 2% of the landscape that they inhabited about 200 years ago (see also Chapter 16). But would this negative trend continue, and thereby lead to endangerment and extinction within the foreseeable future? To address this pivotal question, USFWS investigated several potential threats, and reached the following overlapping conclusions in 2000 (USFWS 2000a):

- Thirty percent of the former geographic range of 200 years ago no longer contained prairie dogs.
- Thirty-seven percent of the former range had been modified for agriculture and was no longer inhabitable by prairie dogs.
- Plague had ravaged populations in 66% of the former range in the 1980s and 1990s (see also Chapter 11).
- Plague had been especially devastating in the western two-thirds of the former geographic range, and appeared to be expanding eastward.
- If threats and population declines continued, the prairie dog's remaining area of occupancy might decrease by 90% over the next 30 years.

For these reasons, USFWS concluded in its 12-month finding that the prairie dog was a candidate for FLETWP as a threatened species, with an LPN of 8 (USFWS 2000a). Two excerpts from the 12-month finding are especially instructive regarding the reasoning of USFWS:

> [The prairie dog] has undergone significant reductions in its historic range and also in the amount of habitat within its range which it presently occupies. Moreover, recent population trends indicate that its overall numbers are declining and will likely continue to decline within the foreseeable future within a significant portion of its range. Accordingly, the species is likely to become endangered in the foreseeable future in a significant portion of its range. (USFWS 2000a, Section 1.1)
>
> At present, occupied habitat has decreased over the past century by two orders of magnitude (from approximately 100 million acres to less than 1 million acres). In 30 years (assuming the spread of plague to currently plague-free areas), occupied habitat could decrease by another order of magnitude to approximately 0.1 percent of historic estimates. (USFWS 2000a, Section 4.1)

Why Did USFWS Reverse Its Decision in 2004?

After designating the prairie dog as a candidate species for FLETWP in 2000 (USFWS 2000a), USFWS completed annual candidate assessments in 2001 and 2002. Both times, USFWS concluded that the prairie dog should remain a candidate species (USFWS 2001, 2002a). In its annual candidate assessment for 2004, however, USFWS concluded that the prairie dog is no longer a candidate species (USFWS 2004). Why the reversal? New information on two issues, in particular—cumulative area of occupancy, and plague—persuaded USFWS to remove the prairie dog from the candidate list.

Cumulative Area of Occupancy

When USFWS adds a species to FLETWP, numerous regulations and restrictions necessarily follow. Individuals, organizations, and state agencies were concerned about these complications after USFWS designated the prairie dog as a candidate species in 2000, and initiated several efforts to avert listing (Chapters 14 and 15). In addition, agencies from each state scrambled, via field surveys, aerial surveys, and remote sensing (Chapter 6), to obtain an accurate estimate of the area inhabited by prairie dogs. Collectively, these state surveys provided the first good estimate in over 40 years of the cumulative area inhabited by prairie dogs across the former geographic range (Table 12.1). The most significant conclusion from these surveys is that USFWS had underestimated the cumulative area inhabited by prairie dogs in 2000 for the designation of the species as a candidate for FLETWP (USFWS 2000a). Specifically, the USFWS estimate for 2000 was 311,000 hectares (768,000 acres), but its estimate for 2004 was 2.5 times higher (766,000 hectares [1.89 million acres]) (Table 12.1). This higher, more accurate, estimate of cumulative area inhabited across the entire geographic range played a major role in the USFWS decision to remove the prairie dog from the candidate list (USFWS 2004). Note that the higher estimate in 2004 did not result because prairie dog populations increased dramatically from 2000 through 2004, but rather because the calculation in 2000 was a serious underestimate.

Some recent state estimates for the area inhabited by prairie dogs are controversial. Forest Guardians et al. (2004), for example, have argued that the recent estimates are inflated, especially for Colorado. Debating the accuracy of state estimates, however, misses the key point, which is that we have more prairie dogs today than USFWS concluded that we had in 2000. More important, we have more prairie dogs today than we had in the late 1950s, when the Bureau of Sport Fisheries and Wildlife (BSFW) estimated that the cumulative area occupied by prairie dogs within the United States was a mere 147,000 hectares (363,000 acres) (BSFW 1961). The estimate for area currently inhabited by prairie dogs in South Dakota alone is higher than the estimate over all states for 1961 (see Table 12.1).

Table 12.1. Estimates, by state or country, used by USFWS for area inhabited by prairie dogs at different times. All estimates are for thousands of hectares. References: USFWS 2000a (for 200 years ago and for 2000), BSFW 1961 (for 1961), USFWS 2004 (for 2004).

	Estimate of area (in thousands of hectares) inhabited by prairie dogs at different times, by state or country			
State or country	*About 200 years ago*	*1961*	*2000*	*2004*
Arizona	263	0	0	0
Colorado	1,200–2,800	39	38	255
Kansas	800–1,000	20	17	53
Montana	600–2,400	11	26	36
Nebraska	2,400	12	24	55
New Mexico	>2,700	7	16	24
North Dakota	800	8	10	8
Oklahoma	380	6	4	26
South Dakota	700	13	59	165
Texas	23,000	11	29	>72
Wyoming	6,500	20	51	51
Total for United States	39,000–43,000	147	274	745
Canada	0.6–0.8		0.8	1
Mexico	560		36	>20
Total for North America	40,000–44,000		311	766

Even if the current estimate from Colorado is inflated by 50%, it is still well above the estimates from 1961 and 2000 (see Table 12.1). Nine of eleven states had larger areas inhabited by prairie dogs in 2004 than in 1961; increases were large (i.e., by a factor of at least 2.5) for all of these nine states, and the increase for South Dakota was especially impressive (by a factor of more than 10) (see Table 12.1). The cumulative area inhabited by prairie dogs across the United States in 2004 was more than five times the cumulative area for 1961 (see Table 12.1).

Table 12.1 does not negate that today's prairie dogs, like prairie dogs in the early 1960s, occupy less than 2% of the terrain that they inhabited 200 years ago (Chapter 16). Regarding possible listing, however, the crucial conclusion from Table 12.1 is that the cumulative area of occupancy has increased over the last 40 years. Prairie dogs thus show no evidence that endangerment and extinction are inevitable in the foreseeable future, and this conclusion played a key role in the USFWS decision to remove the species from the candidate list (USFWS 2004).

Plague

In its 12-month finding, USFWS rated plague as a moderate, imminent threat to the long-term persistence of prairie dogs (USFWS 2000a). This rating resulted mainly from examination of the devastating effects of plague in a few large populations, where mortality approached 100%. With the assumption that plague would be similarly ruinous for smaller populations, USFWS predicted a decline of 50% in overall population size per decade for the foreseeable future (USFWS 2000a). USFWS retracted this prediction in 2004, in response to the following discoveries of the early 2000s (USFWS 2004; see also Chapters 11 and 16):

- Following an outbreak of plague, some populations recover, over several years, to pre-plague levels.
- For some individual prairie dogs, an unusually high initial dosage of plague bacteria might be necessary for infection. Further, a small percentage of prairie dogs shows limited resistance to plague. Consequently, plague might not be as annihilatory for prairie dogs as USFWS envisioned in 2000.
- Today's colonies are smaller and more isolated than they were 200 years ago. These characteristics probably render today's prairie dogs less susceptible to plague.

In addition, USFWS emphasized in 2004 that the eastern one-third of the prairie dog's former geographic range remains plague-free, and that most of today's prairie dogs live there.

USFWS acknowledges that plague continues to ravage some of today's prairie dog populations. Because of the new information just summarized, however, USFWS has concluded that plague is unlikely to cause extinction or endangerment of prairie dogs in the foreseeable future. This conclusion was instrumental in the USFWS decision to remove the prairie dog from the candidate list (USFWS 2004).

The Politics of Prairie Dogs and ESA

The legislators responsible for ESA tried to design a process that would focus on the scientific merits of protecting rare species and would ignore nonbiological considerations. Unfortunately, however, ESA is not immune to politics. Lobbying of politicians by special-interest representatives can creep into the listing process. Information to support listing is always incomplete, and therefore subject to debate by "experts" who sometimes use select information to promote self-serving agendas. Economics also can play a part, when opponents complain that the consequences of listing a species would harm them financially. And because petitioners sometimes threaten to sue, the menace of courtroom costs and delays might influence the listing process as well. Finally, the leanings of each presidential administration can have major impacts on the utility of ESA. "Conservative" politicians tend to oppose ESA listings, whereas "liberal" politicians typically favor listings and a broader application of ESA.

ESA is the only federal law with clear, rigorous standards for protecting species. Opponents sometimes criticize ESA's "inflexibility." But its rigid nature helps ESA to weather politics and to save species from extinction (Stokstad 2005; Woodroffe et al. 2005). More "flexible" laws such as the Clean Water Act (CWA) and the National Forest Management Act sometimes are less effective than ESA in guarding our natural resources. If CWA were more rigid and more effectively addressed the protection of wetlands, for example, then perhaps we would have little need to invoke ESA to protect many aquatic species that are currently in peril (Davison 2001). ESA has provided stopgap protection for many species and habitats, and thereby has helped to conserve ecosystems as well (Chapters 4, 17, and 18; Box to Chapter 12).

BOX 12.1 Why the Prairie Dog Merits ESA Protection

Nicole J. Rosmarino

Along with other biologists involved with efforts to conserve prairie dogs, Rob Manes believes that the United States Fish and Wildlife Service (USFWS) made a good decision in 2004 to remove the prairie dog from the list of candidate species for the Federal List of Endangered and Threatened Wildlife and Plants (FLETWP) (Chapter 12). I disagree. Here I discuss problems that I perceive with the USFWS analysis of population trends and current threats. I also evaluate the role of politics in the listing process, and the importance of protecting ecosystems. I conclude by arguing that the prairie dog deserves recognition as a threatened species.

Problems with the USFWS Analysis of Population Trends and Current Threats

Biologists focus on the area inhabited by prairie dogs to evaluate trends in population size within states and across the geographic range. Past and current estimates of the cumulative area inhabited are elusive, however (Chapter 6). Consider the USFWS (2004) calculation for the area inhabited by prairie dogs in Colorado in 2004, for example (255,000 hectares [630,000 acres]; see

Table 12.1). New information from in-the-field checks indicates that this calculation is a serious overestimate (Forest Guardians et al. 2004; Reading 2004). About one-third of the cumulative estimate of the area within the United States inhabited by prairie dogs (Table 12.1) is therefore suspect. The removal of the prairie dog from the candidate list has weakened incentives to improve estimates of in-state areas of occupancy by prairie dogs—so that future analyses of in-state and range-wide population trends will be difficult.

Table 12.1 indicates that the cumulative area inhabited by prairie dogs has increased over the last 40 years, and this putative trend played a key role in the USFWS decision to remove the prairie dog from the candidate list (USFWS 2004; Chapter 12). But the methods used to estimate the area inhabited by prairie dogs in the 1950s and 1960s (visual observations) differ substantially from the methods of the last decade (aerial photography and satellite imagery, in addition to visual observations; see Chapter 6). Consequently, any trends that result from comparisons of data separated by 40 years are perhaps questionable.

USFWS (2004) has described the threat of plague to prairie dogs as less severe than previously indicated (USFWS 2002a). But the inability of many populations to recover from recurring epizootics of plague continues throughout much of the prairie dog's geographic range (USFWS 2004; Chapter 11). Further, USFWS (2004) recently has characterized threats from poisoning, recreational shooting, and habitat destruction as insignificant—erroneously, in my opinion—and thereby has eliminated the need to consider whether current regulatory mechanisms adequately conserve prairie dogs.

The Role of Politics in the Listing Process

Legislators responsible for the Endangered Species Act (ESA) recognized that economic concerns and patterns of land use can promote extinction. To prevent such extinctions, ESA stipulates that listing decisions must be based on science, not politics. Indeed, to deter the distortion of the listing process by political and economic concerns, Congress amended ESA in 1982 by adding the word "solely" in front of the words "on the basis of the best scientific and commercial data available" (*Congressional Record*, 17 September 1982, page 24153). I submit, however, that politics has played a significant role in the listing process for many plants and animals, and especially for the prairie dog.

While William J. Clinton and George H. W. Bush were presidents of the United States, the number of new listings averaged 65 and 59 species per year, respectively. During the administration of George W. Bush, by contrast, new listings have averaged only eight species per year—all in direct response to court order. Despite a backlog of 311 species on the candidate list, the current Bush Administration has requested inadequate funds for imperiled species (http://endangered.fws.gov)—and now complains that funds are insufficient for new listings (*Federal Register* 69:24876–24904, 4 May 2004).

To discourage listing and to encourage the removal of the prairie dog from the candidate list, three state agencies in Colorado threatened to sue if USFWS added the prairie dog to FLETWP (Walcher et al. 1999). Former Democratic Senator Tom Daschle from South Dakota met with the Secretary of the United States Department of the Interior Gale Norton in May 2004, declaring that he hoped the prairie dog would be off the candidate list by August 2004 (*Rapid City Journal*, 27 May 2004). Daschle got his wish. And on the day after USFWS announced the removal of the prairie dog from the candidate list, South Dakota unveiled a poisoning program that includes colonies of prairie dogs with black-footed ferrets (Chapters 12, 15, and 18).

The Importance of Protecting Ecosystems

Increasingly, scientists, conservationists, and policymakers are advocating the protection of ecosystems to address the continuing loss of biodiversity (United States General Accounting Office (GAO) 1994; USFWS 1997; Chapters 4, 17, and 18). ESA states a dual purpose: to conserve not only threatened and endangered species, but also the ecosystems on which they depend. To better protect ecosystems, USFWS should give higher priority to keystone species (Rosmarino 2002). Listing the prairie dog will help to safeguard its grassland ecosystem as well.

The Prairie Dog Merits Listing as a Threatened Species

Many questions remain regarding the conservation of prairie dogs. We know, however, that loss of habitat, recreational shooting, poisoning, and plague all continue to devastate prairie dog populations throughout much of the geographic range (Chapters 10, 11, 16, and 17). For these reasons, my perspective is that the prairie dog is a threatened species—that is, it is likely to become endangered in the foreseeable future. The prairie dog thus merits listing, and all the protection that results from such listing.

The "Precautionary Principle" guides policymakers to err in favor of caution in the face of uncertainty (Shipworth and Kenley 1996, Foster et al. 2000; Stokstad 2005). USFWS could, and should, apply this principle for the conservation of imperiled species. The ESA provision for threatened species embodies the notion of "better safe than sorry." My perspective is that we should not wait until we have all the necessary information to make the decision about listing the prairie dog, because that time will never come. We know from past experience that inaction is lethal. From 1973 to 1995, for example, 83 species went extinct while awaiting federal protection (Suckling et al. 2004). Without the benefits of listing, threats will continue to diminish prairie dog populations and the grassland ecosystem of western North America.

Regarding the possible listing of the prairie dog, emotions from both sides of the issue run hot, for several reasons: the prairie dog's charismatic appeal (Chapter 2); its keystone status for grassland ecosystems (Chapter 4); its potential to reduce the suitability of terrain for grazing by domestic livestock (Chapter 5); and a long history of poisoning that has involved federal, state, and county governments (Chapter 8). USFWS consequently has been under heavy political pressure from both conservatives and liberals since NWF's and BLF's petitions to list the prairie dog in 1998. My assessment is that, with the information available, USFWS made a reasonable decision in 2000 to designate the prairie dog as a candidate species for FLETWP. I also believe that USFWS made a good decision in 2004 to remove the prairie dog from the candidate list after reviewing new information that accumulated in the four years that followed the USFWS decision in 2000.

What Happens Now?

After USFWS designated the prairie dog as a candidate species for FLETWP in 2000, Native Americans, ranchers, farmers, and state and federal biologists began to cooperate and compromise for the conservation of prairie dogs. In many cases, the ultimate reason for collaboration was to avoid regulations and restrictions that would accompany listing. Regardless of motivation, progress was evident. With the removal of the prairie dog from the candidate list in 2004 (USFWS 2004), however, the future of the prairie dog and its grassland ecosystem is unclear. In South Dakota, for example, poisoning of prairie dogs has resumed at Conata Basin (Buffalo Gap National Grasslands), which contains one of the few populations of black-footed ferrets that consistently has increased since its reintroduction in 1996 (Chapter 4). Poisoning also has resumed at South Dakota's Pine Ridge and Rosebud Native American reservations, and at three of the five largest prairie dog complexes described in Chapter 16. Further, with the threat of ESA regulations and restrictions now gone, the implementation and effectiveness of "A multi-state conservation plan [MSCP] for the black-tailed prairie dog, *Cynomys ludovicianus*, in the United States" (Luce 2003; Chapter 14) are dubious (Chapters 17 and 18).

If new information indicates that the long-term survival of prairie dogs is in danger, then any individual or agency can petition USFWS to reconsider the prairie dog for listing.

Conserving a single species, such as the prairie dog, is difficult, but conserving the prairie dog's grassland ecosystem is a greater challenge. Progress in the conservation of ecosystems probably will require changes in the provisions and administration of state and federal laws and programs. New legislation, and perhaps amendments to ESA as well, also might be necessary for better conservation of ecosystems (Pyare and Berger 2003; Soulé et al. 2003, 2005; Chapters 17 and 18).

Summary

- The purpose of ESA is to conserve wildlife and plants that are, or might soon be, in danger of extinction. Methods to thwart the extinction of species include conservation of suitable habitat and attempts to stop declines in overall population size.
- USFWS and NMFS are responsible for the administration of ESA.
- USFWS (or NMFS) considers a species for listing (i.e., for addition to FLETWP) in response to its own assessment or, more commonly, to a petition from an outside person or organization. In the first part of the listing process, USFWS must make a 90-day finding that indicates whether substantial information exists for possible listing. If the 90-day finding is affirmative, then USFWS solicits additional input and completes a 12-month finding that determines whether listing is warranted, not warranted, or warranted-but-precluded.
- After a designation of warranted-but-precluded, USFWS does not necessarily add the candidate species to FLETWP at a later date. Via an annual candidate assessment, for example, USFWS might remove a species from the candidate list.
- If a candidate species eventually is added to FLETWP, its designation is either endangered or threatened. An endangered species is in jeopardy of extinction throughout all or a significant portion of its geographic range. A threatened species is likely to become endangered within the foreseeable future.
- Because of drastic declines in population size over the last 200 years, and because the declines seemed to be continuing, USFWS designated the prairie dog as a candidate for FLETWP as a threatened species in 2000.
- New data from the early 2000s indicate that USFWS underestimated the cumulative area inhabited by prairie dogs for its designation as a candidate species in 2000, and that USFWS probably overestimated the continuing devastation from plague. Further, the cumulative area inhabited by prairie dogs across the former geographic range has increased over the last 40 years—that is, prairie dogs show no evidence that endangerment and extinction are inevitable in the foreseeable future. For these reasons, USFWS removed the prairie dog from the candidate list in 2004.

- The grassland ecosystem of western North America includes not only prairie dogs, but also many species such as black-footed ferrets, mountain plovers, and burrowing owls that depend on prairie dogs for survival. With the removal of the prairie dog from the candidate list in 2004, the long-term persistence of the grassland ecosystem, for which the prairie dog is a keystone species, is perhaps in question.
- Conserving a single species, such as the prairie dog, is difficult, but conserving the prairie dog's grassland ecosystem is a greater challenge. Progress in the conservation of ecosystems probably will require changes in the provisions and administration of state and federal laws and programs. New legislation, and perhaps amendments to ESA as well, also might be necessary for better conservation of ecosystems.

Acknowledgments

I thank Pete Gober, who has earned gratitude and respect for his bold leadership, hard work, and sound reasoning in advocating responsible conservation of the prairie dog and its grassland ecosystem of western North America.

PART III

Conservation of Prairie Dogs

John L. Hoogland

If prairie dogs are worth saving, how do we proceed? The next six chapters provide possible solutions for politicians, conservation biologists, and wildlife managers.

People move, or translocate, prairie dogs for two reasons. Sometimes we want to move them away from a place of danger—for example, an area designated for a supermarket or commercial housing—to a safer home. Other times we want to start a new colony in a particular area. For years I have been telling people that fewer than 5% of translocated prairie dogs will remain at the recipient-site for more than one week. Most of the others will perish as they disperse in search of their genetic relatives back home. In the past ten years or so, however, biologists have made huge strides to increase survivorship and discourage dispersal of translocated prairie dogs. As they explain in Chapter 13, Dustin Long, Kristy Bly-Honness, Joe Truett, and David Seery have concocted ploys that induce as many as 71% of translocated prairie dogs to remain at the recipient-site for more than two months; further, most surviving individuals rear offspring in the year after translocation. With the methods described in Chapter 13, translocation is now a honed mechanism by which we can initiate a new colony or save prairie dogs that are imperiled at a specific colony-site.

Prairie dogs are social animals that interact frequently and amicably with their genetic relatives of the home territory. Because kinship is so important, moving prairie dogs as family groups probably should increase the success of translocations. Debra Shier's research, which required catching, marking, and observing individuals to determine family (coterie) compositions, supports this hypothesis (Box to Chapter 13). Dustin Long et al.'s research with unmarked individuals, however, suggests that keeping families together does not enhance either survivorship or reproductive success of translocated prairie dogs (Chapter 13). The resolution of this issue will be important, because moving prairie dogs as families takes longer and is more difficult and more expensive than moving mixed-family groups. In the meantime, I like Debra Shier's suggested compromise: let's keep individuals from the same and adjacent burrow-entrances (i.e., presumed families) together and translocate them into the same area of the same recipient-site. This practical suggestion does not require observations of marked individuals, and therefore involves only minimal additional effort and cost. Intriguing, indeed, is Long et al.'s hypothesis that increasing the time held in captivity for mixed-family groups might improve the survivorship and reproductive success of translocated prairie dogs.

In 2000, the United States Fish and Wildlife Service (USFWS) concluded that the prairie dog was a candidate species for addition to the Federal List of Endangered and Threatened Wildlife and Plants (FLETWP). Such addition would guarantee better protection for the prairie dog, but also would necessitate numerous regulations and restrictions for farmers, ranchers, and state and local governments of western states. To avoid such entanglements, states responded in several ways. The ten states with prairie dogs—plus an eleventh state, Arizona, where the prairie dog has been eradicated—formed the Interstate Black-tailed Prairie Dog Conservation Team, which developed "A multi-state conservation plan [MSCP] for the black-tailed prairie dog, *Cynomys ludovicianus*, in the United States." Further, many Native American tribes developed plans to manage prairie dogs on their reservations. In Chapter 14, Bob Luce, Rob Manes, and Bill Van Pelt summarize these encouraging developments.

In August 2004, USFWS ruled that the prairie dog is no longer a candidate species for FLETWP. The long-term implications of this reversal for MSCP are unclear, but the short-term repercussions are lucid: with the threat of regulations and restrictions associated with listing now gone, commitment to MSCP already has begun to diminish (Chapters 17 and 18).

The Farm Security and Rural Investment Act, commonly known as the Farm Bill, sometimes offers financial incentives and assistance to landowners who restore and protect wetlands, streams, wildlife habitats, and other important natural resources. Luce et al. promote the clever notion that similar incentives should be available to landowners who improve and maintain habitats for prairie dogs and those species such as black-footed ferrets, burrowing owls, and mountain plovers that depend on prairie dogs for survival (Chapter 14).

Four federal agencies manage lands with large populations of prairie dogs: the Bureau of Land Management (BLM), the National Park Service (NPS),

USFWS, and the United States Forest Service (USFS). Changes in policies after the prairie dog became a candidate species for FLETWP in 2000 indicated that all four agencies would help to ensure the long-term survival of prairie dogs. But, as noted above, USFWS concluded in 2004 that the prairie dog is no longer a candidate species. In immediate response, USFS resumed poisoning in several areas, including Conata Basin (Buffalo Gap National Grasslands, South Dakota), where black-footed ferrets also live. Will BLM, NPS, and USFWS soon allow poisoning as well? If so, what will be the role of federal lands in the conservation of prairie dogs? In Chapter 15, John Sidle, Greg Schenbeck, Eric Lawton, and Dan Licht discuss these important, vexing issues.

Restoring prairie dogs to their former abundance over the entire geographic range probably is unrealistic. We need to concentrate our efforts in specific areas that are most likely to be successful. In Chapter 16, Jonathan Proctor, Bill Haskins, and Steve Forrest explain and explore the concept of "focal area," which is a site where we can allow prairie dogs to occupy at least 4,000 hectares (9,880 acres)—so that both prairie dogs and those species that depend on them can thrive, and so that ecological processes such as recycling of nutrients and changes in species composition can prevail.

Proctor et al. identify 84 focal areas, ranging in size from 4,300 hectares to 2.4 million hectares (10,600 acres to 5.9 million acres), with a cumulative area of 10.5 million hectares (26 million acres). Of highest priority are the five focal areas with complexes of prairie dogs that currently inhabit more than 4,000 hectares (9,880 acres). Focal areas can provide the habitat necessary for the restoration and long-term survival of both the prairie dog and its grassland ecosystem. And, because most focal areas are within federal lands managed by agencies such as BLM and USFS, interference with ranching and agriculture should be minimal.

In theory, the solution to guarantee long-term survival of prairie dogs is simple, and involves the following steps: prohibit all shooting and poisoning; kill all fleas and thereby deter transmission of plague at colonies threatened by the disease; restore the suitable habitat that has been destroyed over the years by farming, urban development, and other factors; and change negative attitudes toward prairie dogs. In practice, of course, these steps are impractical and unrealistic. In Chapter 17, Brian Miller and Richard Reading propose more feasible, but nonetheless aggressive, actions for the conservation of prairie dogs. Their suggestions merit careful consideration.

In Chapter 18, I examine whether we can save prairie dogs, and whether we should bother.

CHAPTER 13

Establishment of New Prairie Dog Colonies by Translocation

Dustin Long, Kristy Bly-Honness, Joe C. Truett, and David B. Seery

Prairie dogs have disappeared over large portions of their former geographic range (Chapters 12 and 16). Their ability to reclaim lost ground is limited because long-distance dispersers, which usually travel less than 7 kilometers (4 miles) (Garrett and Franklin 1988; Chapter 3), usually do not survive and reproduce unless they find other occupied colony-sites or recently vacated ones. Timely restoration of prairie dogs in abandoned areas distant from existing colonies will require help from wildlife managers.

A translocation is the transfer of an individual from a source colony-site to either another colony-site or a new recipient-site without any prairie dogs. The first translocations of black-tailed prairie dogs occurred in the late 1970s, and these initial attempts used many of the methods developed for translocations of Utah prairie dogs in the early 1970s (Coffeen and Pedersen 1993).

In this chapter we discuss the role of translocations for the conservation of prairie dogs. We start by describing a good source population, and then explain our methods for livetrapping prairie dogs and caring for them before translocation. We describe a good recipient-site and explain methods to make recipient-sites better. We document that large numbers of translocated prairie dogs survive better than smaller numbers, and that the ratio of adults to juveniles, and of males to females, also affects the success of translocations. We investigate whether translocations are more successful if prairie dogs are moved as family groups, and Debra Shier investigates this same issue in her Box to our chapter. Finally, we demonstrate the benefits of short-term monitoring of translocated prairie dogs, and point out that continued management of recipient-sites is usually unnecessary within about one year after translocation.

BOX 13.1 Translocations Are More Successful When Prairie Dogs Are Moved as Families

Debra M. Shier

My research at the Vermejo Park Ranch, New Mexico, indicates that translocations of prairie dogs are more successful when individuals are moved together as family units (Shier 2004). Prairie dogs moved as complete coteries (N = 484 adults [at least one year old] and juveniles into five colonies, 87–100 per colony) survived and reproduced better than prairie dogs moved without consideration of coterie membership (N = 489 adults and juveniles into five colonies, 88–103 per colony).

Before translocations, I determined membership of coteries in April and May by observing behavioral interactions and sleeping patterns of eartagged, dye-marked individuals at large source-colonies. I then transferred family members into the same or adjacent man-made burrows at five recipient-sites with no other resident prairie dogs. Nonfamily members were transferred from three source-colonies into man-made burrows at five other recipient-sites with no other resident prairie dogs (five individuals per burrow). All transfers occurred in the summers of 2001 and 2002. I estimated survivorship by re-trapping all eartagged prairie dogs that were still at the recipient-sites in the spring following release. I estimated female reproductive success by measuring the percentage of females that weaned a litter, litter size at weaning, and the number of weaned juveniles per female (either lactating or non-lactating).

Adult and juvenile prairie dogs translocated as complete families survived better than prairie dogs translocated without attention to family (Figure 13-Box.1, left side), and they also experienced higher reproductive success (Figure 13-Box.1, right side). Further, prairie dogs from large families (at least 12 members, N = 129 from 10 families) survived better than prairie dogs from smaller families (fewer than 12 members, N =169 from 21 families): 55% versus 32%. Finally, prairie dogs translocated as families excavated more burrow-entrances during the first year: 229 (average, N = 5 colonies) versus 55 (N = 5 colonies).

Why do my results differ from the results of Dustin Long et al. (Chapter 13), who found no evidence to support the notion that translocations are more successful when prairie dogs are moved as families? At least three factors probably are important: methods for assessing survivorship and reproduction, timing of assessments, and size and composition of translocated families. Regarding methods and timing, Long et al. and I studied the same individuals translocated into the same recipient-sites in New Mexico, but we estimated survivorship at different times via different methods. Specifically, Long et al. estimated survivorship from visual counts of aboveground, unmarked individuals at two months after the release of translocated prairie

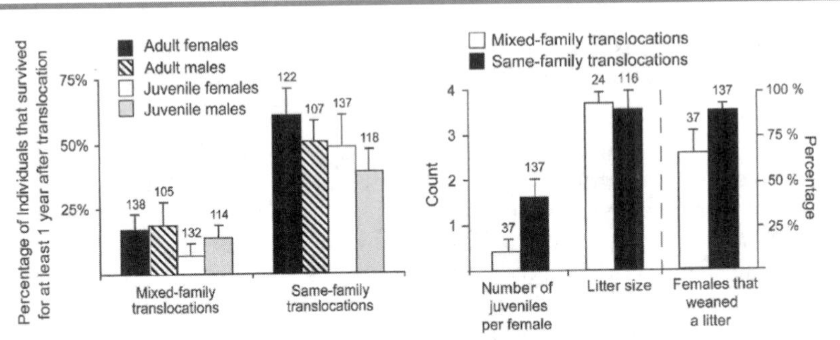

Figure 13-Box.1. *Left side:* survivorship of same-family translocations (into five recipient-sites) versus survivorship of mixed-family translocations (into five recipient-sites). Bars indicate averages, and the line above each bar indicates 1 standard error (SE); the number above each SE line indicates the number of individuals released. *Right side:* annual reproductive success (ARS) of females of same-family translocations (into five recipient-sites) versus ARS of females of mixed-family translocations (into five recipient-sites) as measured by: number of emergent juveniles per female (either lactating or non-lactating), litter size, and percentage of females that weaned a litter. Bars indicate averages, and the line above each bar indicates 1 SE; the number above each SE line indicates the sample size (either the number of females or the number of litters produced).

dogs, but I determined exact survivorship by livetrapping all eartagged individuals and their offspring at 12 months after release. Regarding size and composition of translocated same-family groups, Long et al. livetrapped an average of 5.0 individuals from one burrow, or two adjacent burrows, for their incomplete same-family groups in South Dakota (range = 3–11) (Bly-Honness et al. 2004); by contrast, I livetrapped an average of 11.3 individuals for my complete same-family groups in New Mexico (range = 5–29).

Determination of family compositions probably is not feasible for large-scale translocations (e.g., involving more than about 1,000 individuals), or when other people supply the prairie dogs. Because only members of the same coterie use the same burrow-entrance (Hoogland 1995), one practical solution might be to keep individuals from the same and adjacent burrow-entrances (i.e., presumed family members) together, and then translocate them into the same area of the same recipient-site (see also Robinette et al. 1995; Dullum 2001; Truett et al. 2001a; Roe and Roe 2003, 2004). This method should improve survivorship and reproductive success of translocated individuals, but the additional effort and cost will be minimal.

What Makes a Good Source Population?

The source population is the colony, or group of nearby colonies, that provides prairie dogs for translocations. As explained below, four factors that affect the suitability of source populations are disease, genetics, legal constraints, and removal versus sustainable harvest.

Disease

The disease of greatest concern when translocating prairie dogs is plague. Transmitted by fleas, plague usually is fatal to prairie dogs, and sometimes to humans as well (Chapter 11).

For reasons that are unclear, plague is absent throughout the eastern one-third of the prairie dog's geographic range (Chapter 11). Translocations involving prairie dogs from states such as North Dakota, South Dakota, Nebraska, Kansas, and Oklahoma are therefore less likely to be affected at the outset by plague. For translocations involving prairie dogs from outside the plague-free zone, three procedures can help to assess whether plague might be problematic in a particular geographic area (Truett et al. 2001a): monitoring of potential source and recipient colony-sites, analysis of carnivore blood samples for presence of antibodies to plague, and queries to state agencies that track plague. To reduce the transfer of plague, we recommend quarantine and application of Carbaryl to captured prairie dogs (see below).

Prairie dogs also can contract tularemia (also known as rabbit fever), which infects many other species, including humans, and usually spreads via ticks (Thorne 1982; La Regina et al. 1986). *Francisella tularensis*, the bacterium that causes tularemia, can be lethal for prairie dogs. Because it responds to antibiotics, tularemia among humans is rarely fatal (Texas Department of Health, undated). Further, no human cases of tularemia have arisen from contact with prairie dogs (Texas Department of Health 2002). We know of only two outbreaks of tularemia among prairie dogs, both localized. One occurred in a crowded colony in a city park in South Dakota (E. S. Williams, Wyoming State Veterinary Laboratory, personal communication, 2002), and the other occurred in a captive colony in Texas (Texas Department of Health 2002).

In spring 2003, a viral disease known as monkeypox was introduced into the United States from Africa via other rodents. The most likely culprits were Gambian giant rats imported from Ghana (CDC 2003). In a pet store in Illinois, monkeypox evidently spread from caged Gambian giant rats to prairie dogs in adjacent cages (Gerberding and McClellan 2003). Several persons have contracted monkeypox from their pet prairie dogs. Monkeypox can be fatal for both prairie dogs and humans (CDC 2003), but no human mortalities in the United States from monkeypox have occurred to this point. To deter the spread of monkeypox among captive and wild prairie dogs, the United States Department of Health and Human Services (2003) recently has issued a ruling that prohibits the capture and translocation of prairie dogs. This ruling has far-reaching implications for the restoration of prairie dogs. Exemptions are sometimes available for scientific purposes—for example, for translocations of prairie dogs to improve habitat for black-footed ferrets. If the risk from monkeypox subsides, then capture and translocation of prairie dogs probably will become permissible once again.

Genetics

Prairie dogs show genetic variation within and among populations (Chesser 1983; Foltz et al. 1988; Daley 1992; Roach et al. 2001; Trudeau et al. 2004; Jones et al. 2005). No definitive analysis of range-wide genetic variability of prairie dogs is available, however, and no plans for preserving population- or area-specific genetic variation have emerged. Capturing prairie dogs from the nearest available source-colonies helps to preserve geographically distinct genetic combinations that might exist, and it is also easier and less expensive (Truett et al. 2001a).

Legal Constraints

Because prairie dogs have been regarded as pests for so long and because they and their fleas can transmit plague, many state and local regulations prohibit or discourage translocations (Mulhern and Knowles 1997; Truett et al. 2001a; Chapter 17). As noted above, the recent appearance of monkeypox among captive prairie dogs has precipitated more restrictions for translocations.

Removal Versus Sustainable Harvest

Prairie dog colonies scheduled for partial or total elimination can make good source-colonies—that is, removing individuals from such colonies can promote plans to reduce one colony and to restore another. Landowners who anticipate that all prairie dogs will be removed via livetrapping at source-colonies invariably will be disappointed, however.

Alternatively, wildlife managers and landowners sometimes might want to preserve source-colonies. To prevent overharvest and eventual extinction of valuable source-colonies, annual removal of prairie dogs should not exceed the population's maximal sustainable yield (MSY), which will vary with numerous factors (Chapter 10). Our experience suggests that removal of less than about 25% of adult (at least one year old) and juvenile residents in late summer does not jeopardize the source-colony's long-term survival.

How Should We Capture Prairie Dogs?

Methods for capturing prairie dogs for translocations include livetrapping, flooding the burrows, and vacuuming individuals from burrows (Truett et al. 2001a). Livetrapping probably is the most common method, but the other two methods are locally popular. Regardless of method, we recommend that capture take place only during summer and early fall to minimize mortality. Specifically, we recommend postponing capture until juveniles have been coming aboveground for at least six weeks (i.e., until late June or early July, for most colonies). Mortality among individuals captured too early (e.g., May or early June at most colonies) is high, especially for juveniles—probably because they are not yet fully weaned (Hoogland 1995; J. L. Dullum, personal communication, 2002). Further, we recommend cessation of capture by about October at most latitudes. Otherwise, freezing of the soil in late autumn and winter will impede the excavation of new burrows by translocated prairie dogs at recipient-sites.

Livetrapping

Wire mesh livetraps suitable for prairie dogs measure approximately 15 centimeters (cm) × 15 cm × 60 cm (6 inches [in] × 6 in × 24 in), and can be either single-door or double-door, collapsible or non-collapsible (see also Chapter 2). Collapsible livetraps require less space for transport, but are more prone to damage by domestic livestock. Commercial livetrap vendors include National (Tomahawk, Wisconsin), Tomahawk (Tomahawk, Wisconsin), Havahart (Lititz, Pennsylvania), and Tru-Catch (Fruitdale, South Dakota).

We place livetraps within 1–2 meters (3–7 feet) of burrow-entrances and bait them with mixed grain or whole oats. From our experience, we offer the following observations and suggestions for successful livetrapping (see also Hoogland 1995; Truett et al. 2001a):

- Efficiency of livetrapping varies directly with the density of prairie dogs and with the number of available livetraps.

- Individuals at colony-sites with little or low-quality forage enter livetraps more readily than individuals in areas with abundant, high-quality forage. Livetrapping prairie dogs during late spring and early summer, when green vegetation is most abundant, can be especially difficult.
- Prairie dogs that live in colonies where residents recently have been shot, poisoned, or otherwise harassed are more difficult to livetrap than those in undisturbed colonies (Chapter 10).
- Success improves when prairie dogs have an opportunity to acclimate to livetraps. For several days prior to setting for capture, we place closed livetraps, or livetraps that have been tied open, near burrow-entrances. Either way, we recommend spreading bait in and around the livetraps during the period of acclimation.
- Success of livetrapping increases with experience of the researcher. Recognition of burrow-entrances from which prairie dogs are likely to emerge, optimal spacing of livetraps, and techniques for baiting all improve with practice. Helpful hints include using level spots for placement of livetraps, so they will not move when a prairie dog enters; keeping livetraps in good working order, especially regarding the release mechanism; stringing a thin trail of bait from the burrow-entrance up to the livetrap, and then placing a small handful of bait on and behind the treadle.
- Success with livetrapping often increases to a peak within the first week, and then declines as susceptible individuals are removed. Only rarely do more than 25% of set livetraps capture prairie dogs.
- Overheating in sunny, hot weather is the most common cause of mortality during livetrapping, so frequent checking of livetraps—about every 30 minutes or so—is crucial when temperature exceeds about 21°C (70°F). Frequent checking is not as important during cooler weather (less than about 10°C [50°F]), unless prairie dogs in livetraps get wet from rain or snow—so that hypothermia might result. Hypothermic individuals usually revive quickly after drying under warm conditions (e.g., in a heated van).
- Checking of livetraps is easier—and the possibility of losing a prairie dog to overheating, for example, is therefore lower—if placement of livetraps is deliberate and methodical (in groups of five, for example), and in areas of high visibility.
- We prefer to remain at the colony-site and to carefully watch livetraps when they are open—so that we can act quickly if the weather suddenly changes, and so that we can intervene if American badgers or other predators try to harass captured prairie dogs.

Flooding Burrows

Some workers flush prairie dogs from burrows with water (Truett et al. 2001a). This method is most suitable when copious water from a hydrant or water truck is available. Flooding burrows might drown prairie dogs, however, and unweaned juveniles in spring are especially vulnerable (Dustin Long, unpublished data; see also Coffeen and Pedersen 1993).

Details of the flushing procedure vary among workers. Mark McKee (Bonham, Texas, personal communication, 2002) sends a burst of water into an occupied burrow-entrance for several seconds, then reduces the flow and reaches into the entrance with his hand to catch an emerging prairie dog. Lynda Watson of Lubbock, Texas, uses a similar method (Axtman 2002), but others use a noose to catch the emerging prairie dogs (e.g., see Coffeen and Pederson 1993). One of us (DL) catches 10–30 prairie dogs per hour via flushing.

Vacuuming Prairie Dogs from Burrows

Workers sometimes vacuum prairie dogs from burrows with a customized truck fitted with a flexible tube that inserts into burrow-entrances (Figure 13.1). Gay Balfour of a company called "Dog Gone" sometimes captures more than 100 individuals per day by this method. He pads walls of the truck's receiving chamber with thick foam to minimize injuries to prairie dogs as they are pulled through the tube and ejected against the chamber walls. While watching Balfour in action, one of us (JCT) observed a rate of mortality of about 5% (of about 100 captured), but another of us (DBS) observed a lower rate (22/1,263 = 1.7%). The vacuum method works better in warm weather than in cooler weather, presumably because subterranean prairie dogs remain closer to burrow-entrances in warm weather.

Care of Captured Prairie Dogs Before Translocation

When caring for captured prairie dogs before releasing them into recipient-sites, we have the following four major concerns.

Treatment for Fleas

Immediately after capturing prairie dogs, we treat them with a powder called Carbaryl (Rhone-Poulec, Research Triangle Park, North Carolina) to kill fleas, which transmit plague (Marinari and Williams 1998; Truett et al. 2001a;

Figure 13.1. Capturing prairie dogs with a vacuum truck. Walls of the truck's receiving chamber are padded with thick foam to deter injuries to prairie dogs as they are pulled through the tube and ejected against the chamber walls. Operators open rear door and climb inside for retrieval. Photo by Joe Truett.

Chapter 11). The prairie dogs can be dusted with Carbaryl while they are in livetraps or holding-cages, or by gently shaking them in bags containing Carbaryl.

Holding-Cages

Prairie dogs can be retained in livetraps for transport, but we usually transfer them to holding-cages so that we can immediately reuse the livetraps. Havahart rabbit hutches (60 cm × 60 cm × 45 cm [24 in × 24 in × 18 in]) work well as holding-cages. We are careful to protect prairie dogs in holding-cages from prolonged exposure to direct sunlight, precipitation, and either high (more than 21°C [70°F]) or low (less than 4°C [39°F]) temperatures. Via wire or chains, we suspend holding-cages 0.5–1.0 meters (2–3 feet) off the floor and separate them from adjacent cages by at least 60 cm (24 in). To facilitate cleaning of holding-cages and to deter infestation by fleas, we do not provide nesting material. We stock cages with a continuous supply of water and food (laboratory rodent chow, alfalfa pellets, or low-sodium cattle-cake). Instead of water, we sometimes offer carrots and lettuce.

Requirements for a holding-cage include a floor mesh with holes small enough (less than 1.3 cm × 2.0 cm [0.5 in × 1 in]) to prevent legs and feet from getting stuck. Holding-cages should be tall enough (about 40 cm [16 in]) to allow prairie dogs to stand up. For short trips we have placed as many as 20 prairie dogs in one holding-cage with no obvious adverse effects. To our surprise, housing mixed sexes and mixed ages in the same holding-cage usually involves little aggression—even when housing lasts for as long as 14 days and even when individuals are from different coteries.

Quarantine

We isolate prairie dogs potentially infected with plague and other diseases for at least 14 days prior to release (Marinari and Williams 1998). Holding-cages used for transport, described above, work well for quarantine. Depending on size of the holding-cage and size of the prairie dogs, we sometimes quarantine 15–20 individuals in the same holding-cage. Huddling together and lying on top of one another are normal during quarantine.

Injuries and Sickness During Livetrapping and Quarantine

Invariably a few prairie dogs—less than 1% of all captures—become sick or incur serious injury during livetrapping, transport, or quarantine. Common injuries such as bloody noses and torn claws generally do not require special treatment. Debilitating injuries (e.g., broken bones or paralysis), disease, and serious infections, however, usually require either veterinary care or euthanasia. Cervical dislocation and asphyxiation with carbon dioxide are humane methods of euthanasia (Marinari and Williams 1998).

Prairie dogs that inexplicably perish in livetraps or holding-cages should be submitted to a veterinarian for autopsy. Testing for plague is the primary objective, but documenting other causes of mortality (e.g., tularemia or monkeypox) is also valuable. Most states have agencies that perform autopsies for a nominal charge.

What Makes a Good Recipient-Site for Reintroduction of Prairie Dogs?

The best recipient-sites have intact burrows from recent occupancy by prairie dogs. Such sites often require little preparation before reintroduction, and offer better protection from predators than sites without preexisting burrows. If burrows from recent occupancy are not available, then we use a powered auger to excavate numerous (man-made) burrows that are approximately 2 meters deep.

We do not recommend release of prairie dogs into colony-sites with a recent history of plague, because infected fleas can survive in burrows for as long as one year after all the prairie dogs have died (Chapter 11). Following infusion of vacated burrows with an insecticide-dust called Deltadust (Bayer Environmental Science, Montvale, New Jersey), however, one of us (DBS) has successfully reestablished prairie dogs within burrows where the occupants had succumbed to plague only several weeks previously.

Burrow-entrances at deserted colony-sites disappear over time, but wildlife managers sometimes can detect long-abandoned colony-sites by looking for surface anomalies such as low burrow-mounds, patches of distinctive vegetation, and collapsed burrows (Oakes 2000). Prairie dogs are good at locating and reopening old burrows, and for this reason even long-abandoned colony-sites often are suitable for reintroduction. Historical records and information from local long-time residents can offer good leads for locating former colony-sites (Oakes 2000). We caution, however, that previously inhabited colony-sites are sometimes unsuitable because of tall vegetation.

Prairie dogs also can thrive in sites that do not have evidence of previous occupancy. Biologists have developed criteria for identifying habitat suitable for prairie dogs from analyses of variables such as slope, type of soil, and type and height of vegetation (Truett et al. 2001a; Chapter 16). Prairie dogs generally select deep and well-drained soils of sandy-loam to loamy-clay texture, with slopes less than 10% (Koford 1958; Reading and Matchett 1997; Chapter 16). Soils that are difficult to penetrate with a powered auger probably will pose problems for translocated prairie dogs as well, so we search for a different recipient-site when we encounter ground that seems especially unyielding. Vegetation should be low enough (less than 15 cm [6 in] or so) so that prairie dogs can easily detect predators in all directions. The dominant perennial grasses at release-sites should be resilient to grazing, or they soon will disappear. Grazing-sensitive black grama, for example, disappeared within about three years at one site following colonization by prairie dogs (Joe Truett, unpublished data). Blue grama and buffalo grass, by contrast, are more suitable at release-sites because they are short and resist heavy grazing. Even with grazing-adapted species, however, reduction in vegetative cover invariably occurs over time at colony-sites (Chapter 5).

Preparation of Recipient-Site Before Releasing Prairie Dogs

Recipient-sites, each at least 1–2 hectares (2–5 acres), must have burrows either from previous occupancy by prairie dogs, or from man-made burrows excavated with a powered auger. In our research with the Turner Endangered Species Fund, most of our release-sites have not had burrows from previous occupancy. As explained below, we have discovered two tactics that dramatically improve the success of translocations into release-sites with no natural burrows: mowing tall vegetation, and use of acclimation-cages with man-made burrows. With these ploys, we have translocated more than 7,000 prairie dogs over the last seven years, and have established more than 100 new colonies.

Mowing Tall Vegetation

Recipient-sites are more suitable when all vegetation is shorter than 15 cm (6 in). When necessary, we therefore use a tractor-powered mower to cut vegetation for 50 meters (164 feet) beyond the outermost man-made burrow-entrances of all recipient-sites (Truett and Savage 1998). Via burning or heavy grazing by livestock (Cable and Timm 1988; Ford et al. 2002), vegetation at some recipient-sites is already sufficiently short.

Acclimation-Cages for Man-Made Burrows

To coerce translocated prairie dogs to remain at their new colony-sites, we use a method that involves acclimation-cages in combination with man-made burrows. Otherwise, most translocated prairie dogs would quickly disperse (Truett et al. 2001a). Each acclimation-cage consists of an underground nest-chamber and an aboveground retention-basket connected by flexible, corrugated plastic tubing with a diameter of 10 cm (4 in) (Figure 13.2). This construction allows movement of prairie dogs between the nest-chamber and retention-basket, but deters escape during the period of acclimation. We construct nest-chambers either as full-cylinders to be installed with a powered auger, or as half-cylinders to be installed with a backhoe (Figure 13.2).

The type of nest-chamber (full- or half-cylinder) for acclimation-cages depends on equipment available for installation and personal preference. Rates of abandonment and rates of predation by American badgers seem to depend more on depth, rather than type, of nest-chamber. We recommend a minimal depth of 1.2 meters (4 feet) for each nest-chamber.

Within the mowed areas of each recipient-site, we deploy the acclimation-cages 10–20 meters (33–66 feet) apart in grid fashion. In areas at high risk from plague, we infuse nest-chambers with Deltadust. If livestock are nearby, we repel them by installing a temporary battery-powered electric fence around the mowed recipient-site.

Note that we use acclimation-cages only in combination with man-made burrows. If burrows in good condition remain at a recipient-site from recent

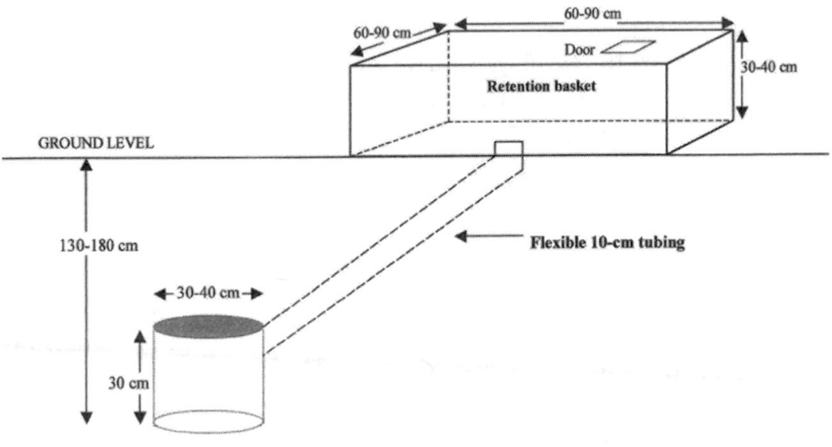

Figure 13.2. Acclimation-cage used to coerce translocated prairie dogs to remain at a recipient-site. Each acclimation-cage consists of an underground nest-chamber and an aboveground retention-basket, connected by flexible plastic tubing with a diameter of 10 cm (4 in). Materials for the construction of full- and half-cylinder nest boxes include non-perforated plastic tubing with a diameter of 10 cm (4 in), particle-board, and 1-cm × 1-cm (0.25-in × 0.25-in) hardware cloth. The retention-basket, used with both full- and half-cylinder nest-chambers, consists of 2.5-cm × 5.0-cm (1-in × 2-in) welded wire, and has a hinged access door in the top, and a 10-cm × 10-cm (4-in × 4-in) hole in the bottom for the plastic tubing. (A) The full-cylinder nest-chamber is installed with a powered auger and trencher. (B) The half-cylinder nest-chamber is installed with a backhoe. The half-cylinder nest-chamber usually takes less time to install than the full-cylinder nest-chamber, but disturbs more soil. Prairie dogs readily use both types of nest-chamber. Details for construction and installation are available from authors.

occupancy by prairie dogs, we do not use either underground nest-chambers or retention-baskets. Rather, we simply release translocated individuals directly into existing burrows.

We use a few simple procedures to deter flooding of nest-chambers during heavy rains. We do not install acclimation-cages in areas likely to collect surface runoff, for example. Further, the tubing that connects the nest-chamber to the surface is non-perforated, and we position the upper end of each tube so that it projects 15–20 cm (6–8 in) above the surface. Packing soil around the protruding end gives it the appearance of a natural burrow-entrance and burrow-mound.

Depending on the size of translocated prairie dogs, we put four to ten individuals inside each acclimation-cage. We provide food in retention-baskets as sodium-free cattle-cake, which eliminates the need for food dispensers. We provide water in large dispensers attached to the exteriors of retention-baskets (Figure 13.3). Water-rich foods such as carrots, cabbage, and lettuce are acceptable substitutes for water dispensers. About a week after introducing prairie dogs into acclimation-cages, we remove the retention-baskets and the electric fence.

How Many Individuals, and What Ratios of Adults to Juveniles and of Males to Females, Are Best for Translocations?

To initiate new colonies, we usually translocate 60–100 prairie dogs (see also Robinette et al. 1995; Dullum 2001). With a few notable exceptions, small translocated groups (fewer than ten prairie dogs) do not survive as well as larger groups.

Under natural conditions, juvenile prairie dogs do not disperse except under extraordinary circumstances (Hoogland 1995). Consequently, because dispersal of translocated prairie dogs away from release-sites can be problematic, biasing translocation groups in favor of juveniles might seem advantageous. Juvenile-biased groups have at least three disadvantages, however:

- Juveniles are less likely than adults to survive until the following year (Chapter 3).
- If they survive, juveniles are less likely than adults to mate and rear offspring in the following year (Chapter 3).
- Juveniles are less likely than adults to excavate new burrows. A translocated group of only juveniles (29 males and 31 females) in New Mexico dug only

Figure 13.3. Prairie dog within retention-basket of acclimation-cage. We remove retention-baskets about one week after release of translocated prairie dogs into the recipient-site. Photo by Melissa Woolf.

two new deep (longer than 2 meters) burrows within the first three months, for example. At nearby release-sites, by contrast, several similar-sized translocation groups containing both adults and juveniles invariably excavated numerous deep burrows within three months.

Copying a tactic used in certain translocations of Utah prairie dogs (Coffeen and Pedersen 1993), we translocated 12 adult male black-tailed prairie dogs into two recipient-sites (6 males per site) in New Mexico in December 2000, with hopes that they would excavate burrows for use by mixed-sex groups released later. Over the next seven months the translocated males dug only two shallow (less than 2 meters long) burrows, both at the same recipient-site. After all 12 males had died or dispersed, we translocated groups containing adults and juveniles of both sexes into the same two sites (at least 12 individuals per site). Within 30 days after these latter translocations, more than 20 new burrow-entrances appeared at each site. With these somewhat anecdotal results, we abandoned the notion of using adult males as "advance diggers" at recipient-sites.

Under natural conditions, the ratio of adult females to adult males is usually about two to one, and the ratio of juvenile females to juvenile males is usually about one to one. Following the first emergences of juveniles from the natal burrows, the ratio of adults to juveniles varies greatly, but usually is slightly adult-biased (King 1955; Tileston and Lechleitner 1966; Halpin 1987; Garrett and Franklin 1988; Hoogland 1995). Previous investigators have translocated groups for which ages and sex ratios approximate those that usually occur under natural conditions (Lewis et al. 1979; Robinette et al. 1995; Dullum 2001). We recommend this strategy as well, but we recognize that the ability to vary ages and sexes within translocated groups depends in large part on the ages and sexes of the prairie dogs captured. For reasons regarding survivorship and excavation of new burrows, we recommend that the number of juveniles within translocated groups always should be less than the number of adults.

Are Translocations More Successful if Prairie Dogs Are Moved as Family Groups?

Social animals might survive better if translocated as family groups (Kleiman 1989; Ackers 1992). Because only members of the same coterie usually forage in the home territory (Hoogland 1995), some workers have attempted to keep families together for translocation by capturing prairie dogs from the same small area (Robinette et al. 1995; Dullum 2001; Truett et al. 2001a; Roe and Roe 2003, 2004). Our recent research suggests, however, that keeping coteries together has little influence on success of translocations.

Using the translocation methods described above, Kristy Bly-Honness et al. (2004) in South Dakota and Dustin Long (in preparation) in New Mexico have compared survival at two months post-release of same-family groups versus mixed-family groups. Each same-family unit in South Dakota contained prairie dogs livetrapped at one burrow-entrance, or at two entrances in close proximity, over several days. Each same-family unit in New Mexico was captured by Debra Shier (2004; Box to Chapter 13) after observations of marked individuals to determine composition of coteries. Mixed-family units in both states contained a random mix of several prairie dogs, livetrapped from distant locations at the same colony-site. Minimal survivorship (i.e., the maximal number of individuals observed over several visual counts) was almost identical two months after translocations for same-family versus mixed-family groups in New Mexico (Table 13.1). In South Dakota during the first two months post-release, mixed-family groups survived (nonsignificantly) better than same-family groups (Table 13.1). At 12 months after translocation, mixed-family groups in South Dakota had (nonsignificantly)

Table 13.1. Minimal percentage of prairie dogs still at the recipient-site two months after translocations at two locations for two types of social groups (Bly-Honness et al. 2004; D. Long, unpublished data). Minimal percentage equals maximal percentage observed over several visual censuses.

Location *Social group*	*Number of release-sites*	*Minimal percentage (%) of translocated individuals still alive at two months after release (average and range)*
South Dakota		
Same-family	4	43 (31–68)
Mixed-family	6	54 (35–67)
New Mexico		
Same-family	3	44 (30–56)
Mixed-family	3	42 (30–52)

higher survivorship than same-family groups, and the ratios of juveniles to adults for mixed-family and same-family groups were almost identical (Table 13.2).

Our censuses at 2 and 12 months after translocations indicate that mixed-family groups survive and reproduce as well as same-family groups. For certain translocations in New Mexico, however, Debra Shier (2004; Box to Chapter 13) found that same-family groups survived and reproduced significantly better during the first year than did mixed-family groups. More research is necessary to determine why same-family groups sometimes survive and reproduce better than mixed-family groups. In the meantime, we will continue to translocate prairie dogs as mixed-family groups, because this method is easier and more economical.

Another key variable that might enhance translocations is time held in captivity prior to release. Our preliminary results indicate that mixed-family groups held together in captivity for at least 14 days during quarantine survive better after release than do mixed-family groups not held in extended captivity. More data are necessary to confirm or reject this provocative, unexpected trend.

Benefits of Short-Term Monitoring and Management

Post-release monitoring of translocated prairie dogs not only measures success of various strategies, but also allows early detection, and correction, of certain

Table 13.2. Adult survivorship and juvenile recruitment at 12 months after translocation for prairie dogs in South Dakota. Same-family groups were translocated as complete families (4–10 individuals per family); mixed-family groups contained prairie dogs from different families (4–10 individuals per group). The percentage of translocated individuals still alive after 12 months is the maximal percentage observed over several visual censuses. We estimated juvenile recruitment by dividing the number of juveniles at the recipient-site by the total number of both adults and juveniles at that site.

Translocations (July 2001)		*Minimum number alive 12 months later (July 2002)*			*Percentage (%) of translocated individuals still alive after 12 months*	*Percentage (%) of residents at release-site that were juveniles at 12 months after translocation*
Release sites	*Number released*	*Adults*	*Juveniles*	*Total*		
Same-family #1	69	49	29	78	71	37
Same-family #2	69	17	15	32	25	47
Same-family #3	71	17	26	43	24	60
AVERAGE	70	38	29	51	40	48
Mixed-family #1	71	26	21	47	37	45
Mixed-family #2	73	31	23	54	42	43
Mixed-family #3	67	43	46	89	64	52
AVERAGE	70	33	30	63	48	47

problems. We have used periodic visual censuses (Knowles 1986b; Severson and Plumb 1998) to assess survivorship and to look for evidence of predation.

During a typical visual census of prairie dogs, some individuals are obscured by vegetation or burrow-mounds, and others are underground (Chapter 6). Estimates of the "observability index"—that is, the percentage of resident prairie dogs that is visible to human observers—ranges from 55% (Severson and Plumb 1998) to 57% (Biggins et al. 1993) to 86% (Knowles 1986b). The average of these estimates is 66%. At about two months after translocation, we usually see about 40%–45% of the individuals that we released. After adjusting for the average "observability index," these numbers indicate that about 61%–68% of our translocated prairie dogs are still resident at their release-sites after two months.

Censuses at three months after translocation have been similar to censuses at two months, for three reasons. First, most escapes and subsequent dispersals usually occur during the first few days after prairie dogs are released into the acclimation-cages, or during the first few days after the removal of retention-baskets. Second, as noted below, translocated individuals sometimes seem disoriented after the removal of the retention-baskets, and thus are more susceptible to predation, but this confusion usually persists for only several days. Third, by the end of two months the prairie dogs usually have excavated many new burrow-entrances, and thus presumably are safer from predation. We usually do not continue monthly censuses beyond the third month, partly because the onset of colder weather reduces aboveground activity.

Our colonies started via translocations usually produce juveniles at rates approximating "normal" in the first year following establishment. Censuses in June 2002 at six South Dakota colonies established via translocation in summer 2001, for example, showed an average of 0.94 juveniles per adult (range = 0.59–1.53). This average compares favorably with the average of 0.72 juveniles per adult (range = 0.36–1.23) observed over 14 consecutive years at the Rankin Ridge colony at Wind Cave National Park in South Dakota (Hoogland 1995, Table 16.1; Chapter 3).

Some of our 100+ colonies initiated via translocation into previously unoccupied recipient-sites have fared poorly—usually because of dispersal or predation—and a few (less than 10%) eventually have failed completely. When initial translocations fail, the released prairie dogs usually survive/remain long enough to excavate new burrows and thereby improve the suitability of the recipient-site. Where such improvement occurs, we commonly translocate additional prairie dogs to recipient-sites with poor initial survivorship. Follow-up translocations are easier and less expensive than initial translocations because the underground nest-chambers are already in place. If enough new burrows excavated by the first translocated individuals are present, then the reattachment of retention-baskets is sometimes unnecessary for the second wave of translocated individuals. We do not perform follow-up translocations if we discover an unacceptable feature of the recipient-site (e.g., evidence of plague) that we did not detect before the first translocations.

In most cases the greatest threat to translocated prairie dogs is predation by enemies such as American badgers, coyotes, ferruginous hawks, golden eagles, and prairie rattlesnakes. Badgers and coyotes are especially troublesome. Badgers sometimes remove retention-baskets or rip open nest-chambers and kill the occupants, for example. Badgers usually do not, however, harass nest-chambers buried at least 1.2 meters (4 feet). Badgers also capture prairie dogs within newly excavated, shallow burrows.

Prairie dogs sometimes seem disoriented for the first few days following the removal of retention-baskets. When disturbed aboveground, they are slow to find entrances to nest-chambers, and consequently are highly susceptible to predation, especially by coyotes. This vulnerability lasts only several days, because the translocated prairie dogs soon learn the precise locations of burrow-entrances.

If successful, badgers and coyotes commonly return to recipient-sites. Over several days, mortality from returning predators can be heavy. If acceptable and legal, removal of returning enemies can reduce predation on translocated prairie dogs. The recommended open terrain at recipient-sites facilitates shooting of problematic badgers and coyotes. Flooding with water promotes the capture of badgers that have usurped prairie dog burrows.

Long-Term Management Following Translocation

The best defense against plague within colonies initiated by translocation is to select source-colonies and recipient-sites with no known history of this ruinous disease. If any sign of plague appears after translocations, then killing fleas via infusions of burrows with Deltadust might halt the disease and thereby save most translocated prairie dogs and their descendants (Seery et al. 2003; Hoogland et al. 2004; Chapter 11).

In addition to killing fleas that transmit plague, Deltadust also kills other arthropods within prairie dog burrows (e.g., other insects; arachnids such as mites, ticks, and spiders). Because of this negative side effect, we only recommend using Deltadust when the colony initiated by translocation is especially important (e.g., key focal colony; Chapter 16).

As noted above, predators—especially American badgers and coyotes—pose the greatest threat to colonies initiated by translocations. Predation is more likely when tall, dense vegetation grows within or near new recipient colony-sites. Without removal of such vegetation—via grazing by livestock and native ungulates, for example, or via human intervention such as repeated mowing—attempts to promote survival of translocated prairie dogs (e.g., by controlling predators, or by providing supplemental food) usually will be futile. Beyond the first year, translocated prairie dogs and their descendants usually survive and reproduce well without any additional intervention—except for infusions of burrows with Deltadust if plague erupts, or mowing if vegetation grows too tall.

Summary

- The best colonies for obtaining prairie dogs for translocation show no evidence of plague and are near the release-sites.

- Livetrapping is the most common method for capturing prairie dogs for translocation; other methods include flooding burrows with water and vacuuming individuals from burrows.
- Before translocation to a release-site, prairie dogs should be treated for fleas with Carbaryl, and then quarantined for at least 14 days to check for plague and other diseases.
- The best recipient-sites for reintroducing prairie dogs have intact burrows from recent occupancy by prairie dogs, and no history of plague.
- When no burrows from recent occupancy are available, preparation of recipient-sites before release of translocated prairie dogs involves excavation of burrows with a powered auger, mowing tall vegetation, and installation of acclimation-cages. Each acclimation-cage consists of an underground nest-chamber and an aboveground retention-basket, connected by nonperforated, flexible plastic tubing. This construction allows movement of prairie dogs between the nest-chamber and retention-basket, but deters escape during the period of acclimation. Retention-baskets are removed about one week after release.
- To initiate new colonies, we recommend translocations that involve 60–100 prairie dogs, for which ages and sexes approximate those under natural conditions (i.e., more adults than juveniles, and more adult females than adult males). We recognize, however, that the ability to vary ages and sexes within translocated groups depends in large part on the ages and sexes of the prairie dogs captured.
- Under some circumstances, prairie dogs translocated together as same-family groups survive and reproduce better than prairie dogs translocated as mixed-family groups. Often, however, mixed-family translocations seem to fare as well as same-family translocations, and the former are always easier and more economical. More research is necessary to better understand the possible importance of keeping families together for translocations.
- Post-release monitoring of translocated prairie dogs measures success of various strategies, and allows early detection, and correction, of certain problems. We use periodic visual censuses after translocations to assess survivorship and to look for evidence of predation.
- American badgers and coyotes pose the greatest threat to colonies initiated by translocation. Predation is most intense in the first two months or so, when the prairie dogs are acclimating to their new colony-site and excavating new burrows. If they endure the first two months, translocated prairie dogs and their descendants usually survive and reproduce well without any additional intervention from wildlife managers—except for infusions of

burrows with Deltadust if plague erupts, or mowing if vegetation grows too tall.

Acknowledgments

We thank the Turner Endangered Species Fund and USFWS for financial support. Matt Hartsough and Melissa Woolf helped to design and test the methods that we describe. We thank Larry Temple, Shawn Russell, Kevin Honness, Kurt Sanders, and Rocky Mountain Arsenal National Wildlife Refuge's staff and volunteers for assistance with translocations. Mike Phillips and Kyran Kunkel reviewed earlier versions of this manuscript.

CHAPTER 14

A Multi-State Plan to Conserve Prairie Dogs

Robert J. Luce, Rob Manes, and Bill Van Pelt

In this chapter we explain how states responded to the petition to add the prairie dog to the Federal List of Endangered and Threatened Wildlife and Plants (FLETWP) in 1998, to its designation as a candidate species for FLETWP in 2000, and to its removal from the candidate list in 2004. We examine how states plan to address the continuing decline of prairie dog populations, and then explore the roles of private landowners and Native Americans in the conservation of prairie dogs.

State Responses to the 1998 Petition to Add the Prairie Dog to FLETWP, and to the 2000 Classification of the Prairie Dog as a Candidate Species

On 31 July 1998, the National Wildlife Federation (NWF) petitioned the United States Fish and Wildlife Service (USFWS) to add the prairie dog to FLETWP (Graber et al. 1998; see also Biodiversity Legal Foundation et al. 1998; Chapter 12). The petition argued that prairie dogs inhabited about 30 million hectares (74 million acres) 200 years ago, and that they currently inhabit about 275,000 hectares (680,000 acres)—that is, less than 1% of their former range. NWF's estimated area of current occupancy probably was an underestimate. More realistic estimates of area currently inhabited by prairie dogs are 631,000 hectares (1.6 million acres; Table 14.1) and 745,000 hectares (1.8 million acres; USFWS 2000a, 2004; Chapter 16). Even with these higher estimates, NWF's claim—that prairie dog populations have drastically declined—is compelling (Table 14.1).

Table 14.1. Area in each state currently inhabited by prairie dogs (2003), and goal for each state for area inhabited by prairie dogs in 2011. All areas are in hectares; 1 hectare = 2.471 acres. For the ten-year objective, Native American tribes in Montana, South Dakota, and North Dakota will set objectives independent of state objectives.

State	*Hectares currently inhabited by prairie dogs (2003)*	*Goal for hectares inhabited by prairie dogs in 2011*
Arizona	0	1,861
Colorado	255,596	103,588
Kansas	52,861	60,181
Montana	36,450	97,349
Nebraska	32,400	55,588
New Mexico	24,300	35,288
North Dakota	8,303	40,723
Oklahoma	26,007	27,806
South Dakota	64,800	80,786
Texas	79,785	118,717
Wyoming	50,625	64,059
TOTALS	631,126	685,946

For most of the last 200 years, loss of habitat, poisoning, and recreational shooting have been primarily responsible for eliminating prairie dogs. Over the last 20 years or so, however, plague has been the factor most responsible for decimating populations (USFWS 2000a; Chapter 11). In Montana, for example, plague reduced the cumulative area inhabited by prairie dogs by about 50% between 1986 and 1998. If this trend continues, plague might reduce the area inhabited by prairie dogs to less than 10% of current estimates over the next 30 years, and the remaining colonies will be small and isolated (USFWS 2000a). The future of prairie dogs is thus unclear, and USFWS responded to this incertitude in 2000 by designating the prairie dog as a candidate for FLETWP as a threatened species (USWFS 2000a; Chapter 12). In 2004, USFWS reversed its earlier designation by concluding that the prairie dog is no longer a candidate species (USFWS 2004; Chapter 12). Regardless of designation, the inescapable conclusion is that prairie dog populations have declined sharply over the last 200 years, are still declining today throughout much of the geographic range, and need better conservation (see also Chapters 12, 16, 17, and 18).

Shortly after NWF filed its petition in 1998, representatives from the eleven states within the former or current geographic range of the prairie dog formed the Interstate Black-tailed Prairie Dog Conservation Team. Delegates from nine of the states (all except Colorado and North Dakota) signed a Memorandum of Understanding in November 1999 to cooperate on range-wide conservation, and each state formed its own committee for in-state management. The committees contained representatives of cattlemen, conservationists, environmentalists, energy-developers, hunters, hunting outfitters, landowners, and urban planners. Most committees also contained representatives from federal agencies such as the United States Department of Agriculture (USDA), USFWS, and the United States Bureau of Land Management (BLM).

An early response by states to NWF's petition was the "Black-tailed Prairie Dog Conservation Assessment and Strategy" (CAS), which relied on range maps, literature, and state and federal publications to delineate the prairie dog's former and current distributions (Van Pelt 1999). CAS also summarized the policies of conservation for each state and evaluated threats to prairie dog populations. Finally, CAS emphasized the importance of establishing long-term goals for the cumulative area inhabited by prairie dogs. CAS eventually led to "A multi-state conservation plan [MSCP] for the black-tailed prairie dog, *Cynomys ludovicianus*, in the United States" (Luce 2003).

Two of the eight Native American tribes whose lands are inhabited by prairie dogs have developed plans for conservation. Cooperation is under way between Native American tribes and the states of Montana, North Dakota, and South Dakota to conserve prairie dogs near boundaries of reservations.

States' Plan to Address the Continuing Decline of Prairie Dog Populations

Here we define the former geographic range as the area inhabited by prairie dogs about 200 years ago—that is, before serious declines in population due to recreational shooting, poisoning, plague, and conversion of colony-sites into cropland. Two data sets define the former geographic range of prairie dogs: recorded localities of collection, capture, and observation (Hall 1981; see also Hollister 1916); and the Bailey Ecoregion Habitat Model (Bailey et al. 1994; Luce 2003). Former range identified in the scientific literature (Hall 1981) includes all specimen records from 1815 through 1977, and defines the extremes of the known range. Individual states' distribution data were compared to Hall (1981) to ensure that no gross errors were present in either (Figure 14.1). Bailey Ecoregions were overlaid on the Hall (1981) range map and the state-delineated range maps to designate ecoregions that currently have colonies, or formerly had them (Figure 14.1).

Even though they might have supported colonies in the past, some ecoregions currently have little suitable habitat for prairie dogs. Due mainly to conversion of so much native prairie to cropland, for example, relatively few

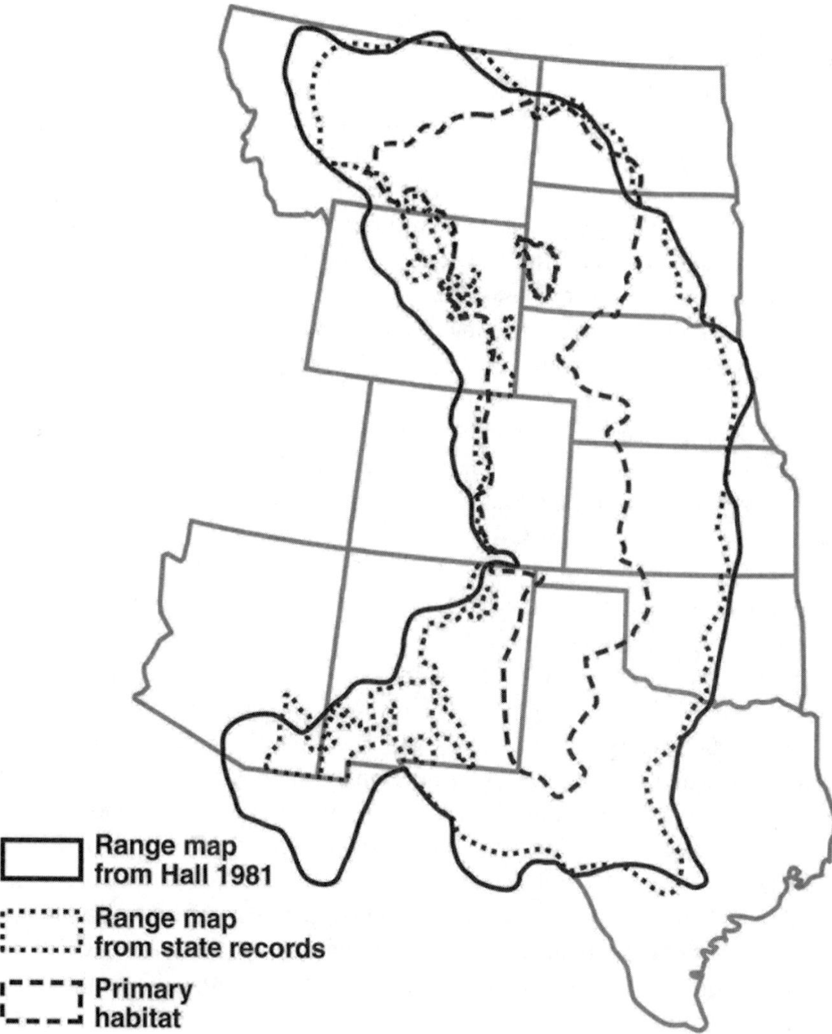

Figure 14.1. Geographic distribution of the black-tailed prairie dog about 200 years ago. References: Hall 1981; wildlife agencies from eleven states. Ecoregions with vegetation indicative of shortgrass prairie and with evidence of former occupancy by prairie dogs are rated as primary habitat (see text).

prairie dogs currently live in the mixed-grass prairie. Rather, most of today's prairie dogs live in the shortgrass prairie. Ecoregions with vegetation indicative of shortgrass prairie and with evidence of current or former prairie dog colonies are rated as primary habitat (or primary range) in MSCP. Ecoregions with vegetation typical of mixed-grass prairie or desert grassland and with evidence of former or current colonies are rated as secondary habitat (secondary range).

MSCP prescribes the following actions for conservation of prairie dogs: complete an inventory in each state to determine the cumulative area occupied by prairie dogs and the distribution and landownership of colonies and complexes (groups of nearby colonies; see Chapter 2); identify "focal areas" that contain suitable habitat, with special emphasis on areas where plague is absent (see also Chapters 11 and 16); provide financial incentives to landowners who agree to conserve prairie dogs; develop mechanisms to regulate recreational shooting and poisoning; set reasonable goals for each state for cumulative area occupied by prairie dogs; and, every third year, recalculate the distribution and cumulative area occupied by colonies and complexes.

Under MSCP, each state will be responsible for developing and managing a portion of the occupied habitat necessary to achieve the range-wide goal. Specifically, the goals for cumulative area inhabited by prairie dogs include the following:

- For now, maintain more than 631,000 hectares (1.6 million acres) of prairie dogs across all states—that is, maintain the same estimated area inhabited by prairie dogs in the United States in 2003 (see Table 14.1).
- By 2011, increase the area inhabited by prairie dogs within the United States to 686,000 hectares (1.7 million acres) (see Table 14.1). Achieving this goal will mean an increase of 9%. If declines in prairie dog populations continue because of plague, poisoning, recreational shooting, and loss of habitat, then reaching MSCP's goal for 2011 will require prudent, aggressive conservation (Chapters 15, 16, 17, and 18).
- Maintain or increase the current area inhabited by prairie dogs in the two complexes of more than 2,000 hectares (4,900 acres) (Conata Basin, Buffalo Gap National Grassland, South Dakota, and Thunder Basin National Grassland, Wyoming).
- Develop and maintain at least ten additional complexes of more than 2,000 hectares (4,900 acres) by 2011, with each state either managing at least one new complex or contributing to at least one new complex via an agreement with another state or with a Native American tribe.
- Maintain more than 10% of cumulative area inhabited by prairie dogs within colonies or complexes of more than 400 hectares (1,000 acres) by 2011.
- Within each state, achieve either of the following: maintain colonies within more than 75% of the counties that formerly had prairie dogs; or maintain colonies within more than 75% of the cumulative area formerly inhabited

by prairie dogs. Of the states that have (or had) prairie dogs, all except Arizona and Nebraska satisfy the first criterion; several states satisfy the second criterion.

MSCP accommodates the states' request to control recreational shooting of prairie dogs. Consequently, individual states and Native American tribes retain the option to close shooting seasons completely or seasonally on lands under their jurisdiction. Colorado, South Dakota, and Montana, for example, have initiated year-round or seasonal restrictions on recreational shooting of prairie dogs on some public lands. Similarly, recreational shooting of prairie dogs for part of the year is now prohibited at Wyoming's Thunder Basin National Grassland, a possible recipient-site for reintroduction of black-footed ferrets.

MSCP regards 400 hectares (1,000 acres) as the minimal size for a colony or complex to meet multi-species needs (but see Chapters 16 and 17). Priority for location of complexes (from highest to lowest) is as follows: (1) public lands; (2) combination of public lands and adjacent private or Native American lands; (3) combination of Native American and private lands; (4) "key private lands" (i.e., private lands with special provisions for the conservation of prairie dogs; see Chapter 16); and (5) typical private lands (Luce 2003).

As noted above, the prairie dog is no longer a candidate species (USFWS 2004; Chapter 12). Even though the threat of listing is gone, we hope and expect that states will continue to support MSCP and to cooperate for the preservation of prairie dogs (but see Chapters 17 and 18).

Role of Private Landowners And Native Americans in the Conservation of Prairie Dogs

Approximately 87% of the area currently inhabited by prairie dogs is privately owned, 5% is on federal lands, and 8% is on Native American reservations (Chapter 16). Private landowners frequently disagree with federal and state agencies regarding the conservation of prairie dogs (Chapters 7, 15, and 17). Most farmers and ranchers favor drastic reduction or total eradication of colonies, as did many of their parents and grandparents. In Wyoming, for example, 54% of landowners with prairie dogs on their domains prefer to completely eliminate them (Wyoming Agricultural Statistics Service 2001; see also Chapter 7). Some farmers and ranchers (9%), however, are willing to maintain the number of prairie dogs occupying their lands, and 18% agree that conservation of prairie dogs is important (Wyoming Agricultural Statistics Service 2001). Reasons that some landowners favor conservation of prairie dogs include concern for the environment; interest in wildlife-dependent recreation; protection from additional restrictions on land use; and financial benefits, through either direct payments or cost-sharing in land improvements.

Federal and state laws grant United States citizens access to wildlife, and this provision has generated public agencies that manage wildlife. Landownership sometimes impedes access to wildlife for recreation or management. Consequently, disagreements among landowners, politicians, wildlife managers, and recreationists sometimes develop. Conflicts escalate when they involve species that are rare or endangered. Conservation of prairie dogs on private lands therefore is a formidable task.

Financial incentives for landowners sometimes are important tools for conservation and management. Several state wildlife agencies, for example, offer payments for recreational access to private lands. In some states, landowners can receive payment for improving habitat for wildlife. Ninety-three percent of Wyoming landowners have indicated interest in a program that would offer financial compensation to farmers and ranchers who agree to maintain prairie dog colonies on their domains (Wyoming Agricultural Statistics Service 2001). Funding for this sort of program is more likely to be available if the prairie dog is a candidate species for, or eventually added to, FLETWP (Chapter 18; Box to Chapter 12).

The nation's largest effort to manage natural resources on private lands involves the Farm Security and Rural Investment Act, commonly known as the Farm Bill. The Farm Bill includes the Conservation Reserve Program, which pays landowners to cease cultivation of crops on targeted lands in order to reduce agricultural surpluses and to protect soil, water, and wildlife. The Farm Bill also offers financial incentives and assistance to restore and protect wetlands, streams, wildlife habitats, and other important natural resources. In each case, landowners receive federal payments to modify use of their lands for specific types of conservation. The Farm Bill probably is the most likely mechanism for funding incentives to landowners who conserve prairie dogs.

In 2001, the Interstate Black-tailed Prairie Dog Conservation Team proposed a program to the United States Department of the Interior that would provide $7.4 million per year for financial incentives for landowners who voluntarily conserve prairie dogs. The program proposed an average of $25 per year per hectare with prairie dogs ($10 per acre) for ten years, and a one-time payment of $250 per hectare ($100 per acre). The proposal contained several components important to landowners, including the following: provisions for flexibility in land management, including grazing by domestic livestock that is compatible with the needs of prairie dogs; protection from new regulations regarding the conservation of prairie dogs; financial benefits, especially direct payments; assistance with reduction of colonies that expand into areas not covered in the incentive program; freedom to use enrolled lands to generate income by means that will not harm prairie dogs (e.g., ecotourism); and allowances for wildlife-based recreational income (e.g., photography, wildlife watching, and off-site recreational shooting of prairie dogs). Stipulations for payment would have prohibited actions such as reduction of protected colonies or cultivation of enrolled lands. The proposal was not accepted, but in 2004 Congress funded the "High Plains Partnership" (HPP). HPP will use conservation funds from the Farm Bill to finance incentives for landowners who improve and maintain grassland habitats for prairie dogs and species such as black-footed ferrets, burrowing owls, and mountain plovers that depend on prairie dogs for survival.

Conservation of prairie dogs and grassland ecosystems will be difficult without assistance from landowners. Financial incentives will help to secure the necessary cooperation.

Summary

- In response to possible addition of the prairie dog to FLETWP, representatives from the eleven states within the former or current geographic range of the prairie dog formed the Interstate Black-tailed Prairie Dog Conservation Team, and then crafted "A multi-state conservation plan [MSCP] for the black-tailed prairie dog, *Cynomys ludovicianus*, in the United States."
- Actions prescribed by MSCP include inventories of in-state cumulative area inhabited by prairie dogs; financial incentives to landowners who agree to conserve prairie dogs; regulation of recreational shooting and poisoning of prairie dogs; and reasonable goals for in-state cumulative area inhabited by prairie dogs.
- For now, MSCP's goal is to maintain 631,000 hectares (1.6 million acres) inhabited by prairie dogs across all states. The goal for 2011 is to increase the area inhabited by prairie dogs by 9%, to 686,000 hectares (1.7 million acres). If declines in prairie dog populations continue because of plague, poisoning, recreational shooting, and loss of habitat, then reaching MSCP's goal for 2011 will require prudent, aggressive conservation.
- Conservation of prairie dogs and grassland ecosystems will be difficult without assistance from landowners. Financial incentives will help to secure the necessary cooperation.

CHAPTER 15

Role of Federal Lands in the Conservation of Prairie Dogs

John G. Sidle, Gregory L. Schenbeck, Eric A. Lawton, and Daniel S. Licht

As populations of black-tailed prairie dogs (hereafter, simply "prairie dogs") continue to decline (Chapter 16), attention is shifting to federal lands and how they might contribute to conservation. As on private lands, prairie dogs on federal lands sometimes have been targets of recreational shooting, poisoning, and loss of habitat (Chapters 8, 10, and 16). Despite such persecution, some of today's largest colonies and complexes of prairie dogs are on federal lands, such as the Charles M. Russell National Wildlife Refuge in Montana, the Thunder Basin National Grassland in Wyoming, and the Buffalo Gap National Grassland in South Dakota.

Ranchers frequently purchase permits so that their livestock can graze on federal lands, especially on lands administered by the United States Bureau of Land Management (BLM) and the United States Forest Service (USFS). Consequently, in addition to favoring the elimination of prairie dogs on their private lands (Chapters 5, 7, and 16), ranchers commonly favor the reduction of prairie dog populations on federal lands as well. Grazing by livestock on federal lands thus complicates the conservation of prairie dogs.

In this chapter we document the areas inhabited by prairie dogs on federal lands under the authority of BLM, National Park Service (NPS), United States Fish and Wildlife Service (USFWS), and USFS. We then explain the policies of these federal agencies before and after the prairie dog became a candidate species in 2000 for the Federal List of Endangered and Threatened Wildlife and

Plants (FLETWP) (USFWS 2000a, Chapter 12). Finally, we discuss the role of federal lands in the conservation of prairie dogs, and how the removal of the prairie dog from the candidate list in 2004 might affect this role.

Federal Lands That Contain Prairie Dogs

As outlined below, prairie dogs currently inhabit 55,100 hectares (136,200 acres) of federal lands managed by four agencies (Figure 15.1) (Table 15.1).

Bureau of Land Management (BLM)

BLM lands include about four million hectares (ten million acres) within the former geographic range of the prairie dog. When managing these lands, BLM must consider numerous factors, including development of sources for minerals and energy; conservation of habitat for fish, burros, wild horses, and other wildlife; grazing by domestic livestock; and numerous federal statutes such as the Federal Land Policy and Management Act (1976). In addition to thousands of other hectares that are probably suitable for colonization, BLM lands include 19,800 hectares (49,000 acres) currently inhabited by prairie dogs (Table 15.2).

National Park Service (NPS)

Most NPS units in the Great Plains were established for reasons other than conservation of wildlife. Fort Larned National Historic Site, for example, was established for cultural resources, Devils Tower National Monument for geologic features, and Badlands National Park for paleontologic treasures. Nevertheless, prairie dogs currently inhabit a cumulative area of about 2,800 hectares (6,900 acres) in three national parks (Badlands, Theodore Roosevelt, and Wind Cave), and small areas (less than 40 hectares [99 acres]) in four other NPS units (Table 15.3). Much of the habitat within NPS units is unsuitable for colonization, but prairie dogs nonetheless inhabit 2% of the total area of the seven units with colonies. Except for the small colony at Bent's Old Fort National Historic Site in Colorado, all colonies within NPS units are in areas with no history of plague (Chapter 11).

United States Fish and Wildlife Service (USFWS)

USFWS manages the National Wildlife Refuge System, for which the conservation of biological diversity is a priority. Prairie dogs currently inhabit about

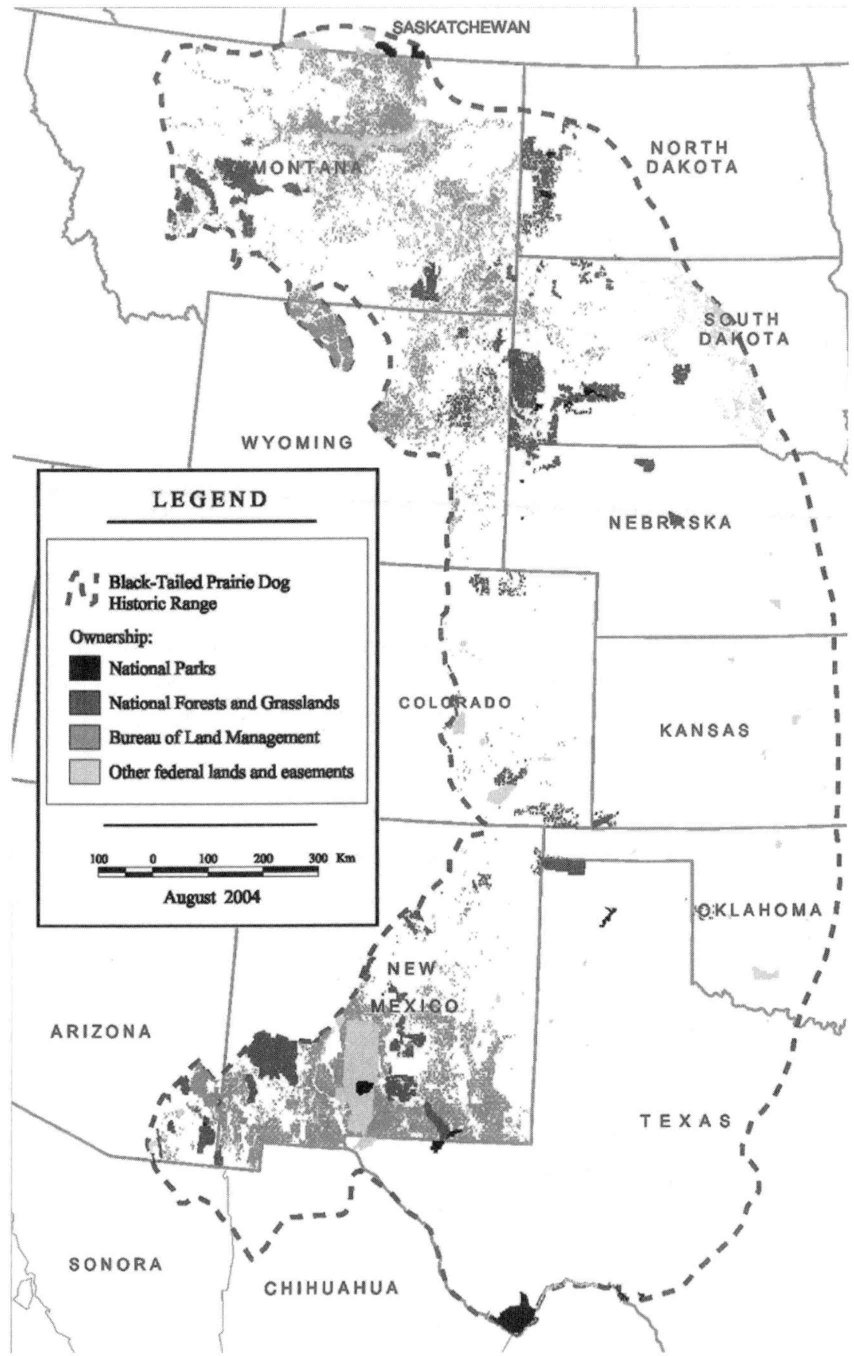

Figure 15.1. Location of principal federal lands administered by BLM, NPS, USFWS, and USFS in the geographic range of the prairie dog.

Table 15.1. Area currently inhabited by prairie dogs on federal lands. Estimates for BLM, NPS, and USFWS are from 2002; estimates for USFS are from 2004.

Area currently inhabited by prairie dogs on federal lands (hectares)	
Bureau of Land Management (BLM)	19,800
National Park Service (NPS)	2,800
United States Fish and Wildlife Service (USFWS)	3,700
United States Forest Service (USFS)	28,800
TOTAL	55,100

Table 15.2. Area inhabited by prairie dogs on BLM lands in 2002.

BLM unit	*Area inhabited in 2002 (hectares)*
Royal Gorge, Colorado	No data
Northeast, Colorado	No data
Billings, Montana	2,260
Big Dry, Montana	2,185
Powder River, Montana	1,457
Lewistown, Montana	318
Lewistown West Hi-Line, Montana	48
West Hi-Line, Montana	1,609
Headwaters, Montana	0.4
Malta, Montana	3,253
Glasgow, Montana	212
White Sands, New Mexico	87
Roswell, New Mexico	236
Carlsbad, New Mexico	4
North Dakota	81
South Dakota	85
Cody, Wyoming	56
Casper, Wyoming	2,023
Buffalo, Wyoming	4,505
Newcastle, Wyoming	1,356
TOTAL	19,775

Table 15.3. Area inhabited by prairie dogs in NPS units in 2004.

NPS unit	*Area inhabited in 2004 (hectares)*	*Nearest colony*	*Issues of management for prairie dogs*	*Future plans for prairie dogs*
Badlands National Park, South Dakota	2,544	Large complexes adjacent to park	Occasional non-lethal control for "good neighbor" purposes, or for protection of park facilities. Park has black-footed ferrets.	Writing new plan for conservation.
Bent's Old Ft. National Historic Site, Colorado	20	About 8 kilometers	None reported.	Writing new plan for conservation.
Chiricahua National Monument, Arizona	0	Unknown	None reported.	None.
Coronado National Memorial, Arizona	0	About 6 kilometers (in Mexico)	None reported.	Some initial efforts at reintroduction of prairie dogs.
Devils Tower National Monument, Wyoming	16	No colonies nearby	Occasional encroachment into campground and visitor areas. Neighbors want control.	Writing new plan for conservation.
Fort Bowie National Historic Site, Arizona	0	120–160 kilometers	None reported.	Reintroduction of prairie dogs under consideration.
Fort Larned National Historic Site, Kansas	13	About 16 kilometers	Burrowing occurs in historic trail ruts.	Maintain current area inhabited by prairie dogs.
Guadalupe Mountains National Park, Texas	0	Unknown	None reported.	Has unsuccessfully attempted to restore prairie dogs. Might try again.
Scotts Bluff National Monument, Nebraska	37	No colonies nearby	Colony has increased from about 2 hectares to 14 hectares in last few years.	None.

Theodore Roosevelt National Park, North Dakota	343	Colonies on national grasslands adjacent to park	Might initiate control for "good neighbor" policy. Moved a picnic area in response to encroachment.	Writing new plan for conservation.
Wind Cave National Park, South Dakota	809	Colonies on state and private lands adjacent to park	Might initiate control near campground and for "good neighbor" purposes. Home for current research on genetics and habitat requirements for prairie dogs.	Writing new plan for conservation. Possible reintroduction of black-footed ferrets.

Table 15.4. Area inhabited by prairie dogs on national wildlife refuge units in 2000, 2001, or 2002.

National Wildlife Refuge System unit	*Area inhabited in 2000, 2001 or 2002 (hectares)*
Big Sag Waterfowl Production Area, Montana	2
Bitter Lake National Wildlife Refuge, New Mexico	2
Buffalo Lake National Wildlife Refuge, Texas	67
Charles M. Russell National Wildlife Refuge, Montana	1,254
Fort Niobrara National Wildlife Refuge, Nebraska	40
Hailstone National Wildlife Refuge, Montana	51
Halfbreed National Wildlife Refuge, Montana	23
Hewitt Lake National Wildlife Refuge, Montana	6
Kingsbury Lake Waterfowl Production Area, Montana	30
Kirwin National Wildlife Refuge, Kansas	24
LaCreek National Wildlife Refuge, South Dakota	121
Lake Mason National Wildlife Refuge, Montana	193
Maxwell National Wildlife Refuge, New Mexico	53
Muleshoe National Wildlife Refuge, Texas	16
Quivira National Wildlife Refuge, Kansas	2
Rainwater Basin Wetland Management District, Nebraska	16
Rocky Mountain Arsenal National Wildlife Refuge, Colorado	127
Sullys Hill National Game Preserve, North Dakota	2
UL Bend National Wildlife Refuge, Montana	1,347
Wichita Mountains National Wildlife Refuge, Oklahoma	38
Willow Creek National Wildlife Refuge, Montana	190
Yellow Water National Wildlife Refuge, Montana	88
TOTAL	3,692

2,600 hectares (6,400 acres) within Montana's UL Bend and Charles M. Russell National Wildlife Refuges, and about 1,100 hectares (2,700 acres) scattered among 20 other national wildlife refuges (Table 15.4). Several refuges contain additional habitat that is probably suitable for colonization by prairie dogs.

United States Forest Service (USFS)

The federal government purchased 65-hectare (160-acre) plots of land from destitute farmers and ranchers in the 1930s and 1940s. These plots originally were given to citizens in the late 1800s via the Homestead Act. The plots are not always contiguous, but rather are intermingled with private lands (Figure 15.2). In 1960, these new federal lands collectively assumed the name of "national grasslands," under the management of USFS. A primary objective within national grasslands is conservation of wildlife.

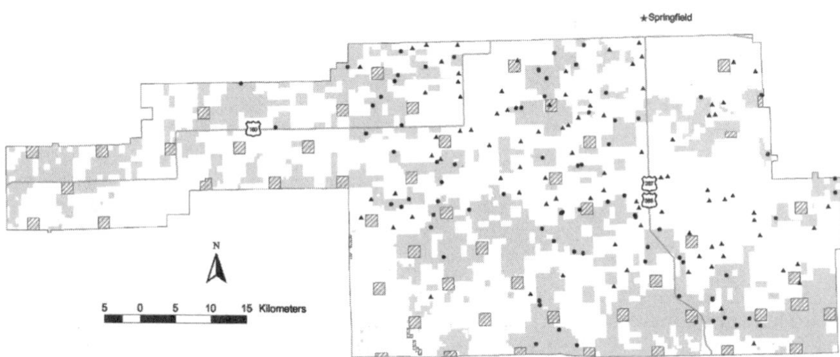

Figure 15.2. The distribution of prairie dog colonies within and near Comanche National Grassland (CNG) in Colorado. As illustrated here, national grasslands are often fragmented and intermingled with private lands. Circles indicate colonies on federal lands, and triangles indicate colonies on state and private lands; white indicates private lands, gray indicates national grasslands, and hatched indicates state lands. Large prairie dog complexes that include both CNG lands and private lands can promote the conservation of the prairie dog and its grassland ecosystem.

Over 75% of the habitat within national grasslands probably is suitable for colonization, but prairie dogs currently inhabit less than 2% (USFS 2001). Specifically, prairie dogs currently occupy about 28,800 hectares (71,200 acres) within national grasslands (Table 15.5).

Policies of Federal Agencies Before the Prairie Dog Became a Candidate Species for FLETWP in 2000

Bureau of Land Management (BLM)

Before 2000, BLM encouraged recreational shooting to reduce prairie dog numbers. BLM also cooperated with Animal and Plant Health Inspection Service (APHIS) of the United States Department of Agriculture (USDA) to poison prairie dogs (Chapter 8).

In the late 1980s, BLM in Montana began to more actively conserve prairie dogs (Flath and Clark 1989). BLM identified an area called the 40 Complex near the Charles M. Russell National Wildlife Refuge, for example, as a sanctuary for prairie dogs and black-footed ferrets.

National Park Service (NPS)

NPS has a rich history of research with prairie dogs. A 15-year study of the behavioral ecology of prairie dogs occurred at Wind Cave National Park, for

Table 15.5. Area inhabited by prairie dogs on USFS lands in 1980, 2002, and 2004. References: Schenbeck1981; USFWS 2002; unpublished reports.

USFS unit	*Area inhabited in 1980 (hectares)*	*Area inhabited in 2002 (hectares)*	*Area inhabited in 2004 (hectares)*
Black Kettle National Grassland, Oklahoma	0	0	0
Buffalo Gap National Grassland, South Dakota	17,240	7,327	10,620
Cimarron National Grassland, Kansas	20	1,344	2,280
Comanche National Grassland, Colorado	730	2,497	4,906
Fort Pierre National Grassland, South Dakota	380	260	535
Grand River National Grassland, South Dakota	610	723	817
Little Missouri National Grassland, North Dakota	550	1,680	1,680
Oglala National Grassland, Nebraska	120	516	909
Pawnee National Grassland, Colorado	180	729	1,158
Kiowa/Rita Blanca National Grassland, Oklahoma and Texas	420	2,185	1,665
Thunder Basin National Grassland, Wyoming	2,550	1,750	3,864
Black Hills National Forest, South Dakota	No data	89	111
Custer National Forest, Montana	No data	218	218
Nebraska National Forest (Bessey), Nebraska	57	26	36
Samuel R. McKelvie National Forest, Nebraska	0	0	0
TOTAL	22,800	19,344	28,799

example (Hoogland 1995). Other notable studies of prairie dogs at Wind Cave have investigated social behavior and population dynamics (King 1955); effects on aboveground biomass and nutrient dynamics (Coppock et al. 1983a, 1983b; Krueger 1986; Detling 1998); nonlethal methods for reducing colony size (Garrett and Franklin 1983); spatial distribution and use of habitat (Wydeven and Dahlgren 1985); dispersal (Garrett and Franklin 1988); influence on the grassland ecosystem (Whicker and Detling 1993); ontogeny of behaviors (Loughry and Lazari 1994); foraging and vigilance (Kildaw 1995); and population genetics (Dobson et al. 1998). Further, several NPS units have in-field displays about the ecology and social behavior of prairie dogs (e.g., Badlands, Wind Cave, and Theodore Roosevelt National Parks, and Devils Tower National Monument). Prairie dog colonies are feature attractions at NPS units where they occur (Figure 15.3). At Devils Tower National Monument, for example, the prairie dog is second only to the tower itself at charming visitors.

Figure 15.3. Children watching prairie dog. Tourists frequently stop to observe the antics of prairie dogs at Badlands, Wind Cave, and Theodore Roosevelt national parks, and at Devils Tower National Monument. Photo by Daniel S. Licht.

Despite mandates and policies that promote natural processes, NPS sometimes reduces wildlife populations for political or other reasons (Sellars 1997). At Wind Cave National Park in the early 1980s, for example, both poisoning (Fisher 1982) and shooting (J. L. Hoogland, personal communication, 2004) of prairie dogs occurred. Park administrators argued that the killings were necessary to conserve the park's biological diversity, and that reduction of the area inhabited by prairie dogs from 728 hectares (1,800 acres) to 283 hectares (700 acres) still would provide sufficient habitat for black-footed ferrets. Poisoning of prairie dogs also occurred in other NPS units prior to 2000, commonly as a "good-neighbor" policy—that is, in response to complaints by neighboring landowners who worried that prairie dogs from the NPS unit would disperse to their private lands (Wilkinson 1994; Roemer and Forrest 1996).

United States Fish and Wildlife Service (USFWS)

Like NPS, USFWS sometimes has struggled with the conservation of prairie dogs. Within national wildlife refuges prior to 2000, for example, USFWS authorized occasional poisoning of prairie dogs. In the late 1990s, however, USFWS made two important changes. First, in 1994, USFWS agreed to prohibit poisoning and to allow reintroductions of black-footed ferrets at prairie dog colony-sites at the UL Bend National Wildlife Refuge in Montana. Second, in 1997, USFWS initiated translocations of prairie dogs into the Charles M. Russell National Wildlife Refuge in Montana.

United States Forest Service (USFS)

Prior to 1972, USFS commonly poisoned prairie dogs on national grasslands and encouraged recreational shooting. Use of nonselective poisons such as Compound-1080 became illegal on federal lands in 1972, however, and prairie dog populations consequently increased on national grasslands in the mid- and late 1970s. Ranchers with permits to allow their livestock to graze on national grasslands protested the expansion of prairie dog colonies, as did neighboring landowners. When a more selective rodenticide (zinc phosphide) became available, poisoning of prairie dogs resumed on the Buffalo Gap National Grassland in 1978 (USFS 1978), and soon on other national grasslands as well.

Policies of Federal Agencies After the Prairie Dog Became a Candidate Species in 2000

Bureau of Land Management (BLM)

In 2000, BLM directed all field offices to improve conservation of prairie dogs, and to ensure that actions authorized, funded, or carried out by BLM do not contribute to possible listing (i.e., addition to FLETWP). Further, BLM initiated several new policies to enhance conservation, including the following: mapping and tracking of all known colony-sites on BLM lands; participation in formulation of "A multi-state conservation plan [MSCP] for the black-tailed prairie dog, *Cynomys ludovicianus*, in the United States" (Luce 2003; Chapter 14); notification of the general public, including ranchers, that unauthorized poisoning of prairie dogs on BLM lands is a violation of BLM policy; consideration for the conservation of prairie dogs in the evaluations of BLM lands for activities such as grazing by livestock, finding and development of oil and gas reserves, granting rights-of-way, and organized recreational events; evaluation of the need to reduce or prohibit recreational shooting of prairie dogs on some BLM lands; and distribution of questionnaires, and sponsoring of workshops and meetings, regarding the importance of conserving prairie dogs.

National Park Service (NPS)

After USFWS's designation of the prairie dog as a candidate species in 2000, NPS improved conservation in several ways. NPS acknowledged in internal memoranda that the prairie dog is a keystone species worth saving, for example, and transferred authority regarding conservation of prairie dogs from its Integrated Pest Management Program to the Natural Resource Stewardship and Science Division.

Park superintendents are responsible for control of prairie dogs within NPS units. Current NPS policy permits control under three circumstances: when prairie dogs threaten human health (e.g., when infected with plague; see Chapter 11); when they jeopardize cultural resources or park objectives; or when their colonies abut private land. Control of prairie dogs since 2000 has involved occasional nonlethal measures, such as barriers that deter expansion of colonies into campgrounds and administrative areas. Control also has involved limited livetrapping either for translocations (Chapter 13) or to provide prey for captive black-footed ferrets. No poisoning has occurred within NPS units since 2000.

Several NPS units are considering actions to promote expansion of prairie dog colonies. Wind Cave National Park, for example, is assessing the feasibility of increasing the number and size of prairie dog colonies to accommodate black-footed ferrets.

United States Fish and Wildlife Service (USFWS)

In 2000, USFWS directed the National Wildlife Refuge System to improve the conservation of prairie dogs. Neither poisoning nor recreational shooting of prairie dogs is currently permitted. Wildlife managers at several refuges (e.g., Rocky Mountain Arsenal National Wildlife Refuge in Colorado and Charles M. Russell National Wildlife Refuge in Montana) have translocated prairie dogs from local private lands into refuges to initiate new colonies, or to reestablish former colonies that disappeared because of plague. Written guidelines for refuge managers regarding the conservation of prairie dogs are now complete (USFWS 2003).

United States Forest Service (USFS)

In 2001, new plans regarding conservation of prairie dogs emerged for national grasslands in Nebraska, North Dakota, South Dakota, and Wyoming (USFS 2001). The new plans deviated sharply from the old plans (USFS 1984). Specifically, the new plans identified habitat components required by prairie dogs, and, with only a few exceptions, prohibited poisoning. Consequently, the cumulative area inhabited by prairie dogs on national grasslands probably would have increased over the next ten years (Table 15.6). In 2005, however, USFS's policies changed—so that poisoning and other methods of eliminating prairie dogs on USFS lands probably will increase (USFS 2005). The predicted increase of cumulative area inhabited by prairie dogs over all national grasslands (Table 15.6) now seems unlikely.

Prairie dog colonies on federal lands in general, and on national grasslands in particular, are fragmented (Figure 15.2), and thus more prone to extinction (Chapter 2). If prairie dogs can survive on private lands adjacent to federal lands, then fragmentation will decrease and large complexes will result—so that extinction of colonies will be less common, and recolonization of deserted colony-sites will be more common (Chapter 16). Private landowners near federal lands thus can play a key role in the conservation of prairie dogs via voluntary cooperation or financial incentives (Chapter 14).

Role of Federal Lands in the Conservation of Prairie Dogs

Federal lands offer enormous potential for the conservation of prairie dogs (Wuerthner 1997; Chapter 16). Changes in policies after the prairie dog became a candidate species for FLETWP in 2000 indicated that BLM, NPS, USFWS, and USFS all would help to promote conservation. But USFWS concluded in 2004 that the prairie dog is no longer a candidate species (Chapter 12). And in 2005, USFS rescinded many of its earlier restrictions (USFS 2001) on the poisoning of prairie dogs. Consequently, in response to increasing prairie dog populations and pleas for presidential intervention, poisoning of prairie dogs has resumed at USFS's Conata Basin (Buffalo Gap National Grasslands, South Dakota) (Chapters 12 and 18), where black-footed ferrets also live. As for USFWS and USFS, will policies for BLM and NPS soon become less favorable for prairie dogs? The answer to this question will determine the role of federal lands in the conservation of the prairie dog and its grassland ecosystem.

Summary

- Prairie dogs currently inhabit 55,100 hectares (136,200 acres) of federal lands managed by BLM, NPS, USFWS, and USFS.
- Prior to the designation of the prairie dog as a candidate species in 2000, BLM, NPS, USFWS, and USFS all authorized occasional or frequent poisoning of prairie dogs, and BLM encouraged recreational shooting as well.
- After the designation of the prairie dog as a candidate species in 2000, policies of BLM, NPS, USFWS, and USFS became more favorable to prairie dogs.
- The role of federal lands in the conservation of the prairie dog and its grassland ecosystem will depend on how BLM, NPS, USFWS, and USFS respond to the recent removal of the prairie dog from the list of candidate species for FLETWP.

Table 15.6. Prairie dogs in the national grasslands and national forests in the northern Great Plains in 1998. Predicted areas of occupancy for prairie dog colony-sites under new management derive from a colony expansion model (USFS 2001). The lower end of the range is expected if normal or above-normal precipitation occurs over the next ten years. The upper end of the range is expected if below-normal precipitation occurs . USFS (2005) recently has rescinded many of its earlier restrictions on the poisoning of prairie dogs, so predictions for certain national grasslands will change.

National grassland or forest	*Total area of national grassland or national forest (hectares)*	*Number of prairie dog colonies*	*Cumulative area inhabited by prairie dogs (hectares)*	*Number of colonies in 1998 that inhabited colony-sites of the following areas (hectares)*				*Predicted cumulative area inhabited by prairie dogs in ten years (hectares)*
				0.4–9.7	*10.1–19.8*	*20.2–40*	*>40.4*	
Little Missouri, North Dakota	462,705	149	1,157	113	18	9	9	2,185–3,804
Grand River, South Dakota	62,717	37	615	9	5	0	5	1,052–1,659
Fort Pierre, South Dakota	46,941	42	291	33	6	1	2	485–769
Buffalo Gap, South Dakota	241,666	296	5,374	133	44	27	28	9,307–14,973
Oglala, Nebraska	38,234	9	300	4	1	2	2	485–769
Nebraska, Nebraska	36,488	8	28	8	0	0	0	Unknown
Thunder Basin, Wyoming	226,688	146	7,421	47	17	26	34	12,545–20,234

CHAPTER 16

Focal Areas for Conservation of Prairie Dogs and the Grassland Ecosystem

Jonathan Proctor, Bill Haskins, and Steve C. Forrest

Biologists disagree about the magnitude of the area inhabited by the prairie dog in the 1800s, and also about the magnitude of the area inhabited today (Wuerthner 1997; Vermeire et al. 2004; Chapter 6). But we all agree on one point: prairie dog populations have plummeted over the last 200 years because of poisoning, recreational shooting, plague, and loss of suitable habitat (Chapters 8, 10, and 11). This decline has precipitated similar declines for black-footed ferrets, mountain plovers, burrowing owls, and other species that depend on prairie dogs for survival (Chapters 4 and 17). Further, today's colonies are so small and isolated that their impact is trivial for the ecosystem processes that are pronounced in larger colonies (e.g., mixing of top- and subsoil, enhanced nitrogen uptake by plants, and changes in floral species composition; see Chapter 4).

In the 1800s, the geographic range of prairie dogs encompassed more than 160 million hectares (395 million acres), and extended from southern Canada to northern Mexico and from eastern Nebraska to the foothills of the Rocky Mountains (Hollister 1916; Hall 1981). Prairie dogs did not live everywhere in this huge range, and here we distinguish between geographic range and area actually inhabited within that range. About 200 years ago, prairie dogs inhabited about 30 million hectares (74 million acres) of the 160 million hectares in their geographic range—that is, prairie dogs inhabited about 19% of their geographic range (Table 16.1; Knowles et al. 2002; Vermeire et al. 2004). Today's prairie dogs, however, inhabit somewhere between 0.5–0.8 million hectares (1.2–2 million acres)—that is, they inhabit less than 0.5% of their former geographic range, and about 2% of the area that they inhabited 200 years ago (Table 16.1; Luce 2002; Chapters 12 and 14).

Despite this population crash (i.e., a reduction by about 98% of the area formerly inhabited), the plight of the prairie dog is not hopeless. Large areas of the former geographic range still contain grasslands suitable for colonization (The Nature Conservancy 2000). Further, relocation of prairie dogs into unoccupied suitable habitat is feasible (Dullum 2001; USFWS 2002b; Chapter 13), and prairie dog colonies will expand if we can protect them from poisoning, recreational shooting, plague, and conversion of colony-sites to farmland (Chapters 8, 10, and 11). For these reasons, we argue in this chapter that

Table 16.1. Past and current estimates of area inhabited by prairie dogs, and estimate of potential suitable habitat currently available, by state or province. References: Lance 1903; Burnett 1918; Anderson et al. 1986; Flath and Clark 1986; Oakes 2000; USFWS 2004; P. Fargey, personal communication, 2002; R. List, personal communication, 2002. Details are available from authors.

State or province	*Area within former geographic range (hectares)*	*Area within former geographic range inhabited by prairie dogs about 200 years ago (hectares)*	*Current area inhabited by prairie dogs (hectares)*		*Estimate of potentially suitable habitat currently available (hectares)*
			2002	*2004*	
Arizona	1,796,400	278,000	0	0	1,379,800
Colorado	11,513,300	2,800,000	87,000	256,000	8,016,100
Kansas	14,740,800	800,000	53,000	53,000	7,156,900
Montana	24,540,000	595,000	36,000	36,000	13,958,100
Nebraska	16,787,300	No reliable data	32,000	55,000	4,655,000
New Mexico	20,036,400	3,480,000	20,000	24,000	16,040,600
North Dakota	5,266,700	No reliable data	13,000	8,000	2,651,500
Oklahoma	9,239,100	No reliable data	9,000	26,000	4,293,700
South Dakota	13,460,900	711,000	65,000	165,000	8,140,200
Texas	33,813,200	23,300,000	35,000	96,000	22,857,200
Wyoming	8,501,300	No reliable data	133,000	51,000	7,006,700
Saskatchewan	854,800	No reliable data	1,000	1,000	557,200
Sonora	775,600	No reliable data	<1,000	<1,000	0
Chihuahua	3,020,500	No reliable data	20,000	20,000	399,300
TOTAL	164,356,300	>32,000,000	504,000	791,000	97,112,300

restoration of prairie dogs to an ecologically functional role is feasible at numerous sites.

But wait: why should we bother to worry about today's prairie dogs when they inhabit more than 500,000 hectares (1.2 million acres) and, as detailed below, number between 25 and 40 million in late spring of each year? Three reasons come to mind. First, as noted above, these numbers, though large, are less than 2% of the numbers of about 200 years ago. Second, most of today's prairie dogs live in small, isolated colonies, and therefore are susceptible to local extinctions (Chapters 2 and 17). Third, and perhaps most important, a healthy grassland ecosystem requires more prairie dogs (Chapters 4, 12, 17, and 18). Black-footed ferrets need *large* prairie dog colonies and complexes (groups of nearby colonies) (see Chapter 2) for survival, for example (Clark 1989; Miller et al. 1996). Similarly, mountain plovers and burrowing owls are especially attracted to large prairie dog colonies (Knowles et al. 1982; Knowles and Knowles 1984; Olson 1985; Griebel 2000).

In this chapter we examine where prairie dogs lived prior to settlement of the Great Plains, and where they live now. We define a focal area and list the criteria for identification of good focal areas. We identify focal areas for western North America in general, and for Montana in particular. We emphasize the importance of establishing and maintaining large prairie dog colonies and complexes—i.e., colonies and complexes that span at least 4,000 hectares (9,884 acres)—because, as in other chapters (e.g., see Chapters 4, 12, 17, and 18), our concern is the persistence of not only the prairie dog, but also its grassland ecosystem.

Where Did Prairie Dogs Live Prior to European/American Settlement of the Great Plains?

Figure 16.1 shows the estimated geographic range of prairie dogs in the 1880s, and Table 16.1 shows occupancy by state or province in the early 1900s.

Not all land within the former geographic range is suitable for prairie dogs. Steep slopes, sandy soil, and tall vegetation, for example, render habitat unsuitable. Flat areas or gentle (less than 10%) slopes, by contrast, are more amenable to colonization and occupancy by prairie dogs (Dalsted et al. 1981; Knowles 1982). Prairie dogs live in most types and textures of soil, but highly sandy and poorly drained soils are unsuitable (Osborn 1942; Reid 1954; Sheets 1970; Knowles 1982). Prairie dog colonies vary in size and location over time in response to drought, fire, grazing, colony age, and plague, and also in response to human disturbances such as recreational shooting, poisoning, and conversion of colony-sites to farmland.

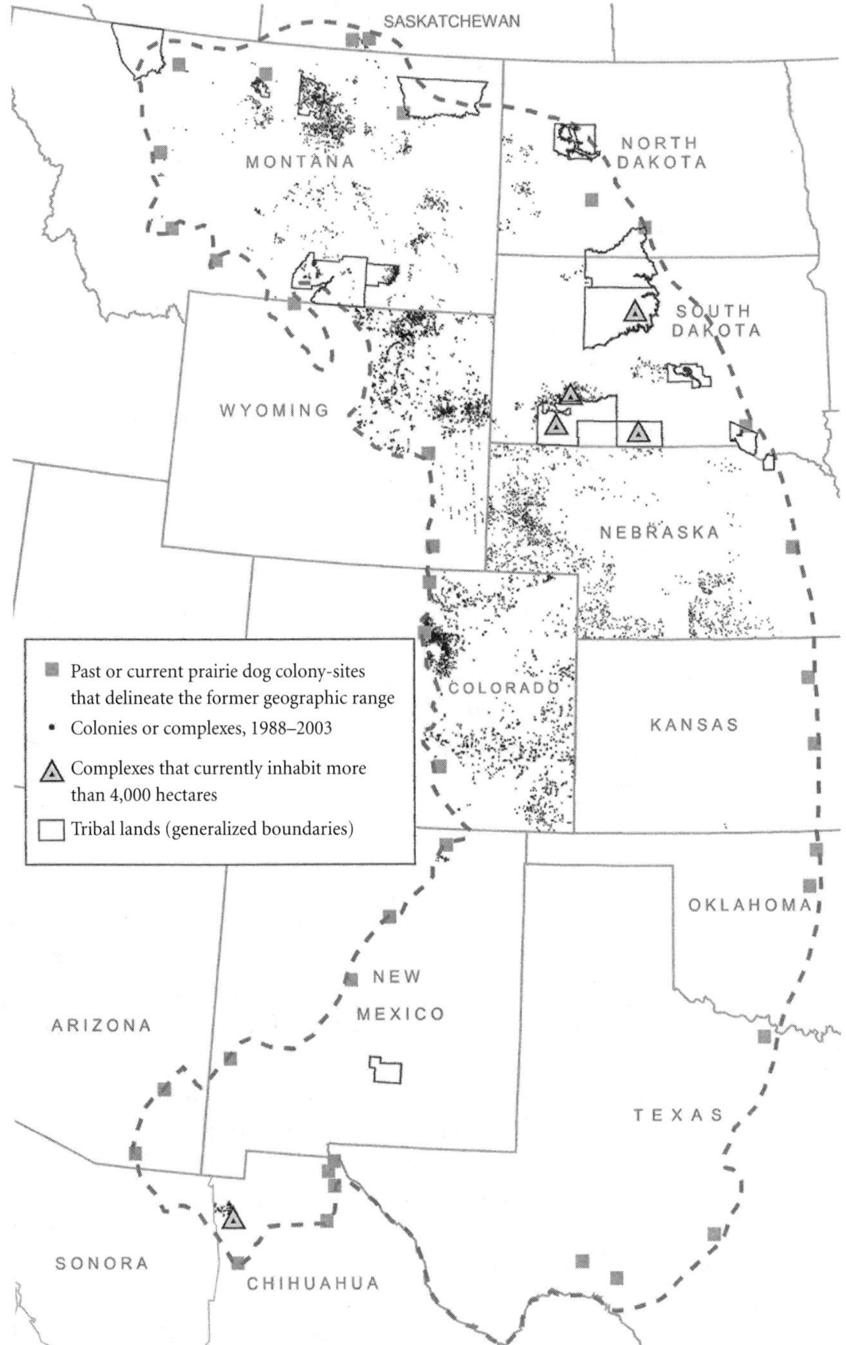

Figure 16.1. Maximal geographic range of prairie dogs about 1880, and distribution of mapped prairie dog colonies and complexes from 1988 to 2003. The dotted line indicates the prairie dog's geographic range of about 200 years ago. References and details are available from authors.

Unfortunately, nobody undertook a systematic inventory of the distribution of prairie dogs prior to the many changes in land use in the late 1800s. Rough estimates from the late 1890s and early 1900s made by the Bureau of Biological Survey (Merriam 1902a) and others (Burnett 1918; Anderson et al. 1986; Oakes 2000; Knowles et al. 2002) yield only an approximate picture of the distribution of prairie dogs by state and province in about 1900. These estimates include information from all five species of prairie dogs and indicate that the five species inhabited roughly 41 million hectares (101 million acres) in the early 1900s. Because the former geographic range of the black-tailed prairie dog is 71% of the former cumulative geographic range for all five species, black-tailed prairie dogs probably inhabited roughly 30 million hectares (74 million acres) in about 1900 (41 million hectares × 0.71 = roughly 30 million hectares) (Nelson 1919; Anderson et al. 1986; Hoffmeister 1986; Vermeire et al. 2004). Good regional maps of areas inhabited by prairie dogs sometimes resulted from surveys, and other times, ironically, from efforts to poison prairie dogs (e.g., Flath and Clark 1986; Oakes 2000; Knowles et al. 2002). These data of varying reliability indicate that prairie dogs occupied 2%–15% of the Great Plains before the late 1800s. Large colonies inhabiting more than 20,000 hectares (49,000 acres) were numerous, and many colonies were exceptionally large. Some colonies, for example, occupied more than 2 million hectares (4.9 million acres) (Knowles et al. 2002).

Where Do Prairie Dogs Live Now?

Table 16.1 shows the area currently inhabited by prairie dogs by state or province, and Figure 16.1 shows the distribution of colonies that have been mapped over the last 20 years or so. Accuracy of mapping varies among states. Certain states (e.g., Texas and North Dakota) and certain Native American tribes (e.g., in North and South Dakota) do not publish information about the size and location of prairie dog colonies. Other states (Oklahoma, New Mexico, and Kansas) are still conducting surveys.

The large colony-sites of yesteryear (more than 20,000 hectares [49,000 acres]) are now gone. Remaining are smaller, scattered colonies, with only a few occupying more than 2,000 hectares (4,900 acres) (Figure 16.1). The cumulative area occupied by today's prairie dogs is between 0.5 and 0.8 million hectares (1.2–2.0 million acres) (Table 16.1). Today's cumulative population of adult and yearling prairie dogs, before the emergences of juveniles from their natal burrows in late spring, is therefore between 12.5 and 20 million. Following the first emergences of juveniles, today's cumulative population is between 25 and

40 million prairie dogs. These estimates assume densities of 25 adults and yearlings per hectare and 25 juveniles per hectare (Hoogland 1995; Chapter 2).

Patterns of land use, land ownership, and disease primarily determine how prairie dogs are distributed today. We estimate, for example, that conversion of grassland habitat to cropland has eliminated 37.6 million hectares (92.9 million acres, or 33%) of grassland within the former geographic range—almost entirely on private lands and primarily in the eastern one-third of the range (see also Choate et al. 1982; Bragg and Steuter 1996; Samson et al. 1998). In Montana—the only state with a rigorous statewide inventory of colonies, including the distinction of colony-sites with live prairie dogs versus colony-sites with no prairie dogs because of plague or poisoning—Native American lands have the highest percentage of occupancy by prairie dogs (1.5%), followed by federal and state lands (0.33%), and then private lands (0.08%). Plague, most prevalent in the western two-thirds of the former geographic range, often prevents prairie dogs from inhabiting or recolonizing certain large areas (Chapter 11). Only about 10% of the former geographic range is both uncultivated and plague-free (USFWS 2002a).

Fragmentation of colonies following population crashes from poisoning, plague, or some other catastrophe also affects the distribution and persistence of prairie dogs (Chapter 8). Small, isolated colonies are more likely than larger colonies to be ignored in poisoning campaigns, for example, but these same colonies are more prone to extinction from other causes such as genetic drift, inability to avoid extreme inbreeding, and predation (Chapter 2). In Oklahoma, the persistence of prairie dog colonies is highest for large, isolated colonies (Lomolino and Smith 2001).

What Are Focal Areas?

Because resources for conservation are always scarce, we need to target operations that are most likely to be successful (Groves 2003). A "focal area" for the restoration and conservation of prairie dogs is a site of sufficient size so that a colony or complex can be large enough to provide suitable habitat for black-footed ferrets, burrowing owls, mountain plovers, and other species that depend on prairie dogs for survival (Chapter 4). But what do we mean by "sufficient size"? Bigger is always better, but an area of 4,000 hectares (9,884 acres) for a colony or complex is probably the minimum necessary for a fully functional grassland ecosystem (Conservation Breeding Specialist Group 2004). Density varies among colonies (Chapters 2 and 6), but a colony that inhabits 4,000 hectares (9,884 acres) usually contains roughly 100,000 adult and yearling prairie dogs and, in late spring, roughly 100,000 juveniles as well; these estimates assume densities of 25 adults and yearlings per hectare and 25 juveniles per hectare (Hoogland 1995; Chapter 2).

Restoring prairie dogs to their former abundance over the entire former geographic range is unrealistic, but finding representative focal areas where prairie dogs can be restored, with complexes of at least 4,000 hectares (9,884 acres), is eminently feasible (see also Miller et al. 1994; Licht 1997; Wuerthner 1997; Gilpin 1999; EDAW 2000; Lomolino et al. 2003; Samson et al. 2004).

Factors That Affect the Suitability of Focal Areas

As described below, at least four factors affect the suitability of focal areas.

Quality of Habitat

Before restoring prairie dogs to a focal area (via translocation, for example; see Chapter 13), we must identify habitat likely to be suitable. For such identification, we used a model designed for Montana that combines information regarding slope, vegetation, and soil-type with a Geographic Information System (GIS) (Proctor 1998). Indications of suitability include slopes of less than 4% and short vegetation classified as grassland, salt-desert shrub, dry salt flats, or mixed barren sites. Two lines of evidence indicate the accuracy of our classification of habitat. First, 95% of known colonies in Montana are in areas classified by our model as suitable. Second, records of poisoning in 1924 show that numerous prairie dog colonies inhabited a large area on the Crow Reservation, Montana (Bureau of Biological Survey, 1924). Our model identified this same area as one of the largest areas of suitable habitat in the state, even though few prairie dogs live there today.

We modified Proctor's (1998) methodology for Montana to accommodate data from throughout the former geographic range of prairie dogs. Because only general information about vegetation was available for most areas, we used categories of preferred vegetation that were somewhat broader, though still consistent, with the Montana categories. Recent research indicates the presence of prairie dog colonies at slopes up to 10% (USGS 1999), so we changed our cutoff for slopes from 4% to 10%. We categorized the Sandhills region of Nebraska as unsuitable because we have found no evidence that large complexes of prairie dogs ever have lived there. We also classified farmland as unsuitable, but recognize that much farmland could become suitable for prairie dogs if agriculture ceases. Our model indicates that about 97 million hectares (240 million acres) of habitat—that is, about 61% of the former geographic range of 160 million hectares (395 million acres)—is currently suitable for prairie dogs (Table 16.1, Figure 16.2).

Opportunities for Management

Opportunities for management improve the suitability of focal areas for restoration and conservation. Public lands, especially those belonging to the Bureau of Land Management (BLM) and United States Forest Service (USFS), offer tremendous potential because: they often occur in large, contiguous blocks and are not cultivated for crops; conservation of biodiversity is a priority there; and large colonies of prairie dogs already live there in many cases. Consequently, when possible, a logical place to restore and conserve large prairie dog colonies and complexes is on public lands (see also Chapter 15).

Many Native American lands also offer excellent opportunities for conservation. Several reservations (e.g., Fort Belknap, Northern Cheyenne, Cheyenne River, and Rosebud) currently have programs for the conservation of prairie dogs and black-footed ferrets. Reservations in South Dakota (Cheyenne River, Pine Ridge, and Rosebud) contain three of today's five largest prairie dog complexes. The Northern Cheyenne Fish and Wildlife Enhancement Department has initiated a program with a goal of restoring complexes of prairie dogs that span 4,000 hectares (9,884 acres).

We use the term "key private land" for terrain that belongs to a landowner who actively promotes the conservation of prairie dogs. Key private lands can foster the restoration of large colonies and complexes, especially in states with only limited public lands (e.g., Kansas, Oklahoma, Texas, and Nebraska). Groups with key private lands include Turner Enterprises (with lands in South Dakota, Kansas, and New Mexico), The Nature Conservancy (Montana, Wyoming and Colorado), the Southern Plains Land Trust (Colorado), and the Gray Ranch (New Mexico).

The Current Existence of Colonies

The presence of prairie dogs in an area eliminates all doubt regarding suitability of habitat. Consequently, the most promising regions for conservation are those areas that already contain numerous colonies and complexes. Unfortunately, as noted above, good information on the existence and location of today's prairie dog colonies is lacking for certain states. Huge complexes that would meet our criteria for focal areas are so conspicuous that they cannot easily escape detection, however, and thus are more likely than smaller complexes to be discovered in states with incomplete inventories.

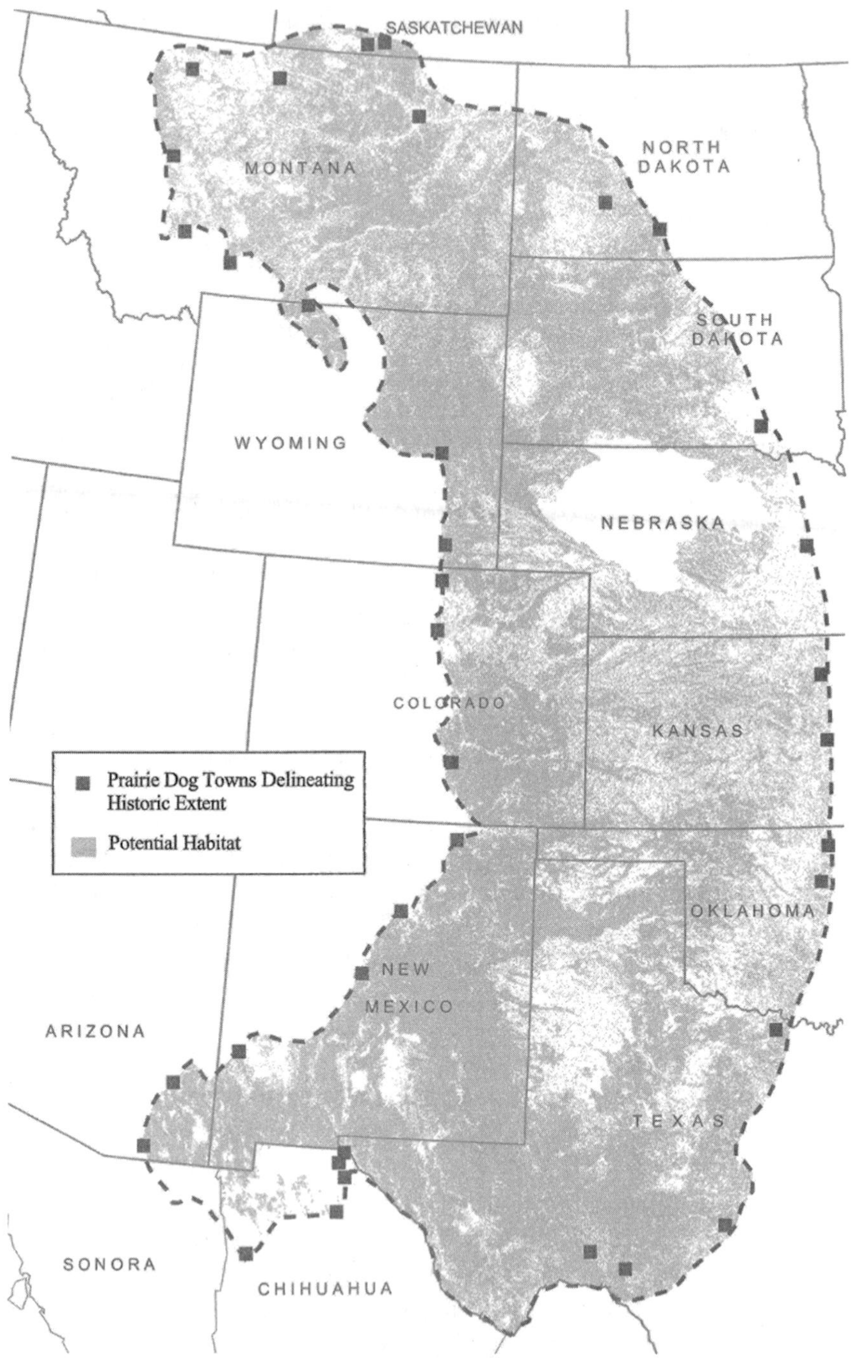

Figure 16.2. Suitable habitat, as determined from slope and vegetative cover, for today's prairie dogs. The dotted line indicates the prairie dog's geographic range of about 200 years ago.

Geography

In order to preserve possible genetic differences associated with geography, plans for conservation of prairie dogs should include focal areas distributed throughout the former geographic range, including the periphery (Lomolino and Smith 2001). Focal areas also should be sufficiently numerous and widespread to maximize the probability of long-term survival against plague. Focal areas in the eastern one-third of the prairie dog's current geographic range are especially promising, because plague is currently absent there (Chapter 11).

Best Opportunities for Restoring and Conserving Prairie Dogs Throughout North America's Great Plains

Using the criteria described above, we have identified 84 focal areas (all more than 4,000 hectares [9,884 acres]) for the restoration and conservation of prairie dogs (Figure 16.3), as follows:

- For 60 focal areas: when possible, we identified the five largest focal areas of suitable habitat on public lands in the eleven states and three provinces that currently have prairie dogs (or had them in the past [Arizona]). Oklahoma has only three focal areas of more than 4,000 hectares (9,884 acres), Kansas has only two, and no information is available for the Sonoran province of Mexico. The other nine states and two provinces all have five focal areas (N = 3 [Oklahoma] + 2 [Kansas] + 45 [9 states × 5] + 10 [2 provinces × 5] = 60 focal areas).
- For 21 focal areas: we also identified the largest focal area on Native American lands in each reservation (N = 13) and all focal areas within key private lands (N = 8).
- For the last three focal areas: because Kansas has only two focal areas (counted above) with at least 4,000 hectares (9,884 acres), we added the largest three blocks of suitable habitat in Kansas (regardless of landownership) as additional focal areas (N = 3).

The 84 focal areas range in size from 4,300 hectares to 2.4 million hectares (11,000 acres to 5.9 million acres) (Figure 16.3), and most focal areas are largely or entirely within federal or state, rather than private, lands. The cumulative area of these 84 focal areas is 10.5 million hectares (26 million acres): 9 million hectares (22.2 million acres) on federal and state lands, 1.3 million hectares (3.2 million acres) on Native American lands, 180,000

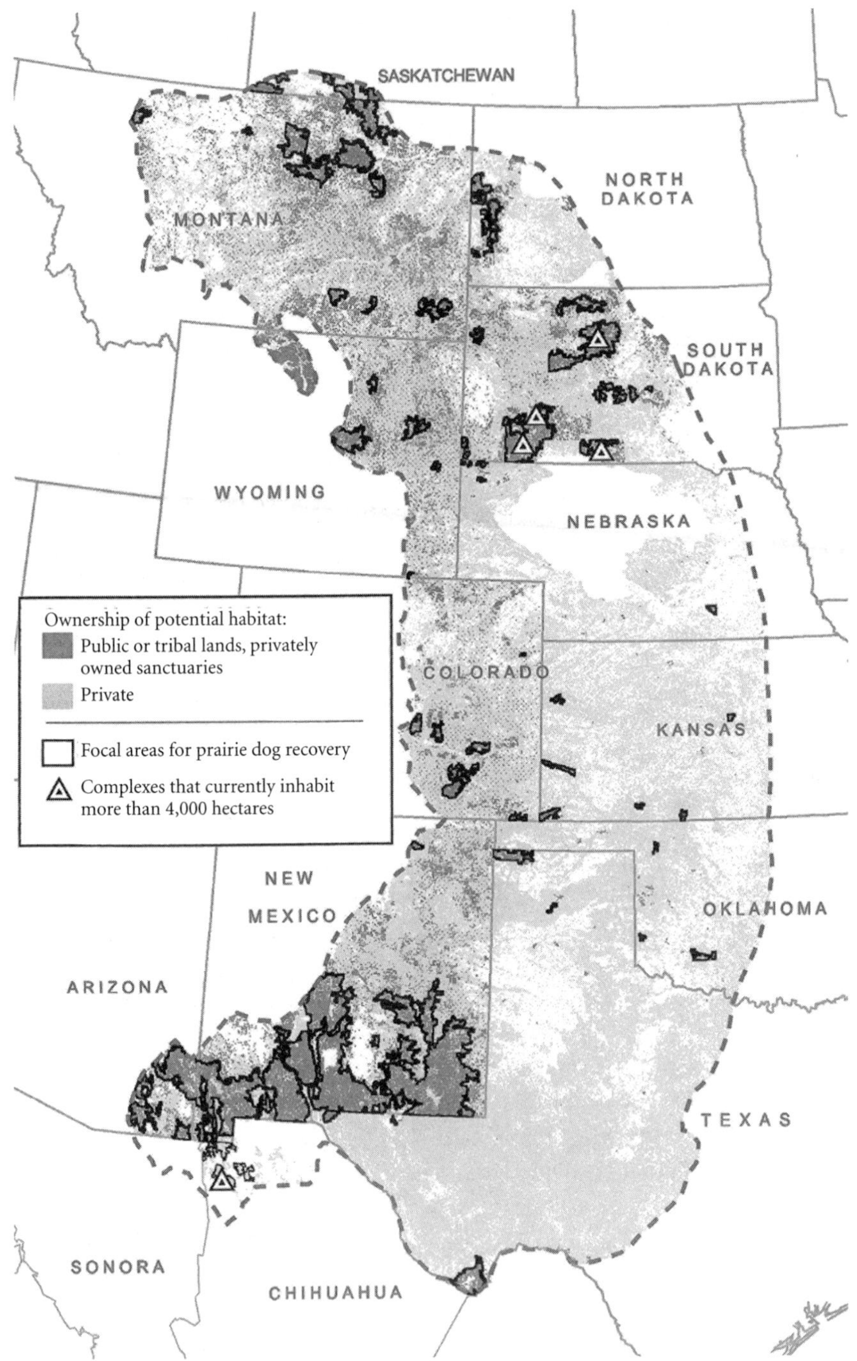

Figure 16.3. Potential focal areas for restoration and conservation of prairie dogs. The dotted line indicates the prairie dog's geographic range of about 200 years ago. References and details are available from authors.

hectares (445,000 acres) on key private lands, and 60,000 hectares (148,000 acres) on the additional Kansas focal areas.

Of the 77 million hectares (190 million acres) of suitable habitat on (non-key) private lands, 1.6% (1.2 million hectares [3 million acres]) occurs within focal areas. Private lands within focal areas are more important than other private lands for the long-term survival of the prairie dog and its grassland ecosystem. Private lands within focal areas therefore should have higher priority for programs that provide incentives (Chapters 14 and 17) to those landowners who support the conservation of prairie dogs.

Of highest priority for conservation are the five prairie dog complexes that currently span more than 4,000 hectares (9,884 acres). These complexes are pivotal because they offer the best immediate opportunities for long-term survival of black-footed ferrets, burrowing owls, mountain plovers, and other species that depend on prairie dogs (Chapter 4). Second in priority are the six focal areas where management currently calls for recovery of a 4,000-hectare (9,884-acre) complex. Recovery efforts are already under way in three of these six: Vermejo Park, New Mexico; Bad River, South Dakota; and the Northern Cheyenne Reservation, Montana (USFWS 2002b). The remaining three second-priority focal areas are within the following national grasslands: Buffalo Gap, South Dakota; Little Missouri, North Dakota; and Thunder Basin, Wyoming (Table 16.2; USFS 2002).

Best Opportunities for Restoring and Conserving Prairie Dogs in Montana

Montana—which, as noted above, is the only state with a systematic statewide inventory of prairie dogs—exemplifies how the availability of good information about the distribution of prairie dogs can improve the identification of focal areas (Proctor 1998). For this state we devised a simple scoring system that credits each pixel (i.e., area of 90 meters × 90 meters) with either 0 or 1 depending on whether the pixel occurs: outside (score = 0) or inside (score = 1) habitat scored as suitable; outside (0) or inside (1) a colony or complex of prairie dogs (i.e., within 0.75 kilometers [0.5 miles] of any colony mapped between 1988 and 2003); and outside (0) or inside (1) an area of more than 4,000 hectares (9,884 acres) of suitable habitat on public lands. Our scoring system also credits each pixel with a value between 0 and 1, depending on whether the pixel is distant from a colony (more than 24 kilometers [15 miles] away, score = 0) or within a colony (score = 1). With this system, the value for each pixel ranges from 0 to 4. Figure 16.4 shows the relative importance for each pixel in Montana.

Table 16.2. Land ownership characteristics for some selected focal areas. All areas are in hectares; 1 hectare = 2.471 acres. Sources of data are available from authors.

Location	*Total potential habitat*	*Key private potential habitat*	*Native American potential habitat*	*BLM potential habitat*	*USFS potential habitat*	*NPS potential habitat*	*USFWS potential habitat*	*State potential habitat*	*Other*	*Maximum area occupied in past 20 years*
Glaciated Plains, Montana	230,939	11,791	0	154,440	0	0	40,839	23,869	0	9,629
Fort Belknap, Montana	169,481	0	163,316	0	0	0	0	6,165	0	6,612
Grasslands National Park, Saskatchewan/Bitter Creek, Montana	217,827	0	357	193,319	0	0	28	24,123	0	281
Little Missouri, North Dakota	125,490	0	0	399	111,310	4,225	0	9,556	0	477
Bad River-Fort Pierre, South Dakota	84,318	47,840	0	0	36,352	0	0	0	126	584
Buffalo Gap, South Dakota	114,058	0	0	0	82,252	26,234	0	5,549	23	7,125
Thunder Basin, Wyoming	139,996	0	0	6,094	117,660	0	0	16,242	0	15,947
Oglala, Nebraska and South Dakota	19,010	0	0	0	18,778	0	0	232	0	216
Comanche-Fort Carson, Colorado	155,198	0	0	83	53,565	0	0	16,991	84,559	383
Cimarron, Kansas, Oklahoma, and Colorado	42,220	0	0	0	42,220	0	0	0	0	unknown
Wichita Mountains, Oklahoma	35,933	0	0	0	0	0	11,158	0	24,775	unknown
Rita Blanca, Texas, Oklahoma, and New Mexico	127,920	0	0	10	121,566	0	0	6,354	0	unknown
Antelope Ridge, New Mexico	742,380	0	0	405,336	0	0	0	328,072	8,972	unknown
San Simon, Arizona	283,527	0	0	174,235	5,951	75	0	103,266	0	unknown
Pancho Villa, Mexico and New Mexico	100,708	0	0	0	0	0	0	0	100,708	20,417

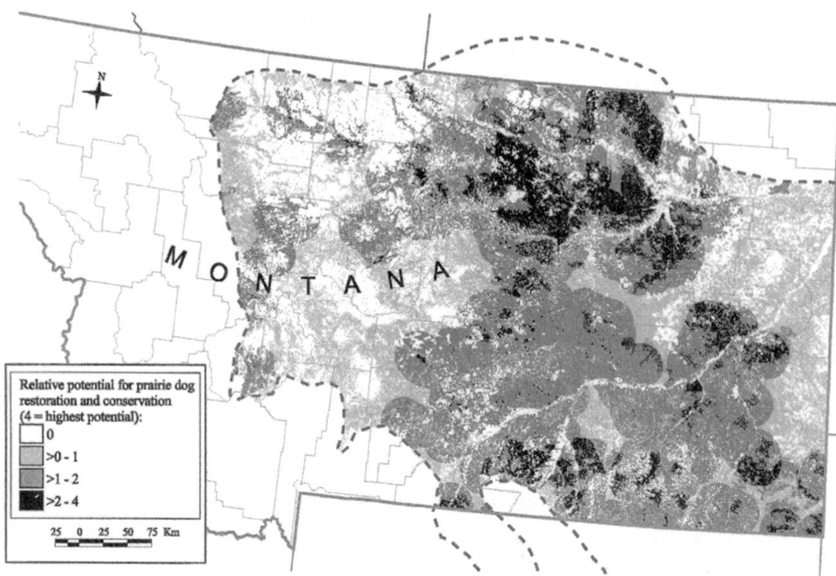

Figure 16.4. Ranking of habitat in Montana regarding suitability for occupancy by prairie dogs.

How Can Focal Areas Promote Restoration and Conservation of the Prairie Dog?

If prairie dogs are restored and conserved within only 15% of the suitable habitat within the 84 focal areas that we have identified (Figure 16.3), the cumulative area occupied will be about 1.6 million hectares (4 million acres)—two to three times the area currently occupied by prairie dogs, but still only about 1% of the 160 million hectares (395 million acres) within their former geographic range, and only about 5% of the 30 million hectares (74 million acres) inhabited by prairie dogs about 200 years ago.

Grazing by livestock often occurs on federal and state lands, but the vast majority of grazing occurs on private ranches. Because most focal areas are largely or entirely within federal or state lands, interference with agricultural and ranching operations should be minimal. We believe that focal areas can provide the habitat necessary for the restoration and long-term survival of both the prairie dog and its grassland ecosystem.

Summary

- In the 1800s, the geographic range of prairie dogs encompassed more than 160 million hectares (395 million acres), and extended from southern

Canada to northern Mexico and from eastern Nebraska to the foothills of the Rocky Mountains. Prairie dogs did not live everywhere in this huge range, but rather inhabited about 30 million hectares (74 million acres), about 19% of their geographic range.

- Today's prairie dogs inhabit somewhere between 0.5–0.8 million hectares (1.2–2.0 million acres)—that is, they inhabit less than 0.5% of their former geographic range, and about 2% of the area that they inhabited 200 years ago.
- Large colonies encompassing more than 20,000 hectares (49,000 acres) were common 200 years ago, and many colonies were exceptionally large; some occupied more than 2 million hectares (4.9 million acres). Today's colonies are smaller and more isolated, and only a few occupy more than 2,000 hectares (4,900 acres).
- Today's cumulative population of adult and yearling prairie dogs is between 12.5 and 20 million. Following the weaning of juveniles each spring, today's cumulative population of adults, yearlings, and juveniles is between 25 and 40 million.
- A "focal area" for the restoration and conservation of prairie dogs is an area of sufficient size so that a colony or complex can provide suitable habitat for black-footed ferrets, burrowing owls, mountain plovers, and other species that depend on prairie dogs for survival. Bigger is always better, but an area of 4,000 hectares (9,884 acres) for a colony or complex is probably the minimum necessary for a fully functional grassland ecosystem.
- Four factors that affect the suitability of focal areas for the restoration and conservation of prairie dogs are quality of habitat, opportunities for management, the current existence of colonies, and geography.
- We have identified 84 focal areas for the restoration and conservation of prairie dogs. These focal areas range in size from 4,300 hectares to 2.4 million hectares (11,000 acres to 5.9 million acres), and their cumulative area is 10.5 million hectares (26 million acres).
- Grazing by livestock often occurs on federal and state lands, but the vast majority of grazing occurs on private ranches. Because most focal areas are largely or entirely within federal or state lands, interference with agricultural and ranching operations should be minimal.
- If prairie dogs are restored and conserved within only 15% of the suitable habitat within the 84 focal areas that we have identified, the cumulative area occupied would be about 1.6 million hectares (4 million acres)—two to three times the area currently occupied by prairie dogs, but still only about 1% of the 160 million hectares (395 million acres) within their former geographic range, and only about 5% of the 30 million hectares (74 million

acres) inhabited by prairie dogs about 200 years ago. Focal areas evidently can provide the habitat necessary for the restoration and long-term survival of not only the prairie dog, but also its grassland ecosystem.

Acknowledgments

For help with the manuscript, we thank D. E. Biggins. For financial assistance, we thank the Predator Conservation Alliance and the J. M. Kaplan Fund.

CHAPTER 17

A Proposal for More Effective Conservation of Prairie Dogs

Brian J. Miller and Richard P. Reading

The Endangered Species Act (ESA) states that decisions about the status of a rare species must be made "solely on the basis of the best scientific and commercial data available" and "without reference to possible economic or other impacts" (Chapter 12). Often in the past, however, scientific data have yielded to political pressure during the listing process (Box to Chapter 12). As a result, decisions sometimes reflect what can be tolerated (by humans) rather than what is best (for the imperiled species). For the conservation of the prairie dog, the primary goal should be to maintain sufficient numbers and widespread distribution for a healthy grassland ecosystem.

In this chapter, we address the following issues regarding the conservation of prairie dogs: area currently occupied; recreational shooting; prairie dogs as pets; plague; current mechanisms for regulation; poisoning; inability to respond adaptively to certain threats; ecological functions; negative attitudes; and evaluation of methods of conservation. The first six are directly relevant to the process of adding a species to the Federal List of Endangered and Threatened Wildlife and Plants (FLETWP) (Chapter 12). Although not officially addressed by an ESA evaluation, the last four are also important for conservation. As we tackle these questions, we consider arguments that led to the designation of the prairie dog as a candidate species for FLETWP by the United States Fish and Wildlife Service (USFWS) (Chapter 12); actions proposed by "A multi-state conservation plan [MSCP]for the black-tailed prairie dog, *Cynomys ludovicianus*, in the United States"(Luce 2003); and the conservation of other species, such as black-footed ferrets, burrowing owls, and mountain plovers, which are directly affected by the conservation of prairie dogs. We conclude by speculating on the long-term prognosis for prairie dogs.

Area Currently Occupied by Prairie Dogs

Today's prairie dogs inhabit somewhere between 0.5–0.8 million hectares (1.2–2 million acres), down by about 98% from the 30 million hectares (74 million acres) they inhabited about 200 years ago (Chapter 16). Further, over two-thirds of today's prairie dogs live in small, isolated colonies (USFWS 2000a). The MSCP goal for cumulative area occupied by prairie dogs in 2011 is 686,000 hectares (1.7 million acres), an area that indicates a ten-year policy of "no net loss" (Chapter 14). While important as an immediate goal, we think that "no net loss" is insufficient as a ten-year goal. Indeed, the USFWS (2000a) designation of the prairie dog as a candidate species for FLETWP implied a need for recovery rather than just the maintenance of current numbers.

In 2001, the United States Ninth Circuit Court of Appeals ruled that recovery of a species must include a significant portion of the former geographic range. To serve properly as a keystone species, the prairie dog must regain a distribution throughout as much of its former range as possible.

USFWS has run out of sites suitable for the reintroduction of black-footed ferrets, and consequently has missed the time frame and goals outlined in the recovery plan for ferrets (USFWS 1998a). Lack of prairie dogs is the reason. Setting low goals for the conservation of prairie dogs impedes the recovery of ferrets. On the other hand, protecting enough prairie dogs so that they can sustain viable populations of ferrets would indicate that the prairie dog is recovering its ecological function (Section 2b of ESA).

Black-footed ferrets survived and reproduced on a 3,100-hectare (7,660-acre) complex of white-tailed prairie dogs near Meeteetse, Wyoming, in the early 1980s (Clark 1989; Miller et al. 1996). Because black-tailed prairie dogs live at higher densities than white-tailed prairie dogs (Hoogland 1995), MSCP speculated that reintroduced ferrets should be able to persist on a 2,000-hectare (4,900-acre) complex of black-tailed prairie dogs (Luce 2003). The population of ferrets near Meeteetse crashed in 1985 because of canine distemper, however (Miller et al. 1996). We should not use a failed example, involving a different species of prairie dog, to estimate the minimal size of a complex of black-tailed prairie dogs necessary to support black-footed ferrets.

The recovery of ferrets probably will require at least ten prairie dog complexes—each with 115,000–160,000 adult, yearling, and juvenile prairie dogs—for short-term survival (USFWS 1998a; see also Groves and Clark 1986; Lacy and Clark 1989; Biggins et al. 1993). At normal densities of prairie dogs (roughly 50 adults, yearlings, and juveniles per hectare [20 adults, yearlings, and juveniles per acre]; see Chapter 2), each of these complexes probably should contain more than 3,000 hectares (7,400 acres). Gilpin (1999) estimated that long-term survival of prairie dogs will require at least 20 sanctuaries, each with at least 104,000 hectares (257,000 acres) of suitable habitat, of which 10%–50% is inhabited by prairie dogs.

A "focal area" for the restoration and conservation of prairie dogs is an area of sufficient size so that colonies and complexes can provide suitable habitat for black-footed ferrets, burrowing owls, mountain plovers and other species that depend on prairie dogs for survival. Jonathan Proctor et al. (Chapter 16) have identified 84 focal areas, which range in size from 4,300 hectares to 2.4 million hectares (11,000 acres to 5.9 million acres). The cumulative area of these 84 focal areas is 10.5 million hectares (26 million acres) of suitable habitat: 9 million hectares (22.2 million acres) on federal and state lands, 1.3 million hectares (3.2 million acres) on Native American lands, and 180,000 hectares (445,000 acres) on key private lands. For better protection of those focal areas that occur on federal lands and contain both ferrets and prairie dogs, we recommend designation as "Federal Wilderness areas," where roads, industry, and motorized equipment would be prohibited.

If prairie dogs are restored and conserved within only 15% of the suitable habitat within the 84 focal areas identified by Proctor et al. (Chapter 16), the cumulative area occupied will be about 1.6 million hectares (4 million acres)—two to three times the area currently occupied by prairie dogs, but still only about 1% of the landscape within their former geographic range of 160 million hectares, and only about 5% of the original 30 million hectares (74 million acres) actually inhabited by prairie dogs about 200 years ago. We recommend 1.6 million hectares (4 million acres) of occupancy as a new ten-year goal for MSCP. We recommend addition of another 1.6 million hectares of occupancy for the 20-year goal of MSCP.

Recreational Shooting

Especially in combination with poisoning or plague, recreational shooting disrupts social behavior and promotes the reduction of prairie dog colonies (Stockrahm and Seabloom 1988; Vosburgh and Irby 1998; Chapter 10). Before the USFWS (2000a) designation of the prairie dog as a candidate species, recreational shooting was unregulated in all states with prairie dogs. Four of eleven states with prairie dogs (currently, or in the past [Arizona]) now regulate shooting in some manner. Two states lack the authority to regulate shooting, and the other five states have not exercised authority to regulate shooting.

The USFWS (2000a) first rated recreational shooting as a low threat to the long-term survival of prairie dogs, but more recently concluded that shooting does not constitute a threat at all (USFWS 2002c, 2004). But shooting can act synergistically with other factors to increase the probability of extinction of colonies (Chapter 10). Further, capricious killing is unnecessary, reinforces a negative attitude toward prairie dogs, probably violates anti-cruelty laws, and tarnishes the image of hunting. Especially while numbers of prairie dogs are still low, we propose a moratorium on recreational shooting. At a minimum, we propose a prohibition of shooting at key focal areas with both prairie dogs and black-footed ferrets.

Prairie Dogs as Pets

If captured when young, prairie dogs make excellent pets and thereby increase public awareness of their charm and importance (Ferrara 1985) (Figure 17.1). Prairie dogs do not readily breed under laboratory or pet-store conditions, however, and catching juveniles in the wild is arduous (Hoogland 1995). Consequently, prairie dog pets have been rare for most of the last 200 years.

In the late 1990s, Gay Balfour designed a truck that can vacuum juvenile prairie dogs from their natal burrows (Chapter 13, Figure 13.1). Since then, thousands of juveniles have been captured from the wild and sold as pets, and national and international interest in prairie dogs as pets has skyrocketed (e.g., Frazier 1999). While not as serious as other threats (e.g., poisoning, recreational shooting, plague, and conversion of habitat to farmland), the pet industry nonetheless poses another obstacle to the long-term survival of prairie dogs.

We do not advocate using wild animals as pets. The pet industry has decimated natural populations of many species of parrots and tropical fish, for example, and efforts to conserve dwindling populations by vendors and pet owners have been negligible. With the current high demand for them as pets, the same result is possible for prairie dogs. Further, funneling prairie dogs through pet stores exposes them to exotic diseases, such as monkeypox (Chapter 13), that might later invade natural populations (e.g., via release of pets into the wild).

Plague

Plague is an introduced bacterial disease whose primary vectors are fleas. Prairie dogs are highly susceptible to plague, and entire colonies usually disappear after plague arrives (Chapter 11). In Montana, plague probably has been

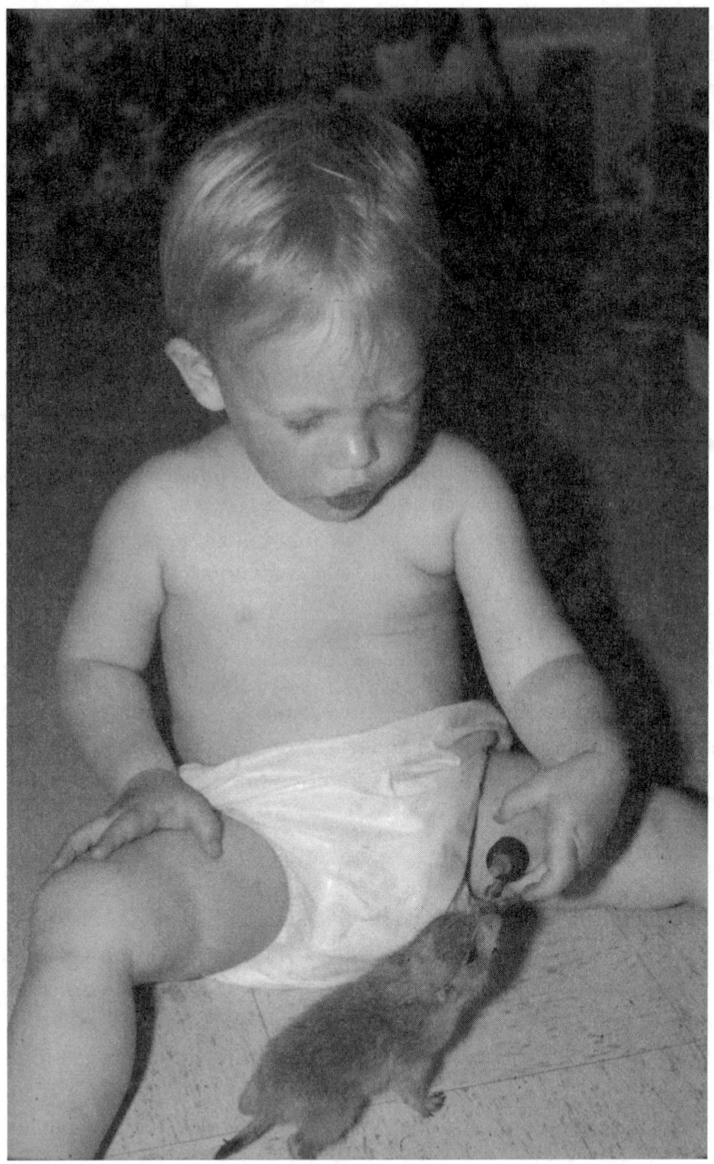

Figure 17.1. Prairie dogs as pets. Here Mark Hoogland bottle-feeds evaporated milk to a six-week-old prairie dog that was given to John Hoogland by a neighbor, who found it weak and disoriented aboveground. If captured at first emergence from the natal burrow or earlier, prairie dogs make dandy pets. Most pets come from natural populations, however, so the pet industry is another threat to the conservation of prairie dogs. Photo by Judy G. Hoogland.

responsible for a 50% decline in area inhabited by prairie dogs over the last ten years (Luce 2003; Chapter 12). Plague among prairie dogs usually does not occur east of the 102nd meridian. Reasons for this abrupt boundary remain unclear, thereby precluding confidence that the boundary will persist.

In its 12-month finding and later candidate assessments, USFWS (2000a, 2001, 2002a, 2004) concluded that plague is a moderate threat to prairie dogs. But we currently have no treatment for prairie dogs infected with plague, nor do we have a reasonable way to deter large-scale outbreaks (Luce 2003; Chapter 11). We think that plague is a serious threat, and concur with Jack Cully et al.'s three suggestions for protecting prairie dogs against plague (Chapter 11): infusions of burrows with Deltadust (Bayer Environmental Science, Montvale, New Jersey) at the first sign that plague might be present; more research with anti-plague vaccines; and the adoption of the "Precautionary Principle" (Johnston et al. 1999; Foster et al. 2000; see also below) in the design of prairie dog sanctuaries—that is, more and larger sanctuaries than might otherwise seem necessary.

Current Mechanisms for Regulating Prairie Dogs

Ideally, federal policy for a particular issue emerges after input from the various agencies that represent all interests. Unfortunately, one interest commonly dominates, and thereby influences policy for its own benefit. The agricultural and ranching industries, for example, have exerted a major impact on the conservation of wildlife for more than 100 years (Dunlap 1988). Many farmers and ranchers have viewed the prairie dog as a problem, and their goal has been eradication (Chapter 8). The result has been a consistent and steep decline of prairie dog populations. As long as agricultural and ranching interests dominate policy regarding prairie dogs, we cannot envision how adequate regulatory mechanisms, as originally intended under ESA, will develop.

Consider the following example of agricultural and ranching influence on the conservation of prairie dogs. MSCP considered both Landsat satellite imagery and the Bailey Ecoregion Model to establish goals for cumulative area occupied by prairie dogs (Luce 2003). Landsat satellite imagery is more precise than the Bailey Ecoregion Model and also more equitable among states (Luce 2003). But the Bailey Ecoregion Model nonetheless was selected for MSCP because "the historic range figures [from Landsat satellite imagery] far exceeded the best acreage estimates derived independently by the states, and therefore would not, in the view of agricultural interests, have been acceptable for use in establishing objectives" (Robert J. Luce, personal communication, 20 March 2002).

Nine of the eleven states within the prairie dog's former geographic range signed a Memorandum of Understanding for MSCP in November 1999 (Luce 2003; Chapter 14). North Dakota and Colorado, however, declined to officially join the multi-state effort. Further, state wildlife commissions of Nebraska and Wyoming recently voted to bar their wildlife agencies from participating in activities related to the conservation of prairie dogs. Finally, Colorado, Montana, Nebraska, and North Dakota have refused to accept the ten-year objectives proposed by MSCP (Robert J. Luce, personal communication, 2003). These actions call into question MSCP's ability to establish adequate regulatory mechanisms for prairie dogs.

Recent changes favorable to prairie dogs resulted directly from the designation of the species as a candidate for FLETWP (Luce 2003; Chapters 14 and 15). Several counties in Colorado, however, have passed or proposed legislation to eliminate financial incentives for landowners who conserve prairie dogs (Reading et al. 2002). When a Colorado environmental group tried to establish a private sanctuary for prairie dogs, the state legislature passed a law requiring approval from county commissioners to move prairie dogs across county lines. In addition, as noted below, most state agricultural agencies retain the designation of prairie dogs as pests. Thus, while federal action has helped in some ways, agencies and regulations of many states and counties still oppose conservation. Much of the progress that resulted from the prairie dog's designation as a candidate species might soon fade away, because USFWS concluded in August 2004 that the prairie dog is no longer a candidate species (USFWS 2004; Chapter 12).

Stakeholders include persons directly affected by the conservation of prairie dogs. As originally defined by ESA, however, stakeholders also include plants (e.g., scarlet globemallow, black nightshade, pigweed, and fetid marigold; see Chapter 4) and nonhuman animals (e.g., black-footed ferrets, mountain plovers, and burrowing owls; see Chapter 4) that depend on prairie dogs for survival. Indeed, prairie dogs themselves are stakeholders. We acknowledge that farmers and ranchers deserve fair consideration, but so do other human and nonhuman stakeholders.

Poisoning

Poisoning of prairie dogs began in the late 1800s because farmers and ranchers viewed the rodents as pests (Chapters 8 and 9). Poisoning soon developed into large-scale, well-organized campaigns that severely reduced and fragmented populations. The federal government began allocating money for poisoning in 1915, and by the 1920s millions of prairie dogs and ground squirrels fell victim annually to oats treated with carbon bisulphide, strychnine, or other toxicants (Chapter 8).

In 2000, USFWS (2000b) estimated that 10%–20% of current prairie dog colonies were poisoned annually—often with assistance from local, state, and federal agencies. Poisoning continues today, primarily on private lands. Some states still require landowners to poison prairie dogs on their lands if neighbors complain. Many county extension services continue to sell poisoned baits and to provide technical assistance to landowners wishing to poison prairie dogs.

The USFWS (2000a) rated poisoning as a moderate, imminent threat to the long-term survival of prairie dogs in 2000, and two years later changed the rating to moderate and non-imminent (USFWS 2002c; see also USFWS 2004). We think that the threat is more serious, and we therefore recommend an immediate halt to poisoning on federal lands and instant termination of all federal subsidies and technical support for poisoning on private lands. Perhaps the federal and state monies currently used to subsidize poisoning could be allocated to financial incentives for persons who agree to maintain prairie dog colonies on their domains (see Miller et al. 1996; Chapter 14). ESA supports and encourages such allocations.

Inability to Respond Adaptively to Certain Threats

Over evolutionary time, prairie dogs have evolved responses to natural threats such as predation and parasites (Hoogland 1995). Prairie dogs have not, however, had sufficient time to evolve meaningful responses to recent unnatural problems such as poisoning, plague, and recreational shooting. Further, today's prairie dogs must confront these recent threats when their numbers, and hence their overall genetic variability, are minimal. Finally, defenses against certain natural threats make prairie dogs especially vulnerable to new, unnatural threats. Consider coloniality, for example. Large, densely populated colonies help to protect prairie dogs from predators such as American badgers, coyotes, golden eagles, and prairie falcons (Hoogland 1995). But these same large colonies are susceptible to massive mortality from unnatural threats such as poisoning and plague (Chapters 8 and 11).

Our recommendations regarding the inability of prairie dogs to respond adaptively to certain threats are straightforward: whenever possible, abolish the threat (e.g., prohibit poisoning); seek solutions to the threat (e.g., vaccine for protection against plague); and allow prairie dogs to increase their cumulative population size and overall distribution, so that they are better able to survive the impacts of novel threats such as plague.

Ecological Functions of Prairie Dogs

ESA was written in 1973 and last revised in 1988. We have learned much about ecological interactions among species and the complexity of ecological webs since 1988, but current ESA policy does not incorporate this new information (Pyare and Berger 2003; Soulé et al. 2003, 2005). A strict legal interpretation of ESA must focus on single species, and cannot easily consider recovery of an imperiled ecosystem. USFWS has argued, for example, that interspecific interactions were not relevant for evaluating the status of prairie dogs under ESA (USFWS 2000a, 2001, 2002a; see also USFWS 2004)—even though black-footed ferrets, burrowing owls, mountain plovers, and other organisms clearly depend on prairie dogs for survival (Chapter 4). Strict legal interpretation of ESA does not require USFWS to consider the role of prairie dogs for the health of the grassland ecosystem, but ESA does allow such consideration. The USFWS Internet Web site lists more than 75 recovery plans that include multiple species. For prairie dogs and the grassland ecosystem, USFWS could write a multi-species recovery plan similar to the South Florida Multi-species Recovery Plan for the Everglades, which considers 68 species (USFWS 1998b).

We agree with Pyare and Berger (2003) and Soulé et al. (2003, 2005) that goals for recovery of a keystone species should explicitly consider densities and distribution needed for a healthy ecosystem (see also Chapter 4). Failure to consider ecosystems under ESA means that we continue to evaluate interdependent species individually, and that we continue to use a version of ESA based on outdated science—a contradiction of the ESA mandate to use "the best scientific and commercial data available." According to Randall Snodgrass of the National Audubon Society (quoted in Primack 2002, page 559), "If the [Endangered Species] Act is truly to prevent further species loss, it's got to evolve into a next generation wildlife law instead of an emergency law that just recovers species from a brink." One solution might involve amendments to ESA. Another might involve new legislation aimed specifically at the conservation of ecosystems rather than single species (Box to Chapter 12; Chapter 18).

Negative Attitudes

Through early 2001, nine states had classified the prairie dog as a pest, and allowed or required eradication (Luce 2003). Such classification promotes and reinforces negative attitudes, and inhibits efforts to inform people about the role of the prairie dog as a keystone species. Positive attitudes toward prairie dogs generally emanate from watching their aboveground antics, recognition of the keystone role that prairie dogs play in grassland ecosystems, and a belief that they have a right to exist (Reading et al. 1999, 2002).

Regarding positive and negative attitudes toward prairie dogs, people on both sides are zealous—so that conflicts are inevitable. Historically, people with negative attitudes have dominated. But people with positive attitudes are increasing in number and banding together for more impact. Table 17.1, for example, lists 50 *organizations* that have a primary concern—the only concern, for many of them—for the conservation of prairie dogs. People with positive attitudes were responsible for the two petitions to USFWS to add the prairie dog to FLETWP (Graber and France 1998; Biodiversity Legal Foundation et al. 1998; Chapter 12). The subsequent designation of the prairie dog as a candidate species (USFWS 2000a) induced a flurry of activity by both groups—one trying to promote eventual listing, the other trying to prevent it. The latter group prevailed, and in August 2004 USFWS removed the prairie dog from the candidate list (USFWS 2004).

Table 17.1. Organizations with a primary concern for the conservation of prairie dogs. The Prairie Dog Coalition is an alliance of nonprofit organizations, concerned citizens, and scientists dedicated to the conservation of prairie dogs and the grassland ecosystem.

Members of the Prairie Dog Coalition
All My Relations, Animal Defense League of Arizona, Animal Protection Institute, Animal Protection of New Mexico, Biodiversity Conservation Alliance, Boulder Environmental Activists Reserve, The Center for Biological Diversity, The Center for Native Ecosystems, Forest Guardians, The Fund for Animals, Great Plains Restoration Council, Habitat Harmony, The Humane Society of the United States, In Defense of Animals, Jews of the Earth, People for the Ethical Treatment of Animals, People for Native Ecosystems, Prairie Dog Action, Prairie Dog Pals, Prairie Dog Rescue of New England, Predator Conservation Alliance, Rocky Mountain Animal Defense, Sinapu, Southern Plains Land Trust, Southern Utah Wilderness Alliance, T & E Incorporated, Texas Public Employees for Environmental Responsibility, Wild Birds Unlimited, The Wild Places Incorporated, and Wildlands Conservation Alliance.
Others that are not members of the Prairie Dog Coalition
Black-footed Ferret Recovery Foundation, Defenders of Wildlife, Denver Zoological Foundation, EDAW, Environmental Defense, Fauna West, Greenwood Wildlife Rehabilitation Sanctuary, Llano Estacado Audubon Society, National Audubon Society, National Wildlife Federation, The Nature Conservancy, Prairie Preservation Alliance, Prairie Hills Audubon Society, Prairie Dog Specialists, Prairie Preserves LLC, Prairie Wildlife Research, Rocky Mountain Bird Observatory, Turner Endangered Species Fund, Wildlife Management Institute, and World Wildlife Fund.

We believe that negative attitudes underlie most of the problems associated with efforts to save the prairie dog and its grassland ecosystem. For successful conservation, we must ameliorate negative attitudes and reduce the dominance of human stakeholders with negative attitudes. Many people are uncomfortable with the idea of trying to influence the values and attitudes of others. If we do not try, however, then we are accepting the status quo and permitting others to wield disproportionate power.

Many laws, regulations, practices of range management, government-sanctioned education programs, and financial subsidies all sustain the notion that prairie dogs are pests. But labeling the prairie dog as a pest makes no biological sense. Indeed, an ecologically valuable native species (the prairie dog) has been declared a pest by powerful groups that favor ecologically degrading exotic species (domestic livestock). Changing practices, laws, and the underlying attitudes will be difficult, but such change is vital if we hope to conserve prairie dogs. Education programs that target adults with strong negative attitudes toward prairie dogs require sensitivity and preparation. Less formidable are education programs for children and others whose views are less rigid, and who therefore are more receptive to scientific findings and innovative strategies for conservation.

Incentives that promote ecologically sound management benefit society as a whole (Farraro and Kiss 2002; Bangs et al. 2005; Nyhus et al. 2005). We recommend a direct link between incentives and the cause of the problem. Incentives thus should aim to improve underlying negative attitudes regarding issues such as threats to lifestyles, control over public and private grazing lands, the prairie dog as a pest, competition between prairie dogs and domestic livestock, and traditional notions of land stewardship. Incentives that merely replace lost income reinforce the notion that prairie dogs are pests.

Some people inevitably will resist efforts to conserve prairie dogs, regardless of education programs and financial incentives. For this minority, legal sanctions might be necessary. Such pressure often ignites conflict, however. We therefore should apply legal pressure only as a last resort.

Evaluation of Methods of Conservation

For the conservation of animals in general, and of prairie dogs in particular, we recommend the "Precautionary Principle": decisions should always err in favor of nature, especially if our actions might lead to changes that are difficult to reverse or to the loss of something irreplaceable, such as a species (Johnston et al. 1999; Foster et al. 2000). Rather than short-term economic gain, the Precautionary Principle emphasizes preservation of ecosystems and evolutionary processes. We recognize the need for compromise, particularly in the early stages of conservation. We only should compromise to make progress toward long-term conservation, however, and we never should regard a compromised strategy as the optimal solution.

Clark (2000) has outlined five steps for conservation: clarify goals; describe trends; analyze conditions; make projections; and evaluate results and select alternatives, if necessary. The absence of one or more of these steps might indicate that somebody or some organization is trying to manipulate the process.

We emphasize the importance of open-mindedness regarding the conservation of prairie dogs. Good ideas and valid concerns can emanate from any source. All opinions deserve a fair hearing. We also affirm, however, that mere opinions are not equivalent to scientific evidence. For evidence and evaluation, we encourage small- or large-scale experiments whenever possible, with designs that minimize confounding variables (Holling 1978; Clark 2000; Chapter 5). Without experiments, we cannot easily learn which strategies work and why—and therefore we cannot easily ensure the long-term survival of the prairie dog and its grassland ecosystem.

What Is the Long-Term Prognosis for Prairie Dogs?

In this chapter we consider ten issues regarding the conservation of prairie dogs. For each issue, we summarize significant problems, and then offer suggestions for improvement. Because prairie dogs have survived various types of persecution for more than 200 years, we are optimistic that, with reasonable protection, their resilience will allow them and their grassland ecosystem to persevere long into the future. Reasonable protection probably will require adding the prairie dog to FLETWP (see also Box to Chapter 12 and Chapter 18).

Summary

- Today's prairie dogs inhabit somewhere between 0.5–0.8 million hectares (1.2–2 million acres), down by about 98% from the 30 million hectares (74 million acres) they inhabited about 200 years ago. Most of today's prairie dogs live in small, isolated colonies. We recommend 1.6 million hectares (4 million acres) of occupancy as a new ten-year goal for the multi-state conservation plan (MSCP).
- We propose a moratorium on recreational shooting of prairie dogs, especially in key focal areas with both prairie dogs and black-footed ferrets.
- We do not advocate prairie dogs as pets.

- Because prairie dogs are so vulnerable to plague and we know so little about the disease, we recommend more and larger sanctuaries than otherwise might seem necessary.
- As long as agricultural and ranching interests continue to dominate policy regarding prairie dogs, we cannot envision how adequate regulatory mechanisms for conservation will develop.
- We recommend an immediate halt to poisoning prairie dogs on federal lands, and instant termination of all federal subsidies and technical support for poisoning on private lands. Perhaps the federal and state monies currently used to subsidize poisoning could be allocated to financial incentives for persons who agree to maintain prairie dogs on their domains.
- Allowing prairie dogs to increase their cumulative population size and overall distribution will help them to survive the impacts of novel threats such as plague.
- We believe that negative attitudes underlie most of the problems associated with efforts to save prairie dogs. For successful conservation, we must ameliorate negative attitudes and reduce the dominance of human stakeholders with negative attitudes.
- For the conservation of prairie dogs, we recommend the "Precautionary Principle"—that is, decisions should always err in favor of prairie dogs. Rather than short-term economic gain, the Precautionary Principle emphasizes preserving ecosystems and evolutionary processes.
- Because prairie dogs have survived various types of persecution for more than 200 years, we are optimistic that, with reasonable protection, their resilience will allow them and their grassland ecosystem to persevere long into the future. Reasonable protection probably will require adding the prairie dog to FLETWP.

CHAPTER 18

Saving Prairie Dogs: Can We? Should We?

John L. Hoogland

Ranchers and farmers are the ones whose lives and livelihoods are usually most affected by prairie dogs. Conservation of prairie dogs will be more successful if we work with ranchers and farmers, and is certain to fail if we consistently work against them. Authors of preceding chapters propose several mechanisms to foster cooperation with ranchers and farmers. In this concluding chapter, I wrestle one last time with the two ultimate questions: Can we save prairie dogs? Should we bother?

Can We Save Prairie Dogs?

When I pondered this question in the first draft of this chapter in fall 2003, the prairie dog was still a candidate species for the Federal List of Endangered and Threatened Wildlife and Plants (FLETWP). For reasons detailed in the previous 17 chapters, I was optimistic about the future of the prairie dog and its grassland ecosystem. Politicians, federal agents, wildlife managers, ranchers, and farmers were cooperating and compromising as they tried to find a solution. Progress for the long-term survival of prairie dogs was unmistakable.

My optimism turned to pessimism in August 2004, when the United States Fish and Wildlife Service (USFWS) concluded that the prairie dog is no longer a candidate species (USFWS 2004). Repercussions have been immediate and devastating (Table 18.1), especially in South Dakota. Poisoning of prairie dogs has begun, for example, at Conata Basin of South Dakota's Buffalo Gap National Grasslands—one of the few areas where black-footed ferrets have consistently increased since their reintroduction (Chapter 4).

Table 18.1. Repercussions through May 2005 since the removal of the prairie dog from the candidate list in August 2004.

REPERCUSSIONS RELATED TO POISONING OF PRAIRIE DOGS

- In fall 2004, poisoning of 1,300 hectares (3,200 acres) at the largest complex on public lands in the Great Plains (Conata Basin, Buffalo Gap National Grasslands, South Dakota), where reintroduced black-footed ferrets have survived and reproduced more successfully than anywhere else.
- In fall 2004, poisoning of 1,500 additional hectares (3,700 acres) at Buffalo Gap National Grasslands.
- In fall 2004, poisoning of 10,931 hectares (27,000 acres) on private lands in South Dakota adjacent to federal lands.
- In fall 2004, poisoning on Pine Ridge and Rosebud Native American Reservations (total areas unknown).
- In December 2004, South Dakota Departments of Agriculture and Game, Fish, and Parks finalized a plan that requires poisoning of prairie dogs on all lands (public and private) within 1.5 kilometers (1 mile) of other lands if the adjacent landowner complains of encroachment.
- In spring 2005, the South Dakota legislature passed two bills regarding prairie dogs, and the governor signed both bills into law. SB-216 reclassifies the prairie dog as a pest under several circumstances. HB-1252 authorizes and funds the widespread poisoning of prairie dogs, including free annual poisoning for landowners adjacent to public lands. The South Dakota Department of Game, Fish, and Parks has allocated an additional $130,000 for poisoning.
- As of May 2005, the Nebraska legislature is considering a bill that reclassifies the prairie dog as a pest and will require poisoning of prairie dogs on most lands.

REPERCUSSIONS RELATED TO RECREATIONAL SHOOTING OF PRAIRIE DOGS

- In fall 2004, South Dakota Department of Game, Fish, and Parks removed its year-round ban on recreational shooting of prairie dogs in Conata Basin, Buffalo Gap National Grasslands.
- As of May 2005, the Colorado Division of Wildlife is considering removal of the year-round ban on recreational shooting of prairie dogs on federal lands in eastern Colorado.

Of the five largest prairie dog complexes—four of them in South Dakota, with each containing more than 4,000 hectares (9,884 acres) (Chapter 16)—three are victims of recent poisoning. Further, with the threat of regulations and restrictions now gone because the prairie dog is no longer a candidate species, the long-term benefits of "A multi-state conservation plan [MSCP] for the black-tailed prairie dog, *Cynomys ludovicianus*, in the United States" (Luce 2003; Chapter 14) are questionable. Indeed, even before the latest ruling by the USFWS, three states (Colorado, Montana, and North Dakota) had refused to accept one or more of MSCP's recommendations and objectives, and one other state (Nebraska) had aborted serious efforts to conserve prairie dogs (Robert J. Luce, personal communication, 6 January 2005).

The grassland ecosystem of western North America includes not only prairie dogs but also the many organisms that depend on them for survival, such as fetid marigolds, scarlet globemallows, black-footed ferrets, mountain plovers, burrowing owls, and ferruginous hawks. A major theme of this book is that conservation is important, not only for the prairie dog, but also for its grassland ecosystem. The two are not necessarily synonymous. A conservation plan that specifies thousands of small colonies scattered throughout the former geographic range, for example, might permit the long-term survival of prairie dogs. But such a plan probably would not ensure the persistence of those ecosystem processes and species that depend on large prairie dog complexes (Chapters 4 and 16).

Regarding the decision to remove the prairie dog from the candidate list for FLETWP (USFWS 2004), it's easy to criticize USFWS. But we must remember that USFWS agents had to follow the inflexible guidelines of the Endangered Species Act (ESA) when trying to determine whether the prairie dog warrants listing. Further, they had to contend with zealots for and against listing, and with pressure from powerful politicians. With these circumstances in mind, I agree with Rob Manes (Chapter 12) that the USFWS decision in 2004 to remove the prairie dog from the candidate list was reasonable. But a reasonable, technically correct decision is not necessarily the best decision for the prairie dog and its grassland ecosystem, as many USFWS agents will readily concede. I share the frustration of Nicole Rosmarino (Box to Chapter 12) on this issue, and I agree with her that somehow we must do more for the preservation of a keystone species and its ecosystem.

ESA focuses on the conservation of single species, with only marginal provision for the conservation of ecosystems. Petitions to list the prairie dog are therefore acceptable, but petitions to list the grassland ecosystem are not acceptable. Conservation biologists who are more concerned about the grassland ecosystem than about the prairie dog thus face a dilemma: must we petition for the listing of the prairie dog (for which, to many, the case seems unconvincing) as a strategy to save the grassland ecosystem (for which the case is more compelling)? We need a better mechanism for the protection of ecosystems. Perhaps the mechanism can come from new legislation, from an amendment to ESA, or from a more liberal interpretation of the current version of ESA. A single recovery plan for the grassland ecosystem will be more effective, and more economical, than separate plans for prairie dogs and the many species and ecological processes that depend on them (Pyare and Berger 2003; Soulé et al. 2003, 2005; Chapters 4 and 17; Box to Chapter 12).

So, what's the bottom line? Can we, or can't we, save the prairie dog and its grassland ecosystem—including one of North America's rarest native mammals, the black-footed ferret? The answer is yes, I think, but recent developments described above (see also Table 18.1) mean that preservation will require bold, persistent conservation. I agree with Jonathan Proctor et al. (Chapter 16) that focal areas will be crucial for such conservation. Focal areas can provide large sanctuaries for prairie dogs on federal and state lands, where interference with ranching, agriculture, and urban development should be minimal. I also agree with Nicole Rosmarino (Box to Chapter 12) and Brian Miller and Richard Reading (Chapter 17) that saving the prairie dog probably will require its addition to FLETWP, with all the protection and funding that accompany listing. Such listing will require a more progressive interpretation of ESA rules for listing than the interpretation used by USFWS in 2004. At a minimum, salvation probably will require classifying the prairie dog as a candidate species once again—with the imminence of later listing. Without listing or redesignation of the prairie dog as a candidate species—or without new legislation or amendments to ESA that target ecosystems rather than single species—significant progress in the conservation of the prairie dog and its grassland ecosystem seems unlikely.

If the prairie dog is added to FLETWP, then new regulations and restrictions regarding land usage, poisoning, recreational shooting, and other issues—and the administration and enforcement of these new rules by state and federal agencies—are inevitable (Chapters 12 and 17). Consequently, most ranchers and farmers do not favor listing the prairie dog. But listing would offer one benefit that many ranchers and farmers do not fully appreciate—namely, funding specifically for conservation. Some of this funding probably would be available to landowners who agree to maintain, rather than eliminate, prairie dog colonies. Several studies indicate that many landowners would accept the restraints and surveillance associated with listing in return for payment for agreeing to preserve prairie dog colonies on their domains (Chapters 7, 10, 14, and 17). With a better understanding of this mechanism for financial compensation, perhaps more ranchers and farmers would favor adding the prairie dog to FLETWP.

Should We Bother to Save Prairie Dogs?

I believe that the conservation of prairie dogs is imperative for many reasons. For organisms in general (Wilson 1988, 2002; Leopold 1989; Noss and Cooperrider 1994; Pullin 2002), and for prairie dogs in particular (McNulty 1971; Miller et al. 1990; Kellert 1996; Wuerthner 1997; Reading et al. 1999, 2002;

Johnsgard 2005), many biologists have argued that species deserve protection in their own right, because of their own inherent value—basically, because they exist. Captivated by the ecology and fascinating social behavior of black-tailed prairie dogs for 16 years, and by the nifty biology of Gunnison's, Utah, and white-tailed prairie dogs for another 16 years, I enthusiastically concur with this opinion (Hoogland 1995, 1999, 2001, 2003a, 2006a).

Organisms sometimes provide important, unexpected benefits for humans (Wilson 2002). Because they frequently develop gallstones, for example, prairie dogs have led medical researchers to a better understanding of diseases and malfunctions of the human gallbladder (e.g., Gurll and DenBesten 1978; Broughton et al. 1991). Prairie dogs also have been useful for physiological research on hibernation (Harlow and Menkens 1986; Harlow and Braun 1995; Lehmer et al. 2001) and the mammalian kidney (e.g., Bakko 1977; Pfeiffer et al. 1979). Perhaps prairie dogs can help us to better understand other aspects of mammalian anatomy and physiology.

Prairie dogs are uniquely social animals that have contributed to our understanding of several key issues in animal behavior, including coloniality, alarm calling, communal nursing, kin recognition, sex ratios, multiple mating, levels of inbreeding, and infanticide (Chapter 2). Additional research with prairie dogs is certain to yield more information, not only about prairie dogs in particular, but about social animals in general.

Prairie dogs change the landscape and soil chemistry, affect the cycling of water and nutrients, alter floral species composition, provide shelter and nesting habitat for many other organisms, and serve as prey for numerous predators (Chapter 4). Conservation of prairie dogs will help to retain these keystone functions of the grassland ecosystem. Indeed, long-term survival of several species—most notably, the black-footed ferret—is contingent on preservation of the prairie dog (Chapter 4).

In Colorado cities such as Boulder, Denver, and Fort Collins, and in Lubbock, Texas, prairie dogs sometimes live within small parks or along highways within city limits, where they can be important prey items for local populations of golden eagles, ferruginous hawks, and red-tailed hawks (Manci 1992; Gietzen et al. 1997; Weber 2004). Regarding numbers of individuals, keystone effects, and overall conservation, the importance of "urban colonies" of prairie dogs is marginal. But urban colonies are nonetheless valuable for at least two reasons. First, urban colonies exemplify Rosenzweig's (2003) vision for "maintaining new habitats to conserve species diversity in places where people live, work, and play." Rosenzweig (2003; see also Daily 2003) appreciates the relevance of large sanctuaries for rare species, but argues that many species will survive only if they have opportunities to evolve mechanisms for living in close contact with humans (see also Mace et al. 1999; Balmford and Whitten 2003; Woodroffe et al. 2005). Second, many people first witness wild prairie dogs at urban colonies. Like pet prairie dogs (Chapter 17), urban colonies increase the public awareness of prairie dogs and those species that associate with them.

The emotional reaction to prairie dogs is rarely lukewarm. People either love 'em, or hate 'em—or do not know what they are. With the realization that I will offend the lovers sometimes and the haters other times, one of my primary objectives as editor of *Conservation of the Black-Tailed Prairie Dog* has been to enlist authors who can propose reasonable plans that will maximize the probability that the prairie dog and its grassland ecosystem will persist long into the future. I have enjoyed writing and editing chapters that deal with issues such as social behavior and demography (Chapters 2 and 3); the prairie dog as a keystone species (Chapter 4); circumstances when competition between prairie dogs and domestic livestock is minimal (Chapter 5); recent techniques that have substantially improved the success of translocations (Chapter 13); ways to change negative attitudes (Chapters 7 and 17); large focal areas for prairie dog sanctuaries (Chapters 15 and 16); and the notion that many ranchers and farmers would embrace listing in return for financial compensation for preserving prairie dog colonies on their domains (Chapter 14). I also have had to tackle several disconcerting issues, however, such as reasons why the prairie dog should be excluded from FLETWP (Chapter 12); methods of killing prairie dogs (Chapter 9); the billions of prairie dogs that have been poisoned over the last 100 years (Chapter 8); and the millions of prairie dogs that have been killed by either recreational shooting (Chapter 10) or plague (Chapter 11). Especially painful for me have been the concession that poisoning of prairie dogs is unlikely to cease (Chapters 8, 9, and 15; Table 18.1), and the realization that perhaps we sometimes should allow ranchers to profit by managing their prairie dog colonies for recreational shooting (Chapter 10). But these concessions are probably necessary, because successful conservation of prairie dogs will require cooperation among people with different convictions. If biologists and wildlife managers understand that prairie dogs sometimes interfere with the raising of crops and livestock, then our recommendations for conservation are more likely to be fair and acceptable to farmers and ranchers. The battle to save the prairie dog and its grassland ecosystem is one that we can win—especially if we act sooner rather than later.

Appendix A. Common and Scientific Names

Bacteria (Schizomycetes)	
sylvatic plague, bubonic plague, plague	*Yersinia [Pasteurella] pestis*
tularemia, or rabbit fever	*Francisella tularensis*
Plants (Plantae)	
aquarius paintbrush	*Castilleja aquariensis*
black grama	*Bouteloua eriopoda*
black nightshade	*Solanum americanum*
blue grama	*Bouteloua gracilis*
bracted spiderwort	*Tradescantia bracteata*
buffalo grass	*Buchloe dactyloides*
curly mesquite or tobasograss	*Hilaria belangeri*
fetid marigold or prairie dog weed	*Dyssodia [Boebera] papposa*
fringed sagewort	*Artemisia frigida*
Graham beardtongue	*Penstemon grahamii*
hairy grama	*Bouteloua hirsute*
honey mesquite	*Prosopis glandulosa*
horseshoe milkvetch	*Astragalus desperatus*
Indian ricegrass	*Achnatherum hymenoides*
Japanese brome	*Bromus japonicus*
little bluestem	*Schizachyrium scoparium*

milkvetch	*Astragalus* spp.
needle-and-thread grass	*Hesperostipa comata*
needleleaf sedge	*Carex duriuscula*
parachute beardtongue	*Penstemon debilis*
pigweed	*Amaranthus retroflexus*
plains pricklypear	*Opuntia polyacantha*
porcupine grass	*Hesperostipa spartea*
prairie dog weed or fetid marigold	*Dyssodia [Boebera] papposa*
prairie junegrass	*Koeleria macrantha*
red threeawn	*Aristida purpurea longiseta*
sand dropseed	*Sporobolus cryptandrus*
scarlet globemallow or scarlet mallow	*Sphaeralcea coccinea*
sedge	*Carex* spp.
sideoats grama	*Bouteloua curtipendula*
silver bluestem	*Bothriochloa saccharoides*
sixweeks fescue	*Vulpia octoflora*
sleeping-ute milkvetch	*Astragalus tortipes*
sun sedge	*Carex inops heliophila*
thickspike wheatgrass	*Elymus macrounus*
tumblegrass	*Schedonnardus paniculatus*
western wheatgrass	*Pascopyrum smithii*
wheatgrass	*Agropyron* spp.
White River beardtongue	*Penstemon scariosus albifluvis*
Internal parasites	
protozoan	phylum Protozoa
roundworm	class Nematoda
spiny-headed worm	class Acanthocephala
tapeworm	class Cestoda

Mollusks (Mollusca)	
common mussel or California mussel	*Mytilus californicus*
Echinoderms (Echinodermata)	
ochre sea star	*Pisaster ochraceus*
Arachnids (Arachnida)	
mites and ticks	order Acarina; the most common species of mites and ticks that parasitize prairie dogs include *Atricholaelaps glasgowi* and *Ixodes kingi*
Insects (Insecta)	
flea	order Siphonaptera; the most common species of fleas that parasitize prairie dogs include *Leptopsylla segnis, Monopsylla exilis, Oropsylla [Opistocrostis] hirsutus, Oropsylla labis, Oropsylla tuberculatus cynomuris, Pulex irritans, Pulex simulans,* and *Thrassis fotus*
lice or sucking lice	order Anoplura
Amphibians (Amphibia)	
boreal toad	*Bufo boreas boreas*
Great Plains toad	*Bufo cognatus*
Plains spadefoot toad	*Scaphiopus bombifrons*
tiger salamander	*Ambystoma tigrinum*
Woodhouse's toad	*Bufo woodhousii*
Reptiles (Reptilia)	
bull snake	*Pituophis melanoleucus*
ornate (or western) box turtle	*Terrapene ornata*
prairie rattlesnake	*Crotalus viridis*
rattlesnake	*Crotalus* spp.

Texas horned lizard	*Phrynosoma cornutum*
western diamondback rattlesnake	*Crotalus atrox*
western plains garter snake	*Thamnophis radix*
Birds (Aves)	
accipiter hawk	*Accipiter* spp.
aplomado falcon	*Falco femoralis*
American kestral	*Falco sparverius*
burrowing owl	*Athene cunicularia*
buteo hawk	*Buteo* spp.
Carolina parakeet	*Conuropsis carolinensis*
chestnut-collared longspur	*Calcarius ornatus*
Cooper's hawk	*Accipiter cooperii*
eared grebe	*Podiceps nigricollis*
eastern meadowlark	*Sturnella magna*
Eskimo curlew	*Numenius borealis*
ferruginous hawk	*Buteo regalis*
golden eagle	*Aquila chrysaetos*
grasshopper sparrow	*Ammodramus savannarum*
Gunnison sage grouse	*Centrocercus minimus*
horned lark	*Eremophila alpestris*
killdeer	*Charadrius vociferous*
ladder-backed woodpecker	*Picoides scalaris*
lark bunting	*Calamospiza melanocorys*
mountain plover	*Charadrius montanus*
northern goshawk	*Accipiter gentilis*
northern harrier	*Circus cyaneus*
parrot	order Psittaciformes

passenger pigeon	*Ectopistes migratorius*
peregrine falcon	*Falco peregrinus*
prairie falcon	*Falco mexicanus*
red-tailed hawk	*Buteo jamaicensis*
western meadowlark	*Sturnella neglecta*
white pelican	*Pelecanus erythrorhynchos*
yellow warbler	*Dendroica petechia*
Mammals (Mammalia)	
Even-toed ungulates (Artiodactyla)	
American bison or bison	*Bison bison*
domestic cow or cow	*Bos taurus*
domestic sheep or sheep	*Ovis aries*
pronghorn, or pronghorn antelope	*Antilocapra americana*
wapiti or elk	*Cervus elaphus*
white-tailed deer	*Odocoileus virginianus*
Odd-toed ungulates (Perissodactyla)	
burro, wild burro, or ass	*Equus asinus*
wild, feral, or domestic horse	*Equus caballus*
Carnivores (Carnivora)	
American badger or badger	*Taxidea taxus*
black-footed ferret or ferret	*Mustela nigripes*
bobcat	*Lynx rufus*
common gray fox	*Urocyon cinereoargenteus*
coyote	*Canis latrans*
domestic cat or house cat or cat	*Felis domesticus* or *Felis silvestris*
domestic dog or dog	*Canis familiaris*
grizzly bear	*Ursus arctos*

long-tailed weasel	*Mustela frenata*
mountain lion or cougar or puma	*Felis [Puma] concolor*
red fox	*Vulpes vulpes*
striped skunk	*Mephitis mephitis*
swift fox	*Vulpes velox*
Rabbits, hares, and pikas (Lagomorpha)	
black-tailed jackrabbit	*Lepus californicus*
eastern cottontail	*Sylvilagus floridanus*
white-tailed jackrabbit	*Lepus townsendii*
Rodents (Rodentia)	
black rat or house rat	*Rattus rattus*
black-tailed prairie dog	*Cynomys ludovicianus*
California ground squirrel	*Spermophilus beecheyi*
chipmunk	*Tamias (Eutamias)* spp.
deer mouse	*Peromyscus maniculatus*
flying squirrel	*Glaucomys* spp.
Gambian giant rat	*Cricetomys gambianus*
ground squirrel	*Spermophilus* spp.
Gunnison's prairie dog	*Cynomys gunnisoni*
house mouse	*Mus musculus*
marmot	*Marmota* spp.
meadow vole	*Microtus pennsylvanicus*
Mexican prairie dog	*Cynomys mexicanus*
mole	family Talpidae
northern grasshopper mouse	*Onychomys leucogaster*
pocket gopher, or gopher	family Geomyidae

prairie dog	*Cynomys ludovicianus* or *Cynomys* spp. In this book other authors and I are referring only to the black-tailed prairie dog (*Cynomys ludovicianus*) when we use the term "prairie dog."
red squirrel	*Tamiasciurus hudsonicus*
rock squirrel	*Spermophilus variegatus*
thirteen-lined ground squirrel	*Spermophilus tridecemlineatus*
tree squirrel	*Sciurus* spp. and *Tamiasciurus* spp.
Utah prairie dog	*Cynomys parvidens*
white-tailed prairie dog	*Cynomys leucurus*
Primates (Primates)	
human	*Homo sapiens*

Appendix B. Acronyms

ADC*	Animal Damage Control
ANPP	Annual aboveground net primary production
APHIS	Animal and Plant Health Inspection Service
AUM	Animal unit month
CBSG	Conservation Breeding Specialist Group
BBS	Bureau of Biological Survey
BLF	Biodiversity Legal Foundation
BLM	United States Bureau of Land Management
BSFW	Bureau of Sport Fisheries and Wildlife
ESA	Endangered Species Act
FLETWP	Federal List of Endangered and Threatened Wildlife and Plants
MSCP	Multi-state conservation plan for the black-tailed prairie dog, *Cynomys ludovicianus*, in the United States
NMFS	National Marine Fisheries Service
NPS	National Park Service
NWR	National Wildlife Refuge
NWF	National Wildlife Federation
PARC	Predatory Animal and Rodent Control
PDU	Prairie Dogs Unlimited
RMA	Rocky Mountain Arsenal National Wildlife Refuge

spp.	Collective term for several species of the same genus: *See glossary*
TNC	The Nature Conservancy
USDA	United States Department of Agriculture
USDI	United States Department of the Interior
USEPA	United States Environmental Protection Agency
USFS	United States Forest Service
USGS	United States Geological Survey
USFWS	United States Fish and Wildlife Service
WHO	World Health Organization
WS*	Wildlife Services

*Wildlife Services (WS) is a program within the Animal and Plant Health Inspection Service (APHIS). Before 1997, WS was called Animal Damage Control (ADC).

Appendix C. Calculations for Chapter 10

In Chapter 10, we use R throughout for "finite rate of population increase." Some readers will be more familiar with the symbol λ (lambda), which is also called the finite rate of population increase and is equivalent to R when the values of survivorship and fecundity do not change. But λ is technically the dominant eigenvalue of the Leslie matrix (Burgman et al. 1993; Akçakaya et al. 1999).

The instantaneous growth rate (r), also called the intrinsic rate of increase (Roughgarden 1979), is related to the finite rate of increase, R or λ, by $R = \lambda = e^{r}$ and is used to predict population growth in continuous time, rather than in discrete time, by the equation $N(t) = N(0) \cdot e^{rt}$ (Burgman et al. 1993, Akçakaya et al. 1999). We discuss R_{max}, the maximal rate of population growth, which occurs when population size is close to zero and growth is unaffected by crowding. Its analog, r_m, represents instantaneous growth under the same conditions. For animals such as prairie dogs that have discrete breeding seasons, density-dependent growth from time t to t + 1 is often written as $N(t + 1) = N(t) + r_m \cdot (1 - (N(t)/K)) \cdot N(t)$ (Johnson 1994).

Knowledge of r_m is also used to estimate maximal sustainable yield (MSY). When renewal of consumable resources is unaffected by prairie dogs, population size necessary to sustain MSY is approximately one-half the carrying capacity (i.e., K/2) and $MSY = r_m \cdot K/4$. When the prairie dogs affect the renewal of consumable resources, on the other hand, then the general rule is $MSY > r_m \cdot K/4$ (Caughley and Sinclair 1994).

Glossary

12-month finding: See *listing process* below.

90-day finding: See *listing process* below.

acclimation-cage: Device used to coerce translocated prairie dogs to remain at a recipient-site. Each acclimation-cage consists of an underground nest-chamber and an aboveground retention-basket, connected by plastic tubing (Figure 13.2).

"active" burrow-entrance: Burrow-entrance with fresh scat (i.e., fecal pellet that is greenish, black, or dark brown, rather than bleached) on the burrow-mound or less than one meter away. Active burrow-entrances help wildlife managers to estimate the number of prairie dogs at a colony-site.

adaptation: A morphological trait (e.g., thick fur to insulate against cold weather) or behavioral pattern (e.g., tendency to run away from predators) that improves either survivorship or reproduction.

adaptive management: A combination of management, monitoring, and research, with an emphasis on learning from successes and failures of current programs, so that future management will be better (Halbert 1993). All authors of *Conservation of the Black-Tailed Prairie Dog* agree with the notion of adaptive management, but the term does not appear in this volume because the word "adaptive" has implications for behavioral and evolutionary ecologists that are unrelated to management.

arachnid: Invertebrate with eight legs (e.g., spiders, ticks, and mites).

alleles: Variations of the same gene. Among humans, one allele of the gene for eye color usually produces brown eyes, but another allele sometimes produces blue eyes.

breeding dispersal: Emigration of an individual from the area where it mated.

breeding territory: Territory in which an individual mates.

candidate assessment: An annual review required for each candidate species to reevaluate its status. The findings of all candidate assessments are published in the *Candidate Notice of Review*.

candidate list: A list of all species of wildlife and plants that qualify as candidate species (i.e., are warranted-but-precluded for addition to FLETWP). Species on the candidate list are reevaluated annually via a candidate assessment.

Candidate Notice of Review: An annual compilation of all candidate assessments. Candidate species are reevaluated each year until a proposed rule is published to list the species, or until a determination is made that listing is not warranted.

candidate species: A species for which vulnerability is sufficient for listing as endangered or threatened, but for which listing is precluded by emphasis on species of higher priority.

colony: Group of individuals of the same species living in the same area. Prairie dog colonies are sometimes called towns or villages. Within colonies, prairie dogs live in territorial subgroupings called coteries.

colony density: Colony size divided by the area inhabited by that colony. The units for colony density are number of prairie dogs per hectare (or per acre).

colony-site: Location inhabited by a colony of prairie dogs.

colony size: Number of prairie dogs that live in a colony. Biologists usually use the term for the number of adults and yearlings within a colony (Hoogland 1995; Chapter 2), but colony size sometimes includes juveniles as well.

competition: Phenomenon that results when sharing of resources by two species adversely affects one or both species (Ricklefs and Miller 2000). Competition does not necessarily occur simply because two species use the same resource, and it is difficult to document under natural conditions. Prairie dogs commonly compete with domestic livestock for forage (Chapter 5).

complex: Group of two or more prairie dog colonies in which each colony is less than 7 kilometers (4 miles) from another colony, so that individuals commonly can disperse between colonies. Complexes are important for the conservation of prairie dogs.

congeners: Species that belong to the same genus. The five species of prairie dogs are congeners, because they all belong to the genus *Cynomys*.

coterie: Territorial family group within a prairie dog colony. A typical coterie contains one breeding male, two to three adult females, and one to two yearlings of each sex. Large coteries sometimes contain two breeding males. The area of a coterie's territory is usually about one-third of a hectare (0.8 acres).

Cynomys ludovicianus: The Latin, scientific name for the black-tailed prairie dog.

demography: Study of issues relating to survival and reproduction. Topics of demography include average and maximal lifespan, litter size, age of first reproduction, senescence, annual and lifetime reproductive success, and causes of mortality.

dimorphism: See *sexual dimorphism.*

domestic livestock: Cattle, horses, and sheep.

diurnal: Active during daylight hours. Most rodents are nocturnal, but prairie dogs and other ground-dwelling squirrels (chipmunks, ground squirrels, and marmots) are diurnal.

ecosystem: A group of plants and animals together with its environment, functioning as a unit; an area that contains organisms interacting with one another and their nonliving environment. Ecologists sometimes talk about forest, grassland, and river ecosystems, but the exact boundaries of most ecosystems are difficult to define.

emergency listing: Immediate assignment to FLETWP for 240 days to protect a species from a threat that could cause immediate extinction. Expected losses during the normal listing process would risk the continued existence of the species that has been emergency listed. A final rule must be published within 240 days of emergency listing to prevent a lapse in protection.

emigration: Movement away from an area; an individual that emigrates is an emigrant. For prairie dogs, emigration is the dispersal away from the home colony-site. Because today's prairie dog colonies are so isolated, most emigrants die before finding another colony-site.

endangered species: Any native species at risk of extinction throughout all or a significant portion of its range.

Endangered Species Act (ESA): Federal legislation, enacted in its present form in 1973, but with later amendments, which promotes conservation of endangered and threatened species and the ecosystems upon which they depend. USFWS and NMFS share responsibility for administration of ESA.

epizootic: Epidemic. For a disease that affects many—sometimes thousands—of individuals in the same area at the same time, biologists sometimes use the term *epizootic* for nonhuman animals, and *epidemic* for humans. Epizootics of plague are common among prairie dogs in the western part of the geographic range.

extinct species: A species no longer found in any portion of its range. Examples of extinct species include the passenger pigeon, Carolina parakeet, and Eskimo curlew.

Federal List of Endangered and Threatened Wildlife and Plants (FLETWP): A list of all species that USFWS or NMFS has determined to be endangered or threatened. Even though a species is not on FLETWP, it might be on a state's list of endangered and threatened species.

Federal Register: A daily publication of regulations and legal notices issued by federal agencies.

final rule: A designation, required within one year after a proposed rule, to list a species as endangered or threatened. A final rule addresses all substantive comments received regarding the proposed rule, including those from selected peer referees.

focal area: Site of sufficient size so that a colony or complex of prairie dogs can be large enough to provide suitable habitat for black-footed ferrets, burrowing owls, mountain plovers, and other species that depend on prairie dogs for survival. Bigger is always better, but an area of 4,000 hectares (9,884 acres) for a colony or complex is probably the minimum necessary for a fully functional grassland ecosystem.

forbs: Herbaceous (i.e., non-woody) plants other than graminoids (grasses or grass-like plants). Graminoids usually predominate at young prairie dog colony-sites, but forbs usually predominate at older colony-sites.

foreseeable future: The time frame during which a threatened species is likely to become endangered. No formal definition exists; the foreseeable future can vary for different species, and for the same species under different circumstances.

former geographic range: The original geographic distribution of a species. Today's range might be larger (e.g., for the coyote) or smaller (e.g., for the prairie dog) than the former geographic range. When biologists say *former geographic range* (or *historic range*), they usually mean the range of about 200 years ago, when accurate estimates of the geographic range for prairie dogs and other organisms became available.

foundation species: Organism that has unique, significant effects on its ecosystem that result from mere abundance. The prairie dog is a foundation species. See *keystone species*.

genetic drift: Process by which alleles decrease (or increase) in frequency because of chance rather than natural selection. Genetic drift is especially pronounced in small populations, which cannot contain as much genetic variation as larger populations. Genetic drift in small populations can cause the loss of substantial genetic variation.

gestation: Pregnancy; period between conception and parturition. For prairie dogs, gestation most commonly lasts for either 34 or 35 days (range = 33–38).

"good neighbor" policy: Elimination or reduction of prairie dog colonies, usually via poisoning, in response to neighboring landowners who worry about invasion of their private lands by dispersing prairie dogs.

gram: Metric unit of mass. One pound is equivalent to 454 grams.

graminoids: Grasses or grass-like plants (e.g., sedges).

ground-truthing: Verification of satellite images and aerial photographs by direct observations from the ground. Without ground-truthing, satellite images and aerial photographs usually do not allow wildlife managers to discriminate between active colony-sites versus colony-sites that recently have lost all prairie dogs (because of plague or poisoning, for example).

hectare: Metric unit of area. One hectare equals 2.471 acres.

historic range: Same as *former geographic range*.

Homestead Act: Legislation passed by Congress in 1862 that granted ownership of a 65-hectare (160-acre) plot of public land to a citizen who had resided on and cultivated the land for five years after the initial claim. Many of these plots are now parts of national grasslands.

immigration: Movement into an area; an individual that immigrates is an immigrant. For prairie dogs, immigration is the arrival into a new colony-site from another colony-site.

immunocontraceptive: Chemical that involves the immune system to prevent conception.

inbreeding: Mating with a close relative such as a parent, offspring, or sibling. Extreme inbreeding, also called incest, commonly produces inferior offspring. Prairie dogs have several mechanisms that discourage extreme inbreeding.

incest: See *inbreeding*.

intercolonial: Between colonies. Intercolonial dispersal occurs when a prairie dog emigrates from one colony and becomes an immigrant into another colony.

intracolonial: Within the home colony. Intracolonial dispersal occurs when a prairie dog moves from one territory to another territory within the same colony.

key private land: Terrain that belongs to a landowner who actively promotes the conservation of prairie dogs.

keystone species: Organism that has unique, significant effects on its ecosystem that are disproportionately large relative to its abundance. The prairie dog is a keystone species. See *foundation species*.

kilogram: Metric unit of mass. One kilogram equals 1,000 grams, and is equivalent to 2.20 pounds.

lactation: Nursing; period between parturition and weaning. For prairie dogs, lactation usually lasts for about 41 days (range = 37–51).

listing: The process of adding an organism to FLETWP.

listing factors: Five factors that provide guidance for determining whether a species should be added to FLETWP. These factors are current or threatened destruction or modification of habitat or range; overutilization for commercial, recreational, scientific, or educational purposes; disease or predation; inadequacy of existing regulatory mechanisms; and other factors that affect continued existence.

listing priority number (LPN): A number from 1–12 that is used to prioritize actions for possible listing of a candidate species. LPN results from the magnitude and immediacy of threats, and also from the degree of taxonomic uniqueness (i.e., the number of similar species). LPN of 1 indicates maximal danger of extinction, and LPN of 12 indicates minimal danger.

listing process: Process of considering a species for addition to FLETWP. The listing process usually begins with receipt of a *petition*. At a minimum, the listing process includes a *90-day finding* that determines whether the petition presents sufficient information for possible listing. If the 90-day finding is affirmative, then a *12-month finding* is mandatory. The 12-month finding asserts that listing is *warranted, not warranted, or warranted-but-precluded*. If a species is added to the *candidate list* (i.e., designated as warranted-but-precluded) in the 12-month finding, then other steps in the listing process might include annual *candidate assessments*, a *proposed rule*, and a *final rule*. Chapter 12 contains a detailed description of the listing process.

livestock: Cattle, horses, and sheep; also called domestic livestock.

maximal sustainable yield (MSY) (regarding recreational shooting): The largest number of individuals that can be shot in one year that will not significantly affect population size in the following year, because the number of individuals shot will be replaced by either births or immigration. Also called *potential yield* or *optimal yield*. Landowners who charge for recreational shooting of prairie dogs try to manage colonies on their domains for MSY, which is difficult to determine.

monkeypox: Viral disease introduced into the United States in spring 2003, probably via Gambian giant rats imported from Ghana. Monkeypox evidently then spread from caged Gambian giant rats in a pet store in Illinois to prairie dogs in adjacent cages. Monkeypox can be fatal for both prairie dogs and humans, but no human mortalities in the United States from monkeypox have occurred to this point.

natal dispersal: Emigration of a young individual from its area of birth.

natal territory: Territory in which an individual is born.

national grasslands: Collection of 65-hectare (160-acre) plots, intermingled with private lands, under management of the United States Forest Service (USFS). Most of the plots originally were given to citizens in the late 1800s via the Homestead Act, and then were purchased by the federal government in the 1930s and 1940s. Several national grasslands contain large colonies and complexes of prairie dogs.

National Marine Fisheries Service (NMFS): A federal agency within the Department of Commerce that works to conserve native marine organisms and their habitats for citizens of the United States. With USFWS, NMFS is responsible for the interpretation and administration of ESA.

not warranted: A conclusion that a species is neither endangered nor threatened.

outbreeding: Mating with an individual who is genetically unrelated, or only distantly related. Prairie dogs have several mechanisms that promote outbreeding.

parturition: Giving birth. For prairie dogs, parturition usually occurs in early morning, after a gestation of about five weeks.

petition: A formal request to consider a species for listing. A petition is submitted to either USFWS or NMFS by either an individual or an organization. Every petition must have supporting documentation.

philopatry: Remaining in the natal territory. Most prairie dog females are philopatric for life, but males typically disperse from the natal territory before reaching sexual maturity.

plague: Disease caused by a bacterium (*Yersinia pestis*) that affects prairie dogs, other rodents, and humans. When plague affects wild rodents, it is called *sylvatic plague*. For humans and probably for other susceptible animals as well, plague has three overlapping stages: bubonic, septicemic, and pneumonic. When plague infects a prairie dog colony, mortality usually approaches 100%.

plague line: Imaginary line that indicates the eastern edge of the incidence of plague among prairie dogs. Plague occurs among prairie dogs west of the plague line in states such as Colorado, Montana, and Wyoming. For unknown reasons, plague is rare among prairie dogs east of the plague line in states such as Kansas, Oklahoma, Nebraska, North Dakota, and South Dakota. The plague line approximately coincides with the 102nd meridian.

Precautionary Principle: Axiom that dictates that decisions should always err in favor of nature, especially if our actions might lead to changes that are difficult to reverse or to the loss of something irreplaceable, such as a species.

proposed rule: A proposal, based on the 12-month finding, to list a species as endangered or threatened. The proposed rule is available to the public for comments, undergoes peer review, and eventually might become a final rule.

protozoan: Single-celled animal such as an amoeba (*Amoeba* spp.) or a paramecium (*Paramecium* spp.).

quarantine: Period of time during which a prairie dog suspected of carrying plague or some other disease (e.g., tularemia or monkeypox) is separated from other prairie dogs. Before translocating prairie dogs into a new colony-site, for example, wildlife managers usually retain individuals in small groups for quarantine that lasts for at least 14 days.

recreation-day: One recreation-day (also called one shooter-day) is one recreational shooter spending one day in the field shooting prairie dogs; four shooters on the same day = four recreation-days.

redundancy (in terms of herbivory): Consumption of plants by several species rather than by a single species.

restoration: Process of returning an ecosystem or a species to its original condition before human disturbance. When wildlife managers and conservation biologists talk about the restoration of prairie dogs, they mean the improvement of conditions so that prairie dogs can live in large colonies and complexes where animals such as black-footed ferrets, mountain plovers, and burrowing owls can also thrive.

senescence: The aging process. For prairie dogs, older individuals weigh less than middle-aged individuals, and consequently rear fewer offspring and are less likely to survive until the following year.

sexual dimorphism: Differences in anatomy related to sex. Prairie dogs show sexual dimorphism in body mass, because males are consistently heavier than females at all ages. Prairie dogs do not show sexual dimorphism in color of the fur.

significant portion of its range: A consideration for threatened or endangered species regarding the extent of range affected by factors that jeopardize continued existence. No formal definition exists; a significant portion of range can vary for different species, or for the same species under different circumstances.

species composition: The types of species in a particular habitat or area.

species richness: The number of species in a particular habitat or area.

spp: Collective term for many species of the same genus. *Spermophilus* spp., for example, includes the different species of ground squirrels of the genus Spermophilus. *Cynomys* spp. includes the five prairie dog species of the genus *Cynomys* (black-tailed, Gunnison's, Mexican, Utah, and white-tailed).

stakeholder: Organism directly affected by the conservation of a species. For prairie dogs, stakeholders include humans such as ranchers, farmers, environmentalists, wildlife managers, outdoor recreationists, Native Americans, and residents of some rural and urban areas. As originally defined by ESA, however, stakeholders also include plants (e.g., scarlet globemallow, black nightshade, pigweed, and fetid marigold) and nonhuman animals (e.g., black-footed ferrets, mountain plovers, and burrowing owls) that depend on prairie dogs for survival. Indeed, prairie dogs themselves are stakeholders.

standard deviation: A statistical measure of variation. Consider the following two sets of numbers: 10, 10, 10 and 5, 10, 15. The average for these two sets is the same (10), but the standard deviation is higher for the second set because it has more variation.

standard error: A statistical measure of variation, related to standard deviation. See *standard deviation*.

subspecies: Distinct population or set of populations within a species. Members of different subspecies usually look different or behave somewhat differently, but can interbreed.

substantial information: Amount of information in a petition that would lead a reasonable person to believe that listing might be warranted, resulting in an affirmative 90-day finding.

sylvatic plague: See *plague*.

taxonomy: Scientific classification. The black-tailed prairie dog's taxonomy is Animalia (kingdom), Chordata (phylum), Vertebrata (subphylum), Mammalia (class), Rodentia (order), Sciuridae (family), *Cynomys* (genus), *ludovicianus* (species).

territorial dispute: An aggressive interaction involving two prairie dogs that usually occurs at the boundary that separates two coterie territories. Territorial disputes include staring, tooth-chattering, flaring of the tail, bluff charges, and reciprocal sniffing of scent glands at the base of the tail. A territorial dispute sometimes escalates into a fight.

threat: An adverse effect on a species that is significant enough to jeopardize its continued existence.

threatened species: Any species that is likely to become endangered within the foreseeable future throughout all or a significant portion of its range.

translocation: Movement of prairie dogs, by people, from one colony-site to another colony-site. Sometimes we translocate prairie dogs away from a place of danger (e.g., an area designated for a supermarket) to get them to a safer home. Other times we translocate prairie dogs to start a new colony in a particular area.

tularemia: Disease caused by a bacterium (*Francisella tularensis*) that affects humans, prairie dogs, other rodents, and rabbits. Also called rabbit fever, tularemia can be fatal for prairie dogs. Because it responds to antibiotics, tularemia among humans is rarely fatal.

United States Fish and Wildlife Service (USFWS): A federal agency within the Department of the Interior that works to conserve and protect native plants and (nonmarine) animals, and their habitats, for citizens of the United States. With NMFS, USFWS is responsible for the interpretation and administration of ESA.

vector: An organism that transfers disease-causing microorganisms from one host to another. Fleas are the most common vectors for the transmission of plague among prairie dogs.

ward: Subcolony. Wards within a prairie dog colony are usually separated by unsuitable habitat such as a hill or tall vegetation. Residents of one ward usually can see and hear residents of an adjacent ward, but movements between wards are uncommon.

warranted: A conclusion that a species is either endangered or threatened. After a species is considered warranted for listing, a proposed rule must be promptly published in the *Federal Register.*

warranted-but-precluded: A conclusion that a species is either endangered or threatened—listing is precluded, however, by emphasis on species with higher listing priority numbers (LPNs). Species that are warranted-but-precluded are called *candidate species.*

References

Note: Full names for acronyms are in Appendix B

Achtman, M., K. Zurth, G. Morelli, A. Guiyoule, and E. Carniel. 1999. *Yersinia pestis*, the cause of plague, is a recently emerged clone of *Yersinia pseudotuberculosis*. *Proceedings of The National Academy of Science (PNAS)* 96:14043–14048.

Ackers, S. H. 1992. Behavioral responses of Utah prairie dogs (*Cynomys parvidens*) to translocation. MS thesis, Utah State University, Logan.

Agnew, W., D. W. Uresk, and R. M. Hansen. 1986. Flora and fauna associated with prairie dog colonies and adjacent ungrazed mixed grass prairie in western South Dakota. *Journal of Range Management* 39:135–139.

Akçakaya, H. R., M. A. Burgman, and L. R. Ginzburg. 1999. Applied population ecology principles and computer exercises using RAMAS® EcoLab 2.0. Sinauer Associates, Inc. Sunderland, Massachusetts.

Alexander, A. M. 1932. Control, not extermination, of *Cynomys ludovicianus arizonensis*. *Journal of Mammalogy* 13:302.

Alexander, R. D. 1974. The evolution of social behavior. *Annual Review of Ecology and Systematics* 5:325–383.

Alexander R. D. 1987. *The biology of moral systems.* Aldine de Gruyter, New York, New York.

Allan, P. F. 1954. Tall grass defeats prairie dogs. *Soil Conservation* 20:103–105.

Allen, D. 1967. *The life of prairies and plains.* McGraw-Hill, New York, New York.

Allison, P. S., A. W. Leary, and M. J. Bechard. 1995. Observations of wintering ferruginous hawks (*Buteo regalis*) feeding on prairie dogs (*Cynomys ludovicianus*) in the Texas Panhandle. *Texas Journal of Science* 47:235–237.

American Society of Mammalogists. 1998. Resolution on the decline of prairie dogs and the grassland ecosystem in North America. Blacksburg, Virginia, 6–10 June 1998.

Andelt, W. F., and T. D. I. Beck. 1998. Effect of black-footed ferret odors on behavior and reproduction of prairie dogs. *Southwestern Naturalist* 43:344–351.

Anderson, E. A., S. C. Forrest, T. W. Clark, and L. Richardson. 1986. Paleobiology, biogeography, and systematics of the black-footed ferret, *Mustela nigripes* (Audubon and Bachman), 1851. *Great Basin Naturalist Memoirs* 8:11–62.

Anderson, S. H., and E. S. Williams. 1997. Plague in a complex of white-tailed prairie dogs and associated small mammals in Wyoming. *Journal of Wildlife Diseases* 33: 720–732.

Anthony, A., and D. Foreman. 1951. Observations on the reproductive cycle of the black-tailed prairie dog (*Cynomys ludovicianus*). *Physiological Zoology* 24:242–248.

Apa, A. D., D. W. Uresk, and R. L. Linder. 1990. Black-tailed prairie dog populations one year after treatment with rodenticides. *Great Basin Naturalist* 50:107–113.

Apa, A. D., D. W. Uresk, and R. L. Linder. 1991. Impacts of black-tailed prairie dog rodenticides on nontarget passerines. *Great Basin Naturalist* 51:301–309.

Archer, S., M. G. Garrett, and J. K. Detling. 1987. Rates of vegetation change associated with prairie dog (*Cynomys ludovicianus*) grazing in North American mixed-grass prairie. *Vegetatio* 72:159–166.

Arizona Game and Fish Department. 1988. *Threatened native wildlife in Arizona.* Arizona Game and Fish Department Publication. Phoenix, Arizona. 32 pages.

Atzert, S. P. 1971. *A review of sodium monofluoracetate (Compound-1080): Its properties, toxicology and use in predator and rodent control.* USFWS, Bureau of Sport Fisheries and Wildlife. Special Scientific Report—Wildlife, Number 146:iv+34 pages. Washington, D. C.

Axtman, K. 2002. The prairie dog: Pest or pet? *Christian Science Monitor,* 13 August 2002.

Bailey, V. 1905. Biological survey of Texas. *North American Fauna* 25:1–226.

Bailey, R. G., P. E. Avers, T. King, and W. H. McNab. 1994. *Ecoregions and subecoregions of the United States.* USFS, Washington, D. C.

Bak, J. M., K. G. Boykin, B. C. Thompson, and D. L. Daniel. 2001. Distribution of wintering ferruginous hawks (*Buteo regalis*) in relation to black-tailed prairie dog (*Cynomys ludovicianus*) colonies in southern New Mexico and northern Chihuahua. *Journal of Raptor Research* 35:124–129.

Bakko, E. B. 1977. Field water balance performance in prairie dogs (*Cynomys leucurus* and *C. ludovicianus*). *Comparative Biochemical Physiology* 56:443–451.

Bakko, E. B., W. P. Porter, and B. A. Wunder, 1988. Body temperature patterns in black-tailed prairie dogs in the field. *Canadian Journal of Zoology* 66:1783–1789.

Balmford, A., and T. Whitten. 2003. Who should pay for tropical conservation, and how could the costs be met? *Oryx* 37:238–250.

Bangs, E. E., J. A. Fontaine, M. D. Jimenez, T. J. Meier, E. H. Bradley, C. C. Niemeyer, D. W. Smith, C. M. Mack, V. Asher, and J. K. Oakleaf. 2005. Managing wolf–human conflict in the northwestern United States. In R. Woodroffe, S. J. Thirgood, and A. Rabinowitz, editors. *People and wildlife: Conflict or co-existence.* Cambridge University Press, Cambridge, United Kingdom.

Barnes, A. M. 1982. Surveillance and control of bubonic plague in the United States. *Symposium of the Zoological Society of London* 50:237–270.

Barnes, A. 1993. A review of plague and its relevance to prairie dog populations and the black-footed ferret. Pages 28–37 in J. Oldemeyer, D. E. Biggins, B. J. Miller, and R. Crete, editors. *Management of prairie dog complexes for the reintroduction of the black-footed ferret.* USFWS Biological Report 13, Washington, D. C.

Bateson, P. 1983. Optimal outbreeding. Pages 257–277 in P. Bateson, editor. *Mate choice.* Cambridge University Press, Cambridge, United Kingdom.

Beard, M. L., S. T. Rose, A. M. Barnes, and J. A. Montenari. 1992. Control of *Oropsylla hirsuta*, a plague vector, by treatment of prairie dog burrows with 0.5% permethrin dust. *Journal of Medical Entomology* 29:25–29.

Bell, H. B., and R. W. Dimmick. 1975. Hazards to predators feeding on prairie voles killed with zinc phosphide. *Journal of Wildlife Management* 39:816–819.

Bell, W. R. 1921. Death to the rodents. *USDA Yearbook 1920*:421–438. United States Government Printing Office, Washington, D. C.

Bell, W. R. 1926. *Report on rodent and predatory animal work, State of Colorado*, 10 September 1926. BBS, USDA, National Archives, Washington, D. C.

Benedict, R. A., P. W. Freeman, and H. H. Genoways. 1996. Prairie legacies—mammals. Pages 135–148 in F. B. Samson and F. L. Knopf, editors. *Prairie conservation*. Island Press, Washington, D. C.

Berry, M. E., C. E. Hock, and S. L. Haire. 1998. Abundance of diurnal raptors on open space grasslands in an urbanized landscape. *Condor* 100:601–608.

Berryman, J. H., and N. C. Johnson. 1973. Ferret and prairie dog programs on public lands: A perspective and some facts. Pages 109–125 in R. L. Linder and C. N. Hillman, editors. *Proceedings of the black-footed ferret and prairie dog workshop*, 4–6 September 1973, Rapid City, South Dakota. South Dakota State University, Brookings, South Dakota.

Biggins, D. E. 2001a. Prairie dog research update #2. Unpublished report, USGS, Midcontinent Ecological Science Center, Fort Collins, Colorado.

Biggins, D. E. 2001b. Prairie dog research update #3. Unpublished report, USGS, Midcontinent Ecological Science Center, Fort Collins, Colorado.

Biggins, D. E., and M. Y. Kosoy. 2001a. Disruptions of ecosystems in western North America due to invasion by plague. *Journal of Idaho Academy of Science* 37: 62–65.

Biggins, D. E., and M. Y. Kosoy. 2001b. Influences of introduced plague on North American mammals: Implications from ecology of plague in Asia. *Journal of Mammalogy* 82:906–916.

Biggins, D. E., B. J. Miller, T. W. Clark, R. P. Reading. 1997. Management of an endangered species: The black-footed ferret. Pages 420–426 in G. K. Meffe and C. R. Carroll editors. *Principles of Conservation Biology*, 2nd edition. Sinauer Press, Sunderland, Massachusetts.

Biggins, D. E., B. J. Miller, L. Hanebury, R. Oakleaf, A. Farmer, R. Crete, and A. Dood. 1993. A technique for evaluating black-footed ferret habitat. Pages 73–88 in J. Oldemeyer, D. E. Biggins, B. J. Miller, and R. Crete, editors. *Management of prairie dog complexes for reintroduction of the black-footed ferret.* USFWS, Biological Report 13, Washington, D. C.

Biggins, D. E., M. H. Schroeder, S. C. Forrest, and L. Richardson. 1985. Movements and habitat relationships of radio-tagged black-footed ferrets. Pages 11.1–11.17 in S. Anderson and D. Inkley, editors. *Proceedings of the Black-footed Ferret Workshop.* Wyoming Game and Fish Department, Cheyenne, Wyoming.

Biodiversity Legal Foundation. 1994. Petition to classify the black-tailed prairie dog (*Cynomys ludovicianus*) as a Category 2 Candidate Species.

Biodiversity Legal Foundation, the Predator Project, and J. C. Sharps. 1998. Petition to the United States Fish and Wildlife Service to list the black-tailed prairie dog. 173 pages.

Bishop, N. G., and J. L. Culbertson. 1976. Decline of prairie dog towns in southwestern North Dakota. *Journal of Range Management* 29:217–220.

BLM. 2001. *Malta Field Office prairie dog shooting program update.* http://www.mt.blm.gov/mafo/info/Pdshootingprogram.html.

Bly-Honness, K., J. C. Truett, and D. H. Long. 2004. Influence of social bonds on post-release survival of translocated black-tailed prairie dogs (*Cynomys ludovicianus*). *Ecological Restoration* 22:204–209.

Bock, J. H., and C. E. Bock. 1989. Ecology and evolution in the Great Plains. Pages 551–577 in J. H. Bock and Y. B. Linhart, editors. *The evolutionary ecology of plants.* Westview Press, Boulder, Colorado.

Boggess, J. E. 1984. Infant killing and male reproductive strategies in langurs (*Presbytis entellus*). Pages 283–310 in G. Hausfater and S. B. Hrdy, editors. *Infanticide: Comparative and evolutionary perspectives.* Aldine de Gruyter, New York, New York.

Bonham, C. D., and A. Lerwick. 1976. Vegetation changes induced by prairie dogs on shortgrass range. *Journal of Range Management* 29:221–225.

Bottoms, K. E., and E. T. Bartlett. 1975. Resource allocation through GOAL programming. *Journal of Range Management* 28:442–447.

Bourland, G., and M. Dupris. 1998. Personal letter to Donald R. Gober, USFWS, Pierre, South Dakota. 27 October 1998.

Bragg, T. B., and A. A. Steuter. 1996. Prairie ecology—the mixed prairie. Pages 53–63 in F. B. Samson and F. L. Knoph, editors. *Prairie conservation.* Island Press, Washington, D. C.

Briske, D. D., and J. H. Richards. 1995. Plant responses to defoliation: A physiological, morphological and demographic evaluation. Pages 635–710 in D. J. Bedunah and R. E. Sosebee, editors. *Wildland plants: Physiological ecology and developmental morphology.* Society for Range Management, Denver, Colorado.

Brizuela, M. A., J. K. Detling, and M. S. Cid. 1986. Silicon concentration of grasses growing in sites with different grazing histories. *Ecology* 67:1098–1101.

Broughton, G., A. Tseng, R. Fitzgibbons, S. Tyndall, G. Stanislav, and E. Rongone. 1991. The prevention of cholelithiasis with infused chenodeoxycholate in the prairie dog (*Cynomys ludovicianus*). *Comparative Biochemical Physiology* 99A:609–613.

Bureau of Sport Fisheries and Wildlife (BSFW). 1961. Prairie dog inventory. Unpublished report. Washington, D. C.

Burgman, M. A., S. Ferson, and H. R. Akçakaya. 1993. *Risk assessment in conservation biology. Population and community biology,* series 12. Chapman & Hall, London, United Kingdom. 314 pages.

Bureau of Biological Survey (BBS). 1924. Record Group 22, United States National Archives, College Park, Maryland.

Burnett, W. L. 1915. *The prairie dog situation in Colorado.* Colorado Office of State Entomologist Circular 17. Fort Collins, Colorado. 15 pages.

Burnett, W. L. 1918. *Rodents of Colorado in their economic relation.* Colorado Office of State Entomologist Circular. 25:1–31.

Burnett, W. L. 1919. Report on rodent control. Pages 40–52 in 10th Annual Report, Colorado Office of State Entomologist, Fort Collins, Colorado.

Burroughs, A. L. 1947. Sylvatic plague studies. The vector efficiency of nine species of fleas compared to *Xenopsylla cheopsis. Journal of Hygiene* 45:371–396.

Burroughs, R. D. 1961. *The natural history of the Lewis and Clark expedition.* Michigan State University Press, East Lansing, Michigan. 340 pages.

Burt, W. H., and R. P. Grossenheider. 1976. *A field guide to the mammals.* Houghton-Mifflin, Boston, Massachusetts. 289 pages.

Buscher, H. N., and J. D. Tyler. 1975. Parasites of vertebrates inhabiting prairie dog towns in Oklahoma. II. Helminths. *Proceedings of the Oklahoma Academy of Science* 55:108–111.

Butts, K. O., and J. C. Lewis. 1982. The importance of prairie dog towns to burrowing owls in Oklahoma. *Proceedings of the Oklahoma Academy of Science* 62:46–52.

Cable, K. A., and R. M. Timm. 1988. Efficacy of deferred grazing in reducing prairie dog reinfestation rates. Pages 46–49 in D. W. Uresk, G. L. Schenbeck and R. Cefkin, editors. *Eighth Great Plains wildlife damage control workshop proceedings.* USFS, Rocky Mountain Forest and Range Experiment Station, 28–30 April 1987, Publication 121, Rapid City, South Dakota.

Cain, S. A., J. A. Kadlec, B. L. Allen, R. A. Cooley, M. C. Hornocker, A. S. Leopold, and F. H. Wagner. 1972. *Predator control—1971 Report to the Council on Environmental Quality and the Department of the Interior by the Advisory Committee on Predator Control.* Council on Environmental Quality and USDI, Washington, D. C. viii + 207 pages.

Calhoun, J. B. 1962. Population density and social pathology. *Scientific American* 206:139–148.

Campbell, J. B. 1996. *Introduction to remote sensing.* The Guilford Press, New York, New York.

Campbell, T. M., and T. W. Clark. 1981. Colony characteristics and vertebrate associates of white-tailed and black-tailed prairie dogs in Wyoming. *American Midland Naturalist* 105:269–276.

Campbell, T. M., T. W. Clark, L. Richardson, S. C. Forrest, and B. R. Houston. 1987. Food habits of Wyoming black-footed ferrets. *American Midland Naturalist* 117:208–210.

Caro, T. 1998. *Behavioral ecology and conservation biology.* Oxford University Press, New York.

Carr, J. F. 1973. A rancher's view towards prairie dogs. Pages 168–171 in R. L. Linder and C. N. Hillman, editors. *Proceedings of the black-footed ferret and prairie dog workshop*, September 4–6, 1973. Rapid City, South Dakota. South Dakota State University, Brookings, South Dakota.

Caughley, G. 1977. *Analysis of vertebrate populations.* John Wiley, New York, New York.

Caughley, G., and A. R. E. Sinclair. 1994. *Wildlife ecology and management.* Blackwell Science, Cambridge, Massachusetts. 334 pages.

Centers for Disease Control (CDC). 2003. *Questions and answers about monkeypox.* http://www.cdc.gov/ncidod/monkeypox/qa.htm (accessed 4 November 2003).

Center for Native Ecosystems, Biodiversity Conservation Alliance, Southern Utah Wilderness Alliance, American Lands Alliance, Forest Guardians, T. T. Williams, Ecology Center, and Sinapu. 2002. Petition to list the white-tailed prairie dog (*Cynomys leucurus*) as a threatened or endangered species and to designate critical habitat under the Endangered Species Act of 1973, as amended.

Ceballos, G., J. Pacheco, and R. List. 2000. Influence of prairie dogs (*Cynomys ludovicianus*) on habitat heterogeneity and mammalian diversity in Mexico. *Journal of Arid Environments* 41:161–172.

Chace, G. E. 1973. Prairie dogs, ferrets and cattle-conflict on the plains. *Animal Kingdom* 76:2–8.

Chace, G. E. 1976. *Wonders of prairie dogs.* Dodd, Mead, and Company, New York, New York.

Chadwick, D. H. 1993. The American prairie. *National Geographic* 184:90–119.

Cheatheam, L. K. 1973. Censusing prairie dog colonies using aerial photographs. Pages 78–88 in *Proceedings of black-footed ferret and prairie dog workshop.* South Dakota State University, 4–6 September 1973, Sioux Falls, South Dakota.

Chesser, R. K. 1983. Genetic variability within and among populations of the black-tailed prairie dog. *Evolution* 37:320–331.

Choate, J. R., E. K. Boggess, and F. R. Henderson. 1982. History and status of the black-footed ferret in Kansas. *Transactions of the Kansas Academy of Science* 85:121–132.

Cid, M. S., J. K. Detling, M. A. Brizuela, and A. D. Whicker. 1989. Patterns in grass silicification: Response to grazing history and defoliation. *Oecologia* 80:268–271.

Cid, M. S., J. K. Detling, A. D. Whicker, and M. A. Brizuela. 1990. Silicon uptake and distribution in *Agropyron smithii* as related to grazing history and defoliation. *Journal of Range Management* 43:344–346.

Cid, M. S., J. K. Detling, A. D. Whicker, and M.A. Brizuela. 1991. Vegetational responses of a mixed-grass prairie site following exclusion of prairie dogs and bison. *Journal of Range Management* 44:100–105.

Cincotta, R. P. 1989. Note on mound architecture of the black-tailed prairie dog. *Great Basin Naturalist* 49:621–623.

Cincotta, R. P., D. W. Uresk, and R. M. Hansen. 1987a. Demography of black-tailed prairie dog populations reoccupying sites treated with rodenticide. *Great Basin Naturalist* 47:339–343.

Cincotta, R. P., D. W. Uresk, and R. M. Hansen. 1987b. A statistical model of expansion in a colony of black-tailed prairie dogs. *Great Plains Wildlife Damage Control Workshop Proceedings* 8:30–33.

Cincotta, R. P., D. W. Uresk, and R. M. Hansen. 1989. Plant compositional changes in a colony of black-tailed prairie dogs in South Dakota. Pages 171–177 in A. J. Bjugstad, D. W. Uresk, and R. H. Hamre, editors. *Ninth Great Plains wildlife damage control workshop proceedings.* USFWS, General Technical Report RM-171, Fort Collins, Colorado.

Clark, T. W. 1977. *Ecology and ethology of the white-tailed prairie dog (Cynomys leucurus).* Publications in Biology and Geology, The Milwaukee Public Museum, number 3, Milwaukee, Wisconsin.

Clark, T. W. 1979. The hard life of the prairie dog. *National Geographic* 156:270–281.

Clark, T. W. 1989. *Conservation biology of the black-footed ferret, Mustela nigripes.* Special Scientific Report, number 3. Wildlife Preservation Trust International, Philadelphia, Pennsylvania.

Clark, T. W. 2000. Interdisciplinary problem solving in endangered species conservation: The Yellowstone grizzly bear case. Pages 285–301 in R. P. Reading and B. J. Miller, editors. *Endangered animals: A reference guide to conflicting issues.* Greenwood Press, Westport, Connecticut.

Clark, T. W., T. M. Campbell, D. G. Socha, and D. E. Casey. 1982. Prairie dog colony attributes and associated vertebrate species. *Great Basin Naturalist* 42:577–582.

Clark, T. W., S. C. Forrest, L. Richardson, D. E. Casey, and T. M. Campbell III. 1986a. Description and history of the Meeteetse black-footed ferret environment. *Great Basin Naturalist Memoirs* 8:72–84.

Clark, T. W., L. Richardson, S. C. Forrest, D. E. Casey, and T. M. Campbell III. 1986b. Descriptive ethology and activity patterns of black-footed ferrets. *Great Basin Naturalist Memoirs* 8:115–134.

Clark, T. W., M. Stevenson, K. Ziegelmayer, and M. Rutherford, editors. 2001. *Species and ecosystem conservation: An interdisciplinary approach.* Yale University, School of Forestry and Environmental Studies Bulletin Series 105:1–276.

Clements, F. E. 1920. *Plant indicators: The relation of plant communities to process and practice.* Carnegie Institution of Washington Publication 290, 388 pages.

Coffeen, M. P., and J. C. Pederson. 1993. Techniques for the transplant of Utah prairie dogs. Pages 60–86 in J. L. Oldemeyer, D. E. Biggins, B. J. Miller, and R. Crete, editors. *Management of prairie dog complexes for the reintroduction of the black-footed ferret.* USFWS, Biological Report 13, Washington, D. C.

Collins, A. R., J. P. Workman, and D. W. Uresk. 1984. An economic analysis of black-tailed prairie dog (*Cynomys ludovicianus*) control. *Journal of Range Management* 37:358–361.

Colorado Division of Wildlife. 2002a. *1998/1999 Small game harvest survey statistics.* http://wildlife.state.co.us.

Colorado Division of Wildlife. 2002b. *Plan to compensate landowners who protect black-tailed prairie dogs.* Wildlife Report, Colorado Division of Wildlife. Denver, Colorado.

Colorado Division of Wildlife. 2002c. *Status of the black-tailed prairie dog (Cynomys ludovicianus) in Colorado.* Report to Interstate Black-tailed Prairie Dog Conservation Team, Las Cruces, New Mexico.

Conservation Breeding Specialist Group (CBSG). 2004. *Black-footed ferret population management planning workshop.* Final report. Apple Valley, Minnesota.

Cook, R. R., J. L. Cartron, and P. J. Polechla. 2003. The importance of prairie dogs to nesting ferruginous hawks in grassland ecosystems. *Wildlife Society Bulletin* 31:1073–1082.

Coppock, D. L., and J. K. Detling. 1986. Alteration of bison and black-tailed prairie dog grazing interaction by prescribed burning. *Journal of Wildlife Management* 50: 452–455.

Coppock, D. L., J. K. Detling, J. E. Ellis, and M. I. Dyer. 1983a. Plant–herbivore interactions in a North American mixed-grass prairie. I. Effects of black-tailed prairie dogs on intraseasonal aboveground plant biomass and nutrient dynamics and plant species diversity. *Oecologia* 56:1–9.

Coppock, D. L., J. E. Ellis, J. K. Detling, and M. I. Dyer. 1983b. Plant–herbivore interactions in a North American mixed-grass prairie. II. Responses of bison to modification of vegetation by prairie dogs. *Oecologia* 56:10–15.

Costello, D. F. 1970. *The world of the prairie dog.* Lippincott, Philadelphia, Pennsylvania.

Coupland, R. T. 1992. Mixed prairie. Pages 151–182 in R. T. Coupland, editor. *Ecosystems of the world 8A. Natural Grasslands. Introduction and Western Hemisphere.* Elsevier, New York, New York.

Cox, M. K., and W. L. Franklin. 1990. Premolar gap technique for aging live black-tailed prairie dogs. *Journal of Wildlife Management* 54:143–146.

Creekmore, T. E., T. E. Rocke, and J. Hurley. 2002. A baiting system for delivery of an oral plague vaccine to black-tailed prairie dogs. *Journal of Wildlife Diseases* 38:32–39.

Crooks, D. R., and M. E. Soulé. 1999. Mesopredator release and avifaunal extinctions in a fragmented system. *Nature* 400:563–566.

Cully, J. F., Jr. 1989. Plague in prairie dog ecosystems: Importance for black-footed ferret management. Pages 47–55 in Clark, T. W., D. Hinkley, and T. Rich, editors. *The prairie dog ecosystem: Managing for biological diversity.* Montana BLM Wildlife Technical Bulletin No. 2. Billings, Montana. 55 pages.

Cully, J. F., Jr., A. M. Barnes, T. J. Quan, and G. Maupin. 1997. Dynamics of plague in a Gunnison's prairie dog colony complex from New Mexico. *Journal of Wildlife Diseases* 33:706–719.

Cully, J. F., Jr., L. G. Carter, and K. L. Gage. 2000. New records of sylvatic plague in Kansas. *Journal of Wildlife Diseases* 36:389–392.

Cully, J. F., Jr., and E. S. Williams. 2001. Interspecific comparisons of sylvatic plague in prairie dogs. *Journal of Mammalogy* 82:894–904.

Curtin, R. A., and P. Dolhinow. 1978. Primate social behavior in a changing world. *American Scientist* 66:468–475.

Daily, G. C. 2003. Time to rethink conservation strategy. *Science* 300:1508–1509.

Daley, J. G. 1992. Population reductions and genetic variability in black-tailed prairie dogs. *Journal of Wildlife Management* 56:212–220.

Dalstead, K. J., J. S. Sather-Blair, H. K. Worchester, and R. Klukas. 1981. Application of remote sensing to prairie dog management. *Journal of Range Management* 34:218–223.

Davic, R. D. 2003. Linking keystone species and functional groups: A new operational definition of the keystone-species concept. *Conservation Ecology* 7:rll [online]. http://www.consecol.org/vol7/iss1/resp11.

Davis, R. M. 1999. Use of orally administered chitin inhibitor (Lufenuron) to control flea vectors of plague on ground squirrels in California. *Journal of Medical Entomology* 36:562–567.

Davison, R. P. 2001. The Endangered Species Act: Looking for help in all the wrong places. Presentation at the Annual Conference of The Wildlife Society. Reno, Nevada.

Dawkins, R. 1976. *The selfish gene.* Oxford University Press, New York, New York.

Day, T. A., and J. K. Detling. 1994. Water relations of *Agropyron smithii* and *Bouteloua gracilis* and community evapotranspiration following long-term grazing by prairie dogs. *American Midland Naturalist* 132:381–392.

Deevey, E. S. 1947. Life tables for natural populations of animals. *Quarterly Review of Biology* 22:283–314.

Degesch America, Inc. 1999. *Applicator's manual for Degesch Phostoxin.* Degesch America, Incorporated, Weyers Cave, Virginia.

Deisch, M. S., D. W. Uresk, and R. L. Linder. 1989. Effects of two prairie dog rodenticides on ground-dwelling invertebrates in western South Dakota. *Ninth Great Plains Wildlife Damage Control Workshop Proceedings* 9:166–170.

Deisch, M. S., D. W. Uresk, and R. L. Linder. 1990. Effects of prairie dog rodenticides on deer mice in western South Dakota. *Great Basin Naturalist* 50:347–353.

Desmond, M. J. 1991. Ecological aspects of burrowing owl nesting strategies in the Nebraska panhandle. MS thesis, University of Nebraska, Lincoln, Nebraska.

Desmond, M. J., J. A. Savidge, and K. M. Eskridge. 2000. Correlations between burrowing owl and black-tailed prairie dog declines: A 7-year analysis. *Journal of Wildlife Management* 64:1067–1075.

Detling, J. K. 1979. Processes controlling blue grama production on the shortgrass prairie. Pages 25–42 in N.R. French, editor. *Perspectives in grassland ecology*. Ecological Studies 32. Springer-Verlag, New York, New York.

Detling, J. K. 1998. Mammalian herbivores: Ecosystem-level effects in two grassland national parks. *Wildlife Society Bulletin* 26:438–448.

Detling, J. K., M. I. Dyer, and D. T. Winn. 1979. Net photosynthesis, root respiration, and regrowth of *Bouteloua gracilis* following simulated grazing. *Oecologia* 41: 127–134.

Diamond, M., and M. Mast. 1978. Crowding, reproduction, and maternal behavior in the golden hamster. *Behavioral Biology* 23:477–486.

Dinsmore, S. J. 2001. Population biology of mountain plovers in southern Phillips County, Montana. PhD dissertation, Colorado State University, Fort Collins, Colorado. 99 pages.

Dinsmore, S. J., G. C. White, and F. L. Knopf. 2001. Annual survival and population estimates of mountain plovers in southern Phillips County, Montana. *Ecological Applications* 13:1013–1026.

Dobson, A., and A. Lyles. 2000. Ecology—black-footed ferret recovery. *Science* 288:985.

Dobson, F. S., R. K. Chesser, J. L. Hoogland, D. W. Sugg, and D. W. Foltz. 1997. Do black-tailed prairie dogs minimize inbreeding? *Evolution* 51:970–978.

Dobson, F. S., R. K. Chesser, J. L. Hoogland, D. W. Sugg, and D. W. Foltz. 1998. Breeding groups and gene dynamics in a socially structured population of prairie dogs. *Journal of Mammalogy* 79:671–680.

Dobson, F. S., R. K. Chesser, J. L. Hoogland, D. W. Sugg, and D. W. Foltz. 2004. The influence of social breeding groups on effective population size. *Journal of Mammalogy* 85:58–66.

Dobson, F. S., and W. T. Jones. 1985. Multiple causes of dispersal. *American Naturalist* 126:855–858.

Dobson, F. S., and B. Zinner. 2003. Social groups, genetic structure, and conservation. Pages 211–228 in Festa-Bianchet, M., and M. Apollonia, editors. *Animal behavior and wildlife conservation*. Island Press, Washington, D. C.

Dobzhansky, T. 1951. *Genetics and the origin of species*. Columbia University Press, New York, New York.

Dolan, C. C. 1999. The national grasslands and disappearing biodiversity: Can the prairie dog save us from an ecological desert? *Environmental Law* 29:213–234.

Dold, C. 1998. Making room for prairie dogs. *Smithsonian* 28:60–66.

Dullum, J. L. D. 2001. Efficacy of translocations for restoring populations of black-tailed prairie dogs in north-central Montana. MS thesis, University of Montana, Missoula, Montana.

Dunlap, T. R. 1988. *Saving America's wildlife.* Princeton University Press, Princeton, New Jersey. 222 pages.

Durant, S. M. 2000. Dispersal patterns, social organization, and population viability. Pages 172–197 in L. M. Gosling and W. J. Sutherland, editors. *Behaviour and conservation.* Cambridge University Press, Cambridge, United Kingdom.

Ecke, D. H., and C. W. Johnson. 1952. Plague in Colorado and Texas. I. Colorado. *Public Health Service Monographs* 6:1–37.

EDAW. 2000. *Black-tailed prairie dog colonies—known locations.* EDAW, Inc. Prepared for Colorado Department of Natural Resources. Denver, Colorado.

Edgar, B., and J. Turnell. 1978. *Brand of a legend.* Stockdale Publishers, Cody, Wyoming. 244 pages.

Ehrlich, P. R., and B. Walker. 1998. Rivets and redundancy. *BioScience* 48:387.

Epstein, H. E., W. K. Lauenroth, I. C. Burke, and D. P. Coffin. 1997. Regional productivity patterns of C_3 and C_4 functional types in the Great Plains of the United States. *Ecology* 78:722–731.

Ernst, A. E. 2001. Changes in black-tailed prairie dog towns on the Texas panhandle determined by GIS. MS thesis, Texas Tech University, Lubbock, Texas.

Eskey, C. R., and V. H. Haas. 1940. *Plague in the western part of the United States.* Public Health Bulletin 254:1–83.

Estes, J. A., M. T. Tinker, T. M. Williams, and D. F. Doak. 1998. Killer whale predation on sea otters linking oceanic and nearshore ecosystems. *Science* 282:473–476.

Fagerstone, K. A. 1982. A review of prairie dog diet and its variability among animals and colonies. *Proceedings of the Great Plains wildlife damage control workshop* 5:178–184.

Fagerstone, K. A., and D. E. Biggins. 1986. Comparison of capture-recapture and visual count indices of prairie dog (*Cynomys* spp.) densities in black-footed ferret (*Mustela nigripes*) habitat. *Great Basin Naturalist Memoirs* 8:94–98.

Fagerstone, K. A., and C. A. Ramey. 1996. Rodents and lagomorphs. Pages 82–132 in P. R. Krausman, editor. *Rangeland wildlife.* Society of Range Management, Denver, Colorado.

Fagerstone, K. A., H. P. Tietjen, and G. K. LaVoie. 1977. Effects of range treatment with 2,4-D on prairie dog diet. *Journal of Range Management* 30:57–60.

Fagerstone, K. A., H .P. Tietjen, and O. Williams. 1981. Seasonal variation in the diet of black-tailed prairie dogs. *Journal of Mammalogy* 62:820–824.

Fagerstone, K. A., and O. Williams. 1982. Use of C_3 and C_4 plants by black-tailed prairie dogs. *Journal of Mammalogy* 63:328–331.

Fahnestock, J. T., and J. K. Detling. 2002. Bison–prairie dog–plant interactions in a North American mixed-grass prairie. *Oecologia* 132:86–95.

Fahnestock, J. T., D. L. Larsen, G. E. Plumb, and J. K. Detling. 2003. Effects of ungulates and prairie dogs on seed banks and vegetation in a North American mixed-grass prairie. *Plant Ecology* 167:255–268.

Falconer, D. S. 1981. *Introduction to quantitative genetics.* Longman, London, United Kingdom.

Farrar, J. P. 2002. Effects of prairie dog mound-building and grazing activities on vegetation in the central grasslands. MS thesis, Colorado State University, Fort Collins, Colorado. vii + 41 pages.

Farraro, P. J., and A. Kiss. 2002. Direct payments to conserve biodiversity. *Science* 298:1718–1719.

Ferrara, J. 1985. Prairie home companions. *National Wildlife* 23:48–53.

Fisher, H. 1982. War on the dog towns. *Defenders Magazine.* October 1982:13–15.

Fisher, R. A. 1958. *The genetical theory of natural selection.* 2nd edition. Dover, New York, New York.

Flath, D., and T. W. Clark. 1989. *The prairie dog ecosystem: Managing for biological diversity.* Montana BLM Technical Bulletin Number 2.

Foltz, D. W., and J. L. Hoogland. 1981. Analysis of the mating system of the black-tailed prairie dog (*Cynomys ludovicianus*) by likelihood of paternity. *Journal of Mammalogy* 62:706–712.

Foltz, D. W., and J. L. Hoogland. 1983. Genetic evidence of outbreeding in the black-tailed prairie dog (*Cynomys ludovicianus*). *Evolution* 37:273–281.

Foltz, D. W., J. L. Hoogland, and G. M. Koscielny. 1988. Effects of sex, litter size, and heterozygosity on juvenile weight in black-tailed prairie dogs (*Cynomys ludovicianus*). *Journal of Mammalogy* 69:611–614.

Foltz, D. W., and P. L. Schwagmeyer. 1989. Sperm competition in the thirteen-lined ground squirrel: Differential fertilization success under field conditions. *American Naturalist* 133:257–265.

Ford, P. L., E. L. Fredrickson, M. C. Anderson, and J. C. Truett. 2002. Fire as a management tool to facilitate expansion of reintroduced black-tailed prairie dog colonies in Chihuahuan Desert grasslands. Society for Conservation Biology 16th Annual Meeting, Canterbury, England, 14–19 July 2002.

Foreman, D. 1962. The normal reproductive cycle of the female prairie dog and the effects of light. *Anatomical Record* 142:391–405.

Forrest, S. C., D. E. Biggins, L. Richardson, T. W. Clark, T. M. Campbell, K. A. Fagerstone, and E. T. Thorne. 1988. Black-footed ferret (*Mustela nigripes*) attributes at Meeteetse, Wyoming, 1981–1985. *Journal of Mammalogy* 69:261–273.

Forrest, S. C., T. W. Clark, L. Richardson, and T. M. Campbell III. 1985. *Black-footed ferret habitat: Some management and reintroduction considerations.* Wyoming Bureau of Land Management Wildlife Technical Bulletin No. 2. Wyoming BLM, Cheyenne, Wyoming. 75 pages.

Forest Guardians, Biodiversity Conservation Alliance, Center for Biological Diversity, Center for Native Ecosystems, and Predator Conservation Alliance. 2004. 60-day notice of intent to sue under the Endangered Species Act. 12 August 2004.

Fortenberry, D. K. 1972. *Characteristics of the black-footed ferret.* USDI, USFWS, Bureau of Sport Fisheries and Wildlife Resource Publication, number 109, Rapid City, South Dakota.

Foster, K. R., P. Vecchia, and M. H. Repacholi. 2000. Science and the Precautionary Principle. *Science* 288:979–981.

Foster, N. S., and S. E. Hygnstrom. 1990. *Prairie dogs and their ecosystem.* Department of Forestry, Fisheries, and Wildlife, University of Nebraska, Lincoln, Nebraska. 8 pages.

Fox, L. R. 1975. Cannibalism in natural populations. *Annual Review of Ecology and Systematics* 6:87–106.

Fox-Parrish, L. 2002. Attitudes and opinions of landowners and general citizens relative to the black-tailed prairie dog. MS thesis, Department of Biological Sciences, Emporia State University, Emporia, Kansas.

Franklin, W. L., and M. G. Garrett. 1989. Nonlethal control of prairie dog colony expansion with visual barriers. *Wildlife Society Bulletin* 17:426–430.

Frazier, D. 1999. Japanese paying top dollar to own prairie dogs as pets. *Rocky Mountain News,* 17 March 1999.

Frederikson, J. K. 2005. A comparative analysis of alarm calls across the five species of North American prairie dogs. PhD dissertation, Northern Arizona University, Flagstaff, Arizona.

Freeman, S., and J. C. Herron. 2004. *Evolutionary analysis.* Pearson Prentice Hall, Upper Saddle River, New Jersey.

Gage, K. L. 1998. Plague. Pages 995–1011 in L. Collier, A. Ballows, and M. Sussman, editors. *Topley and Wilson's Microbiology and Microbial Infections,* 9th ed., Vol. 3. Oxford University Press, New York, New York.

Garrett, M. G., and W. L. Franklin. 1981. Prairie dog dispersal in Wind Cave National Park: Possibilities for control. *Great Plains Wildlife Damage Control Workshop Proceedings* 5:185–198.

Garrett, M. G., and W. L. Franklin. 1983. Diethylstilbestrol as a temporary chemosterilant to control black-tailed prairie dog populations. *Journal of Range Management* 36:753–756.

Garrett, M. G., and W. L. Franklin. 1988. Behavioral ecology of dispersal in the black-tailed prairie dog. *Journal of Mammalogy* 69:236–250.

Garrett, M. G., J. L. Hoogland, and W. L. Franklin. 1982. Demographic differences between an old and a new colony of black-tailed prairie dogs (*Cynomys ludovicianus*). *American Midland Naturalist* 108:51–59.

Gerberding, J. L., and M. B. McClellan. 2003. *Joint order of the Centers for Disease Control and Prevention and the Food and Drug Administration, Department of Health and Human Services, 11 June 2003.* United States Food and Drug Administration, Rockville, Maryland.

Gietzen, R. A., S. R. Jones, R. J. McKee. 1997. Hawks, eagles, and prairie dogs: Population trends of wintering raptors in Boulder County, 1983–1996. *Journal of Colorado Field Ornithology* 31:75–86.

Gigliotti, L. M. 2002. *Wildlife values and beliefs of South Dakota residents report, Executive summary of Report HD-10-02-AMS.* South Dakota Game, Fish, and Parks, Pierre, South Dakota.

Gillette, C.P. 1912. *The pest inspection act.* Colorado Office of State Entomologist Circular No. 2. Pages 1–6.

Gilpin, M. 1999. *An inquiry into the population viability of the black-tailed prairie dog.* http://www.homepage.montana.edu/~mgilpin/prairie_dog.html.

Goodrich, J. M., and S. W. Buskirk. 1998. Spacing and ecology of North American badgers (*Taxidea taxus*) in a prairie dog (*Cynomys leucurus*) complex. *Journal of Mammalogy* 79:171–179.

Gosling, L. M. 2003. Adaptive behaviour and population viability. Pages 13–32 in Festa-Bianchet, M., and M. Apollonia, editors. *Animal behavior and wildlife conservation.* Island Press, Washington, D. C.

Graber, K., T. France, and S. Miller. 1998. Petition for rule listing the black-tailed prairie dog (*Cynomys ludovicianus*) as threatened throughout its range. National Wildlife Federation, Boulder, Colorado.

Grady, R. M., and J. L. Hoogland. 1986. Why do male prairie dogs (*Cynomys ludovicianus*) give a mating call? *Animal Behaviour* 34:108–112.

Green, R.A. 1998. Nitrogen distribution in a perennial grassland: The role of American bison. PhD dissertation, Colorado State University, Fort Collins, Colorado. xii + 126 pages.

Greenwalt, L. 1988. Reflections on the power and potential of the Endangered Species Act. *Endangered Species Update* 5:7–9.

Greenwood, P. J. 1980. Mating systems, philopatry and dispersal in birds and mammals. *Animal Behaviour* 28:1140–1162.

Griebel, R. L. 2000. Ecological and physiological factors affecting nesting success of burrowing owls in Buffalo Gap National Grassland. MS thesis, University of Nebraska, Lincoln, Nebraska. 98 pages.

Grossmann, J. 1987. A prairie dog companion. *Audubon* 89:52–67.

Grossmann, J., and J. L. Hoogland. 1994. Home on the range. *BBC Wildlife* 12: 28–36.

Groves, C .R., 2003. *Drafting a conservation blueprint: A practitioner's guide to planning for biodiversity.* Island Press, Washington, D. C. 457 pages.

Groves, C. R., and T. W. Clark. 1986. Determining minimum population size for recovery in the black-footed ferret. *Great Basin Naturalist* 8:150–159.

Groves, C. R., D. B. Jensen, L. L. Valutis, K. H. Redford, M. L. Schaffer, J. M. Scott, J. V. Baumgartner, J. V. Higgins, M. W. Beck, and M. G. Anderson. 2002. Planning for biodiversity conservation: Putting conservation science into practice. *Bioscience* 52:499–512.

Guber, D. L. 2003. *The grassroots of a green revolution: Polling America on the environment.* Massachusetts Institute of Technology Press, Cambridge, Massachusetts.

Guenther, D. A., and J. K. Detling. 2003. Observations of cattle use of prairie dog towns. *Journal of Range Management* 56:410–417.

Gurll, N., and L. DenBesten. 1978. Animal models of human cholesterol gallstone disease: A review. *Laboratory and Animal Science* 28:428–432.

Hafner, D. J. 1984. Evolutionary relationships of the Nearctic Sciuridae. Pages 3–23 in J. O. Murie and G. R. Michener, editors. *The biology of ground-dwelling squirrels.* University of Nebraska Press, Lincoln, Nebraska.

Halbert, C. L. 1993. How adaptive is adaptive management? Implementing adaptive management in Washington State and British Columbia. *Reviews in Fisheries Science* 1:261–283.

Hall, E. R. 1981. *The mammals of North America.* John Wiley and Sons, New York, New York. 1,181 pages.

Halloran, A. F. 1972. The black-tailed prairie dog: Yesterday and today. *Great Plains Journal* 11:138–144.

Halpin, Z. T. 1983. Naturally occurring encounters between black-tailed prairie dogs (*Cynomys ludovicianus*) and snakes. *American Midland Naturalist* 109:50–54.

Halpin, Z. T. 1987. Natal dispersal and the formation of new social groups in a newly established town of black-tailed prairie dogs (*Cynomys ludovicianus*). Pages 104–118 in B. D. Chepko-Sade and Z. T. Halpin, editors. *Mammalian dispersal patterns: The effects of social structure on population genetics.* University of Chicago Press, Chicago, Illinois.

Hamilton, J. D., and E. W. Pfeiffer. 1977. Effects of cold exposure and dehydration on renal function in black-tailed prairie dogs. *Journal of Applied Physiological, Respiratory, and Environmental Exercise Physiology* 42:295–299.

Hamilton, W. D. 1966. The moulding of senescence by natural selection. *Journal of Theoretical Biology* 12:12–45.

Hamilton, W. D. 1971. Geometry for the selfish herd. *Journal of Theoretical Biology* 31:295–311.

Hanken, J., and P. W. Sherman. 1981. Multiple paternity in Belding's ground squirrel litters. *Science* 212:351–353.

Hanley, T. A., and K. A. Hanley. 1982. Food resource partitioning by sympatric ungulates on Great Basin rangeland. *Journal of Range Management* 35:152–158.

Hansen, R. 1993. Control of prairie dogs and related developments in South Dakota. Pages 5–7 in J. L. Oldemeyer, D. E. Biggins and B. J. Miller, editors. *Management of prairie dog complexes for the reintroduction of the black-footed ferret.* Biological Report 13, USFWS, Washington, D. C.

Hansen, R. M., and B. R. Cavender. 1973. Food intake and digestion by black-tailed prairie dogs under laboratory conditions. *Acta Theriologica* 18:191–200.

Hansen, R. M., R. C. Clark, and W. Lawhorn. 1977. Foods of wild horses, mule deer, and cattle in the Douglas Mountain area, Colorado. *Journal of Range Management* 30:116–118.

Hansen, R. M., and I. K. Gold. 1977. Black-tail prairie dogs, desert cottontails and cattle trophic relations on shortgrass range. *Journal of Range Management* 30:210–214.

Harlow, H. J., and G. E. Menkens. 1986. A comparison of hibernation in the black-tailed prairie dog, white-tailed prairie dog, and Wyoming ground squirrel. *Canadian Journal of Zoology* 64:793–796.

Harlow, H. J., and E. J. Braun. 1995. Kidney structure and function of obligate and facultative hibernators: The white-tailed prairie dog (*Cynomys leucurus*) and the black-tailed prairie dog (*Cynomys ludovicianus*). *Journal of Comparative Physiology [B]* 165:320–328.

Harrison, R. G., S. M. Bogdanowicz, R. S. Hoffmann, E. Yensen, and P. W. Sjerman. 2003. Phylogeny and evolutionary history of the ground squirrels (Rodentia: Marmotinae). *Journal of Mammalian Evolution* 10:249–276.

Haug, E. A., B. A. Millsap, and M. S. Matell. 1993. Burrowing owl (*Speotyto cunicularia*). Pages 1–20 in A. Poole and F. Gill, editors. *The birds of North America,* No. 61. The Academy of Natural Sciences, Washington, D. C.

Haynie, M. L., R. A. van den Bussche, J. L. Hoogland, and D. A. Gilbert. 2003. Parentage, multiple paternity, and breeding success in Gunnison's and Utah prairie dogs. *Journal of Mammalogy* 84:1244–1253.

Heady, H. F., and R. D. Child. 1994. *Rangeland ecology and management.* Westview Press, Boulder, Colorado. xvi + 519 pages.

Hedrick, P. W. 2004. Conservation biology: The impact of population biology and a current perspective. Pages 347–365 in R. Singh and M. Uyenoyama, editors. *The evolution of population biology.* Modern Synthesis. Cambridge University Press, Cambridge, United Kingdom.

Hedrick, P. W., and S. T. Kalinowski. 2000. Inbreeding depression in conservation biology. *Annual Review of Ecology and Systematics* 31:139–162.

Hill, E. F., and J. W. Carpenter. 1982. Responses of Siberian ferrets to secondary zinc phosphide poisoning. *Journal of Wildlife Management* 46:678–685.

Hillman, C. N. 1968. Field observations of black-footed ferrets in South Dakota. *Transactions of the North American Wildlife and Natural Resources Conference* 33:433–443.

Hinkle, N. C., M. K. Rust, and D. A. Reierson. 1997. Biorational approaches to flea (Siphonaptera: Pulicidae) suppression: Present and future. *Journal of Agricultural Entomology* 14:309–321.

Hinnebusch, B. J., A. E. Rudolph, P. Cherepanov, J. E. Dixon, T. G. Schwan, Å. Forsberg. 2002. Role of *Yersinia* murine toxin in the survival of *Yersinia pestis* in the midgut of the flea vector. *Science* 296:733–735.

Hoffmeister, D. F. 1986. *Mammals of Arizona.* University of Arizona Press and Arizona Game and Fish Department, Tuscon, Arizona. 602 pages.

Holbrook, H. T., and R. M. Timm. 1985. Comparisons of strychnine and zinc phosphide in prairie dog control. *Proceedings of the Eastern Wildlife Damage Control Conference* 2:73–79.

Holekamp, K. E. 1984. Dispersal in ground-dwelling sciurids. Pages 297–320 in J. O. Murie and G. R. Michener, editors. *The biology of ground-dwelling squirrels.* University of Nebraska Press, Lincoln, Nebraska.

Holling, C. S., editor. 1978. *Adaptive environmental assessment and management.* John Wiley and Sons, New York, New York.

Hollister, N. 1916. A systematic account of the prairie dogs. *North American Fauna* 40:1–37.

Holt, W. V., A. R. Pickard, J. C. Rodger, and D. E. Wildt. 2002. *Reproductive science and integrated conservation.* Cambridge University Press, Cambridge, United Kingdom.

Hood, G. A. 1972. Zinc phosphide—a new look at an old rodenticide for field rodents. *Proceedings of the Vertebrate Pest Conference* 5:85–92.

Hoogland, J. L. 1979a. Aggression, ectoparasitism, and other possible costs of prairie dog (Sciuridae: *Cynomys* spp.) coloniality. *Animal Behaviour* 69:1–35.

Hoogland, J. L. 1979b. The effect of colony size on individual alertness of prairie dogs (Sciuridae: *Cynomys* spp.). *Animal Behaviour* 27:394–407.

Hoogland, J. L. 1981a. The evolution of coloniality in white-tailed and black-tailed prairie dogs (Sciuridae: *Cynomys leucurus* and *C. ludovicianus*). *Ecology* 62:252–272.

Hoogland, J. L. 1981b. Nepotism and cooperative breeding in the black-tailed prairie dog (Sciuridae: *Cynomys ludovicianus*). Pages 283–310 in R. D. Alexander and

D. W. Tinkle, editors. *Natural selection and social behavior.* Chiron Press, New York, New York.

Hoogland, J. L. 1982a. Prairie dogs avoid extreme inbreeding. *Science* 215:1639–1641.

Hoogland, J. L. 1982b. Reply to a comment by Powell. *Ecology* 63:1968–1969.

Hoogland, J. L. 1983a. Black-tailed prairie dog coteries are cooperatively breeding units. *American Naturalist* 121:275–280.

Hoogland, J. L. 1983b. Nepotism and alarm calling in the black-tailed prairie dog (*Cynomys ludovicianus*). *Animal Behaviour* 31:472–479.

Hoogland, J. L. 1985. Infanticide in prairie dogs: Lactating females kill offspring of close kin. *Science* 230:1037–1040.

Hoogland, J. L. 1986. Nepotism in prairie dogs (*Cynomys ludovicianus*) varies with competition but not with kinship. *Animal Behaviour* 34:263–270.

Hoogland, J. L. 1992. Levels of inbreeding among prairie dogs. *American Naturalist* 139:591–602.

Hoogland, J. L. 1994. Amicable and hostile treatment of juvenile prairie dogs by older conspecifics. Pages 321–337 in S. Parmigiani and F. S. vom Saal, editors. *Infanticide and parental care.* Harwood Academic Publishers, New York, New York.

Hoogland, J. L. 1995. *The black-tailed prairie dog: Social life of a burrowing mammal.* University of Chicago Press, Chicago, Illinois.

Hoogland, J. L. 1996a. *Cynomys ludovicianus. Mammalian Species* 535:1–10.

Hoogland, J. L. 1996b. Why do Gunnison's prairie dogs give anti-predator calls? *Animal Behaviour* 51:871–880.

Hoogland, J. L. 1997. Duration of gestation and lactation for Gunnison's prairie dogs. *Journal of Mammalogy* 78:173–180.

Hoogland, J. L. 1998a. Estrus and copulation for Gunnison's prairie dogs. *Journal of Mammalogy* 79:887–897.

Hoogland, J. L. 1998b. Why do Gunnison's prairie dog females copulate with more than one male? *Animal Behaviour* 55:351–359.

Hoogland, J. L. 1999. Philopatry, dispersal, and social organization of Gunnison's prairie dogs. *Journal of Mammalogy* 80:243–251.

Hoogland, J. L. 2001. Black-tailed, Gunnison's, and Utah prairie dogs all reproduce slowly. *Journal of Mammalogy* 82:917–927.

Hoogland, J. L. 2003a. Prairie dogs. Pages 232–247 in G. A. Feldhamer, B. C. Thompson, and J. A. Chapman, editors. *Wild mammals of North America.* Johns Hopkins University Press, Baltimore, Maryland.

Hoogland, J. L. 2003b. Sexual dimorphism in five species of prairie dogs. *Journal of Mammalogy* 84:1254–1266.

Hoogland, J. L. 2004a. Infanticide. Pages 693–694 in M. Bekoff, editor. *Encyclopedia of Animal Behavior,*Volume 2. Greenwood Press, Westport, Connecticut.

Hoogland, J. L. 2004b. *The Prairie Dog.* World Book Encyclopedia, Volume P, pp. 72–73.

Hoogland, J. L. 2006a. Alarm calling, multiple mating, and infanticide among black-tailed, Gunnison's, and Utah prairie dogs. In J. O. Wolff and P. W. Sherman, editors. *Rodent Societies.* University of Chicago Press, Chicago, Illinois.

Hoogland, J. L. 2006b. Conservation of prairie dogs. In J. O. Wolff and P.W. Sherman, editors. *Rodent Societies.* University of Chicago Press, Chicago, Illinois.

Hoogland, J. L., D. K. Angell, J. G. Daley, and M. C. Radcliffe. 1988. Demography and population dynamics of prairie dogs. Pages 18–22 in D. W. Uresk, G. L. Schenbeck, and R. Cefkin, editors. *Proceedings of the Eighth Great Plains Wildlife Damage Control Workshop.* USFS, Technical Report RM-154. Fort Collins, Colorado.

Hoogland, J. L., S. Davis, S. Benson-Amram, D. LaBruna, B. Goossens, and M. A. Hoogland. 2004. Pyraperm halts plague among Utah prairie dogs. *Southwestern Naturalist* 49:376–383.

Hoogland, J. L., and D. W. Foltz. 1982. Variance in male and female reproductive success in a harem-polygynous mammal, the black-tailed prairie dog (Sciuridae: *Cynomys ludovicianus*). *Behavioral Ecology and Sociobiology* 11:155–163.

Hoogland, J. L., and J. M. Hutter. 1987. Aging live prairie dogs from molar attrition. *Journal of Wildlife Management* 51:393–394.

Hoogland, J. L., R. H. Tamarin, and C. K. Levy. 1989. Communal nursing in prairie dogs. *Behavioral Ecology and Sociobiology* 24:91–95.

Hrdy, S. B. 1979. Infanticide among animals: A review, classification, and examination of the implications for the reproductive strategies of females. *Ethology and Sociobiology* 1:13–40.

Hrdy, S. B. 198l. "Nepotists" and "altruists": The behavior of old females among macaques and langur monkeys. Pages 59–76 in P. T. Amoss and S. Harrell, editors. *Other ways of growing old.* Stanford University Press, Stanford, California.

Hubbard, J. P., and C. G. Schmitt. 1984. *The black-footed ferret in New Mexico.* Endangered Species Program, Department of Game and Fish, Santa Fe, New Mexico. 118 pages.

Hughes, A. J. 1993. Breeding density and habitat preference of the burrowing owl in northeastern Colorado. MS thesis, Colorado State University, Fort Collins, Colorado. 28 pages.

Hurlbert, S. H. 1997. Functional importance vs. keystoneness: Reformulating some questions in theoretical biocenology. *Australian Journal of Ecology* 22:369–382.

Hygnstrom, S. E. 1995. Plastic visual barriers were ineffective at reducing recolonization rates of prairie dogs. *Great Plains Wildlife Damage Control Workshop Proceedings* 12:74–76.

Hygnstrom, S. E., and K. C. VerCauteren. 2000. Effectiveness of five burrow fumigants for managing black-tailed prairie dogs. *International Biodeterioration and Biodegradation* 45:159–168.

Hygnstrom, S. E., P. M. McDonald, and D. R. Virchow. 1998. Efficacy of three formulations of zinc phosphide for managing black-tailed prairie dogs. *International Biodeterioration and Biodegradation* 42:147–152.

Hyngstrom, S. E., and D. R. Virchow. 1994. Prairie dogs. Pages B85–B96 in *Prevention and control of wildlife damage—1994.* Cooperative Extension Division, Institute of Agriculture and Natural Resources, University of Nebraska, Lincoln. http://wildlifedamage.unl.edu/handbook/handbook/allPDF/ro_b85.pdf.

Ingham, R. E., and J. K. Detling. 1984. Plant–herbivore interactions in a North American mixed-grass prairie. III. Soil nematode populations and root biomass on *Cynomys ludovicianus* colonies and adjacent uncolonized areas. *Oecologia* 63: 307–313.

International Hunter Education Association. 1998. 1998 Hunting casualty report. Available through California Department of Fish and Game. http://www.dfg.ca.gov/ihea/ihea98b.

Isaäcson, M., P. Taylor, and L. Arntzen. 1983. *Ecology of plague in Africa: Response of indigenous wild rodents to experimental plague infection.* Bulletin of the World Health Organization 61:339–344.

Jackson, R. T. 1917. *Narrative report for the month of September, October 1, 1917.* BBS, USDA, National Archives, Washington, D. C.

James, P. C., and R. H. M. Espie. 1997. Current status of the burrowing owl in North America: An agency survey. Pages 3–5 in J. L. Liner and K. Steenhof, editors. *The burrowing owl, its biology and management: Including the Proceedings of the First International Symposium.* Raptor Research Report No. 9.

Johnsgard, P. A. 1988. *North American owls. Biology and natural history.* Smithsonian Institution Press, Washington, D. C. 295 pages.

Johnsgard, P. A. 2005. *Prairie dog empire: A saga of the shortgrass prairie.* University of Nebraska, Lincoln, Nebraska.

Johnson, D. H. 1994. Population analysis. Pages 419–444 in T.A. Bookhout, editor. *Research and management techniques for wildlife and habitats.* The Wildlife Society, Bethesda, Maryland.

Johnson, G. D., and K. A. Fagerstone. 1994. *Primary and secondary hazards of zinc phosphide to nontarget wildlife—a review of the literature.* USDA, APHIS, Denver Wildlife Research Center Research Report No. 11-55-005, Denver, Colorado.

Johnson, G. E. 1927. Observations on young prairie dogs (*Cynomys ludovicianus*) born in the laboratory. *Journal of Mammalogy* 8:110–115.

Johnson, J. R., and J. T. Nichols. 1982. *Plants of South Dakota grasslands: A photographic study.* Bulletin 566, Agricultural Experiment Station, South Dakota State University, Brookings, South Dakota.

Johnson, K., L. Pierce, and T. Neville. 2004. *Field verification of black-tailed prairie dog remote sensing survey in New Mexico.* Final Report. Natural Heritage New Mexico, NMNHP Publication Number 04-GTR-61:1-24. University of New Mexico, Albuquerque, New Mexico.

Johnson, W. C., and S. K. Collinge. 2004. Landscape effects on black-tailed prairie dog colonies. *Biological Conservation* 115:487–497.

Johnston, P., D. Santillo, and R. Stringer. 1999. Marine environmental protection, sustainability and the Precautionary Principle. *Natural Resources Forum* 23:157–167.

Jones, C. G., J. H. Lawton, M. Shackak. 1994. Organisms as ecosystem engineers. *Oikos* 69:373–386.

Jones, R. T., A. P. Martin, A. J. Mitchell, S. K. Collinge, and C. Ray. 2005. Characterization of 14 polymorphic microsatellite markers for the black-tailed prairie dog (*Cynomys ludovicianus*). *Molecular Ecology Notes* 71–73.

Karhu, R. R., and S. H. Anderson. 2000. Effects of pyriproxyfen spray, powder, and oral bait treatments on the relative abundance of fleas (Siphonaptera: Ceratophyllidae) in black-tailed prairie dog (Rodentia: Sciuridae) towns. *Journal of Medical Entomology* 37:864–871.

Kays, J. S. 1997. *Recreational access and landowner liability in Maryland.* Extension Bulletin 357. Maryland Cooperative Extension, College Park, Maryland.

Kayser, M. 1998. Have varmint rifle, will travel. *American Hunter* (June): 44–47, 61–62.

Keane, B. 1990a. Dispersal and inbreeding avoidance in the white-footed mouse, *Peromyscus leucopus. Animal Behaviour* 40:143–152.

Keane, B. 1990b. The effect of relatedness on reproductive success and mate choice in the white-footed mouse, *Peromyscus leucopus. Animal Behaviour* 39:264–273.

Keffer, K. K., K. M. Gordon, and S. H. Anderson. 2001. *Effects of recreational shooting on behavior of black-tailed prairie dogs.* Interim Report, Wyoming Cooperative Fish and Wildlife Research Unit, University of Wyoming, Laramie, Wyoming. 14 pages.

Kellert, S. R. 1996. *The value of life.* Island Press, Washington D. C.

Kelso, L. H. 1939. *Food habits of prairie dogs.* USDA Circular 529.

Kelson, K. R. 1949. Speciation of rodents in the Colorado River drainage of eastern Utah. PhD dissertation, The University of Utah, Salt Lake City, Utah.

Kietzmann, G. E. 1987. Ectoparasites of black-tailed prairie dogs (*Cynomys ludovicianus*) from South Dakota. *Journal of Wildlife Diseases* 23:331–333.

Kildaw, S. D. 1995. The effect of group size manipulations on the foraging behavior of black-tailed prairie dogs. *Behavioral Ecology* 6:353–358.

King, J. A. 1955. Social behavior, social organization, and population dynamics in a black-tailed prairie dog town in the Black Hills of South Dakota. *Contributions from the Laboratory of Vertebrate Biology*, The University of Michigan, 67:1–123.

King, J. A. 1959. The social behavior of prairie dogs. *Scientific American* 201:128–140.

King, J. A. 1984. Historical ventilations on a prairie dog town. Pages 447–456 in J. O. Murie and G. R. Michener, editors. *The biology of ground-dwelling squirrels.* University of Nebraska Press, Lincoln, Nebraska.

Kleiman, D. G. 1989. Reintroduction of captive mammals for conservation: Guidelines for reintroducing endangered species into the wild. *Biological Science* 39:152–161.

Knopf, F. L. 1996. Mountain plover (*Charadrius montanus*). Pages 1–16 in A. Poole and F. Gill, editors. *The Birds of North America*, Number 211. The Academy of Natural Sciences, Philadelphia, Pennsylvania, and The American Ornithologists' Union, Washington, D. C.

Knopf, F. L., and J. R. Rupert. 1996. Productivity and movements of mountain plovers breeding in Colorado. *Wilson Bulletin* 108:28–35.

Knowles, C. J. 1982. Habitat affinity, populations, and control of black-tailed prairie dogs on the Charles M. Russell National Wildlife Refuge. PhD dissertation, University of Montana, Missoula, Montana. 171 pages.

Knowles, C. J. 1985. Observations on prairie dog dispersal in Montana. *Prairie Naturalist* 17:33–40.

Knowles, C. J. 1986a. Population recovery of black-tailed prairie dogs following control with zinc phosphide. *Journal of Range Management* 39:249–251.

Knowles, C. J. 1986b. Some relationships of black-tailed prairie dogs to livestock grazing. *Great Basin Naturalist* 46:198–203.

Knowles, C. J. 1987. Reproductive ecology of black-tailed prairie dogs in Montana. *Great Basin Naturalist* 47:202–206.

Knowles, C. J. 1988. An evaluation of shooting and habitat alteration for control of black-tailed prairie dogs. Pages 53–56 in D. W. Uresk, G. L. Schenbeck, and

R. Cefkin, technical coordinators. *Eighth Great Plains wildlife damage control workshop proceedings.* USDA-Forest Service, General Technical Report RM-154.

Knowles, C. J. 2003. *Status of the black-tailed prairie dog in North Dakota.* Report to North Dakota Game and Fish, Bismarck, North Dakota.

Knowles, C. J., and P. R. Knowles. 1984. Additional records of mountain plovers using prairie dog towns in Montana. *Prairie Naturalist* 16:183–186.

Knowles, C. J., and P. R. Knowles. 1994. *A review of black-tailed prairie dog literature in relation to rangelands administered by the Custer National Forest.* USFS report.

Knowles, C.J., and P. R. Knowles. 1999. *The historic and current status of the mountain plover in Montana.* BLM report, Billings, Montana. 57 pages.

Knowles, C. J., C. J. Stoner, and S. P Gieb. 1982. Selective use of black-tailed prairie dog colonies by mountain plovers. *Condor* 84:71–74.

Knowles, C. J., J. Proctor, and S. C. Forrest. 2002. Black-tailed prairie dog abundance and distribution on the Northern Great Plains based on historic and contemporary information. *Great Plains Research* 12:219–254.

Koenig, W. D., D. van Vuren, and P. N. Hooge. 1996. Detectability, philopatry, and the distribution of dispersal distances in vertebrates. *Trends in Ecology and Evolution* 11:514–517.

Koford, C. B. 1958. Prairie dogs, whitefaces, and blue grama. *Wildlife Monographs* 3: 1–78.

Kolbe, J. J., B. E. Smith, and D. M. Browning. 2002. Burrow use by tiger salamanders (*Ambystoma tigrinum*) at a black-tailed prairie dog (*Cynomys ludovicianus*) town in southwestern South Dakota. *Herpetology Review* 33:95–99.

Kotliar, N. B. 2000. Application of the new keystone-concept to prairie dogs: How well does it work? *Conservation Biology* 14:1715–1721.

Kotliar, N. B., B. W. Baker, A. D. Whicker, and G. Plumb. 1999. A critical review of assumptions about the prairie dog as a keystone species. *Environmental Management* 24:177–192.

Kretzer, J. E., and J. F. Cully. 2001a. Effects of black-tailed prairie dogs on reptiles and amphibians in Kansas shortgrass prairie. *The Southwestern Naturalist* 46: 171–177.

Kretzer, J. E., and J. F. Cully. 2001b. Prairie dog effects on harvester ant species diversity and density. *Journal of Range Management* 54:11–14.

Krueger, K. 1986. Feeding relationships among bison, pronghorn, and prairie dogs: An experimental analysis. *Ecology* 67:760–770.

Krysl, L. J., M. E. Hubbert, B. F. Sowell, G. E. Plumb, T. K. Jewett, M. A. Smith, and J. W. Waggoner. 1984. Horses and cattle grazing in the Wyoming Red Desert, I. Food habits and dietary overlap. *Journal of Range Management* 37:72–76.

Kucheruk, V. V. 1965. Paleogenesis of plague natural foci in connection with history of rodent fauna. *Fauna i ekologiya grizunov* 7:5–86.

Lacy, R. C., and T. W. Clark. 1989. Genetic variability in black-footed ferret populations: Past, present, and future. Pages 83–103 in U. S. Seal, E. T. Thorne, M. Bogan, and S. Anderson, editors. *Conservation Biology of the Black-footed Ferret.* Yale University Press, New Haven, Connecticut.

Lacey, J. R., and H. W. Van Poolen. 1981. Comparison of herbage production on moderately grazed and ungrazed western ranges. *Journal of Range Management* 34:210–212.

Lamb, B. L., K. Cline, A. Brinson, N. Sexton, and P. D. Ponds. 2001. *Citizen knowledge of and attitudes toward black-tailed prairie dogs.* Completion report. USGS Open-File Report 01-471. Midcontinent Ecological Science Center, Fort Collins, Colorado.

Lamb, B. L., and K. Cline. 2003. Public knowledge and perceptions of black-tailed prairie dogs. *Human Dimensions of Wildlife* 8:127–143.

Lambeck, R. J. 1997. Focal species: A multi-species umbrella for nature conservation. *Conservation Biology* 11:849–856.

Lande, R., B. Saether, and S. Engen. 1997. Threshold harvesting for sustainability of fluctuating resources. *Ecology* 78:1341–1350.

Lang, J. T., and W. F. Chamberlain. 1986. Methoprene dust for flea (Siphonaptera: Ceratophyllidae) suppression on ground squirrels (Rodentia: Sciuridae). *Journal of Medical Entomology* 23:141–145.

Lantz, C. L. 1903. *Destroying prairie dogs and pocket gophers.* Kansas State Experiment Station Bulletin 116:147–163.

La Regina, M., J. Lonigro, and M. Wallace. 1986. *Francisella tularensis* infection in captive, wild caught prairie dogs. *Laboratory Animal Science* 36:178–180.

Lauenroth, W. K. 1979. Grassland primary production: North American grasslands in perspective. Pages 3–24 in N. R. French, editor. *Perspectives in grassland ecology.* Springer-Verlag, New York, New York.

Lauenroth, W. K., I. C. Burke, and M. P. Gutmann. 1999. The structure and function of ecosystems in the central North American grassland region. *Great Plains Research* 9:223–259.

Lauenroth, W. K., and D. G. Milchunas. 1992. Short-grass steppe. Pages 183–226 in R. T. Coupland, editor. *Ecosystems of the World 8A. Natural grasslands. Introduction and Western Hemisphere.* Elsevier, New York, New York.

Lechleitner, R. R., L. Kartman, M. I. Goldenberg, and B. W. Hudson. 1968. An epizootic of plague in Gunnison's prairie dogs (*Cynomys gunnisoni*) in south-central Colorado. *Ecology* 49:734–743.

Lee, C. D., and F. R. Henderson. 1989. Kansas attitudes on prairie dog control. *Great Plains Wildlife Damage Control Workshop* 9:162–165.

Lehmer, E. M., B. van Horne, B. Kulbartz, and G. L. Florant. 2001. Facultative torpor in free-ranging black-tailed prairie dogs (*Cynomys ludovicianus*). *Journal of Mammalogy* 82:551–557.

Leopold, A. S. 1964. Predator and rodent control in the United States. *Transactions of the North American Wildlife and Natural Resources Conference* 29:27–49.

Leopold, A. S. 1989. *A Sand County Almanac.* Oxford University Press, New York, New York.

Levy, C. E., and K. L. Gage. 1999. Plague in the United States, 1995–1997. *Infections in Medicine* 16:54–64.

Lewis, J. C., E. H. McIlvain, R. McVickers, and B. Peterson. 1979. Techniques used to establish and limit prairie dog towns. *Proceedings of the Oklahoma Academy of Science* 59:27–30.

Licht, D. 1997. *Ecology and economics of the Great Plains.* University of Nebraska Press, Lincoln, Nebraska. 225 pages.

Licht, D. S., and K. D. Sanchez. 1993. Association of black-tailed prairie dog colonies with cattle point attractants in the Northern Great Plains. *Great Basin Naturalist* 53:385–389.

Linder, R. L., R. B. Dahlgren, and C. N. Hillman. 1972. Black-footed ferret–prairie dog interrelationships. Pages 22–37 in *Symposium on rare and endangered wildlife of the Southwestern United States,* 22–23 September 1972, Albuquerque, New Mexico. New Mexico Department of Game and Fish, Santa Fe, New Mexico.

Link, V. 1955. A history of plague in the United States. *Public Health Monographs* 70: 1–120.

List, R., and D. W. MacDonald. 2003. Home range and habitat use of the kit fox (*Vulpes macrotis*) in a prairie dog (*Cynomys ludovicianus*) complex. *Journal of Zoology* (London) 259:1–5.

Livieri, T. M. 1999. Harvest strategies for sustaining fluctuating black-tailed prairie dog (*Cynomys ludovicianus*) populations. Unpublished manuscript, College of Natural Resources, University of Wisconsin–Stevens Point, Stevens Point, Wisconsin. 6 pages.

Lomolino, M. V., and G. A. Smith. 2001. Dynamic biogeography of prairie dog (*Cynomys ludovicianus*) towns near the edge of their range. *Journal of Mammalogy* 82:937–945.

Lomolino, M. V., and G. A. Smith. 2003. Prairie dog towns as islands: Applications of island biogeography and landscape ecology for conserving nonvolant terrestrial vertebrates. *Global Ecology and Biogeography* 12:275–286.

Lomolino, M. V., and G. A. Smith. 2004. Terrestrial vertebrate communities at black-tailed prairie dog (*Cynomys ludovicianus*) towns. *Biological Conservation* 115:89–100.

Lomolino, M. V., G. A. Smith, and V. Vidal. 2003. Long-term persistence of prairie dog towns: Insights for designing networks for prairie reserves. *Biological Conservation* 115:111–120.

Long, M. E. 1998. The vanishing prairie dog. *National Geographic* 193:116–130.

Loughry, W. J. 1987a. Differences in experimental and natural encounters of black-tailed prairie dogs with snakes. *Animal Behaviour* 35:1568–1570.

Loughry, W. J. 1987b. The dynamics of snake harassment by black-tailed prairie dogs. *Animal Behaviour* 103:27–48.

Loughry, W. J. 1988. Population differences in how black-tailed prairie dogs deal with snakes. *Behavioral Ecology and Sociobiology* 22: 61–67.

Loughry, W. J. 1992. Ontogeny of time allocation in black-tailed prairie dogs. *Ethology* 90:206–224.

Loughry, W. J., and A. Lazari. 1994. The ontogeny of individuality in black-tailed prairie dogs, *Cynomys ludovicianus. Canadian Journal of Zoology* 72:1280–1286.

Lower Brule Sioux Tribe. 2002. *Black-tailed Prairie Dog Management Plan.* Lower Brule Sioux Department of Wildlife, Fish, and Recreation, Lower Brule, South Dakota.

Luce, R. J. 2002. *Report of the Interstate Black-tailed Prairie Dog Conservation Team,* 1 September 2002. Interstate Coordinator's Report, Sierra Vista, Arizona.

Luce, R. J. 2003. *A multi-state conservation plan for the black-tailed prairie dog, Cynomys ludovicianus, in the United States.* An addendum to the Black-tailed Prairie Dog Conservation Assessment and Strategy. 79 pages.

Luse, D. R., and S. Wilds. 1992. A GIS approach to modifying stocking rates on rangelands affected by prairie dogs. *Geocarto International* 1:45–51.

Mac, M. J., P. A. Opler, C. E. Puckett Haecker, and P. D. Doran. 1998. *Status and trends of the nation's biological resources.* Volume 2. USDI, USGS, Reston, Virginia. 570 pages.

Mace, G. M., A.Balmford, and H. R. Ginsbergm, editors. 1999. *Conservation in a changing world.* Cambridge University Press, Cambridge, United Kingdom.

Manci, K. M. 1992. Winter raptor use of urban prairie dog colonies. *Colorado Field Ornithology Journal* 26:132.

Manning, R. 1995. *Grassland.* Penguin Books, New York, New York.

Manzano-Fischer, P., R. List, and G. Ceballos. 1999. Grassland birds in prairie-dog towns in northwestern Chihuahua, Mexico. *Studies in Avian Biology* 19:263–271.

Marks, J. S., and I. J. Ball. 1983. Burrowing owl (*Athene cunicularia*). Pages 227–242 in J. S. Armbruster, editor. *Impacts of coal surface mining on 25 migratory bird species of high federal interest.* USFWS, Washington, D. C.

Marinari, P., and E. S. Williams. 1998. *Use of prairie dogs in black-footed ferret recovery programs.* USFWS, National Black-footed Ferret Conservation Center, Laramie, Wyoming.

Marsh, R. E. 1984. Ground squirrels, prairie dogs, and marmots as pests on rangeland. Pages 195–208 in *Proceedings of the conference for organization and practice of vertebrate pest control,* 30 August–3 September 1982 (Hampshire, United Kingdom). ICI Plant Protection Division, Fernherst, United Kingdom.

Matschke, G. H., and P. L. Hegdal. 1985. Efficacy of two lower concentrations of 1080 bait, 0.022% and 0.35%, compared to the standard 1080 bait, 0.0112%, for controlling black-tailed prairie dog populations. Unpublished USFWS report. Denver, Colorado. http://www.fs.fed.us/r2/nebraska/gpng/reports/controlling_pdog_pop .pdf.

Matschke, G. H., K. J. Andrews, and R. M. Engeman. 1992. Zinc phosphide: Black-tailed prairie dog—domestic ferret secondary poisoning study. *Vertebrate Pest Conference Proceedings* 15:330–334.

Matthiessen, P. 1987. *Wildlife in America.* Viking Penguin, New York, New York. 332 pages.

McCain, L. A., R. P. Reading, and B. J. Miller. 2002. Prairie dog gone: Myth, persecution, and preservation of a keystone species. Pages 230–235 in M. Matteson and G. Wuerthner, editors. *Welfare ranching: The subsidized destruction of the American west.* Island Press, Washington, D. C.

McCoy, G. W. 1908. *Plague in ground squirrels.* United States Public Health Service, Public Health Report 23:1289–1293.

McCullough, D. A., R. A. Chesser, and R. D. Owen. 1987. Immunological systematics of prairie dogs. *Journal of Mammalogy* 68:561–568.

McEvedy, C. 1988. The bubonic plague. *Scientific American* 258:118–123.

McNaughton, S. J., and J. L. Tarrants. 1983. Grass leaf silicification: Natural selection for an inducible defense against herbivores. *Proceedings of the National Academy of Sciences* (USA) 80:790–791.

McNaughton, S. J., J. L. Tarrants, M. M. McNaughton, and R. H. Davis. 1985. Silica as a defense against herbivory and a growth promotor in African grasses. *Ecology* 66:528–535.

McNulty, F. 1971. *Must they die?* Doubleday, New York, New York.

Mellado, M., A. Olvera, A. Quyero, and G. Mendoza. 2005. Dietary overlap between prairie dog (*Cynomys mexicanus*) and beef cattle in a desert rangeland of northern Mexico. *Journal of Arid Environments* 62:449–458.

Menkens, G. E. Jr., D. E. Biggins, and S. H. Anderson. 1990. Visual counts as an index of white-tailed prairie dog density. *Wildlife Society Bulletin* 18:290–296.

Menkens, G. E., and S. H. Anderson. 1993. Mark-recapture and visual counts for estimating population size of white-tailed prairie dogs. Pages 67–72 in J. Oldemeyer, D. E. Biggins, B. J. Miller, and R. Crete, editors. *Management of prairie dog complexes for reintroduction of the black-footed ferret.* USFWS, Biological Report 13, Washington, D. C.

Merriam, C. H. 1896. Report of the division of ornithology and mammalogy. Pages 23–25 of *USDA Annual Report for the fiscal year ended 30 June 1896.* Washington, D. C.

Merriam, C. H. 1902a. The prairie dog of the Great Plains. Pages 257–270 in *USDA Yearbook.*

Merriam, C. H. 1902b. Report of chief of BBS. Pages 14–25 in *USDA annual report for the fiscal year ending 30 June 1902.* Washington, D. C.

Messiter, C. A. 1890. *Sport and adventure among the North American Indians.* R. H. Porter, London, United Kingdom. 368 pages.

Metzger, M .E., and M. K. Rust. 2002. Laboratory evaluation of fipronil and imidacloprid topical insecticides for control of the plague vector *Oropsylla montana* (Siphonaptera: Ceratophyllidae) on California ground squirrels. *Journal of Medical Entomology* 39:152–161.

Michener, G. R. 1983. Kin identification, matriarchies, and the evolution of sociality in ground-dwelling sciurids. Pages 528–572 in J. F. Eisenberg and D. G. Kleiman, editors. *Recent Advances in the Study of Mammalian Behavior.* American Society of Mammalogists Special Publication no. 7.

Miles, V. I., M. J. Wilcomb, and J. V. Irons. 1952. Plague in Colorado and Texas. II. Rodent plague in Texas south plains. *Public Health Monographs* 6:39–53.

Miller, B., G. Ceballos, and R. Reading. 1994. Prairie dogs, poison, and biotic diversity. *Conservation Biology* 8:677–681.

Miller, B., R. P. Reading, and S. Forrest. 1996. *Prairie night: Black-footed ferrets and the recovery of endangered species.* Smithsonian Institution Press, Washington, D. C.

Miller, B., R. Reading, J. Hoogland, T. Clark, G. Ceballos, R. List, S. Forrest, L. Hanebury, P. Manzano, J. Pacheco, and D. Uresk. 2000. The role of prairie dogs as keystone species: A response to Stapp. *Conservation Biology* 14:318–321.

Miller, B., R. Reading, J. Strittholt, C. Carroll, R. Noss, M. Soulé, O. Sánchez, J. Terborgh, D. Brightsmith, T. Cheeseman, and D. Foreman. 1999. Focal species in design of reserve networks. *Wild Earth* 11:81–92.

Miller, B., C. Wemmer, D. E. Biggins, and R. Reading. 1990. A proposal to conserve black-footed ferrets and the prairie dog ecosystem. *Environmental Management* 14:763–769.

Miller, L. A., B. E. Johns, and D. J. Elias. 1998. Immunocontraception as a wildlife management tool: Some perspectives. *Wildlife Society Bulletin* 26:237–243.

Miller, S. D., and J. F. Cully, Jr. 2001. Conservation of black-tailed prairie dogs (*Cynomys ludovicianus*). *Journal of Mammalogy* 82:889–893.

Mills, L. S., M. E. Soulé, and D. F. Doak. 1993. The history and current status of the keystone species concept. *BioScience* 43:219–224.

Milne, S. A. 2004. Population ecology and expansion dynamics of black-tailed prairie dogs in western North Dakota. MS thesis, University of North Dakota, Grand Forks, North Dakota.

Moline, P. R., and S. Demarais. 1987. Efficacy of aluminum phosphide for black-tailed prairie dog and yellow-faced pocket gopher control. *Great Plains Wildlife Damage Control Workshop Proceedings* 8:64–66.

Moller, A. P. 2000. Sexual selection and conservation. Pages 161–171 in L. M. Gosling and W. J. Sutherland, editors. *Behaviour and conservation.* Cambridge University Press, Cambridge, United Kingdom.

Mulhern, D. W., and C. J. Knowles. 1997. Black-tailed prairie dog status and future conservation planning. Pages 19–29 in D. W. Uresk, G. L. Schenbeck, and J. T. O'Rourke, editors. *Conserving biodiversity on native rangelands: Symposium proceedings.* USFS, General Technical Report RM-GTR-298, 17 August 1995, Fort Robinson State Park, Nebraska. 38 pages.

Munn, L. C. 1993. Effects of prairie dogs on physical and chemical properties of soils. Pages 11–17 in J. Oldemeyer, D. E. Biggins, B. J. Miller, and R. Crete, editors. *Management of prairie dog complexes for the reintroduction of the black-footed ferret.* USFWS Biological Report 13, Washington D. C.

Myers, K., and W. E. Poole. 1961. A study of the biology of the wild rabbit, *Oryctolagus cuniculus* (L.), in confined populations. II. The effects of season and population increase on behaviour. *Commonwealth Scientific and Industrial Research Organization Wildlife Research* 6:1–41.

Naiman, R. J., J. M Milillo, and J. M. Hobbie. 1986. Ecosystem alternation of boreal forest streams by beaver (*Castor canadensis*). *Ecology* 67:1254–1369.

National Fish and Wildlife Foundation. 2002. Pre-proposal: Western rangeland species conservation initiative. Unpublished document, National Fish and Wildlife Foundation, Washington, D. C.

Nebraska Game and Parks Commission. 2001. Nebraska conservation plan for the black-tailed prairie dog. Draft, July 2001. Nebraska Game and Parks Commission, Lincoln, Nebraska.

Nelson, E. W. 1919. Annual report of chief of BBS. Pages 275–298 in *USDA Annual Report for Fiscal Year Ended 30 June 1919.* Washington, D. C.

Nelson, E. W. 1920. Annual report of chief of BBS. Pages 343–349 in *USDA Annual Report for the fiscal year ended 30 June 1920.* Washington, D. C.

Nichols, F. E., and J. A. Daley. 1995. Prairie dog counts on the Cathy Fromme prairie. Unpublished report submitted to the Fort Collins Natural Resource Department, Fort Collins, Colorado.

Nixon, R. 1972. Environmental safeguards on activities for animal damage control on federal lands. *Federal Register* 37:2875–2876.

Norton, G., and S. Williams. 2003. Responses to interrogatories in Defenders of Wildlife et al. v. Gale Norton and Steven Williams (CIV 02-00163-M DWM).

Noss, R. F., and A. Y. Cooperrider. 1994. *Saving nature's legacy: Protecting and restoring biodiversity.* Island Press, Washington D. C.

Nowak, R., and J. Paradiso. 1983. *Walker's Mammals of the World.* Johns Hopkins University Press, Baltimore, Maryland.

Nyhus, P. J., S. A. Osofsky, P. Ferraro, F. Madden, and H. Fischer. 2005. Bearing the costs of human–wildlife conflict: The challenges of compensation schemes. In R. Woodroffe, S. J. Thirgood, and A. Rabinowitz, editors. *People and wildlife: Conflict or co-existence.* Cambridge University Press, Cambridge, United Kingdom.

Oakes, C. L. 2000. History and consequence of keystone mammal eradication in the desert grasslands: The case of the Arizona black-tailed prairie dog (*Cynomys ludovicianus arizonensis*). PhD dissertation, University of Texas, Austin. 392 pages.

Oldemeyer, J. L., D. E. Biggins, B. J. Miller, and R. Crete, editors. 1993. *Proceedings of the symposium on the management of prairie dog complexes for the reintroduction of black-footed ferrets.* USFWS, Biological Report no. 13. Washington, D. C.

Olendorff, R. R. 1976. The food habits of North American golden eagles. *American Midland Naturalist* 95:231–236.

Olsen, P. F. 1981. Sylvatic plague. Pages 232–243 in J. W. Davis, L. H. Karstadt, and D. O. Trainer, editors. *Infectious diseases of wild animals.* Iowa State University Press, Ames, Iowa.

Olson, S. L. 1985. Mountain plover food items on and adjacent to a prairie dog town. *Prairie Naturalist* 17:83–90.

O'Meilia, M. E., F. L. Knopf, and J. C. Lewis. 1982. Some consequences of competition between prairie dogs and beef cattle. *Journal of Range Management* 35:580–585.

Orent, W. 2004. *Plague: The mysterious past and terrifying future of the world's most dangerous disease.* Free Press, New York, New York.

Osborn, B. 1942. Prairie dogs in shinnery (oak scrub) savannah. *Ecology* 23:110–115.

Otis, D .L., K. P. Burnham, G. C. White, and D. R. Anderson. 1978. Statistical inference from capture data on closed animal populations. *Wildlife Monograph* 62:1–135.

Outwater, A. 1996. *Water: A natural history.* Basic Books, New York, New York.

Owings, D. H., and W. J. Loughry. 1985. Variation in snake-elicited jump-yipping by black-tailed prairie dogs: Ontogeny and snake specificity. *Zeitschrift fur Tierpsychologie* 70:177–200.

Owings, D. H., and S. C. Owings. 1979. Snake-directed behavior by black-tailed prairie dogs (*Cynomys ludovicianus*). *Zeitschrift fur Tierpsychologie* 49:35–54.

Packard, J. M., K. J. Babbitt, P. G. Hannon, and W. E. Grant. 1990. Infanticide in captive collared peccaries (*Tayassu tajuca*). *Zoo Biology* 9:49–53.

Paine, R. 1969. A note on trophic complexity and community stability. *American Naturalist* 103:91–93.

Palmer, T. S. 1899. Report of acting chief of division of biological survey. Pages 59–67 in *USDA Annual Report for the fiscal year ended 30 June 1899.* Washington, D. C.

Palmer, T. S. 1901. Report of the acting chief of the division of biological survey. Page 151 in *USDA Annual Report for the fiscal year ended 30 June 1901.* Washington, D. C.

Peacock, M. M., and A. T. Smith. 1997. The effect of habitat fragmentation on dispersal patterns, mating behavior, and genetic variation in a pika (*Ochotona princeps*) metapopulation. *Oecologia* 112:523–533.

Pfaffenberger, G. S., B. Nygren, D. de Bruin, and C. Wilson. 1984. Parasites of the black-tailed prairie dog (*Cynomys ludovicianus*) from eastern New Mexico. *Proceedings of the Helminthological Society of Washington* 51:241–244.

Pfeifer, S. 1982. Disappearance and dispersal of *Spermophilus elegans* juveniles in relation to behavior. *Behavioral Ecology and Sociobiology* 10:237–243.

Pfeiffer, D. G., and R. L. Linder. 1973. Effects of diethylstilbestrol on reproduction in the prairie dog. *Proceedings of the South Dakota Academy of Science* 52:112–117.

Pfeiffer, E. W., L. N. Reinking, and J. D. Hamilton. 1979. Some effects of food and water deprivation on metabolism in black-tailed prairie dogs. *Cynomys ludovicianus. Comparative Biochemical Physiology* 63:19–22.

Pizzimenti, J. J. 1975. Evolution of the prairie dog genus *Cynomys. Occasional Papers of the Museum of Natural History.* The University of Kansas 39:1–73.

Placer, J., and C. N. Slobodchikoff. 2004. A method for identifying sounds in the classification of alarm calls. *Behavioural Processes* 67:87–98.

Plumb, R., K. Gordon, and S. H. Anderson. 2001. Secondary effects of prairie dog shooting on TBNG raptor populations: Summary of preliminary results from summer 2001. Unpublished report. Wyoming Cooperative Fish and Wildlife Research Unit, University of Wyoming, Laramie, Wyoming. 4 pages.

Plumb, G. E., G. D. Wilson, K. Kalin, K. Shinn, and W. M. Rizzo. 2001. *Black-tailed prairie dog monitoring protocol for seven prairie parks.* USGS, Northern Prairie Wildlife Research Center, Jamestown, North Dakota. 40 pages.

Plumpton, D. L., and D. E. Anderson. 1997. Habitat use and time budgeting by wintering ferruginous hawks. *Condor* 99:888–893.

Plumpton, D. L., and R. S. Lutz. 1993. Nesting habitat use by burrowing owls in Colorado. *Journal of Raptor Research* 27:175–179.

Poland, J. D., and A. M. Barnes. 1979. Plague. Pages 515–597 in H. Stoenner, W. Kaplan, and M. Torten, editors. *CRC Handbook Series in Zoonoses, Section A: Bacterial, rickettsial, and mycotic diseases.* CRC Press, Boca Raton, Florida.

Pollitzer, R., and K. F. Meyer. 1961. The ecology of plague. Pages 433–501 in J. M. May, editor. *Studies of disease ecology.* Hafner, New York, New York.

Polis, G. A., C. A. Myers, and W. R. Hess. 1984. A survey of intraspecific predation within the class Mammalia. *Mammal Review* 14:187–198.

Powell, K. L., and R. J. Robel. 1994. Size and location of black-tailed prairie dog towns in Meade and Gray Counties, Kansas. *Transactions of the Kansas Academy of Science* 97:44–49.

Powell, K. L., R. J. Robel, K. E. Kemp, and M. D. Nellis. 1994. Aboveground counts of black-tailed prairie dogs: Temporal nature and relationship to burrow-entrance density. *Journal of Wildlife Management* 58:361–366.

Power, M. E., D. Tilman, J. A. Estes, B. A. Menge, W. J. Bond, L. S. Mills, G. Daily, J. C. Castilla, J. Lubchenco, and R. T. Paine. 1996. Challenges in the quest for keystones. *BioScience* 466:9–20.

Primack, R. 2002. *Essentials of conservation biology,* 3rd edition. Sinauer Press, Sunderland, Massachusetts.

Proctor, J. D. 1998. A GIS model for identifying potential black-tailed prairie dog habitat in the Northern Great Plains shortgrass prairie. MS thesis, University of Montana, Missoula, Montana.

Pullin, A. S. 2002. *Conservation biology.* Cambridge University Press, Cambridge, United Kingdom. 345 pages.

Pyare, S., and J. Berger. 2003. Beyond demography and delisting: Recovery for Yellowstone's wolves and grizzly bears. *Biological Conservation* 113:63–73.

The Public Information Corporation. 1998. *A study of attitudes of Boulder County, Colorado residents regarding public policy issues.* The Public Information Corporation, Littleton, Colorado.

Quan, T. J., A. M. Barnes, and K. R. Tsuchiya. 1985. Experimental plague in rock squirrels, *Spermophilus variegatus* (Erxleben). *Journal of Wildlife Diseases* 21:205–210.

Quillen, E. 1999. Varmint hunters could save the prairie dog. *Rocky Mountain News,* 30 March 1999. Distributed by Writers on the Range.

Radcliffe, M. C. 1992. Repopulation of black-tailed prairie dog (*Cynomys ludovicianus*) colonies after artificial reduction. MS thesis, Frostburg State University, Frostburg, Maryland.

Rall, Yu. M. 1965. *Natural focality and epizootiology of plague.* Meditsina. Moscow, Russia.

Ramey, C. A., and E. W. Schafer, Jr. 1996. The evolution of the APHIS two-gas cartridge. *Vertebrate Pest Conference Proceedings* 17:219–224.

Randall, D. 1976a. Poison the damn prairie dogs! *Defenders* 51:381–383.

Randall, D. 1976b. Shoot the damn prairie dogs! *Defenders* 51:378–381.

Rayor, L. S. 1985. Dynamics of a plague outbreak in Gunnison's prairie dog. *Journal of Mammalogy* 66:194–196.

Reading, R. P. 1993. Toward an endangered species reintroduction paradigm: A case study of the black-footed ferret. PhD dissertation, Yale University, New Haven, Connecticut.

Reading, Rich. 2004. How many prairie dogs are there? *Grasslands Gazette* 6:5–6.

Reading, R. P., S. R. Beissinger, J. J. Grensten, and T. W. Clark. 1989. Attributes of black-tailed prairie dog colonies in northcentral Montana, with management recommendation for conservation of biodiversity. Pages 13–27 in T.W. Clark, D. Hinckley and T. Rich, editors. *The prairie dog ecosystem: Managing for biological diversity.* Wildlife Technical Bulletin 2. Montana Bureau of Land Management, Billings, Montana.

Reading, R. P., and S. R. Kellert. 1993. Attitudes toward a proposed reintroduction of black-footed ferrets (*Mustela nigripes*). *Conservation Biology* 7:569–580.

Reading, R. P., and R. Matchett. 1997. Attributes of black-tailed prairie dog colonies in north-central Montana. *Journal of Wildlife Management* 61:664–673.

Reading, R. P., B. J. Miller, and S. R. Kellert. 1999. Values and attitudes toward prairie dogs. *Anthrzoös* 12:43–52.

Reading, R. P., T. W. Clark, L. McCain, and B. J. Miller. 2002. Black-tailed prairie dog conservation: A new approach for a 21st century challenge. *Endangered Species Update* 19:162–170.

Reading, R. P., L. McCain, T. W. Clark, and B. J. Miller. 2005. Understanding and resolving the black-tailed prairie dog conservation challenge. Pages 209–223 in

R. Woodroffe, S. J. Thirgood, and A. Rabinowitz, editors. *People and wildlife: Conflict or co-existence.* Cambridge University Press, Cambridge, United Kingdom.

Reid, N. J. 1954. *The distribution of the black-tailed prairie dog in the Badlands of southwestern North Dakota.* State University of Iowa, Iowa City, Iowa. 30 pages.

Restani, M., L. R. Rau, D. L. Flath. 2001. Nesting ecology of burrowing owls occupying black-tailed prairie dog towns in southeastern Montana. *Journal of Raptor Research* 35:296–303.

Ricklefs, R. E., and G. L. Miller. 2000. *Ecology.* Fourth edition. W. H. Freeman and Company, New York, New York.

Roach, J. L., P. Stapp, B. van Horne, and M. F. Antolin. 2001. Genetic structure of a metapopulation of black-tailed prairie dogs. *Journal of Mammalogy* 82:946–959.

Robinette, K. W., W. F. Andelt, and K. P. Burnham. 1995. Effects of group size on survival of relocated prairie dogs. *Journal of Wildlife Management* 59:867–874.

Roe, K. A., and C. M. Roe. 2003. Habitat selection guidelines for black-tailed prairie dog relocations. *Wildlife Society Bulletin* 31(4):1246–1253.

Roe, K. A., and C. M. Roe. 2004. A relocation technique for black-tailed prairie dogs. *Western North American Naturalist* 64(4):445–453.

Roemer, D. M., and S. C. Forrest. 1996. Prairie dog poisoning in northern Great Plains: An analysis of programs and policies. *Environmental Management* 20:349–359.

Rosenzweig, M. L. 2003. *Win-win ecology: How the earth's species survive in the midst of human enterprise.* Oxford University Press, New York, New York.

Rosmarino, N. J. 2002. Endangered Species Act: Controversies, science, values, and the law. PhD dissertation, University of Colorado, Boulder, Colorado.

Rosmarino, N. J. 2004. Petition to list the Gunnison's prairie dog under the Endangered Species Act. Submitted to USFWS on behalf of Forest Guardians and 73 copetitioners. 23 February 2004.

Roughgarden, J. 1979. *Theory of population genetics and evolutionary ecology: An introduction.* Macmillan Publishing, New York, New York.

Russell, R. E., and J. K. Detling. 2003. Grasshoppers (Orthoptera: Acrididae) and black-tailed prairie dogs (Sciuridae: *Cynomys ludovicianus* (Ord)): Associations between two rangeland herbivores. *Journal of the Kansas Entomological Society* 76:578–587.

Sala, O. E., W. J. Parton, L. A. Joyce, and W. K. Lauenroth. 1988. Primary production of the central grassland region of the United States. *Ecology* 69:40–45.

Samson, F. B., F. L. Knopf, and W. R. Ostlie. 2004. Great plains ecosystems: Past, present, and future. *Wildlife Society Bulletin* 32:6–15.

Samson, F. B., F. L. Knopf, and W. R. Ostlie. 1998. Grasslands. Pages 437–472 in J. J. Mac, P. A. Opler, C. E. Puckett Haecker, and P. D. Doran, editors. *Status and trends of the nation's biological resources.* Volume 2. USDI, USGS, Reston, Virginia.

Samuel, M. J., and G. S. Howard. 1982. Botanical composition of summer cattle diets on the Wyoming high plains. *Journal of Range Management* 35:305–308.

Scheffer, T. H. 1937. Study of a small prairie-dog town. *Transactions of the Kansas Academy of Science* 40:391–395.

Scheffer, T. H. 1945. Historical encounter and accounts of the plains prairie dog. *Kansas History Quarterly* 13:527–537.

Scheffer, T. H. 1947. Ecological comparisons of the plains prairie dog and the Zuni species. *Transactions of the Kansas Academy of Science* 49:401–406.

Schenbeck, G. L. 1981. Management of black-tailed prairie dogs on the National Grasslands. Pages 207–213 in R. A. Timm and R. J. Johnson, editors. *Proceedings Fifth Great Plains Wildlife Damage Control Workshop.* University of Nebraska, Lincoln, Nebraska.

Schenbeck, G. L. 1985. Black-tailed prairie dog management on the Northern Great Plains: New challenges and opportunities. *Great Plains Wildlife Damage Control Workshop Proceedings* 7:28–33.

Schenbeck, G. L. 1993. Aerial photograph inventory of black-tailed prairie dog colonies in the Conata Basin/Badlands area of South Dakota. Draft report. USDA, Forest Service, Nebraska National Forest, Chadron, Nebraska. 4 pages.

Schenbeck, G. L., and R. J. Myhre. 1986. Aerial photography for assessment of black-tailed prairie dog management on the Buffalo Gap National Grassland, South Dakota. *USDA, Forest Service, Forest Pest Management, Methods Application Group, Report No. 86-7.* Fort Collins, Colorado.

Schitoskey, F. 1975. Primary and secondary hazards of three rodenticides to kit fox. *Journal of Wildlife Management* 39:416–418.

Schmutz, E. M., E. L. Smith, P. R. Ogden, M. L Cox, J. O. Klemmendson, J. J. Norris, and L. C. Fierro. 1992. Desert grassland. Pages 183–226 in R. T. Coupland, editor. *Ecosystems of the world 8A. Natural grasslands. Introduction and Western Hemisphere.* Elsevier, New York, New York.

Schwartz, A. M. 2002. Surgical sterilization of the black-tailed prairie dog (*Cynomys ludovicianus*): A model for the effects of reproductive inhibition and hormonal reduction in the male. MS thesis, Colorado State University, Fort Collins, Colorado.

Scott, C. M. 1994. USFWS, personal communication to Field Supervisor, USFWS, Ecological Services, Manhattan, Kansas, regarding submission of black-tailed prairie dog as a Category 2 Candidate, 5 January 1994.

Seal, U. S., E. T. Thorne, M. A. Bogen, and S. H. Anderson, editors. 1989. *Conservation biology and the black-footed ferret.* Yale University Press, New Haven, Connecticut.

Seery, D. B., D. E. Biggins, J. A. Montenieri, R. E. Enscore, D. T. Tanda, and K. L. Gage. 2003. Treatment of black-tailed prairie dog burrows with deltamethrin to control fleas (Insecta: Siphonaptera) and plague. *Journal of Medical Entomology* 40:718–722.

Seery, D. B., and D. J. Matiatos. 2000. Response of wintering buteos to plague epizootic in prairie dogs. *Western North American Naturalist* 4:420–425.

Seger, J., and W. D. Hamilton. 1988. Parasites and sex. Pages 176–193 in R. E. Michod and B. R. Levin, editors. *The evolution of sex: An examination of current ideas.* Sinauer Press, Sunderland, Massachusetts.

Sellars, R. W. 1997. *Preserving nature in the national parks: A history.* Yale University Press, New Haven, Connecticut. 380 pages.

Senft, R. L., L. R. Rittenhouse, and R. G. Woodmansee. 1985. Factors influencing patterns of cattle grazing on the shortgrass steppe. *Journal of Range Management* 38:82–87.

Seton, E. T. 1929. *Lives of game animals.* Doubleday, Doran and Company, Garden City, New York.

Severson, K. E., and G. E. Plumb. 1998. Comparison of methods to estimate population densities of black-tailed prairie dogs. *Wildlife Society Bulletin* 26:859–866.

Sexton, N. R., A. Brinson, P. D. Ponds, K. Cline, and B. L. Lamb. 2001. *Citizen knowledge and perception of black-tailed prairie dog management: Report to respondents.* USGS Open-File Report 01-467, Midcontinent Ecological Science Center, Fort Collins, Colorado.

Sharps, J. C., and D. W. Uresk. 1990. Ecological review of black-tailed prairie dogs and associated species in western South Dakota. *Great Basin Naturalist* 50:339–345.

Sheets, R. G. 1970. Ecology of the black-footed ferret and the black-tailed prairie dog. MS thesis, South Dakota State University, Brookings, South Dakota. 33 pages.

Sheets, R. G., and R. L. Linder. 1969. Food habits of the black-footed ferret (*Mustela nigripes*) in South Dakota. *Proceedings of the South Dakota Academy of Science* 48: 58–61.

Sheets, R. G., R. L. Linder, and R. B. Dahlgren. 1971. Burrow systems of prairie dogs in South Dakota. *Journal of Mammalogy* 52:451–453.

Sherman, P. W. 1981. Reproductive competition and infanticide in Belding's ground squirrels and other animals. Pages 311–331 in R. D. Alexander and D. W. Tinkle, editors. *Natural selection and social behavior.* Chiron Press, New York, New York.

Sherman, P. W., and M. L. Morton. 1984. Demography of Belding's ground squirrels. *Ecology* 65:1617–1628.

Shields, W. M. 1982. *Philopatry, inbreeding, and the evolution of sex.* State University of New York Press, Albany, New York.

Shier, D. M. 2004. Social and ecological influences on the survival skills of black-tailed prairie dogs: A role for behavior in conservation. PhD dissertation, University of California at Davis, Davis, California.

Shipworth, D., and R. Kenley. 1996. Fitness landscapes and the Precautionary Principle: The geometry of environmental risk. *Environmental Management* 24:121–131.

Shogren, J. F., and J. Tschirhart, editors. 2001. *Protecting endangered species in the United States: Biological needs, political realities, economic choices.* Cambridge University Press, Cambridge, Massachusetts.

Sidle, J. G. 1999. PPS prairie dog patrol: GPS aerial surveys of dog towns. *GPS World* 10:30–35.

Sidle, J. G., M. Ball, T. Byer, J. J. Chynoweth, G. Foli, R. Hodorff, G. Moraveck, R. Peterson, D. N. Svingen. 2001. Occurrence of burrowing owls in black-tailed prairie dog colonies on Great Plains National Grasslands. *Journal of Raptor Research* 35:316–321.

Sidle, J. G., D. H. Johnson, and B. R. Euliss. 2001. Estimated areal extent of colonies of black-tailed prairie dogs in the northern Great Plains. *Journal of Mammalogy* 82:928–936.

Sidle, J. G., D. H. Johnson, B. R. Euliss, and M. Tooze. 2002. Monitoring black-tailed prairie dog colonies with high-resolution satellite imagery. *Wildlife Society Bulletin* 30:405–411.

Silver, J. 1919. Rodent control operations in the Colorado–Kansas District, Annual Report for the fiscal year 1919. *BBS Annual Report, Colorado.* National Archives, Washington, D. C.

Simberloff, D. 1998. Flagships, umbrellas, and keystones: Is single-species management passe in the landscape era? *Biological Conservation* 83:247–257.

Sims, P. L., and J. S. Singh. 1978. The structure and function of ten western North American grasslands. II. Intra-seasonal dynamics in primary producer compartments. *Journal of Ecology* 66:547–572.

Sims, P. L., J. S. Singh, and W. K. Lauenroth. 1978. The structure and function of ten western North American grasslands. I. Abiotic and vegetational characteristics. *Journal of Ecology* 66:251–285.

Slobodchikoff, C. N., J. Kiriazis, C. Fischer, and E. Creef. 1991. Semantic information distinguishing individual predators in the alarm calls of Gunnison's prairie dogs. *Animal Behaviour* 42:713–719.

Slowik, T. J., R. S. Lane, and R. M. Davis. 2001. Field trial of systemically delivered arthropod development-inhibitor (fluazuron) used to control woodrat fleas (Siphonaptera: Ceratophyllidae) and ticks (Acari: Ixodidae). *Journal of Medical Entomology* 38:75–84.

Smith, G. A., and M. V. Lomolino. 2004. Black-tailed prairie dogs and the structure of avian communities on the shortgrass plains. *Oecologia* 138: 592–602.

Smith, R. E. 1967. Natural history of the prairie dog in Kansas. *Miscellaneous Publications of the Museum of Natural History, University of Kansas* 49:1–39.

Smith, W. J., S. L. Smith, J. G. deVilla, and E. C. Oppenheimer. 1976. The jump-yip display of the black-tailed prairie dog, *Cynomys ludovicianus. Animal Behaviour* 24:609–621.

Smith, W. J., S. L. Smith, E. C. Oppenheimer, and J. G. deVilla. 1977. Vocalizations of the black-tailed prairie dog, *Cynomys ludovicianus. Animal Behaviour* 25:152–164.

Snell, G. P. 1985. Deferred grazing influence on a prairie dog town. *Society for Range Management Annual Meeting* 38:43.

Snell, G. P. 1985. Results of control of prairie dogs. *Rangelands* 7:30.

Snell, G. P., and B. D. Hlavachick. 1980. Control of prairie dogs—the easy way. *Rangelands* 2:239–240.

Society for Conservation Biology. 1994. Resolution of the Society for Conservation Biology: Conservation of prairie dog ecosystems. *Society for Conservation Biology Newsletter* 1:7.

Soulé, M. E., J. A. Estes, J. Berger, and C. M. del Río. 2003. Ecological effectiveness: Conservation goals for interactive species. *Conservation Biology* 17:1238–1250.

Soulé, M. E., J. A. Estes, B. J. Miller, and D. L. Honnold. 2005. Strongly interacting vertebrate species: Conservation policy, management, and ethics. *Bioscience* 55:168–176.

South Dakota Prairie Dog Work Group. 2001. *South Dakota black-tailed prairie dog management plan.* Draft 2, October 2001. South Dakota Department of Game, Fish and Parks, Pierre, South Dakota.

Sperry, C. C. 1934. Winter food habits of coyotes: A report of progress, 1933. *Journal of Mammalogy* 15:286–290.

Stapp, P. 1998. A re-evaluation of the role of prairie dogs in Great Plains grasslands. *Conservation Biology* 12:1253–1259.

Stearns, S. C. 1987. Why sex evolved and the differences it makes. Pages 15–31 in S. C. Stearns, editor. *The evolution of sex and its consequences.* Birkhauser, Boston, Massachusetts.

Stephens, R. M., A. S. Johnson, R. E. Plumb, K. Dickerson, M. C. McKinstry, and S. H. Anderson. 2003. Secondary lead poisoning in birds of prey from scavenging shot black-tailed prairie dogs. Unpublished final report. Wyoming Cooperative Fish and Wildlife Research Unit, University of Wyoming, Laramie, Wyoming. 22 pages.

Stockrahm, D. M. B., and R. W. Seabloom. 1988. Comparative reproductive performance of black-tailed prairie dog populations in North Dakota. *Journal of Mammalogy* 69:160–164.

Stockrahm, D. M. B., B. J. Dickerson, S. L. Adolf, and R. W. Seabloom. 1996. Aging black-tailed prairie dogs by weight of eye lenses. *Journal of Mammalogy* 77:874–881.

Stokstad, E. 2005. What's wrong with the Endangered Species Act? *Science* 309: 2150–2152.

Stolzenburg, W. 2004. Understanding the underdog. *Nature Conservancy* 54: 24–33.

Stubbendieck, J., S. L. Hatch, and C. H. Butterfield. 1992. *North American Range Plants*, 4th edition. University of Nebraska Press, Lincoln, Nebraska.

Suckling, K., R. Slack, and B. Nowicki. 2004. Extinction and the Endangered Species Act. Technical Report, Center for Biological Diversity, Tucson, Arizona.

Sugg, D. W., R. K. Chesser, F. S. Dobson, and J. L. Hoogland. 1996. Behavioral ecology meets population genetics. *Trends in Ecology and Evolution* 11:338–342.

Sullins, M., and D. Sullivan. 1992. Observations of a gas exploding device for controlling burrowing rodents. *Vertebrate Pest Conference Proceedings* 15:308–311.

Summers, C. A., and R. L. Linder. 1978. Food habits of the black-tailed prairie dog in western South Dakota. *Journal of Range Management* 31:134–136.

Sutherland, W. J., and L. M. Gosling. 2000. Advances in the study of behaviour and their role in conservation. Pages 3–9 in L. M. Gosling and W. J. Sutherland, editors. *Behaviour and conservation.* Cambridge University Press, Cambridge, United Kingdom.

Swenk, M. H. 1915. The prairie dog and its control. *Nebraska Agricultural Experiment Station Bulletin* 154:3–38.

Swift, D. M. 1983. A simulation model of energy and nitrogen balance for free-ranging ungulates. *Journal of Wildlife Management* 47:620–645.

Tate, G. H. H. 1947. Albino prairie dogs. *Journal of Mammalogy* 28:62.

Teeri, J. A., and L. G. Stowe. 1976. Climatic patterns and the distribution of C_4 grasses in North America. *Oecologia* 23:1–12.

Terborgh, J., J. Estes, P. Paquet, K. Ralls, D. Boyd, B. J. Miller, and R. Noss. 1999. Role of top carnivores in regulating terrestrial ecosystems. Pages 39–64 in M. Soulé and J. Terborgh, editors. *Continential Conservation: Scientific Foundations of Regional Reserve Networks.* Island Press, Washington, D.C.

Texas Department of Health. Undated. *Basic fact sheet—tularemia in animals.* Available from Zoonosis Control Division, Austin, Texas.

Texas Department of Health. 2002. *Health officials investigating tularemia in captive prairie dogs.* Zoonosis Control Division news release, 6 August 2002, Austin, Texas.

The Nature Conservancy. 2000. *Ecoregional planning in the Northern Great Plains Steppe.* Northern Great Plains Ecoregional Planning Team, The Nature Conservancy. 181 pages. http://www.conserveonline.org/csd;internal&action=buildframes.action.

Thomas, R. E., A. M. Barnes, T. J. Quan, M. L. Beard, G. Carter, and C. E. Hopla. 1988. Susceptibility to *Yersinia pestis* in the northern grasshopper mouse (*Onychomys leucogaster*). *Journal of Wildlife Diseases* 24:327–333.

Thomas, T. H., and M. L. Riedesel. 1975. Evidence of hibernation in the black-tailed prairie dog *Cynomys ludovicianus. Cryobiology* 12:559.

Thorne, E. T. 1982. Tularemia. Pages 63–65 in E. T. Thorne, N. Kingston, W.R. Jolley, and R. C. Bergstrom, editors. *Diseases of wildlife in Wyoming.* Wyoming Game and Fish Department, Cheyenne, Wyoming.

Tietjen, H. P. 1976a. *Zinc phosphide—A control agent for black-tailed prairie dogs.* USFWS, Wildlife Leaflet 509, Washington, D.C.

Tietjen, H. P. 1976b. *Zinc phosphide—Its development as a control agent for black-tailed prairie dogs.* USFWS, Special Scientific Report—Wildlife, Number 195. Washington, D.C.

Tietjen, H. P., J. F. Glahn, and K. A. Fagerstone. 1978. Aerial photogrammetry: a method for defining black-tailed prairie dog colony dynamics. Pages 244–247 in *PECORA IV, Proceedings of the symposium: Application of remote sensing data to wildlife management.* National Wildlife Federation Scientific and Technical Series 3: 1–397.

Tietjen, H. P., and G. H. Matschke. 1982. Aerial prebaiting for management of prairie dogs with zinc phosphide. *Journal of Wildlife Management* 46:1108–1112.

Tileston, J. V., and R. R. Lechleitner. 1966. Some comparisons of the black-tailed and white-tailed prairie dogs in north-central Colorado. *American Midland Naturalist* 75:292–316.

Timm, R. M. 1994. Gas cartridges. Page G42 in S. E. Hygnstrom, R. M. Timm, and G. E. Larson, editors. *Prevention and control of wildlife damage.* Great Plains Agriculture Council and Cooperative Extension Service, University of Nebraska, Lincoln.

Toombs, T. P. 1997. Burrowing owl nest-site selection in relation to soil texture and prairie dog colony attributes. MS thesis, Colorado State University, Fort Collins, Colorado.

Travis, S. E., C. N. Slobodchikoff, and P. Keim. 1996. Social assemblages and mating relationships in prairie dogs: A DNA fingerprint analysis. *Behavioral Ecology* 7: 95–100.

Trevino-Villarreal J., I. M. Berk, A. Aguirre, and W. E. Grant. 1998. Survey for sylvatic plague in the Mexican prairie dog (*Cynomys mexicanus*). *Southwestern Naturalist* 43:147–154.

Trudeau, K. M., H. B. Britten, and M. Restani. 2004. Sylvatic plague reduces genetic variability in black-tailed prairie dogs. *Journal of Wildlife Diseases* 40:205–211.

Truett, J. C., and T. Savage. 1998. Reintroducing prairie dogs into desert grasslands. *Restoration and Management Notes* 16:189–195.

Truett, J. C., J. L. D. Dullum, M. R. Matchett, E. Owens, and D. Seery. 2001a. Translocating prairie dogs: A review. *Wildlife Society Bulletin* 29:863–872.

Truett, J. C., M. Phillips, K. Kunkel, and R. Miller. 2001b. Managing bison to restore biodiversity. *Great Plains Research* 11:123–144.

Tschetter, B. J. 1988. *Estimates of South Dakota prairie dog acreages, 1987.* Report No. 88-01, South Dakota Game, Fish and Parks Department, Pierre, South Dakota. 8 pages.

Ungar, S. 1994. Apples and oranges: Probing the attitude–behaviour relationship for the environment. *Canadian Review of Sociology and Anthropology* 31(3):288–304.

United States Department of Health and Human Services. 2003. Control of communicable diseases: Restrictions on African rodents, prairie dogs, and certain other animals. *Federal Register* 68(213):62353–62369.

United States General Accounting Office (GAO). 1994. *Ecosystem management: additional actions needed to adequately test a promising approach.* GAO-94-111.

United States Ninth Circuit Court of Appeals. 2001. United States Court of Appeals for the Ninth Circuit, Order Numbers 99-56362, 00-55496, D. C. No. CV-97-02330-TJW/LSP.

Uresk, D. W. 1984. Black-tailed prairie dog food habits and forage relationships in western South Dakota. *Journal of Range Management* 37:325–329.

Uresk, D. W., and A. J. Bjugstad. 1983. Prairie dogs as ecosystem regulators on the northern high plains. Pages 91–94 in C. L. Kucera, editor. *Proceedings of the Seventh North American Prairie Conference,* 4–6 August 1980. Southwest Missouri State, Springfield, Missouri.

Uresk, D. W., R. M. King, A. D. Apa, and R. L. Linder. 1986. Efficacy of zinc phosphide and strychnine for black-tailed prairie dog control. *Journal of Range Management* 39:298–299.

Uresk, D. W., R. M. King, A. D. Apa, M. S. Deisch, and R. L. Linder. 1987. Rodenticidal effects of zinc phosphide and strychnine on nontarget species. *Eighth Great Plains Wildlife Damage Control Workshop Proceedings* 8:57–63.

Uresk, D. W., J. G. MacCracken, and A. J. Bjugstad. 1981. Prairie dog density and cattle grazing relationships. *Great Plains Wildlife Damage Control Workshop Proceedings* 5:199–201.

Uresk, D.W., and D.D. Paulson. 1988. Estimated carrying capacity for cattle competing with prairie dogs and forage utilization in western South Dakota. Pages 387–390 in *Management of amphibians, reptiles, and small mammals in North America: Proceedings of the Symposium.* USDA Forest Service, Rocky Mountain Forest and Range Experiment Station, General Technical Report RM-166. Fort Collins, Colorado.

Uresk, D. W., and G. L. Schenbeck. 1987. Effect of zinc phosphide rodenticide on prairie dog colony expansion as determined from aerial photography. *Prairie Naturalist* 19:57–61.

USDA. 2001. Unpublished annual reports of Wildlife Services, 1996–2001. http://www.aphis.usda.gov/ws/tblfrontpage.html.

USEPA. 1995. *Registration Eligibility Decision (RED): Sodium fluoroacetate.* Office of Pesticide Programs, Washington, D. C., EPA 738-R-95-025. http://www.epa.gov/oppsrrd1/REDs/3073.pdf.

USEPA. 1996. *Registration Eligibility Decision (RED): Strychnine.* Office of Pesticide Programs, Washington, D. C., EPA 738-R-96-33. http://www.epa.gov/oppsrrd1/REDs/3133.pdf.

USEPA. 1998. *Registration Eligibility Decision (RED): Aluminum and Magnesium Phosphide.* Office of Pesticide Programs, Washington, D. C., EPA 738-R-98-017. http://www.epa.gov/REDs/0025red.pdf.

USFS. 1978. *Final environmental impact statement for prairie dog management on lands administered by the supervisor of the Nebraska National Forest.* Nebraska National Forest, Chadron, Nebraska.

USFS. 1978. *Management of prairie dogs on lands administered by the supervisor of the Nebraska National Forest.* USDA Final Forest Service Environmental Statement (USDA-FS-R2-FES). Chadron, Nebraska.

USFS. 1988. *Biological assessment, threatened and endangered plants and animals for revised management direction for black-tailed prairie dogs on lands administered by the Supervisor of the Nebraska National Forest.* Chadron, Nebraska.

USFS. 1998. *Analysis of the management situation, Northern Great Plains Management Plan Revisions.* USDA, Custer, Medicine Bow-Routt, and Nebraska National Forests, Chadron, Nebraska.

USFS. 1999. America's National Grasslands, state-by-state listing. www.fs.fed.us/grasslands.

USFS. 2001. *Final environmental impact statement and land and resource management plans: Dakota Prairie Grasslands, Nebraska National Forest units, Thunder Basin National Grassland.* USDA Forest Service, Chadron, Nebraska.

USFS. 2002. *Northern Great Plains management plans revision.* Nebraska National Forest, Chadron, Nebraska.

USFS. 2005. Black-tailed prairie dog conservation and management on Nebraska National Forest and associated units. Final environmental impact statement. USFS, Chadron, Nebraska.

USFWS. 1970. Conservation of endangered species and other fish or wildlife (first list of endangered foreign fish and wildlife as appendix A). *Federal Register* 35:8491–8498.

USFWS. 1984. Endangered and threatened wildlife and plants; final rule to reclassify the Utah prairie dog as threatened, with special rule to allow regulated taking. *Federal Register* 49:22330–22334.

USFWS. 1991. *Utah prairie dog recovery plan.* USFWS, Denver, Colorado.

USFWS. 1997. *Making the ESA work better: Implementing the 10 point plan . . . and beyond.* Denver, Colorado.

USFWS. 1998a. *Black-footed ferret recovery plan.* Denver, Colorado.

USFWS. 1998b. *Multi-species recovery plan for the threatened and endangered species of south Florida.* Volumes I and II: Technical/Agency Draft. Vero Beach, Florida.

USFWS. 1999. 90-day finding for a petition to list the black-tailed prairie dog. *Federal Register* 64:14425–14428.

USFWS. 2000a. 12-month administrative finding, black-tailed prairie dog. 1 February 2000. 107 pages. Summarized in *Federal Register* 65(24):5476–5488.

USFWS. 2000b. Memo from Region 6 Director, 29 November 1999. Denver, Colorado. Description of progress on listing actions. *Federal Register* 67(114):40657–40679.

USFWS. 2001. Candidate and listing priority assignment form. 20 February 2001. 27 pages. Summarized in *Federal Register* 66(210):54808–54832.

USFWS. 2002a. Candidate and listing priority assignment form. 3 June 2002. 46 pages. Summarized in *Federal Register* 67(114):40657–40679.

USFWS. 2002b. *Northern Cheyenne Reservation: Tongue River Enhancement Project.* Lewistown, Montana.

USFWS. 2002c. Endangered and threatened wildlife and plants; Review of species that are candidates or proposed for listing as endangered or threatened; Annual notice of findings on recycled petitions; Annual description of progress on listing actions. Summarized in *Federal Register* 67(114):40657–40679.

USFWS. 2003. *Management of black-tailed prairie dogs on Fish and Wildlife Service lands.*

USFWS. 2004. Species assessment and listing priority assignment form. 12 August 2004. 48 pages. Summarized in *Federal Register* 69(159):51217–51226.

USGS. 1999. 1-degree digital elevation models. EROS Data Center, Sioux Falls, South Dakota.

Vanderhoof, J. L., and R. J. Robel. 1992. Numbers and extent of black-tailed prairie dog towns in western Kansas. *Report to Kansas Department of Wildlife and Parks, Contract No. 221.* 33 pages.

Vanderhoof, J. L., and R. J. Robel. 1994. Numbers and extent of black-tailed prairie dog towns in Kansas. *Transactions of the Kansas Academy of Science* 97:36–43.

Vanderhye, A. V. R. 1985. Interspecific nutritional facilitation: Do bison benefit from feeding on prairie dog towns? MS thesis, Colorado State University, Fort Collins, Colorado. ix + 44 pages.

Van Dyne, G. M., J. D. Hanson, and R. C. Jump. 1983. Seasonal changes in botanical and chemical composition and digestibility of diets of large herbivores on shortgrass prairie. *XIV International Grassland Congress,* pages 684–687.

Van Pelt, W. E. 1999. *The black-tailed prairie dog conservation assessment and strategy.* Arizona Game and Fish Department, Phoenix, Arizona. 55 pages.

Van Pelt, W. E., editor. 2000. *The black-tailed prairie dog conservation assessment and strategy.* Arizona Game and Fish Department, Phoenix, Arizona.

Varela, G., and A. Vázquez. 1954. Hallazgo de la peste selvatica en la Republica Mexicana. Infeccion natural del *Cynomys mexicanus* (perros llaneros) con *Pasurella pestis. Revista del Instituto de Salubridad y Enfermidades Tropicales* 24:219–223.

Vargas, A., M. Lockart, P. Marinari, and P. Gober. 1998. Preparing captive-raised black-footed ferrets *Mustela nigripes* for survival after release. *Dodo* 34:76–83.

Vermeire, L. T., R. K. Heitschmidt, P. S. Johnson, and B. F. Sowell. 2004. The prairie dog story: Do we have it right? *BioScience* 54:689–695.

Vetterling, J. M. 1964. Coccidia (Eimeria) from prairie dog *Cynomys ludovicianus ludovicianus* in northern Colorado. *Journal of Protozoology* 11:89–95.

Vogel, S. 1989. *Life's devices: The physical world of animals and plants.* Princeton University Press, Princeton, New Jersey.

Vogel, S., C. P. Ellington, and D. L. Kilgore. 1973. Wind-induced ventilation of the burrow of the prairie-dog, *Cynomys ludovicianus. Journal of Comparative Physiology* 85:1–15.

Volesky, J. D., J. K. Lewis, and C. H. Butterfield. 1990. High-performance, short-duration and repeated-seasonal grazing systems: Effect on diets and performance of calves and lambs. *Journal of Range Management* 43:310–315.

Vosburgh, T. 2000. Impacts of recreational shooting on prairie dogs on Fort Belknap Reservation, Montana. In T. Vosburgh and R. Stoneberg, editors. 1999 Annual report of black-footed ferret recovery activities. Unpublished report, Fort Belknap Reservation, Montana.

Vosburgh, T. C., and L. R. Irby. 1998. Effects of recreational shooting on prairie dog colonies. *Journal of Wildlife Management* 62:363–372.

Wade, O. 1928. Notes on the time of breeding and the number of young of *Cynomys ludovicianus. Journal of Mammalogy* 9:149.

Wagner, F. H. 1988. *Predator control and the sheep industry.* Iowa State University Press, Ames, Iowa. 230 pages.

Walcher, G., K. Salazar, and D. Ament. 1999. Letter to Pete Gober, USFWS. 3 November 1999.

Walker, B. H. 1991. Biodiversity and ecological redundancy. *Conservation Biology* 6: 18–23.

Waring, G. H. 1970. Sound communications of black-tailed, white-tailed, and Gunnison's prairie dogs. *American Midland Naturalist* 83:167–185.

Waser, N. M. 1993. Sex, mating systems, inbreeding, and outbreeding. Pages 1–13 in N. W. Thornhill, editor. *The natural history of inbreeding and outbreeding: Theoretical and empirical perspectives.* University of Chicago Press, Chicago, Illinois.

Weber, D. A. 2004. Winter raptor use of prairie dog towns in the Denver, Colorado vicinity. Pages 195–199 in W. W. Shaw, L. K. Harris, and L. Vandruff, editors. *Proceedings of 4th international symposium on urban wildlife conservation.* University of Arizona Press, Tucson, Arizona.

Weber, N. S. 1978. *Plague in New Mexico.* Environmental Improvement Agency, Santa Fe, New Mexico. 33 pages.

Weltzin, J. F., S. Archer, and R. K. Heitschmidt. 1997a. Small-mammal regulation of vegetation structure in a temperate savanna. *Ecology* 78:751–763.

Weltzin, J. F., S. L. Dowhower, and R. K. Heitschmidt. 1997b. Prairie dog effects on plant community structure in southern mixed-grass prairie. *Southwestern Naturalist* 42: 251–258.

Wherry, W. B. 1908. Plague among the ground squirrels of California. *Journal of Infectious Diseases* 5:485–506.

Whicker, A. D., and J. K. Detling. 1988a. Ecological consequences of prairie dog disturbances. *BioScience* 38:778–785.

Whicker, A. D., and J. K. Detling. 1988b. Modification of vegetation structure and ecosystem processes by North American grassland mammals. Pages 301–316 in M. J. A. Werger, P. J. M. van der Aart, H. J. During, and J. T. A. Verhoeven, editors. *Plant form and vegetation structure: Adaptation, plasticity and relation to herbivory.* SPB Academic Publishing, The Hague, The Netherlands.

Whicker, A., and J. K. Detling. 1993. Control of grassland ecosystem processes by prairie dogs. Pages 18–27 in J. L. Oldemeyer, D. E. Biggins, and B. J. Miller, editors. *Management of Prairie Dog Complexes for the Reintroduction of the Black-footed Ferret.* USFWS Biological Report 13, Washington D. C.

White, G. C., and K. P. Burnham. 1999. *Program MARK: Survival estimation from populations of marked animals.* Bird Study 46 Supplement, 120–138.

World Health Organization (WHO). 1970. *WHO expert committee on plague.* Technical Report Series No. 447.

Wilcox, B. A., and D. D. Murphy. 1985. Conservation strategy: The effects of fragmentation on extinction. *American Naturalist* 125:879–887.

Wilkinson, T. 1994. Back to the Badlands. *National Parks Magazine* 68:38–42.

Williams, G. C. 1957. Pleiotropy, natural selection, and the evolution of senescence. *Evolution* 11:398–411.

Williams, G. C. 1966. *Adaptation and Natural Selection.* Princeton University Press, Princeton, New Jersey.

Williams, G. C. 1975. *Sex and evolution.* Princeton University Press, Princeton, New Jersey.

Wilson, E. O., editor. 1988. *Biodiversity.* National Academy of Sciences/Smithsonian Institution, Washington, D. C. 538 pages.

Wilson, E. O. 2002. *The future of life.* Alfred A. Knopf, New York, New York. 229 pages.

Winter, S. L., J. F. Cully, and J. S. Pontius. 2002. Vegetation of prairie dog colonies and non-colonized shortgrass prairie. *Journal of Range Management* 55:502–508.

Woodroffe, R., S. J. Thirgood, and A. Rabinowitz. 2005. The future of coexistence: Resolving human–wildlife conflicts in a changing world. In R. Woodroffe, S. J. Thirgood, and A. Rabinowitz, editors. *People and wildlife: Conflict or co-existence?* Cambridge University Press, Cambridge, United Kingdom.

Wuerthner, G. 1997. Viewpoint: The black-tailed prairie dog—headed for extinction? *Journal of Range Management* 50:459–466.

Wydeven, P. R., and R. B. Dahlgren. 1985. A comparison of prairie dog stomach contents and feces using a micro-histological technique. *Journal of Wildlife Management* 46:1104–1108.

Wydeven, A. P., and R. B. Dahlgren. 1985. Ungulate habitat relationships in Wind Cave National Park. *Journal of Wildlife Management* 49:805–813.

Wyoming Agricultural Statistics Service. 2001. *Black-tailed prairie dog management survey: Report of results to Wyoming Game and Fish Department.* Wyoming Department of Agriculture, Cheyenne, Wyoming. 23 pages.

Wyoming Black-tailed Prairie Dog Working Group. 2001. *Wyoming black-tailed prairie dog management plan.* Final Draft. Wyoming Game and Fish Department, Cheyenne, Wyoming.

Young, A.G., and G. M. Clarke, editors. 2000. *Genetics, demography and viability of fragmented populations.* Cambridge University Press, Cambridge, United Kingdom.

Zammuto, R. M., and P. W. Sherman. 1986. A comparison of time-specific and cohort-specific life tables for Belding's ground squirrels, *Spermophilus beldingi. Canadian Journal of Zoology* 64:602–605.

Zeveloff, S. I., and F. R. Collett. 1988. *Mammals of the inter-mountain west.* University of Utah Press, Salt Lake City, Utah.

Zinn, H. C., and W. F. Andelt. 1999. Attitudes of Fort Collins, Colorado residents toward prairie dogs. *Wildlife Society Bulletin* 27:1098–1106.

List of Contributors

Andelt, William F. Department of Fishery and Wildlife Biology, Colorado State University, Fort, Collins, CO 80523, "William F. Andelt" billan@cnr.colostate.edu

Biggins, Dean E. United States Geological Survey, Fort Collins Science Center, 2150 Centre Avenue, Building C, Fort Collins, CO 80526, "Dean E Biggins" dean_biggins@usgs.gov

Bly-Honness, Kristy. Turner Endangered Species Fund, PO Box 1118, Fort Pierre, SD 57532, kblyhonness@montana.edu

Clark, Timothy W. School of Forestry and Environmental Studies, Yale University, 205 Prospect Hall, New Haven, CT 06511, TimClark@yale.edu

Cully, Jack F. United States Geological Survey, Kansas Cooperative Fish and Wildlife Research Unit, 204 Leasure Hall, Division of Biology, Kansas State University, Manhattan, KS, 66506, "Jack Cully" bcully@ksu.edu

Detling, James K. Department of Biology and Natural Resource Ecology Laboratory, Colorado State University, Fort Collins, CO 80523-1878, jimd@nrel.colostate.edu

Ernst, Andrea E. New Mexico Cooperative Fish and Wildlife Research Unit, New Mexico State University, PO Box 30003, MSC 4901, Las Cruces, NM 88003, ernstae@nmsu.edu

Forrest, Steve C. Northern Great Plains Ecoregion Program, World Wildlife Fund-United States, PO Box 7276, Bozeman, MT 59771, scforrest@earthlink.net

Haskins, Bill. Big Sky Conservation Institute, 131 South Higgins Avenue, Suite 201, Missoula, MT 59802, "Bill Haskins" haskins@wildrockies.org

Hoogland, John L. Appalachian Laboratory, The University of Maryland Center for Environmental Science, 301 Braddock Road, Frostburg, MD 21532, hoogland@al.umces.edu

Kotliar, Natasha B. United States Geological Survey, Fort Collins Science Center, 2150 Centre Avenue, Building C, Fort Collins, CO 80526, tasha_kotliar@usgs.gov

Lamb, Berton Lee. Policy Analysis and Science Assistance Branch (PASA), Fort Collins Science Center, United States Geological Survey, 2150 Centre Avenue, Building C, Fort Collins, CO 80526-8118, "Berton L Lamb" lee_lamb@usgs.gov

Lawton, Eric A. Bureau of Land Management, 1849 C Street Northwest, Washington, DC 20240, "Eric Lawton" Eric_Lawton@blm.gov

Licht, Daniel S. National Park Service, 601 Riverfront Street, Omaha, NE 68102, Dan_Licht@nps.gov

Long, Dustin. Turner Endangered Species Fund, PO Box 131, Cimarron, NM 87714, longdh@bacavalley.com

Luce, Robert J. PO Box 2095, Sierra Vista, AZ 85636, bob.luce@earthlink.net

Luchsinger, James C. Middle Niobrara Project Office, The Nature Conservancy, 132 South Hall Street, PO Box 701, Valentine NE 69201, jluchsinger@tnc.org

Manes, Rob. Wildlife Management Institute, 10201 South Highway 281, Pratt, KS 67124, rmanes@tnc.org

Miller, Brian J. Wind River Ranch Foundation, PO Box 27, Watrous, NM 87753, brimill@earthlink.net

Proctor, Jonathan. Defenders of Wildlife, 1425 Market Street, Suite 225, Denver, CO 80202, jproctor@defenders.org

Reading, Richard P. Department of Conservation Biology, Denver Zoological Foundation, 2900 East 23nd Avenue, Denver, CO 80205, rreading@denverzoo.org

Reeve, Archie F. Black-footed Ferret Recovery Foundation and Golder Associates, 309 South 4th Street, Suite 201, Laramie, WY 82070, "Archie Reeve" archiereeve@pictechnologies.com

Rosmarino, Nicole J. Forest Guardians, 312 Montezuma Avenue, Suite A, Santa Fe, NM 87501, nrosmarino@fguardians.org

Schenbeck, Gregory L. Great Plains National Grasslands, United States Forest Service, United States Department of Agriculture, 125 North Main Street, Chadron, NE 69337, "Greg Schenbeck" gschenbeck@fs.fed.us

Shier, Debra M. Department of Ecology and Evolutionary Biology, The University of California at Los Angeles, 621 Charles East Young Drive South, Los Angeles, CA 90095, dmshier@ucla.edu

Seery, David B. United States Forest Service, United States Department of Agriculture, Carson National Forest, Bloomfield, NM 87413, dbseery@fs.fed.us

Sidle, John G. Great Plains National Grasslands, United States Forest Service, United States Department of Agriculture, 125 North Main Street, Chadron, NE 69337, "John Sidle" jsidle@fs.fed.us

Truett, Joe C. Turner Endangered Species Fund, PO Box 211, Glenwood, NM 88039, jotruett@gilanet.com

Van Pelt, Bill. Arizona Game and Fish Department, 2221 West Greenway Road, Phoenix, AZ 85023, bvanpelt@azgfd.gov

Vosburgh, Timothy C. PO Box 1101, Boulder, MT 59632, "Tim Vosburgh" t_vosburgh @onewest.net

Index

Note: Except for common names of other organisms, entries refer to the black-tailed prairie dog. Scientific names for all organisms are in Appendix A.

Island Press Board of Directors